THE VIENNA OPERA

THE
VIENNA
OPERA

MARCEL PRAWY

PHOTOGRAPHS BY
ERICH LESSING,
HENRI CARTIER-BRESSON, ATELIER DIETRICH,
FOTO FAYER, ELISABETH HAUSMANN,
BARBARA PFLAUM AND OTHERS

PRAEGER PUBLISHERS
New York · Washington

BOOKS THAT MATTER

Published in the United States of America in 1970
by Praeger Publishers, Inc., 111 Fourth Avenue, New York, N.Y. 10003

© 1969 in Vienna, Austria, by Verlag Fritz Molden, Wien-München-Zürich

Library of Congress Catalog Card Number: 78-77307

Printed in Austria

Contents

Picture Section

Voll Pietät hüte ich das Alte,
harre geduldig des fruchtbaren Neuen,
erwarte die genialischen Werke unserer Zeit.
La Roche in 'Capriccio'

What justification have I for writing this book? Perhaps only the fact that I have a passionate love for opera. Not just for the Vienna Opera House, which will be the subject of the following chapters, but for the whole art form. My life has been spent almost exclusively in the opera houses of half the world. An excess of vanity makes me reluctant to disclose my date of birth, and I will confine myself to the statement that I have followed the fortunes of the Vienna Opera with close attention since 1924, in other words, for more than forty-five years. My memories begin with the last years of the directorship of Richard Strauss. I have been going to the opera constantly since 1926, and when I say 'constantly', I mean usually not more than seven times a week. If there had been performances twice daily, I should have gone fourteen times.

All in all, the time in Vienna; then the years in the United States, which I spent, when I could, partly as a permanent guest of the Metropolitan Opera, partly in collaborating on operatic productions; then the post-war years when there were my own productions in many countries of Europe to attend to; and latterly my current activity as executive producer at the Vienna Volksoper, which automatically compels me to spend nearly every evening at the opera; adding it all together I come to a total of approximately ten thousand performances. That gives one some sort of perspective.

It might be appropriate at this point to make all sorts of modest gestures, and hastily to add that in Vienna everyone worships the opera, every tram conductor is crazy about it from the cradle on, and every taxi-driver dreams about Anneliese Rothenberger; that to a Viennese, 'Grace' is not the Princess of Monaco but Bumbry and Hoffman, no back-street grocer would cast Reri Grist as Brünnhilde or Birgit Nilsson as Blondchen; in short, to say that no other town in the world is as intimately involved as Vienna is in the life of its opera house, and so on and so forth. But this all has been said a thousand times before. I find it more interesting to approach the whole thing from a different angle: I maintain that all those people who love opera as I do form a worldwide club. A club for which the conditions of entry are more strict than those of the Rotarians, the Freemasons and various international organisations for dabblers in the occult.

My club has certain very special tests to find out whether or not someone really loves opera; and when these tests are rigorously applied one suddenly realises with consternation how few people really do belong to this club, however many may beat their breasts as they loudly proclaim their credentials.

In my opinion the only people who belong to this club are those who love opera so much that every natural form of speech feels basically unnatural, whereas singing is the only natural means of human expression, like the man who is in love with a girl and actually feels compelled to sing to her Rodolfo's aria from *La Bohème* because what he feels cannot possibly be put into ordinary spoken words.

Hence the first test. You are seated in the Theater in der Josefstadt or in the Burgtheater, the curtain rises, actors of the first rank begin to speak, and suddenly you say to yourself: 'How unnatural! Why on earth don't they sing?' You have passed the test.

The reason why opera seems to me to be so natural is not only, I think, because I belong to it body and soul, but also because when a performer sings 'Stride la Vampa' accompanied by the most unutterable ham gestures from grandpa's days, he is never in the same danger of appearing unnatural as his colleague in the theatre who has to deliver a text of similar emotional extravagance. The nature of an opera is created by the music, its melodies dictate movement and gesture. The actor of the spoken word, however, is utterly on his own; there is no music to support him, and so even a touch of pathos can often lapse into bathos.

Even after this first test very few aspiring members are left. But there are still more daunting Sarastro trials to follow, such as this: imagine that, one afternoon, you are among a pleasant gathering of friends, and you and four or five others are talking about the way the Viennese love their opera. You touch on crises in the directorship: there ought to be a strong man at the helm; there ought to be a weak man; Karajan must go; Karajan must stay; that man is to blame for it all, the other is to blame, and so on — and suddenly someone turns on the radio and Birgit Nilsson is singing Isolde's 'Liebestod'. What do you do now? Stop talking and listen — or switch off the radio and continue your discussion?

Nearly everyone turns off the radio. Only those people for whom talk stops here, and listening begins, belong to the club. And that is why I am a bachelor, because I have never yet found anyone who would not switch off. I have seldom noticed a more fierce, irate expression on people's faces than when the Stretta in *Il Trovatore* interrupts them while they are talking.

Real membership in the club begins at an early age: if you haven't made it by the age of seventeen you never will. Notice now and again how typical non-members behave in their youth. A boy or girl going on the first date often doesn't like to publicise the fact at home. So what does he or she say? 'I am going to the Opera.' In my case it was exactly the reverse. I was so embarrassed by being laughed at because of my eternal visits to the Opera that in the end I used to say 'I've got a date', just so that it would look as though I were leading a normal life. Actually, I was on my way to *Meistersinger* or *Palestrina*. And if anyone said to me next day that yesterday's Elsa was fat — for me she was more ravishing than Greta Garbo.

These things all qualify for membership.

The world of opera today can give us genuine cause for rejoicing only if the fact is perfectly clear in our minds that the operatic scene as I knew it in my youth has disappeared without a trace. This has nothing to do with the usual sentimentality of the older generation of opera-goers. I am glad to be engaged in the contemporary world of opera, but after ten thousand evenings one sees and hears in a different way. Just telling oneself that the dead beloved is still alive will not bring her back to life.

In my youth the most important issue was the new operas which were being composed at that time. I was born just early enough to live in the last phase of an era when daily conversation focussed on questions such as: 'What is Puccini working on now? How far has he got with *Turandot*? And what is Richard Strauss doing? Has Pfitzner received his new libretto?' (Minor contemporaries, whose arias we used to whistle, seem like giants today — d'Albert, Mascagni, Korngold etc.)

All this interested us immeasurably, and every success or failure of a new opera at home or abroad was more exciting than the most important political event. We were fully engrossed in the contemporary opera of those days, because it was alive. In my first year at the opera, *Ariadne* was already a classic — and yet it was only eight years old.

This excitement surrounding the world of opera was by no means the case between the Renaissance (when opera was born) and the middle of the eighteenth century. But from the early days of Mozart until the first quarter of the twentieth century, the new musical form was a matter of urgent interest to the general public. During this unique span of time all those classic works were written which have accompanied mankind to this day and have left their mark in hearts and minds. When a person hears *The Magic Flute*, *Aida*, *Tristan and Isolde*, or *Rosenkavalier* for the first time and discovers that a love for opera has been born in him, something in his life has changed.

In the past forty years all this has altered. It is not that there are no more lovers of opera — but where are the new works? Operas so pulsing with life that no one can talk of anything else? And that have a permanent place in international repertoires?

The opera-lover today is living, so to speak, on his capital. Are the cinema and television alone really to blame?

To my mind an opera is a portrayal of a human destiny, serious or gay, borne on the brilliance of the human voice — and at least one of its melodies must stay with us all our lives. It may be that posterity will do more justice to some of the newer works of our time than we have; one thing is certain, since the days of Gluck there has been no period in operatic history with so few successful operas as the last forty years. I read so much about the 'musical theatre', which is supposed to replace old-style opera. But the drawback is this: if there is no system of season tickets to propel the public into its seats, the house stays empty. And just as much in 'unintellectual' Vienna as in all those places where there is so much talk of the 'theatre of the mind'. For here, there, and everywhere, the public invariably comes out on strike when the noblest instrument of all, the human voice, is used like a kettle-drum.

But who in the world wants an operatic hit? The composer has no wish to be labelled as old-fashioned by the avant-garde critics for the sake of a tune (assuming he were able to think of one). If, instead, he tries to be 'modern at all costs', worthwhile possibilities present themselves, for example highly paid commissioned compositions for the top rank houses. True, he will not often be played, but he attracts attention. Our era of the conquest of outer space has also encompassed a world of new sounds, and electronic music has undoubtedly created a new colour, but will it lead to new operas which will attract the public?

Many of these composers fail to pass a different test: they do not recognise their own works when they hear them. After all, with a divertimento for seven broken chamber pots and one viola this is not so easy.

But basically, the director of an opera house can hardly use a genuine popular success either. The very thought of the old director of Vienna's Opera, Hans Gregor, who put on Massenet's *Jongleur de Notre Dame* fifty-two times in the first year (1912) is a never-ending headache to this contemporary successor.

As the comprehensive season-ticket system of today means that a work cannot be performed very often, a success cannot be exploited, and a flop is disguised. This makes for lethargy. Consequently, planning is based on an assumption of failure right from the start. And no one is upset by it — but what chaos is caused by a success! People storm the box office and can get no tickets. The press carries on about bad planning by the director's office. Calmly acting on the assumption that the predetermined flop would materialise, the singers have been allowed to fan out all over the world to fulfil their engagements and cannot be called back. The whole thing makes the director look silly and mildly discomposed.

The entire art form is now in a state of creative crisis, and no one can say when opera will recover. In those days we had everything: the classics and the living moderns. Concurrently with the loss of interest in new works, the dictatorship of scenic production began.

The room in Act One of *Figaro* used to be — a room; sometimes it was well painted and sometimes less so; it had two or it had three doors. But to discuss the subject in terms of the producer's 'concept' would have bored us. Ah yes, I shall be told, but that was in the old days. People were still simple-minded, they were undemanding. Today, people ask for more — no, they quite simply *see* more than they did in bygone days. The visual age of film and television has literally 'opened our eyes' . . . Perhaps. But it has also closed our ears.

And while we are on the subject of the past: the opera used to be taken much more seriously. *Un Ballo in Maschera* was banned by the political censorship, and the 1830 revolution against the Netherlands broke out in Brussels over *La muette de Portici*. And another factor was involved: scenery designers used to hold a high opinion of the audience as individuals and relied on their powers of imagination. When I was young and we went to a performance of Meyerbeer's *Les Huguenots* we saw on the stage a view of a park with a French castle. The scene, thrown together perhaps by a not very capable painter, was hardly a travel poster to attract tourists to France — but the castle was built by Meyerbeer's music and our imagination.

Today, operas no longer launch revolutions; instead they have become the plaything of the producers. We might well expect the producer to place the whole resources of modern technique at the service of the great masterpieces. But how bitterly we have to pay for a few masterly productions by men such as Zeffirelli, Schenk, Rennert and a few others.

Many producers not only mistrust the imagination of the audience and the power of the musical hit, but also feel themselves to be heaven-sent saviours of the opera, which, at bottom, they deeply despise.

Their rescue campaigns are carried out by degrees. For a start, the producers prevent the performance of about half the traditional repertoire: this their authoritarian position within the opera administration empowers them to do. To be able to say, 'Actually, I come from the legitimate stage', fills them with pride (as though a tailor would be proud to say that he was really trained as a shoemaker). The banned operas include all the ones that they don't know, which means the majority, but in particular the so-called static operas. Those are the ones in which such intolerable things as **arias, duets,** and **choruses,** predominate. In the jargon of ignorance disguised as professionalism, this is expressed as '*Aida* just isn't meaningful for me'.

The idea that someone can simply be standing up there singing an aria and not be doing something different at every single moment, is totally incomprehensible to men of this type. If the aria cannot possibly be cut, then they turn the singer into a Mickey Mouse who has to learn to accompany every syllable of 'Largo al factotum' with a whole ballet of movements, with the frequent result that only beginners or third-rate singers put up with it. The rest, when they hear what they have to do, walk off the stage.

When at last a producer finds a work which, unhappily, *is* meaningful for him, he can proceed to a further stage in the rescue operation. This involves totally ignoring the instructions of its authors. I believe that the copyright laws leave a genuine gap at this point. Strauss's *Rosenkavalier* opens with the words 'Wie du warst! Wie du bist!' If I wanted someone to sing 'Wie du bist! Wie du warst!' the publishers would object. But if I play the first act not in the Marschallin's room but on an empty stage in front of a fifteen-foot phallic symbol, no one can stop me. And there is no question but that voices would be heard welcoming this modern innovation. Is there then no copyright protection for scenic instructions? The overriding law is: be different at all costs, banish all visual immobility, express everything as far as possible in optical terms. The music bores many producers to death, which is why the scenic illustration of overtures has become a favourite joke. We have already had

to sit through an overture to *Aida* which was enlivened by promenading camels, mirage-like visions of Egyptian pyramids and similar trash.

In a way I have to be grateful to these gentlemen who distort operas completely beyond recognition. They enable me to earn my bread and butter. When I turn up as a 'guide to the opera' on television and say that *Elektra* takes place in Greece, I am at once rated as an outstanding expert, because in many productions this not entirely irrelevant fact is no longer apparent.

Opera has survived the dictatorship of the primadonnas and the despotism of the star conductors — and now the assassins from without are threatening its innermost nervous system.

The opera houses are full, fuller perhaps than ever before. More people go to the opera than they used to do, but their contact with the house has slackened. A season-ticket holder is entitled to six performances per year; in the old days there used to be *abonnements* for 'every fourth day'. The audience cheers. How often do I look across to the standing area and seek out the place where I grew up: right on the left, where it narrows off, in the lefthand '*Kipfel*'. There stood the élite... I am glad when I watch the faces of young people enjoying the opera. It used to be a bit more uncomfortable in my time. There were no long rails in those days on which one could lean in the standing area. We just stood. It was still standing-room, not leaning-room. And lining up was managed quite differently. If it was a normal performance, we came along to the Opera straight after school, about half past one, and began lining under the arcades in the Kärntner Strasse. The doors opened at five, then we stood inside. One hour before the performance began we received our tickets, burst into the standing-space and stood there until the iron curtain rose. Nowadays it is simpler. At six in the morning numbered tokens are issued. You fetch one, go away, and need not come back until three hours before the performance begins. In the case of sensational performances there is of course no other way but the traditional one: to line up all night so as to be sure of receiving a token in the morning. This system is necessary because most young people nowadays have jobs. But I am still surprised when I walk past at three o'clock and no one is standing there.

People have stacks of records at home, and radio and television bring opera into every house, so that it reaches vast masses of the population which it never reached before. But we used to prepare ourselves for a visit to the opera weeks beforehand, and we went off in our best suits to hear music which we can now listen to while we clean our teeth; the respect we used to have for music is lacking. When we had picked out the pilgrims' chorus on the piano we were more at home in *Tannhäuser* than many people today who possess three stereo recordings of it — opened or unopened. We knew more about the opera.

The talk today is all of the stars, their moods, their fees, their luxurious country houses. Everyone knows whose name is linked with whose, who is angry with whom. There are agitated discussions about the new production of *La Bohème* among people who hardly know what happens in *La Bohème* except that someone has tuberculosis and dies — 'performance ends before ten o'clock p. m.' — the composer's name is Puccini, there are a couple of lovely arias, one about a tiny frozen hand, and it snows in Act Three. What else is there to say about this old warhorse?

Many producers are the allies of ignorance. A young producer in Germany showed Marcel in Act One painting a naked model. Hurrah! Sex is trumps! The stuffy old operas must be brightened up with things that fascinate people today! But as it happens, Marcel's libretto says quite clearly what he is painting: the passage of the Israelites through the Red Sea, at the very moment when the waves close over Pharaoh, their pursuer.

The myth of the 'silly old opera texts' carries on from one generation to another. In my opinion, opera texts are, as a general rule, excellent. The gigantic experiment of making people on the stage sing rather than speak has succeeded approximately seventy or eighty times, perhaps a hundred times, during the past three hundred years. These works are in every respect superlative, and that includes the book. They are usually based either on established works of literature or on brilliant original material. Many libretti originate in effective stage plays. *Il Trovatore*, the case book example of a senseless operatic text, was a very popular play before Verdi set it to music. Did no one understand that either?

Opera books are often thought to be bad because they are only known in clumsy translations. Today, operas are usually sung in the original language, which is certainly more pleasant to listen to. And it is necessary, because operatic performers sing their parts all over the world. But one often finds oneself confronted by a text in Russian, Italian or French which may be incomprehensible: and one then knows still less about the opera.

By rummaging among the shelves of antiquarian music bookshops it is sometimes, with luck, possible to happen on single copies of old pamphlets now rated as unsaleable und unsuitable for re-issue. They are — opera guides. I am not referring to the books which nowadays go by that description, where 'All About *Carmen*' fills one or two pages, which cram a hundred works into one volume, give a résumé of *Madame Butterfly* and point out that the music belongs to the Italian post-Verdian school, has an exotic flavour and is very beautiful. If one rummages deeply enough, ten or fifteen guides to repertoire operas may come to light, many of them up to seventy or eighty pages in length. That hackneyed old thing *Madame Butterfly*, which everyone thinks he knows: there is a great deal to be said about it. Did Madame Butterfly really exist? What did the missionary's report have to say about her? What original Japanese material did Puccini use? And in what way? Surrounded by all that Japanese exoticism, Butterfly makes her entry with the most un-Japanese aria imaginable because she loves the American officer. When Pinkerton leaves her, she dies to a fortissimo of Far Eastern pentatonics. What legal system permitted Pinkerton to marry the little geisha girl in the presence of the American Consul and then to abandon her without further ado? To take another wife without being had up for bigamy? Why is the tenor called Pinkerton in the Italian text and Linkerton in the German? And when Cho-Cho-San prays in the second act, to what gods is she praying? Why does Puccini use the 'Star-Spangled

Banner'? Was it already the national anthem of the United States? What are the contents of the stage play upon which the libretto is based? Why did the audience hiss *Madame Butterfly* at the original first night at the Scala in Milan? What subsequent changes were made by Puccini? Thirty pages of the score were decisive for the failure or international success of the opera. Which were they?

I know perfectly well that one can spend a happy evening listening to *Madame Butterfly* without knowing all that (in the case of *Parsifal* and *Die Frau ohne Schatten* I should venture to doubt it). At any rate, among the students at the places where I teach, at the University and the Reinhardt Seminar of the Vienna Academy of Music, I have often noticed how enormously knowledge enhances enjoyment.

I often hear people say that they can only listen to an opera nowadays if the conductor is one of the greatest in the world and if at least four international stars are singing. The popular, gimmicky expressions 'quality', 'perfection', 'precision' are the favourite props of many unmusical people who hardly know a note of the music and not a word of the plot. This is a product of the stereo age. ('I was listening to stereo for ten hours yesterday — can't remember what.') I too have my hi-fi record player at home and it gives me great pleasure. But the rules of recording are not the same as those that apply to a live performance. Here are human beings, who live, love, die, suffer, laugh, weep, hit their top note or miss it. Every live performance of opera needs to possess some element of the bullfight or of a football match where one is on edge to see into which goal the ball will go. If the audience is tensely involved in a human drama, everything fits in with the excitement of the opera performance, even the cracked note and the missed cue. Verdi said: 'The mania for perfection should not be over-done, because then there is a danger that too little or nothing will be achieved.'

Today, technical reproduction sets the standard. It offers us something quite new: a repetition of the operatic performance. It goes without saying that there can be no irregularities and no botched entries on a record, which can be replayed as often as its life span permits. At the same time the perfectionist standards of the recording should not be carried into the opera house where they will destroy spontaneity.

In the studio, a work is recorded in a series of innumerable small passages. The aria is sung many times, and the best passages out of the many recordings are cut out and assembled. If the high C or F goes adrift at the first take, it may succeed at the second. If even then it fails to come off it can be done again alone, and inserted in the tape of the aria. If it is too short it can be lengthened by technical means. If it is a total failure — a not unknown occurrence — then the one note can be sung by another singer. At the end of all this we admire the perfection and precision of the aria, which never has been sung like this before . . .

It may well happen with a particular section of a recording that the conductor was satisfied, and the singers and the orchestra also. Then the sound supervisor emerges from his cabin and announces that an eighth has been sung in place of the sixteenth called for in the score, and the passage is repeated. The repetition may achieve a higher degree of perfection, but possibly at the expense of dramatic intensity.

The ghost of this sound supervisor haunts live productions as well. No singer can be expected to learn two versions of his part, one for mechanical reproduction and one for live performance. Under the pressure of an insistence upon absolute precision and perfection the effect of immediacy in the presentation is bound to suffer. The days are gone forever when Richard Strauss could say to the oboe 'Just slither over it, I like it better that way', and 'I love Jeritza even when she fluffs'.

Naturally, that only applied to the great artists, who by the power of their personality, raised the temperature to the sizzling point. For a singer who cannot achieve this, accuracy is to be preferred.

To be able to join in the discussion about the world of opera today, certain terms which inevitably crop up must be understood: ensemble theatre, repertory theatre, *stagione* theatre. The whole history of Italian opera is based on the *stagione* theatre. *Stagione* means the time of year, and the opera houses used to play only at certain seasons of the year, above all in the autumn and during the carnival. The opera theatres were fundamentally nothing more than four walls which one impresario or another, with his company, took over season by season. The company was freshly assembled each time. As they were great days of creative activity, the impresario was in the happy position of always being able to order a new opera for his next *stagione* from Signor Donizetti, Signor Bellini or Signor Verdi. Sometimes it was a flop, sometimes it was an *Il Trovatore*. Where the impresario found the money was his affair. The aristocrats were his patrons; if that was not enough he ran a casino in conjunction with the opera. Even in his time, Rossini was entitled by contract to a share of the profits on his operas and on the roulette tables. Operas were financed in much the same way as the musicals in America today, where private 'angels' provide the money. There were no state subsidies. For this reason the operas, like the present day musicals, had to be geared to success from the outset. If the opera flopped, the company had nothing to eat next day. In America, if a musical is a really disastrous failure, the theatre is closed at once and the next morning the postman will look for the cast in vain. The direct opposite to the *stagione* theatre is the ensemble theatre, which is the principle on which opera is run in the whole of German-speaking Europe. It involves a considerable number of singers of all categories who are bound by contract to an opera house for the performance of a broadly diversified repertoire. In Germany and Austria ensemble theatre is considered to be the ethical and rational justification for subsidy by the state. Essentially, it means that at all times the public is able to hear the great operatic masterpieces. It is only in this form that the opera becomes an educational institution, standing for good reason within the jurisdiction of the Ministry of Education.

Which is the better system? That is a matter of taste. But each method represents a different principle of the theatre. *Stagione* theatre only displays a fairly limited selection of works which the company, assembled for a brief period only, is able to perform. It is possible to choose from among the whole range of available singers the very best for these works; on the other hand this method has the disadvantage that one may have to wait for many years before the chance occurs to hear a particular opera. In the ensemble theatre there is the possibility of performing a widely varied repertoire, though the danger exists that a part may not always be ideally cast. *Stagione* theatre still prevails in Italy, and it can happen that at a season in Bologna or Palermo you will not find a single name of a singer from the preceding season. *Stagione* theatre offers the singer no personal involvement with the house. But when in 1916 dear Mimi Peham was engaged by the house manager Emanuel Ritter von Karajan, the conductor's uncle, to work in the office of the Vienna Opera, she had to swear an oath of loyalty *to the house*. (In 1969, gay and bright as a button, and sitting on the same chair, she gave me information for this book.)

One is entitled to expect of ensemble theatre that it will turn into repertory theatre. A visitor to the opera who attends the house regularly for five years ought to become acquainted with the leading works of all eras of operatic history, with baroque opera and with the moderns, with German romantic opera as well as with French *opéra comique*, with Italian *verismo*, with Slav opera and *grand opéra*. The result is bad only when the disadvantages of both systems unite: when an ensemble theatre only puts on the most hackneyed operas and a *stagione* theatre engages second-rate singers.

All over the world nowadays, we always find in actual practice a mixture of the two forms. At the Vienna Opera the difference between an ensemble member of the company who gives thirty performances a year, and a guest artist with a contract for thirty nights, now lies almost solely in the pension rights. At the Scala in Milan the small-part singers (*comprimarii*) are engaged over a longer period of time, but for the leading rôles the *stagione* system prevails entirely.

One of the principal assets of Rudolf Bing, general manager of the Metropolitan, is his talent for successful cadging. He receives nothing from official sources, but he has a sixth sense which tells him when someone, somewhere, is about to shell out. He has his regular supporters, and if he is lucky a well-wisher may even die and leave money to him on condition that he puts on a new production of Flotow's *Martha*. Herbert von Karajan has a passion for flying, so Eastern Airlines financed Karajan's *Ring* at the 'Met'. It is quite extraordinary what interesting programmes for a season can come into existence in this fashion. The usual repertoire operas can be heard at the 'Met', but also American first performances, forgotten delicacies like Bellini's *La Sonnambula* and *Roméo et Juliette* by Gounod — as well as *Wozzeck* with Christa Ludwig, Walter Berry and Karl Dönch.

The great singers of today sing in all the opera houses in the world. The modern generation of singers is tougher and more realistic than its predecessors. The prima donna who slept on till twelve and did not answer the telephone no longer exists. Nor does the star who used to sing twice a week and spent the rest of the time sitting around in coffee houses, had time to study and was able to make his or her voice last for thirty or forty years. Today, in the jet age, they are constantly on the move and work to a twenty-four hour schedule; on the other hand, even top stars often have a career expectation of only ten years.

In this book I shall try to tell the story of the Vienna Opera. No one who comes to Vienna, from whatever part of the world, has ever failed to be captured by the magic of our *Staatsoper*. And yet it is very difficult to put a finger on the precise distinction between the brilliance of the House on the Ring and that of other opera houses. It has so often been written that it was the greatest singers of their time who set their stamp on the Vienna Opera. That is true, but it is also false. The principal figures in operatic history only sang as guest artists in Vienna: Caruso, Gigli, Chaliapin and so on. In the history of the Metropolitan the list of evenings on which singers of this calibre performed is infinitely longer. But there has never been another operatic stage on which magnificent artists with wonderful voices, with charm and personality (even if they were not necessarily the biggest names in the world) worked so long and so intensively for the one opera house alone. Caruso and Gigli shone at the Metropolitan just as they did all over the world, but the artists who created and who still create the magic spell which lies over the Vienna Opera devoted their lives to the House on the Ring and created and developed an operatic entity which exists nowhere else.

One profound secret of the Vienna Opera is this: it has been said before now that the quality of an opera house is dependent in very great measure on all that has happened there in the past. In a sense Piccaver is still singing in the State Opera in Vienna, Richard Strauss is still conducting; there are people in the auditorium who, in certain passages, can still compare Nilsson's phrasing with that of Jeritza; and the markings in the orchestra's parts were made under Krauss and Karajan ... One so often reads that the repertoire of the Vienna Opera has always shown it to be the bastion of Viennese ultra-conservatism. Exactly the reverse is true. It was the conservative press that flayed Richard Wagner and Richard Strauss; as far as the public was concerned, Vienna was a pioneer town for them both. As long as effective operas were being written *for* the public, they were immediately heard in Vienna.

I get around a great deal. I mainly commute between America and Europe, visit this town and that for television and radio or in my capacity as executive producer. Wherever I happen to be, I naturally go to the opera in the evening. That gives me the experience to make comparisons. The Vienna Opera's publicity is very poor; a public relations department in the modern industrial sense does not exist at all. The Viennese love to grumble, and the foreign press sometimes considers our State Opera old-fashioned. On the other hand there are other opera houses with a gleamingly efficient publicity office, but whose quality mostly exists on paper in the form of interviews with rapier-tongued producers who expatiate in speeches and articles on their 'Music Theatre of the Mind', 'Music's Mission in the Twentieth Century' or 'Reshaping the Music Theatre in Tune with the Times'. But heaven help you if you try to hear their *Rigoletto*. If one begs to be given a ticket for tomorrow the contemptuous reply will be, 'But for goodness' sake — *Rigoletto?*' and a ticket will be pressed on one for tonight: it will be a seat for the current commissioned flop. (Several seats would be available if required.)

In Vienna, you can go to *Rigoletto*. There are bad performances here too, but the risk — now and in the past — has perhaps always been less than in any other opera house in the world. No director has ever been able to alter the matter.

This extraordinary lack of dependence on the quality of the director is one of the most remarkable phenomena of the Vienna Opera. In other cities a good director draws the opera up to its zenith, and the next bad one drags it down to its nadir. The fact that this does not apply here is explained by the gigantic inner strength of that colossus, the Vienna Opera and its artists. Naturally, the high subsidies help (the Opera costs the Austrian taxpayer half a million schillings a day), but so do the technical organisation, the chorus (which also gives its own concerts), and the ballet. And when the lights go down — the Vienna Philharmonic plays.

I spent a long time considering how to shape the material of this book. According to social epochs: nobility, middle classes? Or to historical periods: the Ringstrasse era, *fin-de-siècle*, between-the-wars? According to operatic styles: Wagner, *verismo*? I decided at last to place in the centre of each chapter the personality of a director. This enabled me to portray an artistic era in terms of the destiny of a human being with all his dreams, his successes and failures.

It was very difficult to give form to this material. After all, it is the story of singers whom the reader cannot hear, and of performances which he cannot see. For someone with opera mania on the other hand, it is quite easy, because he sometimes feels as though, all through the early and the earliest days, he has always been present everywhere (just as in some former existence; during my own I have nearly always been present). To me it seems like only yesterday that the Emperor Leopold I rode in the great equestrian ballet during his wedding celebrations on the Burgplatz in 1667. And when I read that the baroque opera *Il Pomo d'Oro* by Cesti was performed in a wooden theatre specially built for it on the site of the present Burggarten by Burnacini, that there were one thousand participants and that it was hard to get in, then all I can say is that I certainly would have got in, with or without a ticket. I might have felt thoroughly at home at the Gluck and Mozart premières in the old Burgtheater on the Michaelerplatz, but definitely not in the Freihaus Theatre in the suburb of Wieden where the crush is said to have been appalling. But if, of course, the director Emanuel Schikaneder had invited me personally to attend the world première of *The Magic Flute* I should probably have gone all the same. And, equally, to the first night of *Fidelio* in the Theater an der Wien in 1805 or of *Les Huguenots* in the Theater in der Josefstadt. And I too would have kept on saying that Vienna urgently needed a new opera house. Because I should without a doubt have been a permanent guest of the Kärntnertor Theatre.

That is where I shall begin.

My Thanks to:

Herr Fritz P. Molden for asking me to write this book; his chief editor Dr. Kurt Eigl, without whose self-sacrificing labours this book would never have seen the light of day;

his technical staff;

Herr Erich Lessing for his artistic colour photographs of the rebuilt Vienna Opera and some of its most important new productions, as well as to his wife Frau Traudl Lessing who was responsible for all the pictorial texts together with the laborious research which this entailed;

The Director of the Vienna Opera, Hofrat Dr. Heinrich Reif-Gintl, for an interview with interesting reminiscences;

The Director of the Volksoper, Herr Albert Moser, for talks about many problems arising from his activity as secretary-general of the Opera and for his assistance with proof-reading;

Hofrat Ernst August Schneider, former general manager of the Vienna Opera, for information on the war years, and Fräulein Mimi Peham, secretary to the Director of the Vienna Opera, for her help in exhuming old casts;

Gräfin Christl Schönfeldt for her magnificent help over the chapter on the Opera Ball;

Kammersänger Peter Klein for permission to use his magnificent collection of press cuttings, Kammersänger William Wernigk for allowing me to examine his unpublished sketches on the history of the Vienna Opera, Alfred Jerger for an enlightening talk and Staatsopernsänger Heinz Holecek for several pleasant anecdotes;

Frau Grete von Kralik for permission to use articles by her late husband, Professor Dr. Heinrich von Kralik;

Herr Dr. Götz Kende, founder of the Clemens Krauss archives, for valuable suggestions;

Herr Franz Merkl of the Volksoper for unearthing casts of the State Opera during its era in the Volksoper, and the senior stage manager Herr Adolf Koller for interesting facts;

Frau Dr. Sigrid Wiesmann, Herr Götz Fischer and Herr Paul Vetricek for their help in making excerpts from old critiques and for digging out old pictures, caricatures and press cuttings;

Fräulein Angela Zabrsa for placing her studies on the Opera during the war years, and Fräulein Elisabeth Reisser her seminar writings, at my disposal;

Frau Lilly Marischka for the historical collection of her deceased daughter Mädy and Frau Emmy Becker for critiques and programmes;

Herr Dr. Robert Kittler for his valuable studies on the history of ballet and Herr Hans Rochelt für interesting suggestions on this subject;

Herr Dr. Alexander Witeschnik, who drew my attention to particular documents;

the ladies and gentlemen of the National Library (particularly in the picture archives), of the Imperial and State Archives and the Vienna Municipal Library; my former secretary Fräulein Ina Pope, who typed out the greater part of this book and pointed out mistakes such as (while dictating late at night) my naming Franz Lehár as the composer of *La Bohème* ... and all my friends throughout the world, who during the past 45 years, have talked to me of nothing else but the beloved opera.

And naturally, all those who have written about it. I believe I have read them all — what I have taken from whom I can no longer say. The next author is not required, either, to acknowledge his quotations from me.

M. P.

16

The city gate after which the theatre was named can be seen on the right. The entrance to the theatre was on the Albertina side and the rear entrance in the Kärntnerstrasse was near the 'Komödien-Bierhaus', which was a convenient source of refreshment. Until 1810, the repertoire of the theatre was decidedly mixed, but after 1810 it concentrated on opera and ballet. Among those who conducted here were Beethoven, Donizetti, Nicolai and Verdi. It was razed in 1870 to make way for the Hotel Sacher, which had to abstain from staging opera. (Whether the new Opera House in return had to abstain from making 'Sachertorten' is not known.)

The 'Imperial & Royal Opera House by the Kärnthner Gate'

One of the composers who dominated the repertoire in those days was Giacomo Meyerbeer. Visitors to Meyerbeer operas could always be sure of a lavish spectacle and fine singing. Vienna remained a Meyerbeer stronghold up to the 1930s.

Left above: A scene from Meyerbeer's own production of *Le Prophète* in 1850. Centre: The prison in *L'Africaine*, which was not put on until 1866, after Meyerbeer's death. It immediately inspired a parody entitled *Die Afrikanerin in Kagran (The African Girl from Kagran,* an eastern suburb of Vienna) with Josephine Gallmeyer. Below: A scene from *Les Huguenots* which encountered opposition from the censor in 1848 before being approved for performance at the Imperial Opera.

Right: The auditorium of the Kärntnertor Theatre with its five tiers of boxes and the standing area stretching halfway to the stage. Notice that the orchestra still sit with their backs to the audience. It was from these players that Nicolai formed the Vienna Philharmonic Orchestra.

These were the notables of the Imperial Opera in the mid-nineteenth century — recorded on the next four pages by the leading portrait painters: Kriehuber (12), L'Allemand (1), Dauthage (1), Winterhalter (1) and Leybold (1).

From left to right: Conradin Kreutzer, conductor, and at one time very popular composer, is still remembered for his opera *Das Nachtlager von Granada*. — Otto Nicolai, Kreutzer's successor, bequeathed two immortal creations, *The Merry Wives of Windsor*, and the Vienna Philharmonic Orchestra. The illustration is from 1842, the year in which 'the entire orchestral personnel at the Imperial Opera House' became Vienna Philharmonic. — Heinrich Esser, known as 'the Opera's musical conscience', and virtually a partner in the running of the Opera, conducted the first Vienna performance of a Wagner opera (*Lohengrin*, in 1858). Alois Ander, a tenor extolled by Meyer-

beer as the first Vienna 'Prophète' and by Wagner as the first Vienna Lohengrin, lost his voice during a performance of *Wilhelm Tell* and died insane. — Karl Mayerhofer, formerly an actor at the Burgtheater, later a popular buffo bass, was a member of the Vienna Opera for 40 years and a soloist at the Wagner concerts at the Theater an der Wien in 1863. He sang Masetto in the performance of *Don Giovanni* which opened the new Opera House in 1869. — Johann Nepomuk Beck, a lyric baritone, was Vienna's first Nelusco in *L'Africaine* and first Hans Sachs, and the Don Giovanni of the opening performance in 1869.

Above: Pauline Lucca, a native of Vienna, known as 'the demon wildcat', popularized *Carmen* in the new house. Below: Jenny Lind, 'the Swedish nightingale', incurred the hatred and envy of her less well-paid colleagues at the Kärntnertor Theatre for the astronomical fee she was paid in Meyerbeer's *Vielka* at the Theater an der Wien.

From left centre clockwise: Louise Dustmann-Meyer, the great diva of the last years of the old House and of the first years of the new. She was Vienna's first Elsa and was Donna Anna at the opening performance of the new Opera House in 1869. — Henriette Sontag from the Rhineland, a world-famous and widely-travelled soprano, and Vienna's first Euryanthe. She did not grace the stage of the Vienna Opera for long and she died of cholera in Mexico. — Anna

The brochure announcing the original Viennese Sacher Torte points out that the Hotel Sacher was built on the site of the former Kärntnertor Theatre, which before its demolition in 1870 was where Old Vienna used to foregather for operatic festivals. On the site now occupied by Sacher's the City Council of Vienna erected in 1708 a 'Comödihauss', a private middle class theatre purveying a sort of Viennese *Commedia dell'arte* in which the antics of Hanswurst (a protagonist in Viennese comedy) were interspersed with short operatic interludes. It was eventually burnt down and replaced in 1763 by the Kärntnertor Theatre, which was next to the two city gates known as the 'Kärnthner Thor', sandwiched between one of the narrowest alleys in Vienna on the north side and the 'Bastei' ramparts on the south. The main entrance was about where the Café Mozart is now.

The Viennese had an affection for this theatre that amounted almost to veneration, although it was, from the very first, a distinctly primitive affair. As time went on adjoining houses were acquired or rented, connected with the main building by bridges or corridors, and used for offices and wardrobes. These outside premises were perpetually permeated with odours from adjacent hostelries, notably the popular 'Komödienbierhaus' near the stage door where actors and actresses euphemistically described as 'resting' used to wait for something to turn up in the way of agents on the look-out for talent. To round up the singers hanging about in the beer-house and get them back on to the stage for rehearsals in the Hofburg Redoutensaal was also a laborious business.

The interior of the Kärntnertor Theatre was elegantly fitted out, and it was an intimate little theatre with no fewer than five tiers of boxes, but terrifyingly narrow exits and entrances. What would have happened in a fire hardly bears thinking about. Pauline Lucca, whose *Carmen* was one of the sensations of the new theatre, related how as a young girl she used to sit up in the gods during the Italian *stagione* and how, from their lofty eminence, she and her friends used to join, wholeheartedly, in the choruses. Those were the days . . . It was the cosiest Opera House in the world.

The Kärntnertor Theatre was a Court theatre and had

the good fortune to coincide with a golden age when wonderful operas were being written and the world's greatest composers had them performed by the world's finest singers. It was here in 1814 that Ludwig van Beethoven conducted the final version of *Fidelio* and, in 1824, by which time he was stone-deaf, the first performance of his Ninth Symphony.

During the eighteenth century the two Court theatres — the other one was the Hof-Burgtheater in what is now the Michaelerplatz — offered a hotch-potch of operas, ballets and straight plays. At first the more important musical occasions took place in the Burgtheater, where Gluck was the *Kapellmeister*. It staged the first performances of Mozart's *Die Entführung*, *Le Nozze di Figaro*, *Don Giovanni*, and *Così fan tutte*. For some time there was an attempt to swell the Burgtheater's takings by associating it with a Casino. In 1810 a distinction was drawn between 'theatre' and 'music': the former was allotted to the Burgtheater, and opera and ballet became the prerogative of the 'Imperial House by the Kärnthner Thor'. From now on, opera, instead of being the preserve of the aristocracy, was to be the entertainment of the rising middle-classes.

Until 1848, the year of revolutions, the Court Opera was leased to administrators who were given larger and larger subsidies and came under the Court Chamberlain. The present-day custom of appointing salaried directors and placing them under contract, only dates from 1848. Many of these lessees were Italians, and the mistrust with which they were regarded by the Viennese authorities led, before 1848, to the police being given full powers in the theatre world. All budgets, fees and engagements were scrutinised by the Chief of Police, Graf Sedlnitzky, who also made a point of knowing about the actors' political opinions and previous records. The Opera was further plagued by censorship. *Les Huguenots*, which was about the religious conflict between Catholics and Protestants, was political dynamite, so it was rehashed under the title of *The Ghibellines of Pisa* and set in a completely alien milieu. One quaint result of this was the singing of Protestant chorales long before Luther was born! Again, after the battle of Solferino use of the word

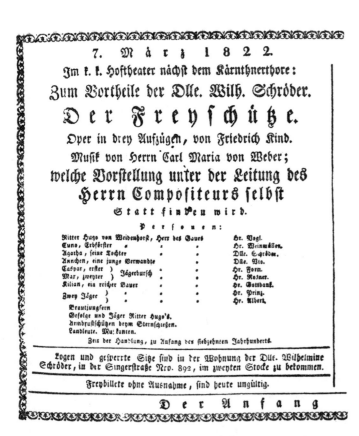

Rome was forbidden in the 1859 productions of *Tannhäuser:* it was replaced by the simple word *dort* (there). (Whether Tannhäuser's narrative, the Rome-narrative, was also referred to as the *dort* narrative is not known.) Less culpable was the ban on muskets in the 1821 production of *Freischütz:* Max and Kaspar used bows and arrows instead, because the Emperor Franz couldn't abide shooting on the stage.

Some of these lessees were distinctly bizarre figures, very different from the present image of an Opera Director. Many of them had previously been managers of unsubsidised theatres, but nearly all of them outgrew their humble start in life. There was a good deal of scepticism when Domenico Barbaja, a figure much derided for his turkey-cock complexion, prodigious girth and dandyish attire, acquired the lease of the Court Opera in 1821. Barbaja started life as a waiter, became a café proprietor, and eventually took over the Teatro San Carlo

in Naples, which had a Casino attached to it. Barbaja soon turned it into a highly lucrative undertaking, one of his most successful coups being his commissioning of the youthful Rossini to compose operas for the San Carlo. His relations with the 'Swan of Pesaro' were somewhat ambivalent, as Rossini's wife, the famous singer Isabella Colbran, was the queen of Barbaja's heart as well as of his theatre. Rossini's operas had enjoyed great popularity in Vienna ever since 1816, and the climax came when Barbaja persuaded Rossini and his wife to come to Vienna. The Rossini craze of 1822 spread like wildfire. Even Grillparzer, Schubert, and the philosopher Hegel succumbed to it. In the same year Carl Maria von Weber conducted two performances of *Freischütz*, and the cast of *Die Zauberflöte* included a new Sarastro named Johann Nestroy! It was now that Barbaja brought off a stroke of genius: he commissioned Weber to write an opera specially for Vienna. Within a year (in 1823) Weber, deathly pale and racked with coughing, was conducting the first performance of *Euryanthe*. So the origin of this important precursor of Wagner's *Lohengrin* was due at least in part to the initiative of a paunchy ex-army caterer.

Barbaja terminated his lease after eight years and was succeeded by the ballet composer Robert Graf Gallenberg.

Famous composers have conducted in the Kärntnertor Theatre. Their names were on the theatre posters even then, long before Felix von Weingartner introduced the practice of making daily announcements of Kapellmeister. — Posters of performances under Weber, Marschner, and Verdi.

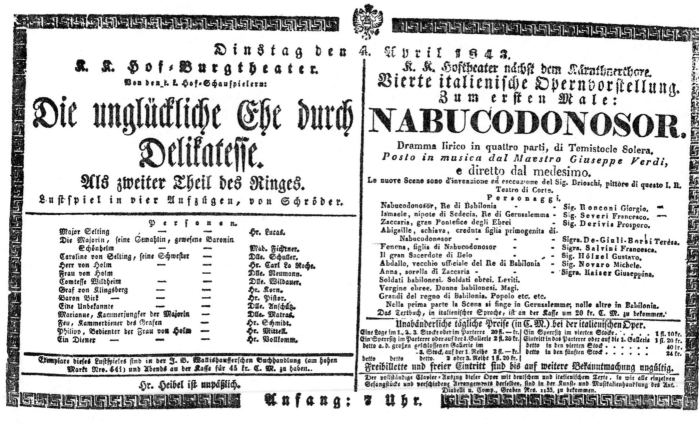

Gallenberg's wife was the Countess Giulietta Guicciardi, the lady to whom Beethoven dedicated his *Moonlight Sonata*. She may even have been his 'unsterbliche Geliebte' (immortal beloved). Gallenberg induced the 'divine' Fanny Elssler to return to Vienna from Italy, and she continued to enchant admirers from all over the world at the Kärntnertor Theatre. Her greatest triumph in opera was the name-part in Auber's *La muette de Portici*, an opera about the revolution in Naples in 1647.

A fascinating sequel to the Barbaja years was the period from 1836 to the revolution of 1848 during which the Vienna Opera and the Milan Scala were under joint administration in the persons of Carlo Balocchino, by profession a 'pantaloon-tailor', and Bartolomeo Merelli, a highly venturesome impresario with extraordinary flair and an uncanny knack of just managing to keep out of prison. Merelli ran a gambling-den or two in Milan as well as the Scala. It was not until the middle of the 19th

century that this curious entente between opera houses and casinos was done away with (though there is still a modern version of it at Monte Carlo).

Balocchino and Merelli provided Vienna with one sensation after another. To start with, they secured the appointment of Donizetti as 'Court and Chamber Composer'. Donizetti moved to Vienna and in 1842 and 1843 conducted his delightful *Don Pasquale* as well as two operas specially composed for Vienna, *Linda di Chamonix* and *Maria di Rohan*. In the same year, 1843, these two resourceful Italians brought off an even greater coup: the sensation of the current season at the Scala being Verdi's *Nabucco*, they persuaded the young Verdi to come and conduct it in Vienna. Before 1843 was out, they had also invited a young composer in Dresden to compose a new opera for Vienna. The composer's name was Richard Wagner, but the project unfortunately came to nothing. By and large, this remarkable pair of Italians did a great deal for German opera. Although Otto Nicolai, who was taken on as a *Kapellmeister* in 1841, never succeeded in getting his opera *The Merry Wives of Windsor* accepted by the Vienna Opera, he was enabled in 1842 to realise his brilliant idea of forming the orchestra of the Court Opera into the 'Artists' Republic' nowadays known as the Vienna Philharmonic Orchestra, so providing Vienna with its first professional orchestra for the performance of symphonic music. In 1846 Heinrich Marschner conducted his *Hans Heiling;* and in 1847 a work commissioned from Friedrich von Flotow, *Martha*, scored a triumph.

With the outbreak of revolution in 1848 everything Italian was condemned as 'reactionary' and Balocchino and Merelli withdrew. For some considerable time the theatre remained closed, the roof having been damaged by gunfire, but later it was re-opened by an 'action committee' of singers, who ran it as a private theatre without a subsidy. There was no money for scenery, and on one occasion Donizetti's *La fille du régiment* had to make do with National Guard uniforms. The revolution also brought Richard Wagner to Vienna, full of revolutionary ardour. In certain subversive circles there was even a plan to make him Director of the Opera.

Shortly after his accession the young Emperor Franz Joseph restored the Opera's standing as a Court Theatre with a subsidy. Once the revolution had been put down, however, the administration of the Opera underwent far-reaching changes. The new Court Chamberlain, Graf Lanckoronski, was a man of initiative and vision. The practice of leasing the theatre was done away with, and salaried Directors in the present-day sense were appointed. This effectively put an end to the powers of the police in all matters pertaining to the theatre.

The first few Directors lasted no longer than many of their successors. Franz Ignaz von Holbein, a descendant of the painter, scored a pronounced success with the first performance of Meyerbeer's *Prophète* under the composer's personal supervision, while the year 1851 saw Fanny Elssler's farewell performance as Gretchen in a ballet based on Goethe's *Faust*. After five years in office Holbein fell into disfavour in high places, and his suc-

Rossini's opera 'Wilhelm Tell' used to be played without cuts in two performances.

cessor, a producer named Julius Cornet, was a Tyrolean peasant whose arrogance made him heartily disliked by the entire staff. He was dismissed when the singer Louise Meyer (who later became the great Wagner singer Dustmann-Meyer) successfully sued him for slander. He came to a terrible end: he used some poisonous black pigment to conceal his baldness and went blind. His successor was (for the first time) a musician of stature, the conductor Carl Eckert, who in 1857 brought with him from Potsdam the first Wagner operas (1858 *Lohengrin*, 1859 *Tannhäuser*). But though an artist of taste and discernment, he was a very poor administrator, and his term of office lasted only until 1860.

It was in May 1861 that Richard Wagner heard *Lohengrin* in Vienna for the first time, conducted by *Kapellmeister* Heinrich Esser and with a cast including Dustmann as Elsa and Alois Ander as Lohengrin. He was so impressed that he was all for doing *Tristan* in Vienna with the same cast. But to establish exploratory contacts took more than two years, and after no fewer than 77 rehearsals, including an orchestral rehearsal conducted by Wagner in person, the work was finally abandoned in 1863 as 'unperformable'. Deeply disapppointed, Wagner retaliated in the same year with a tract on the Vienna Court Opera aimed at the new Director, Matteo Salvi. Veering completely round from his enthusiasm over the *Lohengrin* and *Fliegender Holländer* performances of May 1861, he now castigated the Opera as slovenly and completely out of date. After exhaustive suggestions as to methods of production, training and a reduction of the number of weekly performances to Paris proportions, he propounded the remarkable theory that as the Opera was given a subsidy it should confine itself to German operas (or French operas sung in German). Italian opera and French comic opera should be relegated to seasons in privately financed theatres and sung in the original language. One cannot help wondering whether, if Wagner had been its Director, the Vienna Opera would ever have staged Verdi's *Aida?*

Matteo Salvi, who was at the helm of the Vienna Opera from 1861 till 1867, was an obscure teacher of singing and second-class composer from Bergamo. His contract included the humiliating clause that under no circumstances would he be the Director of the new Opera House on the Ring. The longer the new house took to build, the more acrimonious became the criticism levelled at Salvi. He had some original ideas, but most of them fell through. In 1864 he put on Offenbach's first opera, *Die Rhein-Nixen*, of which all that survives is a melody which later became the famous Barcarolle in *The Tales of Hoffmann*. For the running of the training school that he had in mind, Salvi was certainly not the right man. Many of the quaint pronouncements emanating from this resourceful trouper soon went the rounds in Vienna, as for instance his suggestion: 'To hear the chorus better you'll have to reduce it by half. The people at the back just go through the motions!' French opera was in its heyday in Vienna, and here Salvi was a good deal more successful: 1862 saw the arrival of Gounod's *Faust* damned by some critics as 'musical high treason' and 'desecration of Goethe'; while 1865 was notable for Meyerbeer's *Dinorah* and even more so for his *L'Africaine*.

Salvi's successor, who was to be in charge of the move to the new house, came from Weimar. Franz Dingelstedt was an accomplished amateur pianist and writer and an aristocrat of the art-world. His pretentiousness earned him the nickname of 'Dünkel stets' (always a snob). Despite his cynial pronouncement that the Opera was merely 'a necessary evil' he did at least bring a 'wind of change' to Vienna. He contributed a great deal to smartening up the scenery and costumes and rejuvenating the chorus, which had always been the last resort of aspirants with more influential patronage than voice. As a producer in the elaborate Makart style he was particularly successful with Wagner's version of Gluck's *Iphigenie in Aulis*. Other feathers in his cap were two first performances in 1868. Gounod, warmly applauded, conducted his new opera *Romeo and Juliet* 'as if sitting down to a sumptuously laid table', and the last new opera to be given its first performance in the old Kärntnertor Theatre was another highly successful 'desecration of Goethe', this time Ambroise Thomas' *Mignon*, with two rising young stars named Bertha Ehnn and Gustav Walter.

The golden age of Belcanto was also the golden age of the youthful prima donna, even if it meant chivalrously stretching a point in the matter of the dates of birth submitted by many of the singers in question. Anna Milder, later Napoleon's innamorata, was twenty (or twenty-four) when she created the rôle of Fidelio. Wilhelmine Schröder (later Schröder-Devrient), so much admired by Wagner, was only seventeen when she created a furore as Agathe in *Der Freischütz* of 1821. When she sang in the first performance of *Euryanthe*, Henriette Sontag was seventeen (or nineteen). In those days it was held that the theory that a singer had to gradually 'grow into' exacting roles only applied to mediocrities.

Italian operas were nearly always given by Italian singers in Italian, but with the Court Opera Orchestra, during an annual Italian season. The German season usually ended on Easter Sunday. On Easter Monday the Prater opened with its traditional brilliant *Korso*. On the following day the Italians used to take over the Opera for two or three months and earned frenetic applause with a season of Rossini, Bellini, Donizetti and the latest operas by Verdi — *Rigoletto, Il Trovatore*, and *La Traviata* (which were given an almost unanimous roasting by the Viennese critics). The season usually ended with a 'Pasticcio', an assortment of individual acts from different operas. The reason for Press opposition to the Italians was a patriotic one: they wanted German opera. Actually, the managers and Directors were required by the Court to give priority to German opera, but the public response to the Italians was an uncompromising *Evviva*. Italian operas in German with Viennese casts had difficulty in establishing themselves in the repertoire of the German season. (There was considerable criticism of the way the *stagione* were organised. They were often run by outside impresarios who were paid a lump sum, whereas the cost of the singers was debited to the Court Opera. But as the impresarios also took 'commission' from the singers, quite a lot of unsolicited 'development aid' found its way into certain pockets . . .)

Statistics show that the repertoire of the Kärntnertor Theatre from 1840 to 1850 consisted of 45 French, 25 Italian, and 23 German operas. It was a period during which French opera was in its heyday, Italian opera was forging ahead, and German opera was struggling to establish itself. Statistics of the number of performances as opposed to the titles of the works performed would show up German opera in an even more unfavourable light.

The Viennese singers protested vehemently against the enormous fees paid to their Italian colleagues. Up to the

closing of the Kärntnertor Theatre, the highest salary paid to any singer on its permanent payroll was 10,000 guilders, whereas the Italian stars often got 14,000 guilders for two to three months' work. In 1867 Matteo Salvi paid the brilliant prima donna Desirée Artôt 24,000 guilders for two months (his own salary as Director being a mere 4,200 guilders a year). *Kapellmeister* Heinrich Esser, the theatre's 'musical conscience', earned 3,000 guilders a year, and the orchestral players five to six hundred.

And how much did the Opera cost the State in those days? The subsidy, then known as the *dotation*, in the Balocchino-Merelli era amounted to 75,000 guilders, but by the 1860s it had risen to 230,000 guilders.

Many of the problems which we nowadays glibly associate with the advent of the jet age were already being acrimoniously debated in the good old days. Were operas to be given in the original language, for instance, or in translation? And how should the fees of the visiting stars compare with the salaries of those on the local payroll? There was even talk of a project that has given rise to heated discussion in recent times, namely collaboration between various international opera-houses, a project branded with the hideous and totally un-Austrian designation of an 'Opera Trust', a monstrosity run on American big-business lines. In 1956 Herbert von Karajan put out feelers in this direction, and similar plans were outlined by Rudolf Bing during the negotiations in 1968 about the possibility of his being offered the post of Director of the Vienna Opera. But it was as long ago as 1857 that the Austrian Minister of the Interior instructed the Governors of Venice and Milan to examine the possibility of three months' spring seasons of Italian opera in Milan, Vienna, Venice, Verona and Trieste, all run by a single director, 'an Italian of course', who was to have at his disposal all the subsidies granted to these five cities, all of which in those days belonged to Austria. What eventually caused the abandonment of this grandiose scheme was the loss of all the Austrian possessions in northern Italy. A precursor of this plan was one put forward by a certain Dr. Josef Bacher in 1853. Bacher was a Viennese and so passionately found of music that he acquired the nickname of 'Meyerbeer-Bacher'. What he envisaged was a joint repertoire for the opera houses of London, Paris and Vienna. Bacher was prepared to run the Vienna Opera himself with a subsidy of only 100,000 guilders a year (and also to build a new opera house out of the takings at his own expense). 'Meyerbeer-Bacher' died in a lunatic asylum.

Even in the nineteenth century 'The Imperial and Royal Opera House by the Kärnthner Thor' was by no means the only theatre where Viennese audiences could enjoy opera. From 1845 to 1848 there was also 'grand opera' at the Theater an der Wien, built by Emanuel Schikaneder in 1801, where *Leonora*, the first version of Beethoven's *Fidelio*, was first performed in 1805. It was at this theatre that Jenny Lind, 'the Swedish nightingale', scored one of her greatest triumphs as Norma (at a fee of 1,000 guilders a night), as 'The Daughter of the Regiment' (the conductor being Franz von Suppé!), and in Meyerbeer's latest opera *Vielka*, the composer himself conducting. It was here too that in 1846 Lortzing conducted the

first performance of his *Waffenschmied*. The 'Theater in der Josefstadt' staged amongst other operas the first Vienna performances of *Oberon* (1827), *Robert le diable* (1833), und *La Juive* (1835). It was at a wooden summer theatre, the Thalia Theatre in Neulerchenfeld, that *Tannhäuser* became the first Wagner opera to be given in Vienna (1857). Grillparzer, who had joined in the adulation of Rossini, said the overture 'gave him earache'. The performance of an opera was often followed by a parody of it. The most celebrated parody of all was after the first performance of *Tannhäuser* in November 1857 at the Carl Theatre, on the other side of the Danube Canal. It was written by Nestroy, the scene was set in Grinzing, and the Venusberg was portrayed as a champagne orgy. The Carl Theatre was also on one occasion able to welcome the great coloratura diva Adelina Patti: after the battle of Solferino the Court Opera banned the Italian *stagione*, so the Carl Theatre stepped into the breach.

'The Imperial and Royal Court Opera by the Kärnthner Thor' was the product of a bygone Austrian synthesis, the link with the Italian Provinces. After Meyerbeer's *Prophète* and the eruption of Wagner on to the scene, it was obvious that the technical shortcomings of the Kärntnertor Theatre alone made the building of a new Opera House imperative. Director Holbein complained that 'there isn't even machinery to project the difference between night and day ...'. Madame de Stael once described Venice as an elegy in marble: now there was talk of a 'satire in stone'. The new Opera House opened its doors on the twenty-fifth of May 1869 — but the affections of the Viennese remained obstinately attached to the old one. The last performance in the old house, Rossini's *William Tell*, was on the seventeenth of April 1870.

The work of demolition was supervised by the son of a once celebrated tenor named Josef Erl. One balmy summer evening the sixty-year-old Erl clambered on to what was left of the stage that had been the scene of so many of his triumphs, and to a small group of his former 'fans' sang for the last time Rossini's aria 'O Matilda'.

A great chapter in local Viennese history had come to an end. What followed was part of world history.

Ever since Wagner gained a foothold in the Kärntnertor Theatre, there had been general agreement among the experts that Vienna needed a modern Opera House. Back in the early 1850s Merelli had submitted a plan for a new house near the old Burgtheater in the style of the big Italian opera houses. The year 1857 saw the birth of Franz Joseph's far-reaching plans for the expansion of Vienna; from romantic old Vienna there was to arise a new up-to-date Vienna (which by now has come round again to being looked upon as romantic . . .). In those days the Inner City was still huddled inside a medieval system of walls, moats and bastions which had long ceased to be of any military value. In Biedermeier times, the Viennese used to enjoy taking the air on the 'Glacis', an open expanse of ground between the bastions and the suburbs. The Emperor's plan included the razing of the bastions to make way for a magnificent new thorough-fare in the shape of a horse-shoe, the Ringstrasse, which has given its name to a whole chapter in the history of Vienna. Plenty of space, plenty of money, a touch of the South in its appeal to the senses and admirable taste all contributed to the construction of one of Europe's finest streets, lined by the Renaissance University and Museums, the neo-Gothic Rathaus, the Hellenistic Parliament, and the felicitous blend of styles in the new Opera House. It is surely a vindication of the majesty of its lay-out that the Ringstrasse still defies modernisation. Has it really 'no style'? Or is it not the very embodiment of the 'Viennese style'?

The Emperor lent a willing ear to the claim that the culmination of the splendid buildings along the Ringstrasse must be a new Imperial Opera House. The 'All-Highest' choice of a site fell upon a spacious rectangular area at the apex of the 'horse-shoe', where the future Ringstrasse would cross the southern end of the Kärntner Strasse, formed by the demolition of the two 'Kärntner' city-gates and the filling-in of the adjacent moats. The cost was to be defrayed out of the 'City Expansion Fund', which had been set up for converting the former Glacis into building sites. On the tenth of July 1860, architects at home and abroad were invited to submit anonymous designs for a new Opera House to the Court Chamberlain by the tenth

of January 1861. Instead of the architect's name, which was to be enclosed in a sealed envelope, the designs were to be indentifiable by a motto.

The 'Regulations for the construction of a new Imperial Opera House in Vienna' included the following stipulations. There were to be tiers of boxes, and the theatre was to seat an audience of about 2,500. It was to be suitable for opera and ballet as well as for the Opera Ball. The choice of style was left to the architect, but he was to bear in mind when designing the workshops and storage-space that 'there are always forty or fifty operas, as well as a number of ballets, to be completely equipped'. For members of the Court there was to be a separate covered approach 'not on the same side as the main approach', and an Imperial box with an adjoining salon (and an ante-room for attendants). Thus the new house was to have two separate grand approaches; one from the Opern-gasse for the Emperor, and one from the Kärntner Strasse for the Archdukes.

On the twenty-eighth of October 1861 a jury scrutinised thirty-five entries and selected one submitted under the device 'Fais ce que je dois, advienne ce que pourra'. The architects in question were both professors at the Imperial Academy of Fine Arts, Eduard van der Nüll and August Siccard von Siccardsburg. Both were Viennese and just under fifty years of age. They were also close friends, and had jointly designed the Carl Theatre in 1847, the Sophien Baths in 1848, and the Arsenal in 1856. Van der Nüll was well known at Court for his illustrations for the Empress Elisabeth's missal. Work on excavating the site started in December of the same year.

And so the old bastions were duly razed and the foundations of the new House were laid, up to the level envisaged for the new Ringstrasse. And then, one gusty spring day in 1863, on the twentieth of May to be exact, came the ceremonial laying of the foundation stone. The whole area was flagged, emblazoned and decorated with pine-sprigs, while the onlookers included Ministers, leading citizens from various walks of life, and all the workmen engaged on the site, amongst whom 4,000 guilders were distributed. The actual stone, which was of Istrian marble, came to light in 1952 during the excavations pre-

Poster with information for guests at the opening performances in the new house on May 25, 26, and 29, 1869.

ceding the rebuilding of the house after its destruction during the Second World War. Attached to it was a golden casket containing a parchment document which included an apt description of the house's function: 'To be a monument to the Arts and a place where they are cultivated'. By the seventh of October 1865 the outer structure was completed to roof level, but the interior decoration was not finished until the spring of 1869. The house took seven and a half years to build (the Paris Opera took eleven, from 1863 to 1874, but during the Franco-Prussian War the half-finished building was used first as a hospital and later by the Commune as a propaganda centre).

The building of the new Vienna Opera House coincided with an era of extreme political tension. Austria had lost Lombardy in 1859, and in 1866 had proceeded to lose Venetia, as well as being defeated by Prussia. It was high time for Austria to put her house in order. So in 1867 the 'Compromise' with Hungary was worked out, constituting the basis of the Austro-Hungarian Monarchy until its disintegration in 1918. Yet the Austrians, though keenly aware of the decline of their political prestige, had no inkling of the far greater prestige their new Opera House was to bring them.

At the time, the Viennese viewed any project emanating from 'them', the authorities, with the utmost suspicion. Freedom of thought and liberalisation had led to a habit of saying no simply for the pleasure of doing so. So as the new house neared completion the Press, the experts, and the artistic world in general indulged in a crescendo of scathing criticism of anything and everybody. Some of the popular lampoons about van der Nüll and Siccardsburg were particularly ingenious. The former was derided as having 'no style', and the latter as one to whom Gothic, neo-classical and Renaissance were all the same. There was criticism too of the jumble of styles and even of the site: it would have been much better to build the Opera House at the highest point of the Ringstrasse, on the corner of the Babenbergerstrasse. While the house was being built the Imperial Office of Works, with which Siccardsburg and van der Nüll were on far from friendly terms, had been obliged to raise the level of the Ringstrasse by just over three feet above the original plan. The Viennese immediately started talking about a 'versunkene Kiste' (literally 'a sunken crate', an allusion to the Opera House being at, or slightly below, street level, whereas most others are above it). Another uncomplimentary expression that went the rounds was 'an architectural Königgrätz' (the battle at which Austria was defeated by Prussia in 1866). Ludwig Speidel called the Opera House a 'digesting elephant'. The moody and introspective van der Nüll, who had attempted suicide once before, lost all confidence in his work and hanged himself on the third of April 1868 at a Mariahilf villa belonging to a friend of his. Siccardsburg, normally a robust and cheerful character, was just getting over a serious operation, and his end was undoubtedly hastened by the news of his friend's suicide: he died on the eleventh of June 1868. After these two tragic deaths the Emperor ordered two marble plaques bearing relief busts of the two architects to be placed above the first landing of the main stairway, where they can still be seen.

So even before its opening the Vienna Opera claimed two lives that had been dedicated to its service. They were not to be the last.

Between them, Siccardsburg and van der Nüll had designed a superb opera house, a perfect blend of beauty and absolute functionalism. The ground-plan was simple and clear, and the building was easy to find one's way about in, which meant less danger in the event of fire. It was the perfect realisation of a felicitous phrase in the foundation-stone document: 'of noble proportions'. As among the Gothic, Renaissance and Romanesque elements, no one could decide which style the house was really built in. By and large the house was in a style of its own, the original 'Ringstrasse' style without any of the bogus irrelevancies that characterise so many other buildings of the same period.

The exterior reflected the cultural power of a great Empire, while the interior, a paradoxical blend of modesty and exuberance, was pervaded with an atmosphere of music. Just as in the old days people used to talk of a painter 'composing' a painting, so now the new Opera House was a highly original blend of music and architecture. The famous stairway, the red and pale-gold auditorium, the two soaring amphitheatre galleries, the four tiers of boxes and the vast stage, with its (for those days) ultra-modern set of eight traps, all combined to form a noble environment for noble music. Some of Vienna's foremost painters and sculptors contributed to the interior decoration. The foyer (with the two marble fireplaces that look so like kitchen dressers) ablaze with gold and black-white-red-yellow marble from Belgium, Italy and Salzburg, brought back memories of the past glories of the Habsburg Empire. In this foyer are Moritz von Schwind's reproductions, in egg-tempera on canvas, of scenes from various well-known operas — *Freischütz, Fidelio, The Barber of Seville, Don Giovanni.* Some of Schwind's choices are distinctly odd. He can be forgiven for including *Der häusliche Krieg;* after all, he was a personal friend of Schubert's. But Spontini's *La Vestale,* but no Donizetti! Spohr's *Jessonda* but no Verdi. And no Wagner whatsoever!

From this foyer five glass doors lead to a loggia above the Ringstrasse approach, decorated by the same Schwind with frescoes of scenes from *Die Zauberflöte.* All these frescoes can still be seen, as the Ringstrasse side, including the loggia and the foyer, was the only part of the Opera House that survived the air-raid destruction of March 1945.

A few figures: the new Opera House cost six million guilders (the Kärntnertor Theatre cost 300,000!). Officially it seated an audience of 2,324, but 3,100 could be squeezed in with five to a box and the standing-room for 1,200 packed tight. It covered an area of 28,565 square feet (33,246 including the grass outside). The roof level was 128 feet above the street, and the lowest part of the foundations 55 feet below it. The stage was 95 feet wide and (with the backstage) 157 feet deep.

Endless rehearsals were held to find the right level for the orchestra. The pit eventually agreed upon was somewhat below the Italian, but above the German level.

For the ceremonial opening with Mozart's *Don Giovanni* on the twenty-fifth of May 1869 all the leading dress-shops were sold out, but despite the brisk demand for tickets (the official price was twenty-five guilders for a stall seat) the touts were left with a good many expensive tickets on their hands. The same thing happened at the re-opening in November 1955.

The gala opening was attended by the Emperor and the Archdukes in the Imperial box. But not everything went without a hitch on that twenty-fifth of May 1869. The proceedings opened with a Prologue by Director Dingelstedt declaimed by Charlotte Wolter, a native of Cologne, dressed as Vindobona and bearing aloft the Imperial banner. Since her great triumphs as Iphigenia and Maria Stuart she had been the uncrowned queen of the Burgtheater. The backcloth for the Prologue was a portrayal of 'the murky arches of the Kärntner Tor where not a ray of sunshine ever penetrated'. This was to fade out gradually into a vision of the future Ringstrasse. Unfortunately the stage machinery had a bad day and the transformation never came off. The Prologue itself was a primitive political panegyric, an emotional appeal for peace and unity among all the races and peoples of Austria-Hungary. Finally, Charlotte Wolter made her way down a staircase to the strains of the old Austrian National Anthem and called upon the aforesaid races and peoples to form a circle as a symbol of concord. Unfortunately the accompanying text was blue-pencilled by the censor at the last moment. Another item the police would not sanction was Wolter brandishing a black-red-gold flag, and nobody seemed able to lay hands on a black-yellow Habsburg one at such short notice. Nevertheless, the festively attired audience rose to its feet and acclaimed both Wolter and the Emperor. The Empress Elisabeth was not present, but she came a day or two later to see *La muette de Portici.*

After the Prologue came Mozart's *Don Giovanni* with

Das Orchesterg'frett im neuen Opernhause.

Sehen genug — aber hören nig!

(Schon bei der Generalprobe entdeckter Uebelstand.)

Hören genug — aber sehen nig!

(Nachdem das Orchester gehoben wurde.)

Um zu hören und zu sehen, wird also nichts Anderes überbleiben, als entweder das Orchester auf die III. Gallerie zu postiren (wo man ohnedieß nicht gut hören soll) und die Besucher dieser Gallerie in den Orchesterraum zu stecken,

oder man beläßt das Orchester auf seinem gehobenen Standpunkte und räumt den Sängern und Tänzern dafür eine höhere Stellung ein, indem man sie im Flugwerck arbeiten läßt.

„Da unten aber klingt's fürchterlich."
(Frei nach Schiller's „Taucher.")

Ihr wißt, auf unsern deutschen Bühnen probirt ein Jeder, was er mag.
(„Faust," Vorspiel auf dem Theater.)

Weh mir, wenn Du nichts Besseres weißt.
Schon ist die Hoffnung mir verschwunden.
(Citat aus „Faust", von den Oekonomen des Theaters gemacht.)
Auf das kömmt „Kikeriki" mit seinem letzten und pfiffigsten Vorschlag:

und sagt: Gebt dann stets das Ballet „Die Tochter der Luft"!

Freilich könnte das Orchester auch mittelst einer neuen Erfindung des „Kikeriki" geleitet werden, aber im neuen Opernhaus werden nur Erfindungen des Herrn Hofraths Dingelstedt eingeführt, und

die neueste, glorreichste und vielbesprochenste Erfindung dieses Herrn Hofraths läßt sich auch nicht verdunkeln! Wir meinen nämlich die berühmten Generalproben im Neglige!

A SPOT OF BOTHER OVER THE ORCHESTRA IN THE NEW OPERA HOUSE

Top left: Can see all right — but can't hear a thing! (Unpleasant discovery made at dress rehearsal.)

Top centre left: Can hear all right — but can't see a thing! (After the orchestra had been raised.)

Top center right: To be able both to see and to hear there will be no alternative but either to transfer the orchestra to the third gallery (where one does not hear well in any case) or to dump the occupants of this gallery in the orchestra pit,

or to leave the orchestra where it is but waft the singers into a higher sphere of operations altogether.

'How horrid are the sounds below' (with apologies to Schiller).

Upon our German stages, all may rehearse what they will (with apologies to Goethe).

Woe is me, if thou canst not solve this problem, then all hope I must abandon (with renewed apologies to Goethe).
Hereupon Kikeriki hits on his latest and brightest idea:

and says: Let's put on the same ballet every time: 'Die Tochter der Luft!' (the daughter of the air).

Below left: The orchestra could certainly be conducted by means of a new invention by Kikeriki, but in the new opera house only inventions by Hofrat Dingelstedt are permitted, and ...

Below right: ... the latest, most glorious and most promising invention conceived by Herr Dingelstedt must never be lost sight of: we are referring to the celebrated dress rehearsals in négligé.

new scenery and the most illustrious cast that Vienna could muster. There was another performance of *Don Giovanni* next evening with an equally splendid cast, conclusive evidence of the wealth of singers at the Opera's disposal.

This strange hotch-potch of art and politics, particularly the attempts by the police to assert their crumbling authority in the theatre, was soon taken up by the satirical periodicals. *Der Floh* published an imaginary report by the Director of Police to the Minister of Public Safety, including the following passage:

'The people of Vienna are definitely not yet ready for the blessings of freedom. Thirty-four women and girls were handed over to the authorities for defying the strict regulations whereby the cloak-room attendants are allowed to earn 10 Kreuzer for each outer garment. They stubbornly refused to divest themselves of their coats with the flimsy excuse that they had nothing on underneath except their shifts... A woman who had fainted was arrested for failing to comply instantly with an order to come to her senses. Finally eighty-three persons were removed from the premises for speaking their minds about people who sing out of tune, and showing every intention of not taking the customary lenient view of the first few performances.'

The second performance of *Don Giovanni* in the new

From the series of caricatures 'Kikeriki in the new Opera House'.

That is the way to use the hole!
The mystery has been cleared up!
They have remembered the tortures suffered by the owner of a top hat when he has to hold it in his hands for three hours — Bravo! Not bad at all.
Kikeriki silently presents a laurel wreath to the inventors and places his brand new top hat in this safe place.

But we are accustomed in the theatre to stretch out our legs under the seat of the fellow in front. So Kikeriki, hearkening to the strains of Mayerhofer's music, and admiring the fawn trousers of Hofrat Dingelstedt, lapsed into his old habit and extended his spindly shanks, as is his wont, straight out in front of him.

So muß man das Loch benützen!
Da liegt der Hund begraben!
Man hat nämlich sich an die Qualen erinnert, die ein Cylinderbesitzer auszustehen hat, wenn er seinen Hut drei Stunden lang in der Hand halten soll — Bravo! die Geschichte ist nicht übel.

Kikeriki widmet den Erfindern im Stillen ein neu Lorbeerkranz und bringt seinen funkel nagelneuen Cylinder in Sicherheit.

Weil man aber im Theater gewohnt ist, seine Füße gerade vor sich hin, d. h. unter den Sitz seines Vordermannes zu strecken, so verfiel auch Kikeriki, den Tönen Mayerhofer's lauschend und die lichten Hosen des Hofrathes Dingelstedt bewundernd, in seine alte Gewohnheit und er streckte seine beiden »Eilfer«, wie sonst, gerade vor sich hin.

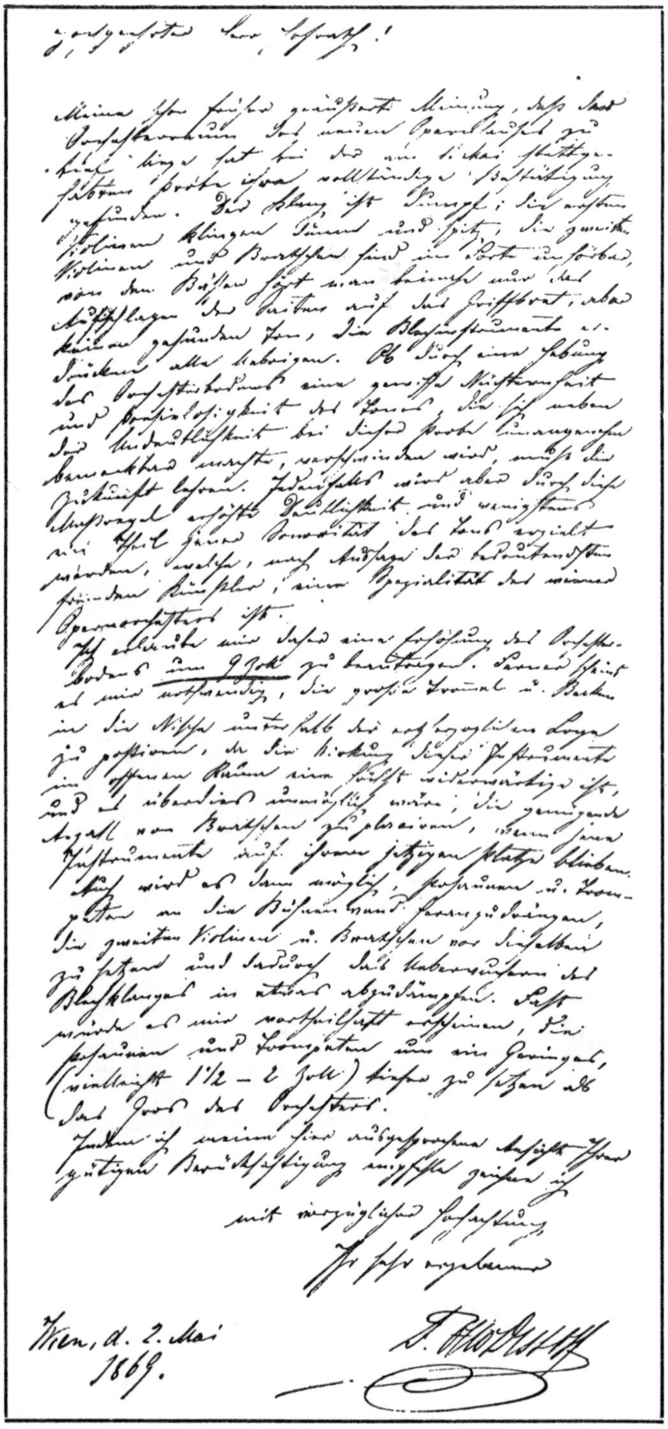

Memorandum by Kapellmeister Otto Dessoff dated 2 May 1869 with suggestions that the orchestra platform be raised.

Transcription:

My previously expressed opinion that the level of the orchestra space in the new Opera House is too low was fully confirmed during the rehearsal which took place on 1 May. The tone is muffled; the first violins sound thin und shrill, the second violins and cello are inaudible when playing forte, from the double bass little is heard beyond the strike of the strings on the finger-board but no healthy tone, the wind instruments smother all the rest. If, by raising the orchestra platform, the sobriety and want of poetic contrast in the tone — which, in addition to lack of clarity, were unpleasantly evident at this rehearsal — would then disappear, only the future will show. Certainly, however, to follow this course would achieve an enhanced clariy and would at least restore some measure of that sonority of tone which, according to the most distinguished foreign artists, is a speciality of the orchestra of the Vienna Opera.

I take the liberty therefore of requesting that the orchestra platform be raised by 9 inches. In addition it appears to me advisable to place the big drum and cymbal in the niche beneath the archducal box. The effects produced by these instruments when standing in an open space are most unpleasant, and besides it would be impossible to accomodate the required number of cellos if those other instruments were to remain where they are. This would also enable the trumpets and trombones to be compressed up against the wall of the stage, the second violins and cellos would be placed in front of them, and by so doing the sound of the brass, which tends to overpower all others, would be subdued. I should almost consider it an advantage to seat the trombones and trumpets at a slightly lower level (1½ to 2 inches) below the rest of the orchestra. I commend my opinions as stated above to your kind consideration, and remain etc. etc.

Otto Dessoff

Vienna, 2 May 1869

house was very poorly attended. Criticism of the building continued unabated for many years to come. One body of opinion found it 'without style' and downright ugly; another found fault with the failure to adopt the Paris idea of building an avenue (from the Opera House to the Wieden district) with splendid views of the façade. Another maintained that it was impossible to see or hear what was going on on the stage.

The first reaction to these complaints was an attempt to rescue the old Kärntnertor Theatre (the same series of events took place and with the same negative result after the opening of the new Metropolitan Opera in New York in 1966). There were plans for turning the Kärntnertor Theatre into a theatre for comic opera — in fact, its very last première was a step in this direction, an Offenbach operetta in January 1870. Or it could be a new home for the Burgtheater! But before the year was out it was pulled down and the site was sold for 300,000 guilders (indirectly to the Hotel Sacher). The props went to the Stadttheater at Brünn (Brno).

It was some twenty-five years before it at last dawned on the Viennese that they now had an Opera House that (acoustically, too) was almost perfect, though there were one or two complaints that were not unjustified: the ventilation plant for instance fed in air from the Kärntner Strasse, which meant that in later years the auditorium was pervaded with a smell of petrol and exhaust fumes. Again, the ceiling of the third tier was definitely too low, and as the pillars supporting the roof were based on the fourth tier, from many of the seats — the dreaded 'pillar seats' — there was practically no view of the stage at all. In those days the processes of democracy were still in their infancy, and people wanting cheap seats were not catered for. But Siccardsburg and van der Nüll had shown their consideration for 'the rank and file' by providing the Operngasse and Kärntner Strasse covered approaches with protection against rain and splashing by passing vehicles.

Vienna's Opera House soon took on an atmosphere of vitality and good humour. Its hospitable doors were open to all and sundry. Later, during the Republic, it became the pride and joy of the people at large. Or as Dingelstedt put it in his Prologue: 'A plaything of the universal spirit whose words have greatness even in the smallest things'.

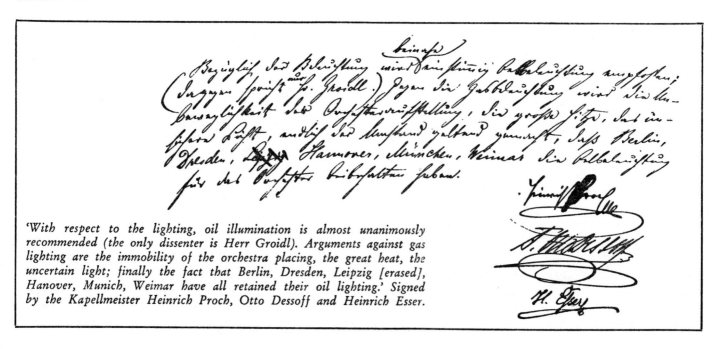

'With respect to the lighting, oil illumination is almost unanimously recommended (the only dissenter is Herr Groidl). Arguments against gas lighting are the immobility of the orchestra placing, the great heat, the uncertain light; finally the fact that Berlin, Dresden, Leipzig [erased], Hanover, Munich, Weimar have all retained their oil lighting.' Signed by the Kapellmeister Heinrich Proch, Otto Dessoff and Heinrich Esser.

It was not long before the routine performances of the new House attained a more brilliant standard than the opening ones, which were not an unqualified success. At first audiences were somewhat sparse, as the Viennese continued to patronise the old house, but as the opening season got into its stride attendances began to pick up. The lavish scenery and technical marvels of the ballet *Sardanapalus* had shown that the 'sunken crate' was able to cater to the Viennese love of spectacle far more effectively than had been expected, and although it was a good many years before criticism of the acoustics died down, the management speeded up the transfer of as many operas as possible from the old house to the new. The difference between the sizes of the stages in the two houses meant that the first performances in the new house were tantamount to premières. Meantime at the Kärntnertor Theatre audiences got smaller and smaller: 'le roi est mort, vive le roi'.

Franz von Dingelstedt — he called himself 'Baron' long before he was entitled to do so — came through the ordeal of managing the transfer with flying colours. Yet this remarkable man was never popular in Vienna; he was too unfeeling. Before coming to Vienna he had been Director in Munich and Weimar, where he had done a lot for Hebbel (the very first performance of *Lohengrin*, at Weimar in 1850, started with a Prologue by Dingelstedt) but his unfortunate idea of repeating the innovation at the opening of the new Vienna Opera House with a political prologue showed his lack of feeling for Viennese taste. One of his earliest successes as a writer was his 'Songs of a Cosmopolitan Night Watchman', and caricatures of him as a night-watchman dogged him for the rest of his life.

The General Intendant of the Court Theatres had promised him the Burgtheater: his post at the Opera was to be only a provisional one to tide him over until the Burgtheater post was vacant. 'In Austria nothing is impossible' was Dingelstedt's maxim.

Although he regarded the Opera as merely 'a necessary evil', during his short term of office (summer 1867 — December 1870) he did at least succeed in coming to grips with some of the artistic problems of a form of art he found so uncongenial. He augmented the orchestra to

111 players (Paris had only 85!), the chorus to 90, and the ballet to 80. His elaborate stage designs à la Makart for '*Die Zauberflöte*' made use of some interesting scenery by Joseph Hoffmann and lasted until after the First World War.

Dingelstedt's worst headache was his conductors. Heinrich Proch, a popular song-composer, retired after thirty-three years of service; Heinrich Esser, the Director's musical adviser, was taken ill in 1870 and died two years later; while Felix Otto Dessoff of Leipzig stayed on but was overworked, as he was also the permanent conductor of the Philharmonic Concerts. So Dingelstedt secured the services of Vienna's most popular conductor, *Kapellmeister* Johann Herbeck, who in July 1869 was appointed 'for the space of one year to join in the conduct of the musical affairs of the Imperial and Royal Opera House', and in April 1870 to the post of 'Adviser and Director of the Musical Establishment of the Imperial and Royal Opera House'. Eventually Dingelstedt's dream came true and he was appointed Director of the Burgtheater, whereupon the General Intendant, Graf Wrbna, appointed Johann Herbeck Director of the Court Opera.

Herbeck was a good-looking man, and Vienna had to wait until 1929 before it got another good-looking Director in the person of Clemens Krauss. With his great mane of hair, and his Franz Joseph beard, Herbeck had an almost hypnotic effect on women, who went into raptures over his head ('like an Old Testament prophet') and his Christ-like eyes. When he became Director of the Opera Herbeck was just under 40 (this he had in common with Clemens Krauss and incidentally with Gustav Mahler as well). Hitherto he had been the much-admired 'perpetuum mobile' of Vienna's musical life, having for some time combined the conductorship of the concerts organised by the 'Gesellschaft der Musikfreunde', the Vienna Male Voice Choir, and the *Singverein* Choir with his duties as Head of the Court Musical Establishment. Herbeck was Viennese born and bred, and having in his youth been a choirboy at Heiligenkreuz Monastery in the Vienna Woods he remained essentially choral-minded all his life. His new appointment meant that he was free to devote himself to the training of his choirs and choruses, now

The Vienna Opera, seen here in an etching by Rudolf von Alt. The absence of any broad avenue of approach, similar to the boulevard in Paris, was the subject of furious criticism even at the planning stage. We have come to love the Opera the way it is.

This series of coloured woodcuts by Petrovits-Bader is entitled: 'The Vienna Ringstrasse in its final form, and the Franz Josephs Kai.' It shows the Ringstrasse, laid out over the debris of the former ramparts, as it looked on the day of its opening. — Top: The Stock Exchange side of the Schottenring. On that terrible 'black Friday' during the World Exhibition of 1873, the Stock Exchange, and indeed Austria as a whole, was shaken to its foundations by the great depression. Millionaires became beggars overnight, the theatres were almost empty, and only Franz Jauner, the Director of the Carl Theatre, managed to fill his theatre night after night with performances of operetta. This gave the General Intendant the idea of entrusting the State Opera to this resourceful manager. The idea paid off, the Opera embarked upon one of its most illustrious periods, and Jauner made Vienna the centre of the Wagner cult. — Below left: The opposite side of the Schottenring, showing the Ring Theatre which Jauner took over after resigning

from the Opera. It burnt down in 1881 and the so-called 'House of
Atonement' was erected on the site. Hessgasse No. 7, opposite the left wing
of the theatre, was where Anton Bruckner was living during the fire, which
he witnessed at uncomfortably short range. — Below right: The old Fran-
zensring, now the Dr. Karl Lueger Ring, near the Schottentor. On the left is
the beginning of the Schottengasse, and on the right the gap in the row of
houses that led up to the Mölkerbastei and the Pasqualatihaus where Beethoven lived for a time. The Ringstrasse was part of the route of the great
procession in 1879 in observance of the silver wedding of the Emperor and
Empress. The procession was designed and arranged by the painter Hans
Makart, who rode at its head on a white horse. Makart's pompous style
was typical of his time and decisively influenced stage-design. He was a
friend of Wagner's and in 1876 gave a banquet for him in Vienna which
was a brilliant social event.

Above: The Opernring, one section of the Ring at least which is not likely to have its name changed. The building on the left of the Opera House with its awnings out is the former Opern Café where artists used to gather after the performances. It was also a favourite meeting-place for a quick snack before the performance. People who found it too expensive used to meet their friends at the 'Sirk Corner' (right-hand edge), well known for its association with the writer Karl Kraus. In musical centres like Vienna or Milan the Opera is always a favourite place to meet. (Unlike New York

or Zurich, where, as I know from experience, not every taxi-driver knows where the opera house is.) — Below: The other side of the Opernring, showing the old Heinrichshof where Leo Slezak lived (Opernring 23, a few houses further along, was the home of Franz von Suppé). As children we used to hang about outside waiting for Slezak to come out or look in at the Café Heinrichshof, which was his regular haunt. The great singers of today have no 'regular haunts'; their schedule of engagements does not include that luxury.

Above: The Kärntnerring on the Grand Hotel and Hotel Bristol side; and the corner looking down the Schwarzenbergplatz. This stretch of the Ring might well be called Vienna's 'Music Street'. In former times the pavements between the Opera House and the Schwarzenbergplatz were thronged with the late-morning 'Ringstrasse Corso'. Nowadays, it connects Vienna's three foremost musical institutions, the Opera House, the Musikverein and the Konzerthaus. It was also along this stretch that Hugo Wolf and some

kindred spirits unharnessed the horses of Wagner's cab and pulled it themselves from the Opera House to the Hotel Imperial. — Below: The Hotel Imperial, before the top stories were added. Wagner stayed here in 1875 and again in 1876 when he was conducting and producing at the Opera on his last visit to Vienna. The Café Imperial on the left of the hotel's main entrance was a regular haunt of Mahler's.

The Kolowrat Ring, now Schubert Ring, showing in the right foreground the former mansion of Archduke Ludwig Viktor which in 1911 was turned into an Imperial Officers' Mess. This was the most fashionable section of the Ringstrasse where the aristocracy and the *nouveaux riches* had their mansions.

The Park Ring and the former 'Gartenbau Gesellschaft', a favourite place of amusement, with flower-shops (and a fine flag). In the background, to the right of the tower of St. Stephen's, is the Palais Coburg, irreverently known among the Viennese as 'Asparagus Hall' from its row of slender pillars. On the opposite side of the Ring are the Stadtpark and Kursalon, a favourite place of amusement during the years between the completion of the Ringstrasse and the outbreak of World War I.

A front view of the future Imperial Opera, an original drawing from the design submitted by the architects Siccardsburg
and van der Nüll for the competition announced on 10 July
1860. Entries were to be submitted to the Court Chamberlain
in a sealed envelope marked with a motto, in this case 'Fais ce
que dois, advienne que pourra' ('Do what you must, come
what may').

III/1

These two lithographs (1851) by Josef Kriehuber depict August von Siccardsburg (left) and Eduard van der Null. Both were natives of Vienna, close friends and colleagues, and both achieved fame long before building the Opera House. Van der Null was born in 1812 and Siccardsburg in 1813, the same year as Wagner. They both completed their architectural studies in Vienna in the same year (1839) and their careers devel-

III/2

oped along extraordinarily parallel lines. Both went to study first in Rome and later in France and Berlin, where they were in contact with Schinkel, and they returned to Vienna together in 1843 to take up appointments on the teaching staff of the Academy of Arts. Together they built the Upper House in Budapest (1844), the Carl Theatre (1847), the Sophiensäle and the Arsenal (all in Vienna), as well as one or two private mansions. Van der Nüll also designed a portfolio for Queen Victoria and a missal for the Empress Elisabeth. The culmination of their careers was to be the Vienna Opera House, but neither of them lived to see its completion. Deliberately malicious criticism drove van der Nüll to suicide in April 1868, and Siccardsburg died two months later, literally of a broken heart.

III/3

Above: Part of a photograph of the Opera House's foundation-stone being ceremonially laid at 10 a.m. on 20 May 1863. The site is best described in a document of the same date: 'The All-Highest's choice fell on a large open space of 3,000 Quadrat-

klafter (about 147,000 square feet) between the south end of the Kärntnerstrasse and the recently approved Ringstrasse which includes the area formerly occupied by the two Kärntner gates and their adjoining bastions'. The same document goes on: 'And thus may the Opera House come into being as one of those monumental buildings in days to come that will keep alive the grateful memory of its august initiator; itself a monument to the arts and a place of their cultivation.'

From a contemporary account of the opening of the new Opera House: 'And when at last the monumental new Opera took over from the ageing Kärntnertor Theatre there seemed to be no place in these vast gilded halls for the old Vienna atmosphere that the Burgtheater cultivated right up to the end. Everything in the new Opera House is too magnificent and splendid; without a telescope one hardly knows where one is, and the fourth gallery, the home of the real objective enthusiasts, is as high as the top of St. Stephen's tower, and from those dizzy heights even the most substantial soprano looks like a dwarf.'

The opening performance of *Don Giovanni* on 25 May 1869 was conducted by Heinrich Proch, who had been a *Kapellmeister* at the Kärntnertor Theatre since 1840. It is to his German translation of *Il Trovatore* that we are indebted for the famous 'Lodern zum Himmel seh' ich die Flammen'. The picture (especially in the right-hand sector) is a good illustration of where the conductor used to station himself in those days, right on the edge of the stage, from where he could conduct the singers and could also attend to the orchestra in an emergency. This gala performance was attended by the Emperor Franz Joseph and the King of Hanover. The absence of the Empress occasioned a good deal of comment.

'Attenzione!
Stagione
italiana!
Sgra. Adelina
Patti.
Il Barbiere
di Siviglia.
In the second
act an inserted
song:
A Romance by
Baroness
W. Rotschildt.
The libretto
can be obtained
at the
ticket-office
and in the
book-store
L. Rosner
(Tuchlauben 22)
for the price
of 30 Kreuzer.
Time: 7 p.m.'

(Woodcut after
J. W. Frey).

The interior of the old Opera House, though lost forever, will always be fresh in the minds of those who knew it as it was from 1869 until its destruction just before the end of the Second World War in 1945. One can only be thankful that the loggia above the Ringstrasse, with its lovely frescoes by Schwind, together with a few adjoining rooms survived the holocaust and now constitute a precious link between yesterday and today.

The Interior of the Old Opera House

'Hier bist du an geweihtem Ort' ('Here you are on sacred ground') says Gurnemanz to Parsifal. The artist has managed to recapture all that went to make up the elusive nimbus of the old Opera House. He portrays it empty, which merely enhances the impression; what emerges is the interior's 'personality', and the reader is free to people it in his imagination from memories of Mahler conducting, or Schalk, or Knappertsbusch, or Clemens Krauss, or Bruno Walter, or any of the other celebrities who officiated here. On the extreme left in the top row, recognisable by its low ceiling and wide frontage, was the artists' box (men only, the ladies' one being in a corresponding position on the other side of the house). Both of course were always raked by hundreds of opera-glasses. Only those who used the box knew of a secret acoustic phenomenon: one had only to tilt one's chair back about three feet and whisper 'Lehmann' to see Lotte break into a smile of acknowledgement from the ladies' box (the story is vouched for by Kammersänger Alfred Jerger). — Over: The royal box, for the use of the Emperor and Empress, their closest relations and other distinguished personages. Together with the Emperor's staircase and royal box drawing-room it was the focal point of the 'precincts reserved for the use of the All-Highest and His Court'.

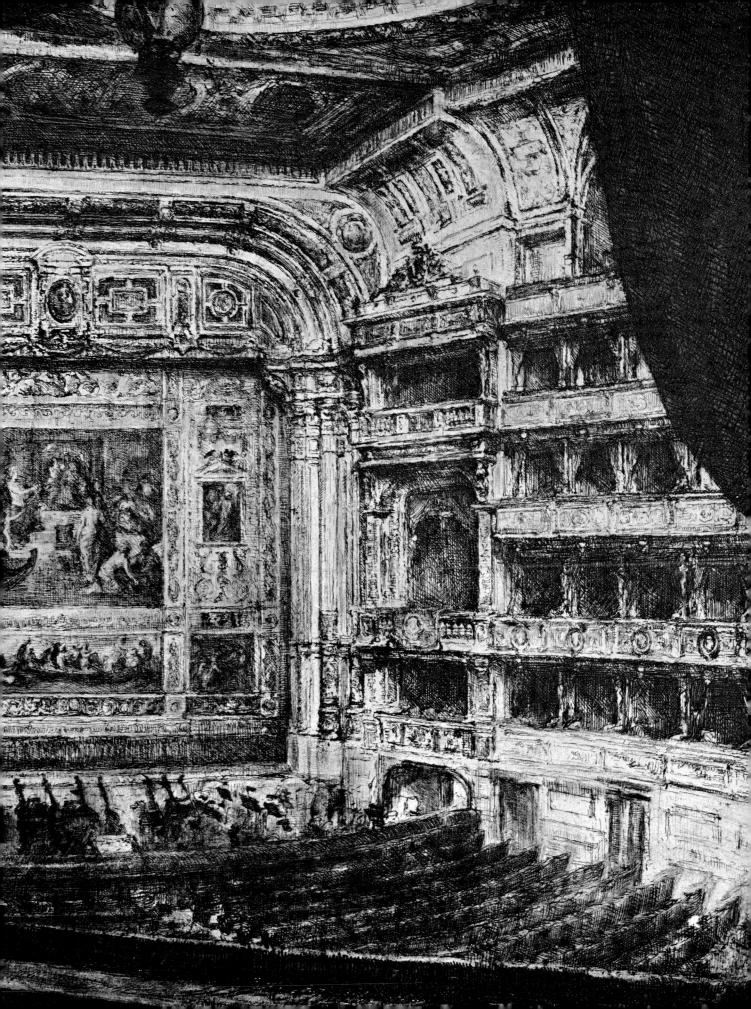

The Ceiling and Mural
Frescoes in the Foyer

How many visitors to the Vienna Opera enjoying a stroll in the foyer during the interval
ever take the trouble to look up at the ceiling
and appreciate Friedrich Sturm's painting 'The
Contest for the Laurels, and Victory'? This orna-
mental and floral painter also executed the
garlands in the loggia according to designs by
Schwind.

Moritz von Schwind, a romantic Viennese painter who was a friend of Schubert's as well as of the architects who built the Opera House, decorated the loggia with frescoes of scenes from *Die Zauberflöte* and also painted fourteen murals in egg-white on canvas of scenes from other well-known operas.
Above: a scene from Gluck's tragic opera *Armide* based on Tasso's 'Gerusalemme liberata'. — Below: a scene from Rossini's Cinderella-opera *La Cenerentola* in which the composer's wife, the contralto Isabella Colbran, gave a brilliant performance, as did Christa Ludwig over a hundred years later. — Right: a scene from Boieldieu's *La dame blanche*, the comic equivalent of Grillparzer's *Die Ahnfrau*.

Schwind's choice of composers in 1869 seems somewhat bizarre by today's standards, for although Mozart, Beethoven, Weber and Meyerbeer are amongst those present, there is not a sign of Wagner or Verdi. On the other hand Schubert is represented by his opera *Der häusliche Krieg* (below) and Haydn by his oratorio *The Creation* (above).

that the days of Metternich and police-chief Sedlnitzky were over (they had been against male-voice choirs because 'everything that involves communal activities and aspirations encourages, directly or indirectly, freedom').

Herbeck was Vienna's darling. The dreaded critic Eduard Hanslick, who was a friend of his, described him as 'a conductor of genius with a demagogic effect'. Herbeck was also a great attraction on the concert platform. In 1866 he conducted a series of mammoth concerts (1,600 performers) in the Spanish Riding School between what are now the Josefsplatz and the Michaelerplatz. His Schubert discoveries are part of musical history. In the 'Spina'schen' music-shop in the Graben in Vienna he discovered the 'Gesang der Geister über den Wassern' among a jumble of manuscripts which the proprietor described as 'just a lot of junk'. In 1865 he visited Anselm Hüttenbrenner, a friend of Schubert's, who was then an eccentric old invalid living near Graz. In a cupboard he found a 'symphonic fragment' in B minor which had been languishing there for no fewer than forty-three years. It proved to be the *Unfinished Symphony*.

Herbeck's great sorrow was that nobody took his own compositions seriously. Neither his four symphonies nor his seven Masses and Oratorios nor his male-voice choruses (including a 'War-song against the Italians' and a 'Festival chorus for the unveiling of the Maria-Theresia memorial'), nor his thirteen-movement incidental music to Goethe's *Faust*, nor his parody *Beethoven's Tenth Symphony* had any success at all.

What Herbeck lacked in theatrical experience he made up for in idealism and imagination. His great achievements were the first Vienna performances of *Die Meistersinger*, *Aida* and *Die Königin von Saba* with which he increased by three the list of what were called 'Divine Service operas' (*Le Prophète*, *La Juive* etc.).

Herbeck was co-founder of the 'Akademischer Wagnerverein' and an out-and-out Wagnerite, though he lacked the intellectual equipment to make much of *Tristan* and the *Ring*. Shortly after Johann Strauss and his band in the early 1850s played excerpts from Wagner's operas for the first time in Vienna, Herbeck introduced into his Male Voice Choir concerts his own arrangements of the Pilgrims' Chorus from *Tannhäuser*, the Sailors' Chorus from the *Fliegender Holländer*, and the Battle Hymn from *Rienzi* long before the Vienna premières of these operas.

Herbeck had been delegated to take over the first performance of *Die Meistersinger* before the departure of Dingelstedt, who didn't think much of it. It was performed on the twenty-seventh of February 1870 in an atmosphere of considerable tension — Vienna was the seventh city *Die Meistersinger* had been performed in, and *Die Meistersinger* was Vienna's fourth Wagner opera (it goes without saying that Johann Strauss and his band had for some time been giving extracts from it). The evening of the first performance happened to be the last Sunday in Carnival, which led to a good deal of horse-play, especially in the Café Walch opposite the Opera, which was the regular haunt of the singers and orchestral players. At the Burgtheater there was a farce called *Rosenmüller und Finke* in which the following exchange occured: Cashier: 'I hear they're rehearsing a new opera, *Meistersinger*.' Clerk: 'Yes, I shall hear it.' Cashier: 'You won't; by the time it actually reaches the stage the entire cast will have lost their voices!'

At the première both the Wagnerites and the anti-Wagnerites in the audience were ready for a scrap. Applause in those days was frequent and uninhibited so of course there was applause after the Overture, though Wagner had directed that it lead straight into the church-scene. There were also salvoes of heavy applause after the song 'Am stillen Herd'. But Beckmesser's Serenade in Act Two gave the anti-Wagnerites their chance to set up a chorus of boos and catcalls. Johann N. Beck, the Hans Sachs, lost his nerve completely and Herbeck, himself a trained singer, had to sing his part while conducting. But Campe, as Beckmesser, stuck it out manfully, and by the end of Act Two the anti-Wagnerites were clearly in a minority. The performance ended in a blaze of triumph — at least as far as the audience was concerned — but most of the critics were hostile. In the *Fremdenblatt* Ludwig Speidel wistfully commented: 'The valiant few who remained true to their convictions expect satisfaction and vindication during the years that lie ahead.'

The humourist Daniel Spitzer wrote commentaries on cultural life in Vienna in his 'Wiener Spaziergänge' (Walks through Vienna), which appeared in the 'Neue Freie Presse'. On 6 March 1870 he wrote about the première of 'Die Meistersinger'. (From Spitzer's 'Gesammelte Schriften', published in 1912.)

Die Zukunftsmuſik-Deklaranten wollten nicht den Ausgleich, nur den vollen Sieg; jede Trivialität, ja ſelbſt die widerliche Bell- und Miau-Muſik des zweiten Aktes, wurde von den muſikaliſchen Tſchechen mit enthuſiaſtiſchem Beifalle begrüßt; wenig hätte gefehlt, und ſie würden bei den wirklich ſchönen Stellen aus reiner Oppoſitionsluſt zu ziſchen begonnen haben. Der Ouvertüre nach zu ſchließen, hätte wenigſtens einer der im Ueberfluß vorhandenen Schuſter ein tragiſches Ende erreichen ſollen, aber dieſe Erwartung wurde getäuſcht. Gevatter Schneider und Handſchuhmacher balgen ſich zu den Klängen einer marcia funebre. — Man denke ſich „Lumpacivagabundus" auf der Bühne, während das Orcheſter die „Eroica" dazu aufſpielt.

Die Sprache ſelbſt der Honoratioren dieſes Opernluſtſpiels, welche hin und wieder neben dem Geſindel zu Worte kommen, iſt, um eine Wagnerſche Ausdrucksweiſe anzuwenden, ein wahres „Geſchlamb und Geſchlumbfer", ſie ſchwatzen reinen Unſinn; manchmal glaubt man, Berauſchte lallen zu hören, und es gereicht denſelben kaum zur Entſchuldigung, daß ſie ſich ſelbſt wiederholt der „Dummheit" zeihen.

So erklärt der ehrenfeſte Herr Veit Pogner, allerdings „halb für ſich": „Ei werd' ich dumm"; Hans Sachs richtet an ſeinen Lehrbuben David die freundliche Einladung: „Verſchlaf deine Dummheit", was ein um ſo ſchlechteres Licht auf die anderen wirft, da beſagtem David von dem Chor der Lehrbuben nachgerühmt wird, daß er „der Allergeſcheit'ſt ſei; der Intrigant und Stadtſchreiber Beckmeſſer richtet an ſich die Gewiſſensfrage: „Darum, darum wär' ich ſo dumm?" und „das Volk" erklärt in gerechter Würdigung der geiſtigen Beſtrebungen desſelben: „Gott, iſt der dumm"! Endlich kann ſelbſt die Heldin Eva nicht umhin, das Bekenntnis abzulegen: „Ich bin wohl recht dumm!" und im Hinblicke auf das Duett, welches ſie mit Walter von Stolzing, ihrem Freier, ſingt, ſcheint ſie ſich auch in der Tat zwar ſtreng, aber gerecht beurteilt zu haben. Es klingt wie der Schwanengeſang des geſunden Menſchenverſtandes, wenn ſie in die leidenſchaftlichen Worte ausbricht: „Ja ihr ſeid es, nein du biſt es, alles ſag' ich, denn ihr wißt es, alles klag' ich), denn ich weiß es", uſf. uſf.

Es iſt weiſe eingerichtet von der Natur, daß die menſchliche Stimme der Wagnerſchen Muſik nicht gewachſen iſt, und daß ſie ſo die Heiſerkeit vor die Taubheit geſetzt hat!

The *avantgardistes* cared not for compromise but only for complete victory: each triviality, indeed even the disgusting barking and mewing of the music in the second act was hailed by a round of applause from the musical 'Tschechen'; little more was wanting, and they would have begun to hiss during the really beautiful sections, this out of sheer love of contradiction. To judge by the Overture, at least one of the superabundant throng of cobblers should have met an unhappy end, but this expectation proved false. The rough and tumble between the smaller tradesfolk took place to the strains of a *marche funèbre*. We may picture 'Lumpazivagabundus' on the stage with 'Eroica' as an orchestral accompaniment.

The language in this operatic comedy, even of the persons of quality who occasionally manage to break into the chatter of the lower orders, is, to use a Wagnerian term, 'a real huddle-muddle', they talk utter nonsense; at times it resembles nothing so much as the babbling of drunkards, and the fact that they repeatedly accuse themselves of 'stupidity' can scarcely be accepted by way of justification.

Thus, the prestigious Veit Pogner, admittedly *sotto voce*, declares: 'Nay, but I am losing my wits'; Hans Sachs offers his apprentice, David, the friendly advice to 'sleep off your stupidity', which casts an even more dubious light upon the others, as the said David is alleged by the chorus of apprentices to be 'the cleverest of all'; the intriguer and town scribe Beckmesser examines his own conscience: 'Hence, ah hence my folly?' and 'the people' exclaim in a just appraisal of the mental efforts of that gentleman: 'Oh Lord, what a fool is he!' At length even the heroine Eva cannot refrain from placing it on record: 'I am indeed most stupid!' And having regard to the duet which she sings with her suitor Walter von Stolzing, she appears to have judged herself strictly, but not unjustly. It sounds like the swansong of commonsense when she breaks out into the passionate words: 'Ah, it is thou, nay, but it is thou, I shall say all, for thou knowest it, all sorrows tell, for I know it' and so on and so forth.

It is a wise provision of nature that the human voice cannot contend with Wagner's music and that, in consequence, hoarseness precedes deafness.

The performance lasted three and a half hours (the first performance in Munich had lasted five). Among the drastic cuts made in Vienna were David's narrative in the first act and the Sachs-Stolzing conversation in the third. Wagner himself was not present, but in his lakeside villa near Lucerne he was given far from objective reports by over-zealous friends, and vented his wrath by bombarding Herbeck with letters and telegrams. He was as furious about the cast as he was about the cuts. Berta Ehnn (Eva) he called 'a baggage from the Salvi-Offenbach school' (he had not forgotten that it was Matteo Salvi, Herbeck's predecessor, who had dropped *Tristan* in favour of Offenbach's *Rhein-Nixen*). Wagner was also incensed about the night-watchman's horn being played by 'a quaking trombonist' instead of on a bull's horn as Wagner himself prescribed. In point of fact it was a bass cornet, as Herbeck was afraid that a bull's horn might grate and ruin the whole scene. Another thing that Wagner protested about was Beckmesser's Serenade's being accompanied by 'an insipid guitar'. In fact it was a mandolin, because the steel-harp of the kind prescribed by Wagner did not arrive from Munich in time. Nowadays of course the harp and bull's horn are always strictly adhered to. Wagner even threatened to complain about Herbeck to 'the highest authority'.

The real reasons for Wagner's wrath lay deeper. He wanted a performance without cuts, as in Munich, and he had naturally expected to be invited to Vienna to supervise the preparations for the première: it was Dingelstedt who stopped his coming. Another bone of contention was that back in the 1850s, when he was living in exile, he had let the Vienna Opera have *Tannhäuser*, *Lohengrin* and *Der Fliegende Holländer* for a relatively modest lump sum without royalties. He thought it unfair that now that his operas were being given in the new house he was still not getting any royalties. After a long struggle with the General Intendant, Herbeck at last got Wagner his royalties, but without back-payments. This was why Wagner refused for the time being to let Vienna have his latest operas, including the Paris version of *Tannhäuser*.

Herbeck, a native of Vienna and a pioneer champion of Wagner, was extremely put out; but this did not stop his efforts on behalf of Wagner's music. In 1871 he designed a production of *Der Fliegende Holländer* himself (the extremely clever lighting-plan is still extant). There was nothing unusual in this; before the appeal to the eye assumed so much importance in the 20th century, *Kapellmeister* often acted as producers as well, Jahn and Mahler at the Vienna Opera for instance, and Toscanini at the Scala in Milan.

In this same year 1870 *Rienzi* became the fifth Wagner opera to find its way into the Vienna repertoire, twenty-nine years after its first performance. Its success was sensational — even the Emperor loved it — and this colourful spectacle was a first choice for the entertainment of visiting potentates until well on into the Mahler era. Wagner saw *Rienzi* in Vienna and was disgusted. He waited only until the first trumpet-call in the Overture before storming out of his box into the buffet, where he cooled down over some ice-cream. He then returned to his box, and kept quiet until the interval, when he castigated the scenery as all wrong historically. What he saw was not the first Vienna performance but a revival in May 1872, when he was conducting in the *Musikvereinssaal* the three famous concerts he organised to raise funds for his Bayreuth plan. The programmes included the *Eroica* and excepts from his own operas. During the 'Magic Fire Music' a violent thunderstorm started, and in his speech after the concert Wagner took this as a good omen. The popular actress Pepi Gallmeyer was so thrilled that she swore never to act in Nestroy's parody of *Tannhäuser* again.

Herbeck saw Verdi's latest opera, *Aida*, at the Scala in Milan and at once secured it for Vienna. The Vienna première in 1874 was a great success, and a critic named Helm wrote that the scenery was so true to life that there was now no need for Crown Prince Rudolf to take a course in Egyptian archaeology. Another oriental opera, Goldmark's *Die Königin von Saba* (1875), proved to be Herbeck's last première. The General Intendant refused to sanction the cost of new scenery, so the production had to make do with the well-worn sets of the ballet *Sardanapalus*.

Both these operas were tremendous box-office attractions, though Hanslick denied that *Aida* possessed a spark of creative genius or that it was even the work of a master. As for *Die Königin von Saba*, some of his colleagues called it the 'music of the future', 'like Wagner's amorphous form'.

With his other premières Herbeck's fortunes varied, but he always set himself the same lofty artistic standards. He put on a lavish production of Weber's *Oberon* and also introduced Schumann's totally undramatic *Genoveva* (to a half-empty house). Another innovation was *Der Widerspenstigen Zähmung (The Taming of the Shrew)* by Hermann Goetz, whose premature death was a great tragedy. It is an attractive work with echoes of *Die Meistersinger*, though Goetz stoutly denied he had ever heard Wagner's masterpiece. At the first performance at Mannheim, Katharina and Petrucchio had had to make do with a horse with a specially built double saddle, but in Vienna Herbeck provided them with a one-horse cab. In 1873, the year of the World Exhibition, the Opera was open the whole year without a break. The summer's first novelty was Ambroise Thomas' *Hamlet* which, like his *Mignon*, was a great favourite with the public but was ridiculed by the critics. Among characteristic 'Herbeckisms' which upset the purists was the addition of altos in the Hunting Chorus in *Freischütz*. I can myself remember having heard in my younger days a survival from the days of Herbeck, namely the insertion of Herbeck's orchestration of Mozart's 'Turkish March' before the last act of *Die Entführung*, and I must confess that I still miss it! Herbeck was also responsible for a performance of *A Midsummer Night's Dream* with Mendelssohn's music as *théâtre paré*, and a concert performance of Gluck's *Orfeo* with the contralto Caroline Bettelheim (who was also Vienna's first Salica in Meyerbeer's *L'Africaine*).

One thing Herbeck inherited from Dingelstedt and the much-maligned Matteo Salvi was an admirable ensemble. The two casts of *Don Giovanni*, with which the new house opened its doors in 1869, were the backbone of his resources, whether in their former rôles or in new ones. Johann N. Beck took the part of Hans Sachs but relinquished it after the first few performances. The first Stolzing was Gustav Walter, who also gave recitals. Berta Ehnn was brilliant as the 'Shrew', and Luise Dustmann, whose vocal powers were declining sharply, created the rôle of Genoveva. The first Aida and Sulamith was Marie Wilt. Her voice was phenomenal, but her ample proportions gave rise to a certain amount of ribaldry (such as 'Round the Wilt in 80 days') which could hardly help coming to her ears. She ended her life by jumping out of her window ...

Capellmeister Herbeck in:

„Die Meistersinger von Nürnberg". Erster Akt.

Capellmeister Herbeck in:

„Die Meistersinger von Nürnberg". Zweiter Akt.

Capellmeister Herbeck in:

„Die Meistersinger von Nürnberg". Dritter Akt.

As well as Amalie Materna from Styria, Vienna's first Amneris and Queen of Sheba, Herbeck engaged another Styrian in the person of Emil Scaria, who developed into one of the greatest Wagnerian basses of all time. Among other useful acquisitions were the coloratura soprano Ilma von Murska, the Ophelia in Thomas' *Hamlet;* Minnie Hauck, a charming soubrette and the first American to appear at the Vienna Opera; and Pauline Lucca, who made her début as Margarethe. She was Viennese born and bred and a pupil of the *Chef du chant* Richard Lewy. Herbeck only took her on to pacify Lewy, who was his arch-enemy, and had no inkling of the sensational Carmen she was to develop into.

In 1873 the coloratura diva Adelina Patti delighted all and sundry as Lucia, one year after her appearance in an Italian *stagione* at the Theater an der Wien. Herbeck, who was a lifelong champion of the orchestral players and got their salaries raised twice during his term of office, prevailed upon Patti to sing at a charity performance for the orchestra's pension fund, a project of his own which he had started in 1872 and always had very much at heart. It was financed out of the proceeds of the six annual charity performances, the subsidy, contributions from members of the orchestra, and the capital of the existing private fund.

In his conscientious attempts to do away at long last with the claque Herbeck was no more successful than his predecessors, nor did he manage to enforce a ban on curtain-calls while the curtain was up.

The last years of Herbeck's term of office were clouded by the great slump, culminating in that Black Friday when there was a crash on the Stock Exchange in which fortunes were wiped out, leading to the collapse of many industrial undertakings and a period of depression, despair and suicides. Takings at the theatres plunged: the only shows to profit from the all-pervading gloom were Johann Strauss operettas at the Theater an der Wien and the French operettas at the Carl Theatre. Yet although attendances at the Opera were smaller than ever, salaries and the costs of production continued to rise.

This was the situation that Herbeck's enemies turned to their advantage, and they launched a campaign to which

his sensitive nature and abhorrence of intrigue eventually succumbed. In the house itself his greatest enemy, as we have seen, was Richard Lewy, the first horn player in the orchestra whom Herbeck had appointed *chef du chant* along the lines postulated by Wagner. The Emperor Franz Joseph was very fond of Herbeck and conferred on him during his illness the Order of the Iron Crown (third class), which meant his elevation to the nobility. But even the Emperor could do nothing to save Herbeck, because what finally toppled him was the all-powerful office of the General Intendant.

This department had been set up in 1867 by the Emperor himself and was intended to act as a link between the Court Theatres and the First Court Chamberlain, whose duties included the administration of the subsidies or *dotations* allotted by the Ministry of Finance. But in this capacity the General Intendant's office encroached more and more greedily on purely artistic domains. It not only exercised control *(de facto)* over rises in expenditure but also had a say in the programme for the season and in the engagement of singers. Of one General Intendant, Graf Wrbna, it was said that he had his eye on the box-office during the daytime and on the ballet in the evening.

Johann Herbeck may have been pathologically touchy, but his conscience as a Civil Servant prevented him from resorting to open revolt. In April 1875 he was finally driven to his resignation, which was virtually tantamount to dimissal. His last act in office was to recommend the great conductor Hans Richter. Herbeck went back to running the 'Gesellschaft der Musikfreunde' concerts, which during his period as Director of the Opera had been in the hands of Anton Rubinstein and Johannes Brahms. (Would an Opera Director to-day give up the conductorship of his concert-series on his appointment to the Opera?)

Two years later Johann Herbeck was dead. With his death, said one of the singers, poetry had departed from the house. And so the term of office of the first star-conductor to become Director of the Vienna Opera ended not so very differently from that of many of his successors.

K. K. Hof-  Operntheater.

Sonntag den 11. Februar 1872.

232. Vorstellung im Jahres-Abonnement.

Die lustigen Weiber von Windsor.

Komisch-phantastische Oper in drei Akten, nach Shakespeare's gleichnamigen Lustspiel, von
S. H. Mosenthal. Musik von Otto Nicolai.
Die Recitative und die Ballade der Frau Reich (3. Akt) von H. Proch.

(Erste Aufführung im neuen Hause.)

Sir John Falstaff	. . .	Hr. Hablawetz. –
Herr Fluth, } Bürger von Windsor	. . .	Hr. Mayerhofer.
Herr Reich, }	. . .	Hr. Krauß.
Fenton	. . .	Hr. Müller. –
Junker Spärlich	. . .	Hr. Regenspurger. –
Dr. Cajus	. . .	Hr. Lay. –
Frau Fluth	. . .	Fr. Dustmann.
Frau Reich	. . .	Frl. Gindele.
Jungfer Anna Reich	. . .	Frl. Siegstädt.
Der Kellner im Gasthause zum Hosenbande	. . .	Hr. Lucca. –
Pitt, } Bürger	. . .	Hr. Wessely.
Pott, }	. . .	Hr. Haag.

Bürger und Frauen von Windsor. Knechte. Kinder.
Masken als Elfen, Fliegen, Wespen und in verschiedenen anderen
abenteuerlichen Gestalten.

Ort der Handlung: Windsor. Zeit: Das 15. Jahrhundert.

Im 3. Akte. **Elfentanz,** komponirt von C. Telle. (Musik aus der Oper „Die Rhein-
Nixen" von J. Offenbach.) Die Fräulein Jacksch, Wildhack, Mauthner,
Minna, Olzer, das weibliche Balletcorps und die Eleven.
Ballabile. Die Fräulein Jacksch, Wildhack, Mauthner, Charles, Minna,
Olzer und das Balletcorps.

Die zur Oper „Die lustigen Weiber von Windsor" vorver-
kauften Sperrsitze sind heute giltig.

K. K. Hof- Operntheater.

Dinstag den 15. April 1873.
Mit Allerhöchster Genehmigung Sr. Majestät des Kaisers.
Zum Vortheile des Fondes der den Allerhöchsten Namen führenden Stiftung zur
Versorgung kaiserlicher und königlicher Offiziers-Witwen und Waisen.
Mit aufgehobenem Abonnement.

Ouverture zu der Oper „Rienzi", von Richard Wagner.

Unter Leitung des Directors **J. Herbeck.**
Das Orchester der kais. königl. Hof-Oper.

Das Weib des Kriegers.

Dramatischer Prolog von Josef Weilen. Musik von Franz Doppler.

Gertrud	Fr. Gabillon.
Ihre Kinder	{ Therese Link. / Sofie Link.

1. Tableau: **Auf dem Schlachtfelde.** Die Herren Mitterwurzer, Ricchini, Birkmeier Ig.', Hassis, Horvath, Klaß Jos., Manzantini B., Manzantini C., Recke.
2. Tableau: **Segen der Mildthätigkeit.** Frl. Vreheisen, Fr. Telle, Petermann, die Fräulein Schömanek, Ricchini, Gebrer, die Herren Beau und Kiriabaum.
3. Tableau: **Heimkehr und Friede.** Die Fräulein Jacksch, Wildhack, Buchs, Löscher, Minna, Dobrauer, Neumann M., Rimus, Stublik, Tomaschütz, Scholz, Biz, die Herren Frayparr, Brice, Hazreiter, Caron, Frappart L., Klaß A., Hassa, Runzianti, Winkler und Rina.
Die Tableaux entworfen und arrangirt von Franz Gaul.

CONCERT.

1. C. M. Weber. Concertstück mit Orchesterbegleitung. Frau Sophie Meuter.
2. Lieder: a) „Das Mädchen und der Schmetterling", von Gustav Scharfe. } Herr Emil Scaria,
   b) „Abschied", Lied von August Horn. k. k. Hof-Opernsänger.
3. Arie aus „Hernani". Fr. Wilt, k. k. Kammer- und Hof-Opernsängerin.

Aus der komischen Oper.

Lustspiel in einem Akte nach dem Französischen des Henri Murger von C. Zell.

Raoul Gerard	Hr. Sonnenthal	Rose, Kammermädchen . . . Frl. Wagner.
Dubreuil, ehemals Schiffskapitän . . Hr. Mizner.		Scene: Paris 1860.
Juliette de Santeuil, seine Nichte . Frl. Janisch.		

Fünfundzwanzig Mädchen und kein Mann.

Komische Operette in 1 Akt von Carl Treumann. Musik von Franz v. Suppé.

Hr. v. Schönhahn, Gutsbesitzer	Hr. C. Treumann.	Bärbele, die Schwäbin, } Töchter Fr. Hartmann.
Danubia, die Oesterreicherin,	Frl. Janisch.	Preziosa, die Arragoneserin, Frl. Scholz.
Hidalga, die Castilianerin,	Frl. Salvioni.	Marianka, die Böhmin, Frl. Buck.
Britta, die Engländerin,	Frl. Ehnn.	Sidonia, Wirthschafterin . . Frl. Gindele.
Maschinka, die Baierin, } seine Töchter	Frl. Tremel.	Agamemnon, Thierarzt . . . Hr. Blasel.
Giletta, die Portugiesin,	Frl. Mauthner.	Dienstmädchen . Damen vom Hof-Opernballet.
Almina, die Tirolerin,	Frl. Dillner.	Pensionärinnen . Damen vom Hof-Opernchor.
Limonia, die Italienerin,	Fr. Fr. Materna.	

Die Handlung spielt auf Schönhahns Gut, in der Nähe einer großen Stadt.

Kassa-Eröffnung 6 Uhr. — Anfang 7 Uhr.

In the old days it was not unusual to include excerpts from other operas. The programme of this performance of Otto Nicolai's 'The Merry Wives of Windsor' mentions the 'Ballade der Frau Reich' in Act Three with music by the Hauskapellmeister Heinrich Proch. One oddity was: Act Three contained a 'dance of the elves' with music from Jacques Offenbach's opera 'Die Rhein-Nixen' — years later this melody became world-famous as the 'Barcarolle' in 'Les Contes d'Hoffmann'.

The first operetta in the new house was 'Fünfundzwanzig Mädchen und kein Mann' by Franz von Suppé.

The Viennese half expect the unexpected as far as their theatres are concerned. But even for a city as accustomed to spectacular developments as Vienna is, the four and a half years following Herbeck's resignation were something of a novelty, for as the new Director of the Court Opera, Franz Jauner, managed to combine his duties with running the Carl Theatre, a 'suburban' establishment, at the same time. At the latter he put on popular pieces such as *Mein Leopold*, painstaking and successful productions of popular comedies. At the former he embarked upon the last round in his campaign to get Wagner established. If the Director's rooms at the Carl Theatre were too small for a first-night party after a new Johann Strauss operetta, he would entertain the king of the waltz in his rooms at the Court Opera. Earlier, the general opinion had been that Jauner was, to put it mildly, a lowbrow who was concerned only with the business side of the theatre. This was not fair. Jauner may have been eccentric, but he was one of the most brilliant Directors the Vienna Opera ever had. He was a *bon vivant* too, and remained one right up to the day he blew his brains out.

The immediate occasion of Jauner's appointment was a purely budgetary consideration. Vienna was still suffering from the after-effects of the Stock Exchange crash in 1873, and the Opera's deficit was by now almost out of control. As the official responsible for the Court theatres, the Court Chamberlain was bound to submit to the Emperor the names of possible Directors. At this critical juncture, Constantin Prinz zu Hohenlohe-Schillingsfürst, who held the office of Court Chamberlain for thirty years (a list of his titles and distinctions, from 'Knight of the Golden Fleece' to 'Honorary Member of the Arts and Crafts Association', would take a whole page), showed how well he knew his job. Himself an art lover and practising musician as well as a shrewd business-man, he realised the necessity of following the producer Dingelstedt and the conductor Herbeck with an administrative expert who would keep an eye on the box-office and not only on the score. Furthermore, Vienna's operetta theatres had been far less badly hit by the slump than the others, nor had it escaped the Lord Chamberlain's notice that the Carl Theatre was making record

profits out of its operettas, farces and popular comedies. It was for this reason that in February 1875 he offered Franz Jauner the post of Director of the Court Opera (after Jauner had already refused it twice). Just imagine: if *Fledermaus* had been a more lucrative box-office attraction at the Theater an der Wien in 1874, Marie Geistinger, a co-director of the Theater an der Wien, might well have been appointed Director of the Court Opera!

Franz Jauner was the son of a Viennese Court engraver. In his early years he made one or two appearances at the Burgtheater and in various German towns, and later became an actor and producer at the Carl Theatre before taking over as its Director in 1872. In his portraits he looks like a character out of Schiller, or like Wagner (whom he admired so much) in his younger days. He was as clever as paint, resourceful, shrewd and full of ideas. He staged and produced everything, from Raimund's *Verschwender* to Jules Verne's *Round the World in 80 Days*. His great ambition was to find some way of challenging Johann Strauss ascendancy at the Theater an der Wien. At one time he thought he had found an 'anti-pope' in the person of the French composer Charles Lecocq, who was hailed as Offenbach's successor. He accordingly put on Lecocq's latest operettas, *La fille de Madame Angot* and *Giroflé, Giroflà* at the Carl Theatre.

Jauner always had a sixth sense for original experiments, and in his very first year (1872) as Director of the Carl Theatre he put on an operetta by Delibes, *Confucius IV*. After his appointment to the Court Opera he gave the first performance of Suppé's operetta *Fatinitza* at the Carl Theatre, and capped all his previous successes by fixing a contract tying Johann Strauss to the Carl Theatre, where *Prinz Methusalem* was given its first performance.

So on the fifteenth of April 1875 this imaginative and brilliantly practical man of the theatre was appointed Director of the Court Opera; he took over on the first of May at the age of forty-three. Being well aware of the snags a Vienna theatre director can trip over, he made it a condition of his acceptance that the post of General

Intendant should be done away with. The General Intendant came between the Court Chamberlain and the Director of the Opera, and it was over this influential official that many of Jauner's successors were to come to grief. Jauner got his way, largely because the post had been only provisionally filled since the death of the tight-fisted Graf Wrbna the year before. Jauner also demanded — and it was granted — that the subsidy should be increased to 300,000 guilders a year and his own salary to 12,000 guilders; a 25 per cent share in the profits; a right to a pension after two years in office (did he have an inkling that he wasn't going to last long?); and sundry guarantees for the implementation of his artistic policy, the principal plank in which was a reconciliation with Richard Wagner in financial as well as artistic matters.

In a telegram from Pola, the Emperor also agreed to Jauner's most awkward stipulation, permission to run the Carl Theatre as well as the Opera, at least for the time being, which meant that there was no conflict between Jauner's interests on either side of the Danube Canal.

Immediately after his appointment Jauner sent a theatrical agent named Gustav Lewy off on a talent-spotting tour of Western Europe to scent out attractions for both his theatres. Within a few days of setting out Lewy wired from Paris: '...OPERA COMIQUE CARMEN BY MEILHAC AND HALEVY MUSIC BY A GIFTED YOUNG COMPOSER... ALSO VERDI CONDUCTING REQUIEM.' Jauner's answer was 'GET THEM ALL'.

Within forty-two days of his appointment Jauner fired his first bombshell: on the eleventh of June 1875 Verdi conducted his brand-new *Requiem* at the Court Opera the first time he had conducted in Vienna for thirty-two years (since *Nabucco* in 1843). As well as four performances of the *Requiem*, Verdi also conducted two of *Aida*. For the *Requiem* he had sent sketches in advance showing how he wanted his forces deployed on the stage, and Franco Faccio, a leading conductor at the Scala, had been going through the work with the chorus. The soprano and alto soloists had sung at the first performances of *Aida* and the *Requiem* in Milan: Teresa Stolz, a Viennese and a distant relation of Robert Stolz, and

Extract from 'The Imperial & Royal Court Opera in Vienna. A statistical review of personnel and artistic activities during the period from 25 May 1869 to 30 April 1894', Vienna 1894.

Oberster Hoftheater-Director:

Seiner Oesterreichisch - Kaiserlichen und Königlich Apostolischen Majestät Erster Obersthofmeister.

Se. Durchl. Herr **Constantin Prinz zu Hohenlohe-Schillingsfürst,** Ritter des gold. Vliesses, Gr. Kr. d. kgl. ung. St. Stephan-O., Bes. der Kriegsmedaille und d. Militär-Dienstzeichens II. Cl. für Officiere, Gr. Kr. d. toscan. O. vom heil. Josef, Gr. Kr. und Ehren-Bailli d. souv. Johanniter-O., Bes. des Marianerkreuzes des deutschen Ritter-O., Ritter des russ.-kais. St. Andreas-O. (in Brillanten), d. St. Alexander-Newsky-, d. weissen Adler-, d. St. Annen- u. d. russ.-kais. königl. St. Stanislaus-O. I. Cl., Ritter des kgl. preuss. schwarz. Adler-O., Adler-O. I. Cl., Grkr. des franz. O. d. Ehren-Legion u. d. kais. brasil. O. vom südlichen Kreuze, Bes. d. ottoman. Osmanié- u. des ottoman. Medschidjé-O. I. Cl., Ritter d. k.-italien O. der Annunziata, Bes. d. Portrait-Decoration d. Schah von Persien (in Brillanten) u. d pers. Sonnen- u. Löwen-O. I. Classe, Grosscordon d. k. japan. O. »der aufgehenden Sonne«, Ritter d. kgl dän. Elephanten-O., Gssk d kgl. portug. Thurm- u. Schwert-O. u. d. kgl. span. O. Carl III. (mit der Colane), Ritter d. kgl bayer. St. Hubertus-O. u. d. kgl. säch. O. d. Rautenkrone, Gkr. d. kgl. säch. Albrecht-O., d. kgl. württemb. Friedrich-O. und des Ordens der königl. württembergischen Krone, Ritter des königl. schwedischen Seraphinen-O., Gkr. d. kgl belg Leopold-O. (in Brillanten), d. kgl. griech O. vom heil. Erlöser, d. kgl. O. »Stern von Rumänien«, d. kgl. serb. weissen Adler-O, d. kgl. serb. Takowa-O. u. d. päpst. Pius-O., Ritter d. kgl. sicilian. St. Januarius-O., Gkr. d. königl. hannoverischen Guelphen-O., des kurfürstl. hessischen Wilhelm-O., d. grossh. hess. Ludwig-O., des grossh. sachsen-weimar'schen O. der Wachsamkeit oder vom weissen Falken und des grossh. mecklenburg. O. d. wendischen Krone, Ritter d. herzgl. nassau'schen Haus-Ordens vom goldenen Löwen, Grosskreuz d. herzgl. sächs.-Ernestinischen Haus-Ordens, Bes. d. fstl. montenegr. Danilo-O. I. Cl., Ritter des kgl. preuss. Kronen-O. II. Classe, Commandeur d. kgl. sicilian. O. Franz I., Ritter d. russ.-kais. St. Wladimir-O. IV. Cl., d. Civil-Verdienst-O. d. kgl. bayer. Krone, d. päpstl. Christus-O. u d. fürstl Hohenlohe'schen Haus- u. Phönix-O., Bes. d. päpstl. Erinnerungs-Medaille pro Petri sede; k. u. k wirkl. Geh. Rath und Kämmerer, Oberst sämmtlicher k u..k. Leibgarden, General der Cavallerie und Inhaber des k. u. k. Infanterie-Regimentes Nr. 87, lebenslängliches Mitglied des Herrenhauses des österr. Reichsrathes, Ehren-Curator des k. k. österr. Museums für Kunst und Industrie, Ehren-Mitglied der k. k. Akademie der bildenden Künste und des Kunstgewerbevereines in Wien.

Maria Waldmann. It was a triumph for Verdi, who was fêted like a king. He was delighted with Vienna but was surprised at the way the lights in the auditorium were dimmed before the performance (a practice Toscanini also introduced at the Scala, but not till many years later). Nowadays 'purists' frown on applause after Verdi's *Requiem*, but in 1875 Verdi himself entered whole-heartedly into repeating the 'Ricordare', 'Offertorium' and 'Agnus Dei'. The Emperor attended one of the performances and received Verdi in audience. The days when the name VERDI was the symbol of the revolt of the Italian Provinces against Austrian rule (Vittorio Emanuele Re d'Italia) seemed forgotten ... Just before the last performances a bust of Verdi was brought from Milan and took its place in the foyer among the busts of other great composers.

Thus Jauner came, saw and conquered. Even the dreaded Hanslick found nothing on which to vent his irony. But there was one outrageous pun by the violinist Josef Hellmesberger: it was June, and Jauner made his annual trip to Marienbad for the cure, or as Hellmesberger put it: 'Er fährt leberleidend nach Marienbad und kommt leider lebend zurück.' (A pun, roughly meaning: 'He is suffering from his liver and we are suffering from his living.')

The first real première (twenty-third of October 1875) of the Jauner era was the opera by the 'gifted young composer' referred to in Lewy's telegram. Sadly, Bizet was not to be the conductor, as Jauner had hoped; he had died in June at the age of thirty-six. It was the first performance of *Carmen* outside France after the far from successful first performance in Paris in March 1875. It was also the first performance in which the spoken dialogue was replaced by recitative. How much Jauner himself contributed to this innovation is not clear: all that is known with certainty is that for the Vienna performance of *Carmen* he insisted on sung recitatives composed by Bizet's friend Guiraud. They were not ready in time, so at the first Vienna performance there was a mixture of sung recitative and spoken dialogue, and it was not until Mahler's day that the whole of the dialogue was converted to recitative.

Carmen, like nearly all the other new works he introduced, was produced by Jauner himself, with a great deal of imagination and resource, though much of it was rather overdone and there was a slight tang of the circus about it. The brilliant cast included Bertha Ehnn as Carmen, Emil Scaria as Escamillo, and the Frankfurt tenor Georg Müller as Don José, a part which unfortunately gave him no opportunity of getting off his famous top C sharp. The notices were 'friendly': Ludwig

Speidel coined his famous expression 'operetta with dancing', while Hanslick allowed that 'the production displayed an interesting blend of spirit and talent'. The only critic to perceive the work's real stature was Ambros in the *Wiener Zeitung*. The first performances took no less than 8,200 guilders — new record — but for the time being *Carmen* was not a real box-office attraction.

But it did become one in January 1879, in Jauner's penultimate year as Director, when he discovered a sensational new Carmen in the person of Pauline Lucca, who despite her Italian stage-name was Viennese born and bred. She was piquant and she was 'sexy' (long before the word was invented). Her natural and uninhibited vivacity foreshadowed the later *verismo*. She had studied the rôle of Elsa with Wagner in Prague, and of Gretchen with Gounod in Paris.

Both on the stage and off it Lucca always seemed to be in the limelight. When some indiscreet photographs began to circulate showing her with Bismarck at Gastein there was almost a renewal of the 1866 war. In America she once sang the parts of both Leonora and Azucena in the same performance of *Il Trovatore*, and for singing the two rôles was paid for three. It was not a beautiful voice in the accepted sense, nor did she specialise in any way. She sang Donna Anna und Despina, Mignon, Katherina — anything that was offered.

But Verdi and *Carmen* were only the preliminaries to the realisation of Jauner's lifelong ambition, which was to make Vienna the home of authentic productions of the works of Richard Wagner. Jauner was shrewd enough to realise that Viennese audiences were going over to Wagner with flying colours; one had only to see how the attendance figures soared whenever a Wagner opera was put on, or to experience the salvoes of applause at the 'Bayreuth Fund' concerts in the *Musikvereinssaal* in the spring of 1875, with Wagner himself conducting.

One of the first things Jauner did after his appointment as Director was to secure the services of the conductor Hans Richter, whose engagement turned out to be one of the milestones in the annals of Viennese music. With his giant stature, flowing blond beard and blue eyes, Richter was a magnetic conductor and was regarded as

Wagner's closest confidant. Richter's friendship with Wagner was due to a curious chance. In 1866 Wagner was working on *Die Meistersinger* in his lakeside villa at Triebschen near Lucerne. Part of the score was smudged and the notes were barely legible, so Wagner was on the look-out for a particularly good copyist. Among those recommended to him was the son of the *Kapellmeister* at Esztergom Cathedral in Hungary who was at present a horn-player in the Vienna Philharmonic Orchestra. Their first acquaintance led to a lifelong friendship which culminated in 1876, when Richter conducted the first performances of the *Ring* at the first Bayreuth Festival. In 1875 Jauner summoned Richter to Vienna from Budapest, where he was Director of the Opera, and Richter became the pillar of Jauner's Wagner policy. As permanent conductor of the Philharmonic concerts from 1875 to 1898 he was an equally authoritative champion of Brahms, Bruckner and Richard Strauss.

Wagner's grudges against Vienna (including those atrocious cuts in *Die Meistersinger* and the long dispute about royalties) were assuaged step by step. Jauner made a conciliatory gesture to Bayreuth on the very first day of his official appointment, the first of May 1875, by arranging for Hans Richter to make his Vienna début with a performance of *Die Meistersinger* without any cuts in the first two acts. The dispute about royalties went right back to 1859 and 1860, when Wagner sold the Vienna performing rights of *Tannhäuser*, *Lohengrin* and *The Flying Dutchman* to the Court Chamberlain's office for a lump sum of 3,620 guilders 'without the right to make any further claims whatsoever against the Imperial Opera in Vienna'. Within a few weeks of Jauner's taking office this tedious dispute was settled on Wagner's terms: a part payment of 10,000 guilders on past performances and 7 per cent royalties from then on.

Jauner proved a genius at handling geniuses, and a brilliant theatrical manager in the present-day sense. In return for the concession on royalties he secured from Wagner the performing rights of *Tristan* (though he never managed to get it put on). An even more sensational coup was the way he positively blackmailed Wagner into personally superintending new Vienna pro-

In his memorandum to the Emperor Franz Joseph I on the ninth of April 1875 the Lord Chamberlain Prince Hohenlohe-Schillingsfürst writes that he would never again wish to let out the Court Opera House, in case it might fall into the hands of 'some swindler'. He recommends Franz Jauner, Director of the Carl Theatre, provided that he 'place the Direction of the Carl Theatre, presently in his hands, in those of another' (which Jauner put off for a long time). Hohenlohe reports Jauner's conditions to the Emperor, which are that he shall run the Court Opera without General Intendant, directly under the Lord Chamberlain, play only four times a week and confine the activities of the ballet to intermezzi in the operas; and also his request that he receive a 25 per cent share in the box-office revenues, a point which Hohenlohe supports because Jauner has proved his administrative ability at the Carl Theatre. We show the first and the last two pages of the text (including the transcription). On the last page of the document, beneath the dateline, is the Emperor's signature with which he confirms Jauner's appointment.

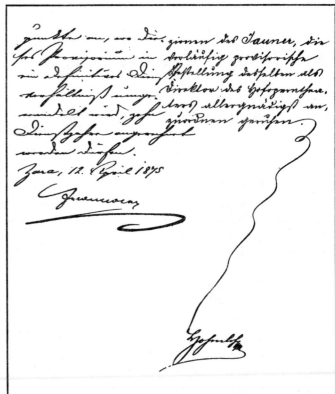

Transcription: left: *I empower you to appoint Franz Jauner, Director of the Carl Theatre in Vienna, as provisional Director of the Court Opera. The suggestions for a reorganisation of the Court Opera, together with the remunerations requested by Jauner, are sanctioned. I further permit that, as from the date on which this provisional appointment will be transformed into a definitive contract of service, Director Jauner shall be entitled to ten years of service retrospectively.*

Zara, 12 April 1875
Franz Joseph

right: *...has delivered proof that he is able to maintain such an Institution in a state of solvency even in difficult circumstances. Convinced as I am that the right man has been found and that, equipped with the necessary authority, he would be capable of leading the Court Opera into an era of prosperity, I humbly presume to submit for consideration that consent be given to Jauner's proposition and that your Majesty be graciously pleased to command his temporary appointment as provisional Director of the Court Opera.*

Hohenlohe

ductions of *Lohengrin* and the Paris version of *Tannhäuser* (its first performance) before the year was out. On the seventh of November 1875 there was an official welcome for Wagner at the Vienna Opera, and the first round was clearly Jauner's.

Wagner started rehearsals on the tenth of November and the first performance was on the twenty-third. Wagner was bound by contract 'to attend to the production in person'. New scenery and costumes were not needed, as the Dresden version of *Tannhäuser* was already in the repertoire. Wagner's responsibility was a thorough overhaul of the music and the stage-action. The conductor was Hans Richter and the cast included Leonard Labatt as Tannhäuser, Amalie Materna as Venus, Bertha Ehnn as Elisabeth, Emil Scaria as the Landgrave, and Louis von Bigno as Wolfram.

The new *Tannhäuser* was an unqualified success, and the Court Chamberlain assured Jauner of the full support of the 'powers that be' in his campaign on behalf of Wagner. Audiences were enthusiastic, but the inevitable chorus of ironic and even venomous criticism in the Press continued unabated. Wagner was castigated for putting animals on the stage, and for leaving so little to the imagination in the erotic Venusberg orgies. Five days after the first night Daniel Spitzer wrote in his 'Wiener Spaziergänge' of Wagner's efforts: '... with the collaboration of a swan, a number of horses, a pack of hounds, and all the Wagnerites in Vienna. The horses and hounds were exceedingly well-behaved, but the same cannot be said of the swan, which tucked a Leda under his wing and subjected her to molestations that must surely be the most risqué representation of mythology ever witnessed on the stage of the Imperial Opera House. Yet hopes that Leda would speed the departing swan with Lohengrin's "All thanks to thee, my faithful swan" were unfortunately not fulfilled ...'

Next came *Lohengrin* on the fifteenth of December, without cuts and in a completely new production supervised by Wagner himself. Hans Richter was again the conductor, and the cast included Amalie Materna as Ortrud, Mila Kupfer as Elsa, Georg Müller as Lohengrin, Georg Nollet as Telramund, and Emil Scaria as King

K. K. Hof- Operntheater.

Freitag den 11. Juni 1875.
Abends halb 8 Uhr
Unter persönlicher Leitung des Komponisten
GIUSEPPE VERDI.
Bei aufgehobenem Abonnement.

REQUIEM
für Soli, Chor und Orchester.
(Erste Aufführung in Wien.)

Soli:
Sigra. Teresa Stolz.   Sigr. Angelo Masini.
Sigra. Maria Waldmann,   Sigr. Paolo Medini.

Chor: (150 Mitwirkende) der gesammte Chor der k. k. Hofoper, verstärkt durch Mitglieder des akademischen Gesangvereines.
Instrumentale: Das Orchester der k. k. Hofoper.

Erste Abtheilung:
Nr. 1. Requiem und Kyrie (Ewige Ruhe gib ihnen). 4stimmig.
Nr. 2. Dies irae (Soli und Chor):
a) Dies irae (Tag des Schreckens). Chor.
b) Tuba mirum (Die Posaune hinmlisch tönend). Chor.
c) Liber scriptus (Ein geschrieben Buch). Mezzo-Sopran u. Chor.
d) Quid sum miser (Ach was werd' ich Armer). Sopran, Mezzo-Sopran und Tenor.
e) Rex tremendae (Herr dess' Allmacht). Quartett und Chor.
f) Recordare (Lieber Jesu! ach gedenke). Sopran u. Mezzo-Sopran.
g) Ingemisco (Schuldvoll tönt dir'). Tenorsolo.

h) Confutatis (Wenn Verfluchte, wenn Verdammte). Solo für Bass.
i) Lacrimosa (Thränenreichster). Quartett und Chor.

Zweite Abtheilung:
Nr. 3. Domine Jesu (Herr der Welt). Offertorium 4stimmig.
Nr. 4. Sanctus (Heilig) Doppelfuge, 2chörig.
Nr. 5. Agnus Dei (Lamm Gottes). Sopran, Mezzo-Sopran und Chor.
Nr. 6. Lux aeterna (Aetherschwingen erhellensie). Mezzo-Sopran, Tenor und Bass.
Nr. 7. Libera me (Befreie mich). Sopransolo, Chor, Schlussfuge.

Die Mitglieder des akademischen Gesang-Vereines haben ihre Mitwirkung freundlichst zugesagt.

Das Textbuch in lateinischer und deutscher Sprache ist an der Kassa für 20 kr. zu bekommen.
Der freie Eintritt ist ohne Ausnahme aufgehoben.
Das Billeten-Vorverkauf zur zweiten Aufführung findet an der Tages-Kassa statt.
Morgen Samstag den 12. Juni 1875. Zweite Aufführung unter des Komponisten persönlicher Leitung.
Kassa-Eröffnung halb 7 Uhr. — Anfang halb 8 Uhr.

K. K. Hof- Operntheater.

Donnerstag den 2. März 1876.
Anfang halb 7 Uhr.
Zum Besten des Chorpersonales. Mit aufgehobenem Abonnement.
Unter Richard Wagner's persönlicher Leitung.

Lohengrin.
Romantische Oper in drei Akten von Richard Wagner.

Heinrich der Vogler, deutscher König	Hr. Scaria.
Lohengrin	Hr. Müller.
Elsa von Brabant	Fr. Kupfer.
Herzog Gottfried, ihr Bruder	L. Yang.
Friedrich von Telramund, brabantischer Graf	Hr. Nollet.
Ortrud, seine Gemalin	Fr. Friedrich-Materna.
Der Heerrufer des Königs	Hr. Say.
Erster	Hr. Schittenhelm.
Zweiter (Edler)	Hr. Schmitt.
Dritter	Hr. Neumann.
Vierter	Hr. Hablawetz.

Sächsische und thüringische Grafen und Edle.
Brabantische Grafen und Edle. Edelfrauen. Edelknaben.
Mannen. Frauen. Knechte.
Ort der Handlung: Antwerpen. — Zeit: Die erste Hälfte des zehnten Jahrhunderts.
Sämmtliche Dekorationen vom Maler Herrn J. Kautsky.
I. Akt: An der Scheide. II. Akt: Burghof. III. Akt: Brautgemach. Verwandlung: An der Scheide.
Kostüme nach Zeichnungen des Historienmalers Herrn Franz Gaul.

Das Textbuch ist Abends an der Kassa für 50 Kreuzer zu haben.
Der freie Eintritt ist heute ohne Ausnahme aufgehoben.

Freitag den 3. März 1876. Geschlossen.
Samstag den 4. März 1876. I. italienische Vorstellung (dispari). Margherita (Faust).

Im k. k. Hof-Operntheater findet eine italienische Opern-Saison statt, welche vom 4. März bis 4. Mai d. J. dauern und 36 Abonnement-Vorstellungen enthalten wird. Die B. L. Abonnenten genießen das unbedingte Recht der Cession ihrer abonnirten Plätze. Anmeldungen und Vormerkungen für Abonnements werden an der Kassa des k. k. Hof-Operntheaters täglich während der gewöhnlichen Amtsstunden entgegengenommen.

Die Tageskassa ist täglich von 9 Uhr Früh bis 5 Uhr Abends geöffnet.

Kassa-Eröffnung halb 6 Uhr. Anfang halb 7 Uhr.

K. K. Hof- Operntheater.

Samstag den 19. Juni 1875.

Abends 7 Uhr.

Unter persönlicher Leitung des Komponisten

GIUSEPPE VERDI

und unter Mitwirkung der Damen **Teresa Stolz Maria Waldmann**, der Herren **Angelo Masini**, und **Paolo Medini.**

Bei aufgehobenem Abonnement.

(Erste Aufführung in italienischer Sprache.)

AIDA.

Opera in quattro Atti. Versi di A. Ghislanzoni.

Personaggi:

Amneris, figlia del re	Sigra. Teresa Stolz.
Aida, schiava etiope	Sigra. Maria Waldmann.
Radames, capitano delle guardie	Sigr. Angelo Masini.
Ramfis, capo dei sacerdoti	Sigr. Paolo Medini.
Amonasro, re d'Etiopia e padre di Aida	Sigr. Bignio.
Il Re	Sigr. Mayerhofer.
Un messagiero	Sigr. Lay.

Sacerdoti, Sacerdotesse, Ministri, Capitani, Soldati, Funzionarii, Schiavi e prigionieri etiopi, Popolo egizio.

L'azione ha luogo a Menfi e a Tebe all' epoca della potenza dei Faraoni.

Das Textbuch in italienischer und deutscher Sprache ist an der Kasse für 20 kr. zu bekommen.

Der freie Eintritt ist ohne Ausnahme aufgehoben.

Kassa-Eröffnung 6 Uhr. — Anfang 7 Uhr.

Montag den 21. Juni 1875.

Zweite Aufführung der Oper „AIDA."

in italienischer Sprache unter persönlicher Leitung des Komponisten.

Die P. T. Abonnenten, welche ihre Logen und Sperrsitze für diese Vorstellung zu behalten gesonnen sind, werden ersucht, die Theaterkasse hiervon längstens bis Sonntag den 20., Mittags 12 Uhr, in Kenntniß zu setzen.

K. K. Hof- Operntheater.

Samstag den 23. Oktober 1875.

137. Vorstellung im Jahres-Abonnement.

Zum ersten Male:

CARMEN.

Oper in vier Akten. Text nach P. Mérimé's gleichnamiger Novelle von H. Meilhac und S. Halévy. Musik von Georges Bizet.

Carmen	—	Fr. Ehnn.
Micaela	—	Fr. Kupfer.
Mercedès	—	Frl. Tagliana.
Frasquita	—	Frl. Morini.
Don José	—	Hr. Müller.
Escamillo, Toreador	—	Hr. Scaria.
Zuniga, Lieutenant	—	Hr. Hablawetz.
Moralès, Sergent	—	Hr. Nollet.
Dancairo,) Schmuggler	—	Hr. Lay.
Remendado,)	—	Hr. Schmitt.
Lillas Pastia	—	Hr. Neumann.
Ein Führer	—	Hr. Pucca.

Soldaten, Straßenjungen, Zigarrenarbeiterinnen, Zigeuner, Zigeunerinnen, Schmuggler, Volk.

Die Handlung spielt in und bei Sevilla.

Die Tänze, komponirt von Carl Telle, ausgeführt von den Fräulein Jaschk, Mauthner, Löscher, Minna, Olzer, Schäger, den Herren Caron, Bütgenbach, Leon Frappart, Thurian, und dem Balletcorps.

Die neuen Dekorationen von C. Brioschi. Kostüme nach Zeichnungen des Historienmalers Franz Gaul. — Das Textbuch ist Abends an der Kassa für 50 kr. zu haben.

Sonntag den 24. Carmen. — Montag den 25. Brahma.

Der freie Eintritt ist heute ohne Ausnahme aufgehoben.

Eine Loge im Parterre, 1. oder 2. Stod	fl 25.—	Ein Parterresit			fl 3.—
Eine Loge im 3. Stod	15.—	Ein Sitz 2. Stod 1. Reihe			4.—
Ein Sitz in der Fremdenloge 1. Reihe	5.—	Ein Sitz 3. Stod 2. Reihe			4.—
Ein Sitz in der Fremdenloge 2. Reihe	4.—	Ein Sitz im 3. Stod, 3.—4. Reihe			1.50
Logensitz aus den vergitterten Logen	3.—	Ein Sitz im 4. Stod			1.50
Logensitz aus vergitterten Logen 3. Stod	3.—	Kassersitz Sitz im 4. Stod			1.20
Ein Sitz im Parquet 1. Reihe	5.—	Eintritt in das Parterre			1.20
Ein Sitz Parquet 2, 3, 4, 5, 6. Reihe	4.—	Eintritt in den 3. Stod			1.—
Ein Sitz Parquet in der 7. bis 13. Reihe	3.50	Eintritt in den 4. Stod			—.80

Die Tageskassa ist täglich von 9 Uhr Früh bis 3 Uhr Abends geöffnet.

Kassa-Eröffnung 6 Uhr. Anfang 7 Uhr.

K. K. Hof- Operntheater.

Donnerstag den 24. Jänner 1878.

20. Vorstellung im Abonnement.

Zum ersten Male:

Das Rheingold.

Vorspiel zu der Trilogie „Der Ring des Nibelungen" in zwei Abtheilungen von

Richard Wagner.

Personen der Handlung:

Wotan,	)		Hr. Scaria.
Donner,	) Götter		Hr. Nawiasky.
Froh,	)		Hr. Schittenhelm.
Loge,	)		Hr. Walter.
Alberich,	) Nibelungen		Hr. Beck.
Mime,	)		Hr. Schmitt.
Fasolt,	) Riesen		Hr. Rokitansky.
Fafner,	)		Hr. Hablawetz.
Fricka,	)		Fr. Kupfer.
Freia,	) Göttinnen		Fr. Dillner.
Erda,	)		Fr. Reicher-Kindermann.
Woglinde,	)		Frl. Siegstädt.
Wellgunde,	) Rheintöchter		Frl. Kraus.
Floßhilde,	)		Frl. Gindele.

Nibelungen.

Schauplätze der Handlung:

1. In der Tiefe des Rheines. (1. Scene.)
2. Freie Gegend auf Bergeshöhen, am Rhein gelegen. Im Hintergrunde „Walhalla". (2. und 4. Scene.)
3. Die unterirdischen Klüfte Nibelheims. (3. Scene.)

Sämmtliche Dekorationen (neu) von den k. k. Hoftheatermalern C. Brioschi, H. Burghardt und J. Kautsky. — Die Maschinerien vom k. k. Maschinen-Inspektor G. Dreilich. — Kostüme und Requisiten nach Zeichnungen von Franz Gaul.

(Zwischen der 1. und 2. Abtheilung eine Pause von 10 Minuten.)

Die Dichtung ist an der Kassa für 50 kr. zu haben.

Der freie Eintritt ist heute ohne Ausnahme aufgehoben.

Freitag den 25. **Das Rheingold.** — Samstag den 26. **Margarethe (Faust).** Letztes Auftreten der Frau Ehnn vor ihrem Urlaube. — Sonntag den 27. **Das Rheingold.**

Der Vorverkauf der Sitzbillette zu den „Rheingold"-Aufführungen findet täglich für die 2., 3. und die folgenden Vorstellungen statt.

Kassa-Eröffnung 6 Uhr. Anfang 7 Uhr.

K. k. Hof- Operntheater.

Sonntag den 2. November 1879.

222. Vorstellung im Abonnement.

Anfang 7 Uhr.

Unter persönlicher Leitung des Komponisten

Johannes Brahms.

Ein deutsches Requiem

nach Worten der heiligen Schrift

für Soli, Chor, Orchester und Orgel.

Soli: Fräulein Anna d'Angeri, Herr L. v. Bignio.

Chor: Der gesammte Chor der k. k. Hofoper, verstärkt durch 60 Herren und Damen, welche ihre gefällige Mitwirkung freundlichst zugesagt haben.

Instrumentale: Das Gesammt Orchester der k. k. Hofoper.

Orgel: Herr Emil Rotter, Mitglied des k. k. Hofopern-Orchesters.

(Der Text ist an der Kassa für 10 kr. zu haben.)

Vorher:

Ouverture zu „Athalia"

von Mendelssohn-Bartholdy.

Zum Schlusse:

„Sinfonia eroica"

von L. v. Beethoven.

Dirigent: Hans Richter.

Montag den 3. **Wiederholung des Requiems** unter persönlicher Leitung des Komponisten. (Anfang 7 Uhr.) Concertpreise.

Dinstag den 4. **Philemon und Baucis.** Hierauf; **Dyellah.** (Anfang 7 Uhr.)

Die Tageskassa ist von 9 Uhr Früh bis 5 Uhr Abends geöffnet.

Kassa-Eröffnung 6 Uhr. Anfang 7 Uhr.

Henry. Wagner is said to have gone through the first act with each individual member of the chorus to ensure that everybody on the stage took an active part in the arrival of the swan. What would he have thought of his grandson Wieland's production of this particular scene, with the chorus declaiming 'Ein Schwan, ein Schwan' while gazing fixedly at the audience as if they were singing an oratorio? On the other hand Wagner so obscured the combat between Lohengrin and Telramund that all the audience could see was the tops of their helmets. Hanslick wrote that 'by the time it was all over I felt as if I'd been pole-axed', and said that it would not be possible to 'survey the full extent of the damage' until after Wagner had left Vienna.

Jauner's original invitation to Wagner was to supervise the productions: now he wanted the composer to conduct. As Wagner had got on very well with the chorus during the *Lohengrin* rehearsals Jauner managed to coax Wagner into conducting a benefit performance of *Lohengrin* for the chorus. Wagner was prepared to forgo half his royalties, and Jauner agreed to make over a substantial proportion of the takings to the chorus. Jauner was a bit worried about the number of orchestral rehearsals Wagner might ask for. In fact, he did without any. He arrived in Vienna on the first of March 1876 and conducted the very next day. He was fêted, made his usual curtain-speech (I remember how his son Siegfried also used to make speeches from the conductor's rostrum during concerts), and left Vienna after only two days. The chorus saw him off at the station to the strains of 'Wacht auf' from Act Three of *Die Meistersinger*. It was to be Wagner's last visit to Vienna. Back at Bayreuth, he plunged straight into the preparations for the first Bayreuth Festival, for which the *Ring* was exclusively reserved. But Jauner was determined to get *Die Walküre* for Vienna ...

Fortunately for Vienna, Wagner desperately needed some of his Vienna cast for the Bayreuth Festival, especially Amalie Materna as Brünnhilde, and of course Hans Richter to conduct. Present-day Opera Directors must look back wistfully at those far-off days when the artists on their payroll were at their entire disposal the whole year round. In his dealings with Wagner Jauner

Richard Wagner selected many members of his Bayreuth cast from among the singers at the Vienna Opera. Brünnhilde was Amalie Materna.

Damen werden dann nur acceptirt, wenn sie sich über eine kräftige Walkürengestalt ausweisen können.

Ladies will be taken into consideration only if they can display a valkyrian frame.

manoeuvred himself into a very strong position and exploited it with the utmost acumen. 'No *Walküre* for Vienna, no Materna or Richter for Bayreuth.' Wagner had to give in, and Vienna heard *Die Walküre* on the sixth of March 1877.

Technically, as well as musically, the evening was a sensation: the start of the performance and the end of the intervals were signalled by an electric bell (electric light was not installed until 1887). The more conservative elements were as outraged by the bell as they were by Wagner's music: 'Surely to goodness opera-goers can be credited with enough intelligence to know when it's time to go back to their seats.'

At this first Vienna performance of *Die Walküre* the Siegmund was Leonard Labatt and the Sieglinde Bertha Ehnn, with Emil Scaria as Wotan. Inevitably, the conductor was Hans Richter. But the greatest triumph of the evening was scored by Amalie Materna as Brünnhilde. From her early successes at the Carl Theatre as an operetta diva the young Styrian had worked her way up, until she was now Wagner's favourite singer. She was the first Bayreuth Brünnhilde and the first Kundry. She was of medium height and distinctly plump, and whenever Wagner wanted to annoy her he used to call her his 'consumptive little Brünnhilde'. But she was gifted with flashing black eyes, a superb voice and with that aura that all the first generation of Wagner singers had.

The Viennese *Walküre* earned golden opinions. Wagner had insisted on the use of the Bayreuth scenery by the Viennese painter Josef Hoffmann. Critics who had seen the Bayreuth production the year before were unanimous in awarding the palm to Vienna. Hanslick's notice was remarkably mild, probably because he was hearing the work for the second time, and included such phrases as 'thunderous applause' and 'Wagner is the darling of German-speaking audiences'. He even waxed enthusiastic over Jauner's production: 'The Valkyries riding about all over the stage on their speedy horses are a wildly romantic picture, whereas at Bayreuth the dismounted Amazons kept boasting about their horses but never actually appeared in the saddle.'

In the 'Ride of the Valkyries' Jauner surpassed himself as a producer. He had engaged the Empress Elisabeth's riding teacher to help in the production, and this official managed to commandeer eight army horses and eight Polish horsemen to act as the Valkyries' doubles. They were dressed as Valkyries, wigs, helmets and all, and were instructed how to 'ride through the air'. In the background an approach was cleared for the horses between wisps of cloud and strewn with thick mattresses to deaden the sound of their hooves. The horses started the 'Ride' from the stage-door on the Kärntner Strasse side and 'landed' at the opposite one on the Operngasse side.

Richard Wagner used live dogs in his Vienna production of 'Tannhäuser' in 1875 — as did Herbert von Karajan many years later.

Hau! Hau! Hoher Herr! Sie haben uns Hunde in die Oper gebracht, und die „Oper" werden Sie bald auf den Hund bringen. Wir danken Ihnen für diese Würdigung unseres Geschlechtes. Hau! Hau! Hunding!

Wow! Wow! Sire! Through you, dogs have come to the Opera and through you, the Opera will soon go to the dogs. We thank you for the appreciation of our race. Wow! Wow!

Across the Valkyries' saddles were slung outsize dummies representing Wagner's 'fallen heroes' on their way to Valhalla.

The Poles found the music 'very noisy', but their generous wages convinced them that this Wagner must be a genius. Grane, Brünnhilde's steed, gave Amalie Materna a lot of trouble by refusing to stand still, especially in the scene in Act Two where she tells Siegmund that he is to go to Valhalla with her. So Jauner stationed a soldier from the Army Service Corps behind a rock, provided him with a liberal supply of oats, and told him to produce them as occasion demanded. Malicious tongues maintained that every now and then a great red orb came bobbing out from behind the rock; it was generally assumed to be the rising sun — in fact it was only the seat of the soldier's trousers.

In this year 1877 *Die Walküre* was performed nineteen times, and during the 'Ride of the Valkyries' the casualty list grew longer at each successive performance. Eventually the minor Valkyries had their horses taken away from them and Grane was alone in his glory. And then came the inevitable day when he was certified by the army as due for retirement. It was Amalie Materna who paid for him to be put out to pasture.

After *Die Walküre*, Jauner filled the Carl Theatre with L'Arronge's *Hasemann's Töchter*. A day or two later, in December 1877, he organised the first 'Opera Soirée', the equivalent of to-day's Opera Ball. It was attended by the Emperor and by eminent politicians and financiers as well as by all the leading lights in the theatrical and artistic worlds, and was certainly an indescribably brilliant scene. On either side of the Imperial box splendid stairways led down to the dance-floor. The Imperial Opera Orchestra was deployed below the Imperial box, and the stage was transformed as if by magic into a gorgeous salon, with palm trees from Asia and exotic-looking banana trees (said to have been temporarily requisitioned from the props for *L'Africaine* and *Die Königin von Saba*). The back-stage was lined with splashing fountains, and from here, for the first time, the entranced spectators could enjoy seeing the auditorium from the other side. The artistic fare provided was varied and lavish, and one of the most entertaining sights was that of *Kapellmeister* Wilhelm Gericke, who looked like the Flying Dutchman, conducting his orchestra with daemonic gestures and, so to speak, by remote control. Up in the fourth gallery a mixed chorus, plus Amalie Materna and Marie Wilt as soloists, sang pieces by the ballet conductor Franz Doppler. Just before midnight Johann Strauss put in an appearance and conducted his waltzes.

The moment he heard of the first Bayreuth Festival's (1876) colossal deficit, Jauner brought off another coup.

Wagner could not possibly hope for another Festival in the near future: he would have to pay off his debts first. And his idea of keeping the *Ring* reserved for Bayreuth would have to be abandoned. Jauner grasped the situation in a flash and quickly made the most of it; he agreed to pay Wagner ten per cent royalties, and got the whole of the *Ring*.

First came *Rheingold* on the twenty-fourth of January 1878 with Emil Scaria as Wotan. Jauner is said to have been particularly anxious to stage *Rheingold* and to have promised even before taking office: 'I'll have the waves of the Rhine splashing the audience!' Ludwig Speidel, the famous critic, wrote in the *Fremdenblatt* of the twenty-seventh of January: 'Personally I should like to heave the whole of the Rheingold back into the deepest part of the Rhine.' In point of fact Jauner seems rather to have overreached himself. The portrayal of the river was adequate, but the gleam of the gold came from above the surface of the water, and the bank of the river is said to have been visible below water level. Hanslick found Wagner's idiom 'indigestible' and described the music as 'vast expanses of desert without any bountiful oases'. But he admitted that the Viennese timbre of the orchestra under Hans Richter was 'incomparably finer and freer than in the musical *Nibelheim* the orchestra are shut up in at Bayreuth'. (Incidentally, as early as 1875 Jauner had followed Bayreuth's example and slightly lowered the orchestra pit.) Hanslick had already seen *Rheingold* in Munich and Bayreuth and found the Vienna production far the best from a technical point of view. He had nothing but praise for the swimming and diving of the Rhine Maidens and for Alberich's transformations into a dragon and a toad. But he ridiculed the rainbow: like a painted bridge in the Vienna Stadtpark or a liversausage in seven stripes... The ultra-conservative Hanslick concluded with a prophetic observation: 'Surely the best solution would be to project this beastly rainbow horizon like *Dissolving Views*.'

In 1878 *Rheingold* was given ten performances, a great credit to Vienna audiences as well as to Jauner. *Siegfried* followed on the ninth of November and was

Two great friends were quite unable to agree over Wagner. Johann Strauss was a Wagnerite and was the first to introduce the Overture to *Tannhäuser* to the concerts in the Volksgarten. Wagner referred to him as 'the most musical character I have ever come across'. Brahms on the other hand signed in his younger days a manifesto against 'the music of the future', a gesture obviously directed against Wagner. Wagner once said of Brahms that 'sometimes he appears in a Handelian *Halleluja* wig, and at other times he goes off to strike up a Csárdás with the gipsies'.

Wagner and Vienna

Shortly after *Tannhäuser*
had made its Vienna
debut at the Thalia Theatre
in Neulerchenfeld (right)
in 1857, Johann Nestroy
brought out a parody of it
in which he played the part
of the Landgrave Purzel
(left), who addresses
'Heinrich Tannhäuser,
member of the Landgrave's
male-voice choir' with the
winged words: 'My son,
your behaviour has been
lousy: I never heard of
such a thing!'

In 1849 a warrant was
issued for Wagner's arrest on
a charge of having
'played a substantial part
in the revolutionary
movement' in Dresden. The
warrant (right) describes
him as '37 or 38 years of
age': in fact he was 36.
During 1848, the year of
revolutions, Wagner was
in Vienna, and revolutionary circles wanted to
install him as Director of the
Kärntnertor Theatre.
If they had succeeded, the
Vienna Opera could boast
of having had Wagner,
Mahler and Strauss as
Directors. In all probability
the idea of Wagner as
Director would have come
up against considerable
opposition because,
as he himself admitted later
in his tract on the
Vienna Opera, he wanted to
have almost the whole
of the non-German
repertoire banned from any
theatre that enjoyed
a subsidy.

Politisch gefährliche Individuen.

Richard Wagner
*chemal. Kapellmeister und politischer Flüchtling
aus Dresden.*

Steckbrief.

Der unten etwas näher bezeichnete Königl.
Capellmeister
Richard Wagner von hier
ist wegen wesentlicher Theilnahme an der
in hiesiger Stadt stattgefundenen aufrühre-
rischen Bewegung zur Untersuchung zu ziehen, zur Zeit aber nicht zu erlangen gewesen. Es werden daher alle Polizeibehörden
auf denselben aufmerksam gemacht und ersucht, Wagnern im Betretungsfalle zu ver-
haften und davon uns schleunigst Nachricht
zu ertheilen.
Dresden, den 16. Mai 1849.
Die Stadt-Polizei-Deputation.
von Oppell.
Wagner ist 37—38 Jahre alt, mittler
Statur, hat braunes Haar und trägt eine
Brille.

In May 1861 Wagner heard *Lohengrin* for the first time at the Kärntnertor Theatre, and was delighted. Alois Ander (top left) was Lohengrin and Louise Dustmann-Meyer (below left) was Elsa. She was also the Vienna Opera's first Elisabeth. Wagner was all for giving the first performance of *Tristan und Isolde* in Vienna with these two, but the plan came to nothing, as half-way through the rehearsals the work was abandoned as 'unperformable'. Gustav Walter (top right) and Bertha Ehnn (in oval) were the lyrical leads in French operas in Vienna *(Romeo and Juliet, Faust, Mignon)*. Walter, seen here as Lohengrin, was also Vienna's first Stolzing in *Die Meistersinger*, while Bertha Ehnn, seen here as Elisabeth, was the first Eva in *Die*

Meistersinger. Hermann Winkelmann, seen here as Parsifal (top left on the right-hand side) was Vienna's leading Wagner tenor during the Jahn era, while of Emil Scaria (top centre), the mighty bass from Graz seen here as Wotan, the Viennese used to say that 'when Scaria sings an aria you can hear it at the Bellaria'. Theodor Reichmann (top right), seen here as the Flying Dutchman, was the leading Wagner baritone during the first years of Jahn and Mahler. The three last-named, as well as Amalie Materna, all sang in the first performance of *Parsifal* at Bayreuth in 1882. Leonhard Labatt (right), seen here as Tannhäuser, was a Swedish tenor who was highly thought of by Wagner and made frequent appearances at the Vienna Opera during Jauner's term.

In this House at Hadikgasse 72 in what was then the suburb of Penzing and is now Vienna's Fourteenth District, not far from Schönbrunn and the Kennedy Bridge, Wagner spent a good part of 1863 and 1864 working on *Die Meistersinger*. Among his copyists were Peter Cornelius, the composer of *Der Barbier von Bagdad*, and allegedly Johannes Brahms. Financially these were desperate years for Wagner, who eventually had to leave Vienna in a hurry to escape his creditors. Fortunately for him it was not long before he was receiving munificent support from King Ludwig II of Bavaria. The villa at Penzing was placed at his disposal by a Baron Rochow, and despite his precarious financial situation Wagner had the whole villa redecorated from top to bottom. He also acquired a dog, a majestic animal that one day suddenly disappeared, much to Wagner's distress, and only came back three days later. Meticulous Wagner research has still not discovered what exactly the dog was doing all this time. A glance at the satirical portrait (right) by an unknown Viennese artist in the style of Arcimboldo leaves one amazed at all the visions milling around in Wagner's head — Valkyries, Rhine Maidens, and of course a swan. Under it is Wagner's signature and some lines from 'O Star of Eve' from *Tannhäuser*.

In the matter of Wagner, Viennese audiences, but not always Viennese critics, proved definitely avant-garde, and it was the audiences that really made Vienna so pro-Wagner from the very first. Here is the well-known engraving after an original drawing by Ro-gelio de Egusquize, the Spanish artist living in Paris who also did portraits of Schopenhauer and Ludwig II, and painted numerous scenes from Wagner operas: Alberich, the Rhine Maidens, Kundry, the Death of Isolde, etc.

This was the 'authentic' background by Th. Jachimowics against which Johann Herbeck conducted the *Flying Dutchman* in 1871. Wagner was inspired to write this opera during a rough voyage to England. In his own words: 'The sea takes up most of the stage.' Nowadays of course we have come a long way from the realism and the ultra-romanticism of our forefathers. Yet to produce the *Flying Dutchman* without putting the sea first is to violate the spirit of the whole work.

Felsige Meeresküste in Norwegen.

Oper Fliegender Holländer Act 1. Dect. gemalt von H. Jachimovig

The scenery for the first Vienna performance of *Tristan* looks as if it might have done duty for an opera by Meyerbeer, all very lavish and colourful in accordance with Wagner's designation of 'a bright summer night' for Act Two. It is said that the first-night audience broke out into its customary applause in the middle of the big love duet. It was not until the next day that they learned from the critics that they had been applauding in the wrong place.

During the last hundred years *Tristan und Isolde*, Wagner's most revolutionary work, has been subjected to all sorts of different interpretations by producers and stage-designers alike. Here are some designs for the Imperial Opera by C. Brioschi (left) for Act Two; by H. Burghart (above) for Act One; and by J. Kautsky (below) for Act Three.

This was C. Brioschi's scenery for the first Vienna performance of *Die Meistersinger* on Carnival Sunday 1870; the first time the work was applauded in Vienna and the last time it was hissed. Curiously enough, Wagner's own sketches for the scenery of *Die Meistersinger* have hardly ever been altered. Although we have been given productions of the *Ring* with abstract scenery, in *Die Meistersinger* Hans Sachs's house has nearly always been on the left and Pogner's on the right.

'Nun sei bedankt, mein lieber Schwan'

There must be millions of Mozart-lovers all over the world who first came to opera via *Lohengrin,* swan and all. There are also thousands of opera-singers who have made that famous entrance in tow behind a swan. The first in our gallery is the Polish tenor Nikolaus Rothmühl, who appeared in Vienna in 1881 and treated the bird with notable gentleness and courtesy. Perhaps he had it on a lead? And does the crown that has slipped almost round the bird's neck really belong to the Duke of Brabant, who had been transformed into a swan?

'Sein Ritter, ich, bin Lohengrin genannt.' There is still enough of the child in all of us to enjoy this poetic and legendary figure as keenly as ever. Admittedly, one swan is enough: we can do without the other one on the helmet. Or can we? In former times it was Lohengrin's beard that made many a young lady's heart beat faster, and how furious they were with that silly inquisitive Elsa who kept putting the same question over and over again to (right) Ernest van Dyck, favourite lyrical tenor of the Jahn era, or (below left) Gottfried Krause, who is obviously thinking of his 'Heil, König Heinrich', or (below right) Hermann Winkelmann, the incomparable Wagner tenor of the 1870s and 1880s, or (left-hand side, above) Georg Müller and Erik Schmedes, or (left-hand side below) Heinrich Vogl and the then slim and youthful Leo Slezak, who on one occasion when the swan moved off without him shouted to the stage-manager: 'What time does the next swan leave?'

'Nie sollst du mich befragen,' but we recognise him straight away as the new jet-age Lohengrin. Though the helmet and the beard have mercifully disappeared, he has as little difficulty in fluttering the hearts of the teenagers as his predecessors had. Sometimes he even comes on without a swan (is this what is known as 'intellectual' theatre?). In Wieland Wagner's production the swan is represented by a gigantic projection, the kind of *kitsch* that would have made the authoress Hedwig Courths-Mahler blush for shame. Logically, Lohengrin would have to sing 'Nun sei bedankt, mein liebes Diapositiv.' The Lohengrin here is Jess Thomas of South Dakota, a prominent representative of the youngest generation of American Wagner singers in Bayreuth, Vienna, etc.

dismissed by Ludwig Speidel as 'an outrageous bore'. The Siegfried was Wagner's own choice, Ferdinand Jäger: Wagner was always against having the same tenor for Siegmund and Siegfried. Amalie Materna was Brünnhilde and Emil Scaria was the Wanderer. Against Wagner's wishes Jauner broke right away from the Bayreuth concept and, as in *Götterdämmerung*, entrusted the scenery to his own staff of stage-designers. Once again the stars of the production were the scenery and the stage-machinery. The dragon, whose antics were manipulated by eight stage-hands in the wings, almost had to take a curtain-call. Despite a number of cuts the performance lasted over five hours, but Jauner had had the foresight to provide buffets of hot food specially for the occasion. The anti-Wagnerites, now definitely in a minority, expressed their gratitude for this 'act of mercy towards the exhausted listener'. In its first year *Siegfried* was performed eight times.

By the time the last work of the *Ring* tetralogy, *Götterdämmerung*, was given its first Vienna performance on the fourteenth of February 1879 Wagner's supremacy, as far as audiences were concerned, was virtually undisputed. Even the critics had changed their tune. Materna was superb as Brünnhilde, and Ferdinand Jäger, though his voice was failing, was still the ideal Siegfried as far as acting was concerned. Jauner made some slashing cuts, including the Norns and half the scene between Hagen and Alberich. At the second performance the whole of Alberich's scene was cut, as well as Waltraute's entry and half the scene between Siegfried and the Rhine Maidens, so that whereas the première lasted five hours, the second performance lasted only four. It should be emphasised that these cuts were suggested by Wagner himself and communicated to Hans Richter for the Vienna production. Wagner was sufficiently realistic to appreciate that it was still too early for uncut productions except at Bayreuth.

Jauner claimed that Wagner's triumph in Vienna was due to his own foresight, and his finest hour came in 1879 when the Court 'on the occasion of the celebration of the silver wedding of their Imperial and Royal Apostolic Majesties the Emperor Franz Joseph I and the Empress Elisabeth' commanded a performance of the closing scene from *Die Meistersinger*, preceded by a pageant by Saar.

Yielding to the mounting pressure of public opinion in 1878, Jauner had to give up running the Carl Theatre in addition to the Opera. At his gala departure from the Carl Theatre Johann Strauss conducted *Prinz Methusalem*. From then on Franz Jauner was 'only' Director of the Imperial Opera.

Establishing Wagner was by no means the only interesting feature of Jauner's term of office. In 1880 he put on a series of Mozart's more important operas, including *Idomeneo* and *Titus*. Yet he could never quite belie his Carl Theatre past, and *Titus* was followed by a patriotic epilogue entitled *Salzburg's greatest son* in which leading Burgtheater actors joined singers and dancers from the Opera in a dramatic portrayal of scenes from Mozart's life. The audience was offered a scene of 'Salzburg bathed in moonlight, one radiant moonbeam symbolically falling upon the house where Mozart was born'. Jauner took curtain-calls in person, and incurred the grave displeasure of the Court for such a serious breach of etiquette.

There were also a good many Italian seasons of operas by Verdi, Rossini, Donizetti, etc. The bright particular star was the wonderful coloratura soprano Adelina Patti, especially in *La Traviata*. The conductor was usually Luigi Arditi, whose 'Kiss-Waltz' is still a popular encore with many a prima donna. Other important premières Jauner was responsible for were Kretzschmer's *Die Folkunger* and a delightful popular Austrian opera by Ignaz Brüll entitled *Das goldene Kreuz*.

Jauner had a predilection for composers, and he managed to secure a number of leading lights (besides Wagner and Verdi) to conduct at the Opera. Delibes, with whom he had been on terms of friendship since his Carl Theatre days, conducted his ballet *Sylvia*, and Anton Rubinstein conducted his opera *Die Makkabäer*, which ran for three nights. Jauner had also officially announced Saint-Saëns' *Samson et Delila* for the 1877 season (to coincide with *Die Walküre*), but the first Vienna performance did not materialise until 1907.

Die Absagungsmisère in der Hofoper.

Cancellation troubles at the Opera

Vormittags ist Herr Director Jauner — wie man hier sieht — pumperl gesund,

In the morning Director Jauner — as we can see — is as fit as a fiddle,

und die Sängerinnen lassen der Reihe nach wegen Unpäßlichkeit absagen.

and one after another the lady singers declare themselves indisposed.

However, Saint-Saëns conducted his oratorio *Le Déluge* in the Opera House in March 1879, and also appeared as the soloist in Beethoven's G major Piano Concerto. Jauner's relations with Johannes Brahms had been somewhat chilly ever since Brahms joined the violinist Joachim in putting his signature to a manifesto against Wagner's 'music of the future'. Nevertheless, during Jauner's term Brahms did conduct at the Opera (apparently with extreme listlessness) a performance of his *Requiem* in November 1879.

Before the new Burgtheater opened in 1888 the company gave occasional performances in the Opera House. One of the outstanding curiosities of the Jauner era was a Singspiel — *Am Wörthersee* by Thomas Koschat, a Carinthian composer of popular songs. It was his first and last excursion into the domains of the Imperial Opera.

Among the singers introduced by Jauner two became particular favourites. Christine Nilsson — like her famous namesake Birgit, a Swede — scored a particularly striking success in Vienna as Ophelia in Ambroise Thomas'

Hamlet, and achieved world-wide fame as Marguerite at the opening performance of the Metropolitan Opera in New York in 1883. Bianca Bianchi (her real name was Bertha Schwarz and she came from Heidelberg) was a coloratura virtuoso without any particular depht of expression, yet in Vienna she brought the house down as Lucia.

The agitation that has toppled so many Directors of the Vienna Opera eventually numbered Jauner, too, among its victims. The deficit had mounted again and he was held responsible for over-lavish productions. In April 1880 the Court Chamberlain again conjured up the spectre of a General Intendant in the person of Leopold Friedrich Freiherr von Hofmann. Jauner regarded this as a breach of his contract and handed in his resignation. On his withdrawal he was almost unanimously acclaimed by the Press as an Opera Director of real stature. And of course there was the consolation of the customary retirement honours.

Franz Ritter von Jauner, to give him his new title, left the Opera on the thirtieth of June 1880 after five years as Director. His last years were even more dramatic

50

Abends ift Jauner aus Wuth darüber, daß er ein Dutzendmal das Repertoire ändern mußte, krank geworden,

When night falls, Jauner is ill in bed, from fury at having had to alter the repertoire a dozen times,

und die Sängerinnen find — wie man hier fieht — wieder pumperl gefund.

and the lady singers — as we can see — are once again as fit as fiddles.

R. W. is taught by the critic Eduard Hanslick how to compose (silhouette by O. Böhler).

than the earlier ones. After leaving the Opera he took over the Ring Theatre on the Schottenring, opposite the Stock Exchange. It had been built in 1874 for comic opera, and in 1881 Jauner introduced a sensational novelty, Offenbach's posthumous opera *The Tales of Hoffmann*. But after only one performance of it the theatre was completely gutted by fire and several hundred people lost their lives. Jauner was found guilty of failing to take adequate security precautions. But he could not live without the theatre, and after a period as co-director of the Theater an der Wien, he found himself back in his old Carl Theatre in 1895.

It looked like the dawn of a second Jauner era. One of his ideas was the concoction of the operetta *Wiener Blut* out of tunes by Johann Strauss. His talent-spotting activities were still employed as assiduously as ever — his operetta *Kapellmeister* was a man called Arnold Schoenberg! But times had changed, and Jauner was well aware that the new century was not going to be his. On the twenty-third of February 1900 he blew his brains out at his desk at the Carl Theatre.

Franz Jauner was succeeded by Wilhelm Jahn, whose term of office established three records. No other Director of the Vienna Opera has ever been in office so long (seventeen years), made fewer enemies or introduced so many new works of lasting value. Between 1888 and 1896, for instance, no fewer than ten new works established themselves in the repertoire for good. Granted, those were the days of plenty, with composers turning out one box office 'smash-hit' after another. The success of these new works showed once again that so long as the new operas were of the type that was sure to catch on, Vienna was definitely an avant-garde operatic centre; the conservatism so often laid at Vienna's door only set in when the contemporary works no longer appealed to the general public.

Wilhelm Jahn often showed how well he understood Viennese taste. He knew all about Vienna's predilection in those days for surface brilliance and the appeal to the senses: though I personally believe that this surface brilliance can excite a good deal more depth of feeling than what is sometimes hailed as profundity. Was it really a case of Jahn's knowing what audiences wanted, or was it that during his term of office he moulded 'Viennese taste' himself?

And how did Jahn come to be Director at all? When Jauner's fortunes began to wane, the authorities decided to resurrect the *General-Intendanz* which Jauner had stipulated should be done away with. The appropriate official at Court, Prince Hohenlohe-Schillingsfürst, advised the Emperor to appoint Baron Leopold Friedrich Hofmann as Intendant. Hofmann was exceptionally good company, shrewd, intelligent and artistically-minded. He was a University lecturer, had been Minister of Finance for a time, and was always on the side of the Director and the artists when problems arose. He was as interested in the running of the Opera House as he was in that of the Burgtheater. He was as ubiquitous as God Himself, and there are many contemporary caricatures of him poking his nose into every corner of the building. One of these cartoons shows him peering out of every single box in the house; and this was hardly an exaggeration, because during the performance he was forever popping into the dressing-rooms and listening to complaints from singers in negligé about not having enough work or being underpaid. During the intervals he would stroll from box to box urging the inmates to renew their subscriptions. He would defer with the utmost blandness to the insults of hot-tempered singers. He was everywhere at once, sometimes even up in the flies.

When Jauner departed, the post of Director was offered as a matter of course to Hans Richter, who had been a conductor at the Opera since 1875 and knew how to get what he wanted. But though Richter was an exceedingly versatile musician, as has been pointed out in the chapter on Jauner, he had no administrative ambitions whatever. In its early days he had been Director of the Budapest Opera and had had administration enough to last him a lifetime. Clearly, this huge, blond, bearded and blue-eyed giant was not the man, and Baron Hofmann had to start all over again. Hofmann seems to have shared Julius Caesar's preference for 'men about me that are fat': at all events his choice fell on another huge, blond, bearded and blue-eyed giant named Wilhelm Jahn, a German-speaking Moravian from Hof who had spent some time singing in opera at Temesvár in Hungary, where he sang parts for every type of voice. Like Richter, Jahn could play a good many instruments, and before coming to Vienna had been a *Kapellmeister* in Amsterdam, Prague and Wiesbaden. He was also an extremely talented producer. Where he differed in appearance from Richter was in the cut of his beard, which was elegantly trimmed, whereas Richter's beard would have done credit to Wotan. His gold-rimmed spectacles made him look more like a schoolmaster than anything else. Jahn accepted the post, and the official appointment followed in 1880. He was on terms of close friendship with Richter, and the latter exerted such a powerful influence on the running of the Opera that he was virtually co-Director. The two men worked out a wonderful system of how to divide up the work between them, which was all the more remarkable as, despite the similarity in their outward appearance, their musical likes and dislikes were totally different. Jahn had a great love for French and Italian opera and also for German light opera such as Lortzing's *Waffenschmied* and *Wildschütz*, while Richter had always been the champion of Richard Wagner and remained so under Jahn, one of his most brilliant successes being the first Vienna performance of *Tristan* in 1883, exactly 22 years after Wagner's own abortive attempt to have it staged in Vienna. This performance of *Tristan* meant that all Wagner's operas had now been given in Vienna except *Parsifal*, which was still reserved for Bayreuth. The first complete Wagner cycle was put on in 1893.

Richter's *Tristan* was a brilliant performance, despite the slashing cuts amounting to about 600 bars, or one fifth of the whole work. Even so, the critic Speidel still complained of the 'deadly boredom', and Hanslick wrote: 'a blue pencil is not enough, what is needed here is a sword'.

The leading parts were sung by the Operas's great Wagner ensemble, that had been schooled by Wagner himself. The *Tristan* was Hermann Winkelmann, the greatest 'heroic' tenor of the 1880s and 1890s. He came to Vienna from Brunswick, and was the son of a piano-maker. There was a kind of softness about his voice which made it ideal for Florestan and for Meyerbeer characters as well as for Wagner. Later, in 1888, he was Vienna's first Otello. The Isolde was Amalie Materna from Styria, who together with Winkelmann, Theodor Reichmann and Emil Scaria had studied with Wagner himself for the first performance of *Parsifal* at Bayreuth. Scaria (King Mark), Vienna's first Wotan, was one of the mightiest of the old Wagner basses. People used to say that 'when Scaria sings an aria it can be heard at the Bellaria' (about half a mile away). He was also one of the many Styrians at the Opera during Jahn's term. Three years later, in 1886, he suddenly began to suffer from lapses of memory: as the Landgrave in *Tannhäuser* he was all at sea, began to flounder,

Hans Richter (right) took charge of the Wagner repertoire during the era of Wilhelm Jahn. Wilhelm Jahn himself concentrated on the French and Italian operas. In this silhouette we see how he used to sit in a cane chair in the middle of the orchestra.

and never recovered. Before the year was out he died of creeping paralysis in a Dresden sanatorium. He was the first of the great Winkelmann-Reichmann-Scaria trinity to depart from the scene, those three great Wagner singers who really knew how to make an impressive entrance down a stairway; who really knew how to wear a beard or a cloak, how to wield a spear or a sword. Scaria was only one of many figures associated with the Vienna Opera who came to a tragic end.

The audience gave *Tristan* a rapturous reception: there was even thunderous applause (imagine!) in the middle of the duet 'O sink hernieder, Nacht der Liebe' in Act Two. But the critics still obstinately refused to share the audience's transports. Daniel Spitzer wrote: 'Anyone who can survive the ordeal of Act Three without closing his eyes is amply qualified to apply for a job as a nightwatchman.' And Max Kalbeck, an exceedingly gifted translator of a whole series of Italian libretti, wrote: 'Simply reading the libretto is enough to give one spots in front of one's eyes. It is a good thing that the verse is for singing and not reading, which means that only about one word in ten is intelligible.' Speidel surpassed them both: 'In order to concentrate on what the singers were doing I shut my eyes during a passage in the second act. The first thing I heard was a cavalry charge riding down 100 defenceless women. There was a terrible mêlée of groans and screams and cries for help, and behind it all the roar of artillery. What had happened? I cautiously opened my eyes. Isolde had heaved a sigh.'

Another notable feature of this *Tristan* production was that for the first time in Vienna the name of the producer was given; Karl Tetzlaff, Jahn's newly appointed chief producer.

In this same year 1883, the year Wagner died, Jahn put on a series of all Wagner's operas between the first and the twentieth of December, including *Rienzi* but not of course *Parsifal*, and without a single imported singer.

Among the most important new operas Vienna was treated to during the next few years were Cimarosa's *Il matrimonio segreto*, Ponchielli's *Gioconda*, and Boito's *Mefistofele* (the two latter as part of the Italian spring season). These were followed by Rubinstein's

Nero (1885), which was a fiasco, *Der Bauer, ein Schelm* (1886), the first Dvořák opera to find its way to Vienna, and Victor Nessler's *Der Trompeter von Säckingen*, about which Hugo Wolf wrote in the *Salonblatt*: 'This opera needs a comprehensive cut, from the first bar to the last.' But Viennese audiences loved its famous aria 'Behüt' dich Gott, es wär' so schön gewesen', sung by Reichmann.

Among the novelties of 1888 was a curious medley entitled *Im Feldlager* on the occasion of the unveiling of the Maria Theresia Memorial. Lead by a General on horseback, the leading singers marched on to the stage in exact replicas of the uniforms of Maria Theresia's day; patriotic songs were sung and there was a projection

of the Vienna of the future, with the splendid new buildings lining the Ringstrasse.

The year 1888 was notable for ushering in the great period of Jahn's term that lasted until 1896. During these eight years the Viennese were regaled with one masterpiece after another. The feast started with two works that were totally different from one another in everything except their popularity: Verdi's penultimate masterpiece *Otello*, and Josef Bayer's ballet *Die Puppenfee*. At the first Vienna performance of *Otello*, in a German version by Max Kalbeck, Winkelmann was Otello, and Theodor Reichmann, the great Hans Sachs and Wolfram, was Iago. Reichmann was a native of Rostock and had a host of admirers who eventually

formed a 'Theodor Society', just as Winkelmann's admirers formed a 'Hermann Society'. The Desdemona was Antonia Schläger, a Viennese, not exactly slim at the best of times, who was later particularly well known for her Santuzza in *Cavalleria Rusticana*. 'Toni', as she was always called, was very popular for a while, but unfortunately she grew stouter and stouter and left the stage to run a restaurant, which she did equally well.

The first night of *Otello* was a sensation, the greatest since the introduction of electric light the year before.

Hans Richter was by no means the only conductor at Jahn's disposal. There was Wilhelm Gericke, for instance, from Styria, who later went to Boston as a *Kapellmeister*. There was also Johann Fuchs (from Styria, of course), who conducted the first performance of *Evangelimann*: he was also Director of the Conservatorium. Last, but by no means least, there were the excellent Franz Doppler and the highly talented ballet-conductor Josef Bayer, the composer of the delightful *Puppenfee*. The choreography of *Puppenfee* was in the hands of Josef Hassreiter, who served the Vienna Opera for no fewer than fifty years in various capacities from dancer to choreographer. *Puppenfee* is still as alive and fresh today as it ever was.

To follow up these two great successes Jahn had the brilliant idea of securing for the Vienna Opera some new works by Jules Massenet, the latest idol of the French Opera he loved so much. Jahn had put on Massenet's *Le Cid* back in 1887, but its success had been not exactly overwhelming. Nevertheless, Jahn held fast to his 'Massenet for Vienna' plan and eventually reaped the reward of his persistence: the Vienna première of *Manon* in 1890 was an outstanding success, and *Manon* is still a favourite in Vienna. But Jahn also realised that what the Vienna Opera really needed, if other operas were to be as popular with his audience as Massenet's were, was a new soprano-tenor constellation of the first magnitude. There had been many such in years gone by, notably Louise Dustmann and Alois Ander in the old Kärntnertor Theatre days, but they had tended more to the 'heroic', and their principal vehicle had been *Lohengrin* (much to the satisfaction of Wagner himself).

Later, there had been Berta Ehnn and Gustav Walter, who had enchanted their audiences in French operas ranging from Gounod's *Faust* and *Romeo and Juliet* to Ambroise Thomas' *Mignon*. In the end, Jahn discovered a wonderful young pair with all the natural charm in the world: Marie Renard and Ernest van Dyck. Marie, despite her French-sounding name, was a native of — you may have guessed it already — Styria. Her real name was Pöltzl and she was the daughter of a Graz cabman. Born in 1864, she had an enchanting stage presence and was as pretty as a picture, somewhat buxom perhaps, but that was what people liked in those days. She had chestnut-coloured hair and a retroussé nose à la Jeritza. It is said that literally everyone in Vienna was in love with her. She was certainly a fascinating Manon and an equally fascinating Carmen with her hair drawn up and a costly Spanish shawl draped over her head. Her acting too was less vulgar than Pauline Lucca's. She was also entrancing as Rose in *Glöckchen des Eremiten* and as Hänsel in Humperdinck's *Hänsel und Gretel,* to name only two of her particular successes. Her only Wagner part was Fricka. In 1900, still on the right side of forty, she decided to quit the stage to marry a Count Kinsky, and at her farewell performance as Carmen she had over a hundred curtain-calls. I can still remember her as a prominent figure in Viennese society in my young days, adored by her thousands of admirers until well on into old age.

Her partner, Ernest van Dyck, a Belgian by birth, was rather too portly to merit the description good looking, and he had, moreover, an unattractive, round head. He started life as a journalist and writing was his main hobby all his life. He even wrote a ballet, *Das Glockenspiel,* which was performed in the Vienna Opera in 1892 to music by no less a composer than Jules Massenet — a gesture of gratitude for van Dyck's superb Des Grieux.

Van Dyck's career as a singer started with Lohengrin in Paris, and he was soon recommended to Cosima Wagner. Later he scored a success as Parsifal at Bayreuth, but he was never really at home singing Wagner, and he had considerable trouble with the language. He

K. K. Hof- Operntheater.

Mittwoch den 19. November 1890.

225. Vorstellung im Jahres-Abonnement.

Zum erstenmal:

MANON.

Oper in 5 Akten und 6 Bildern. Text von Henri Meilhac und Philippe Gille
Deutsch von Ferdinand Gumbert. Musik von J. Massenet.

Manon Lescaut		Frl. Renard.
Poussette)		
Javotte) Manons Freundinnen		Frl. v. Artner.
Rosette)		Frl. Staudthartner.
Der Chevalier Des Grieux		Hr. van Dyck.
Der Graf Des Grieux, dessen Vater		Hr. Greugg.
Lescaut, Garde-du-Corps, Manons Cousin		Hr. Sommer.
Guillot-Morfontaine, ein reicher Pächter		Hr. Horwitz.
von Brétigny		Hr. Felix.
Der Wirth		Hr. Frei.
Ein Sergeant		Hr. Hablawetz.
Erster) Gardist		Hr. Schubert Jr.
Zweiter)		Hr. Hinkelmann.
Ein Soldat		Hr. Schubert Jos.
Der Thürsteher im Seminar von Saint-Sulpice		Hr. Mazzantini.
Dienerin bei Manon		Frl. Erich M.

Edelleute, vornehme Damen, Spaziergänger, Bürger und Bürgerinnen, Soldaten, Reisende, Postillone, Gepäckträger, Spieler, Verkäufer und Verkäuferinnen.

Ort der Handlung: 1. Akt. Der große Hof einer Gastwirthschaft in Amiens. 2. Akt. Zimmer bei Manon und Des Grieux. 3. Akt. (1. Bild.) Die Promenade Cours la Reine. (2. Bild.) Das Sprechzimmer im Seminar von St. Sulpice. 4. Akt. Das transylvanische Hotel. 5. Akt. Auf der Landstraße nach Hâvre. Zeit: 1721.

Vorkommende Tänze von J. Haßreiter, ausgeführt von den Fräulein Hauffe, Allesch, Rathner Well und dem Balletcorps.

Costüme nach Zeichnungen von Franz Gaul. Die neuen Decorationen von J. Brioschi, k. k. Hoftheatermaler. Das Textbuch ist an der Kassa für 50 kr. zu haben.

Der freie Eintritt ist heute ohne Ausnahme aufgehoben.

Donnerstag den 20. Die lustigen Weiber von Windsor. Hierauf: Die Puppenfee. Freitag den 21. Der Cid. Samstag den 22. Zum zweitenmal: Manon.	Sonntag den 23. Die Hugenotten. Montag den 24. Aida. „Amnerie" Frl. Irene v. Chavanne von k. sächs. Hoftheater in Dresden a. G.

Zu jeder im Repertoire angekündigten Vorstellung erfolgt Tags vorher bis 1 Uhr Nachmittags die Ausgabe der Stammsitze; von 1/2 bis 5 Uhr Nachmittags der allgemeine Vorverkauf der restirenden Logen und Sitze gegen Entrichtung der Vorkaufsgebühr.

Diese beträgt je 3 fl. für eine Loge im Parterre oder 1. Rang; 2 fl. für eine Loge der 2. Galerie; 1 fl. für eine Loge der 3. Galerie; 1 fl. für einen Fauteuil im Parquet 1. Reihe; 50 Kreuzer für alle übrigen Sperrsitze und Logensitze; 30 Kreuzer für die numerirten Plätze.

Kassa-Eröffnung 6 Uhr. Anfang 7 Uhr. Ende gegen 10 Uhr.

was much more himself in the French and Italian lyric parts with which Jahn was only too glad to entrust him.

In short, Jahn was a brilliant 'talent-spotter' and a wonderful mentor as well. He was constantly on the look-out for new talent — in schools, in the Provinces, at operetta theatres, even in factories. Antonia Schläger for instance was working as a cutter in a printing-works when Jahn discovered her.

To follow up the success of *Manon*, which was given fifty-four times in its first four years, Jahn was anxious to get his hands on another opera by Massenet as soon as possible, as Massenet had rapidly become Vienna's

favourite composer. Massenet did have an opera to offer: *Werther*, which was to have had its first performance at the Opéra Comique. It had fallen through because of the great fire there that year (1887). Jahn asked Massenet for it, and in 1892 Vienna enjoyed the world-première of *Werther* in the composer's presence, with the enchanting couple Marie Renard and Ernest van Dyck in the leading rôles.

Some of the critics who were against Massenet wrote that although Manon and Lotte were completely different characters the music was always the same. And of course there were the same old voices saying that Goethe must be turning in his grave, etc., just as they had at

the Vienna première of Gounod's *Faust*. However, *Werther* is probably the best 'Goethe' opera there is; at any rate, it made a very great impression in Vienna.

Jahn's versatility and flair were unparalleled, but in one of his speculations he was distinctly less fortunate than usual, and that was his acceptance of Johann Strauss's opera *Ritter Pasman* on New Year's Day 1892. It was at Jahn's own instigation that Strauss sat down to write an opera at all. But *Ritter Pasman* only ran for nine nights. People said that Strauss was aspiring to tread in the footsteps of the Mastersingers, and that his opera was as full of their fingerprints as, say *Hänsel und Gretel* or *Evangeliman*. Speidel wrote that the best way to drown one's disappointment over *Ritter Pasman* would be to go and see *Fledermaus* again. And two years later (1894) *Fledermaus* really did find itself being presented in the Vienna Opera House, even if only at matinées for the time being. All that survived of Johann Strauss's failed opera was the ballet music. The libretto by Ludwig Doczi is mediocre to the point of ineptitude. It is a story about a knight of old who considers his honour has been sullied because the King once gave his wife a kiss on the forehead, so the knight gave the Queen a kiss on the forehead, which annoyed the King ... At the party after the first night Doczi presented Johann Strauss with a huge chocolate cake covered with icing in the shape of passages from Strauss's music, upon which the waltz-king said: 'My dear Doczi, this is the first time that you have provided my music with something tasty to go with it!'

1892 was the year of an important event in Vienna's history, the International Music and Theatre Exhibition at the Prater, and Jahn seized the opportunity with both hands. The Exhibition included a wooden theatre in which for five months a series of highly interesting performances were given.

The whole Jahn era, like the ascendancy of the Habsburgs, was one long sunset splendour. It was the age of middle-class prosperity, of 'Ringstrasse' opulence, in which outwardly the Habsburg era seemed assured of eternity, despite the cracks which were beginning to appear in the edifice. Accordingly, this Exhibition was meant to demonstrate to the world that the Austro-Hungarian partnership was still very much a going concern as far as culture was concerned. It offered Italian opera given by Italian ensembles, Czech operas in Czech, and Polish operas given by the Lemberg (Lwow) opera, all of which made their impact on Viennese taste.

It opened with performances by the Bohemian National Theatre of Prague, of Smetana's *The Bartered Bride*, which had already had two hundred performances in Prague. Its success in Vienna was overwhelming, due largely to a wonderful Kezal named Wilhelm Heš. It was this performance that really made Jahn Smetana-conscious, though it was with *Kuss* and *Geheimnis*, not

The Bartered Bride, that he introduced Smetana to the Vienna Opera. The only thing the critics had to find fault with in the Vienna Opera's production of *The Bartered Bride* was the scenery, which was more like a French summer resort than a Bohemian village. The opera was sung in German, and the Kezal (coloured handkerchiefs, red umbrella and all) was Wilhelm Hesch, as Heš now spelled his name. Jahn had acquired him from Prague. The Hans was Fritz Schrödter, a captivating tenor who had started as a painter in Leipzig and had then been a baritone at the Ring Theatre and in operetta. Jahn turned him into a tenor, and Schrödter became one of the best Davids in *Die Meistersinger* ever known. In later life he was one of the ringleaders in the intrigues against Mahler. The Marie was Paula Mark, a Viennese who, like her attractive and celebrated colleague Lola Beeth, was originally a pianist; but the lovely Paula retired from the stage at a relatively early age to marry the well-known doctor Edmund von Neusser. As Paula Mark-Neusser she was one of the showpieces of Viennese high society and became a successful singing teacher.

But to go back to the International Music and Theatre Exhibition at the Prater. *The Bartered Bride* was followed by Smetana's *Dalibor*, and then the Czech company made way for a Polish company from Lemberg, which offered two operas by Stanislaw Moniuszko, the Director of the Warsaw Opera: *Halka* and *The Haunted Manor*.

But the most interesting and successful visitors to the Exhibition were the Italian ensemble, sponsored largely by the Italian publishers Sonzogno. It was they who introduced *verismo* to Vienna, *verismo* being a new trend in opera which originated in Italy and created an immense, if short-lived, sensation all over the world. It was an attempt to get away from Wagner and evolve a new form of music-drama altogether; to step down from the lofty world of gods and heroes and to depict the 'reality' of bourgeois everyday life. Most of the operas in this genre can only be described as 'thrillers', with flashing knives and plenty of blood, and the stories were by no means as realistic and true to life as they claimed to be.

At the Exhibition Pietro Mascagni (described by the

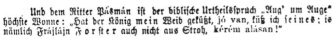

Und dem Ritter Pásmán ist der biblische Urtheilsspruch „Aug' um Auge" höchste Wonne: „Hat der König mein Weib geküßt, jó van, küß ich seines; is nämlich Fräjláin F o r s t e r auch nicht aus Stroh, kérém alásan!"

Ritter Pasman took great delight in following the words of the Script: 'Eye for eye, tooth for tooth.' 'If the king kissed my wife I shall do the same with the queen.'

Director Jahn was a great admirer of Johann Strauss, and suggested to him that he should write a work for the Opera. After it had flopped he consoled him by admitting 'Die Fledermaus' into his repertoire (to begin with, only at matinées).

critic Theodor Helm as an 'Italian Anzengruber') conducted his *Cavalleria Rusticana,* which Jahn himself had conducted at the Vienna Opera a year before (1891) when he had had to repeat the celebrated Intermezzo. The Santuzza had been 'Toni' Schläger, and the Turiddu Georg Müller, a tenor with a dazzling C sharp and a repertoire extending from Mozart to Wagner. Hard on the heels of *Cavalleria* at the Opera came a parody at the Theater an der Wien entitled *Krawalleria musicana* with the great Alexander Girardi as Duriduri-Salamucci.

Mascagni's opera was a tremendous success. It was played a hundred and twenty-three times in three years, and over two hundred times in ten years.

Thus the Italian performance at the Exhibition provided a good opportunity of a comparison with Jahn's at the Opera. The Italian Turiddu was Roberto Stagno, and the Santuzza was the celebrated Gemma Bellincioni; both had sung at the first performance in Rome in 1890.

Mascagni's *L'Amico Fritz* was also given at the Exhibition, and later in the same year at the Opera (the repertoire in those days was well abreast of the times).

Another Italian opera that enjoyed its first Vienna performance in the Prater was *Mala Vita* by Umberto Giordano, the composer of *André Chénier.* But the greatest sensation of all was Leoncavallo's *Pagliacci* (with the famous Prologue), which is perhaps the finest commentary of all on the essence of *verismo.* It was immediately snapped up by Jahn and given at the Opera (in German) the following year. It was another sensational success. The conductor was Hans Richter, to whom the work meant very little. The critics had a good deal to say about Leoncavallo's 'deafening orchestration' which forced the singers to overstrain their voices. The Canio was Ernest van Dyck, and the Nedda was the charming Paula Mark, who after the performance received a note from her colleague Lola Beeth: 'My dear

Paula; as Nedda you are really incomparable. I say incomparable, though my friends say that even I couldn't have played the part better ...'

The first performance was on the Empress Elisabeth's name-day, the nineteenth of November 1893, and there was such a huge audience that people said it was 'like a Wagner audience'. It was a gala performance, with the boxes crammed with the leading figures in high-society and exalted political circles. The people in the stalls looked as though they had come to a gala ball and up in the gallery there was that atmosphere of hectic impatience which is always a harbinger of an important theatrical occasion. After the performance the Lord Steward, Prince Hohenlohe, gave a dinner for Leoncavallo in the Augarten Palace, from where there was a wonderful view of the skating-rink all lit up with the new electric lighting.

Jahn produced *Pagliacci* himself, just as he had produced *Manon* and *Werther,* and there was universal admiration of the enthusiasm and verve with which this stout, ungainly figure would demonstrate to each singer exactly how he wanted him or her to move. He even showed Marie Renard exactly how he wanted Manon to expire. Older people used particularly to enjoy recalling how Jahn not only invented Nedda's 'dance of death' for Paula Mark but also danced it for her himself. In the 'play within a play' he made Mark express the action in dancing and saw Nedda as a girl who knew she was going to die soon.

And all this in 1893! It is hard nowadays to believe that such palmy days ever existed in the world of opera.

The second great masterpiece of Verdi's last years, *Falstaff,* reached Vienna in the year of its first performance at the Milan Scala. It was billed as a 'Performance by the entire solo contingent of the Teatro alla Scala, Milano, conducted by Maestro Edoardo Mascheroni, but with the Vienna Opera orchestra. The Falstaff was Viktor Maurel, the Scala's first Iago, whose fee was in proportion to the exorbitant cost of tickets: but he did at least sing his aria 'Quand'ero paggio del Duca di Norfolk' three times.

Falstaff showed Verdi in yet another quite different light and aroused great enthusiasm, though some disappointed critics made no bones about their dismay that Verdi, Italy's most illustrious composer, had also turned his back on melody, a hit of course at Richard Wagner.

During the remainder of Jahn's seventeen years in office there was at least one more highly successful première, that of Engelbert Humperdinck's fairy-tale opera *Hänsel und Gretel* (first performed at Weimar under Richard Strauss in 1894) with Marie Renard as Hänsel and Paula Mark as Gretel. Ludwig Speidel wrote that 'Renard sang like a nightingale and Mark like a lark'. This was Jahn's first attempt at broadening the repertoire in a post-Wagner German direction.

The Press carried an account of an 'intermezzo' during the première which is well worth recalling. In the scene where the two children bundle the witch into the oven, tongues of flame were seen shooting out of the oven door. Some embers, probably of colophonium, fell on to the stage and continued to burn merrily in an ever-increasing circle. The audience thought it was a deliberate 'stunt' and remained calm. In due course the firemen in attendance noticed the fire on the stage, and when a helmeted head was seen protruding from the oven door, it was at first taken for the witch's. It was not until a fireman started putting out the fire with a wet blanket that people realised the danger they had been in.

Humperdinck's charming work was given an enthusiastic reception, but the critics were divided. The *Neues Wiener Tagblatt* called the 'Witches' Ride' a 'Children's Hour Ride of the Valkyries', and Hanslick wrote: 'The redemption by gingerbread at the end of the opera seems to be a parody of Wagner.'

In 1896 came '*Der Evangelimann*' by Wilhelm Kienzl, which Theodor Helm called 'a compromise between Wagner and Mascagni'. It was a great success. The Johannes was Reichmann, and the part of Magdalena, with the moving aria 'O schöne Jugendtage' was sung by the American contralto Edith Walker. The Evangelimann, with his great aria 'Selig sind, die Verfolgung leiden', was Ernest van Dyck. There was great applause for the scenery of Act Two Scene 2, dominated by Vienna's Karlskirche.

Among other curiosities during Jahn's term were Franz von Suppé conducting his Singspiel *Franz Schubert*

'Krawalleria' — a pun on the name 'Cavalleria', meaning a rough-house. In the cast was Alexander Girardi.

(1886), which ran for one night only; and the cry of the Burgtheater actress Charlotte Wolter echoing round the Opera House: before the Burgtheater moved into its new home in 1888 the ensemble often played in the Opera, in order to get accustomed to acting in a big house. Among the rôles that Charlotte Wolter played in at the Opera were Antigone, Lady Macbeth, Fedora, Lady Maria Stuart. On one occasion in 1884 the Philharmonic Orchestra wanted more money for playing at ballet matinées: Jahn and the General Intendant, Baron Hofmann, refused and engaged Eduard Strauss and his orchestra instead. But 'Handsome Eddy's' side-line lasted for a short time on, because Jahn soon made up his quarrel with the Philharmonic.

To sum up: Jahn's term of office was one of the most brilliant periods in the history of the Vienna Opera. No other Director ever accumulated such a brilliantly assorted repertoire as Jahn did, and no other Director was so universally beloved. Opinion was almost unanimously in his favour, and even the critics left him (on the whole) alone. The only implacable enemy to his dying day was the composer Hugo Wolf, a fanatical adherent of Wagner and the music critic of the *Wiener Salonblatt*. He once wrote: 'Vienna possesses a priceless vase in the form of an orchestra, but the vase is filled with salt water, vinegar, caustic soda, acqua fortis, and sulphuric acid.' He was referring to the popular operas of Jahn's time.

Nevertheless, in all probability, Jahn was also the most successful Director the Vienna Opera has ever had. Among Jahn's ensemble, which was wholly attuned to the sensual appeal of superlative voices, the proportion of Austrian and German artists was astonishingly high. They included Marie Wilt, Rosa Papier, and many others.

Rosa Papier was a native of Baden bei Wien and her best rôles were Orfeo, Amneris, Brangäne and Waltraute. She was a wonderful Lieder singer too. She was at the Vienna Opera for only ten years; she lost her voice and took up teaching at the Conservatoirum, where she trained a whole generation of female singers, among them stars such als Anna Mildenburg, Lucy Weidt, and Rose Pauly. She was also influential in getting Mahler appointed Director. Her son is Dr. Bernhard Paumgartner, an eminent Mozart scholar and the grand old man of the Salzburg Festival.

In 1895 the great Lili Lehmann, whose unusual repertoire ranged from La Traviata to Isolde, came to Vienna to sing Brünnhilde in *Götterdämmerung*.

Jahn was always the artists' true friend (especially the female ones). He used to play billiards in coffee houses or sit down to a beer-session with them, and was always at their disposal with advice and assistance in personal as well as professional problems. But in his later years he was not quite so approachable: his health was none too good, he became morose and anti-social, and towards the end it was almost impossible to get a word out of him. The Opera was run *de facto* by his nephew Hubert Wondra. It was the beginning of what we now look back on as the *fin de siècle*, the end of the nineteenth century, the dawn of a new and completely different world. Of the great figures in the history of music, one after another departed from the scene: Bruckner in 1896, Brahms in 1897, and Johann Strauss in 1899. And Hugo Wolf, Jahn's implacable foe, was confined in an asylum.

Fin de siècle. The times were ripe for a decisive and sweeping change. This was soon forthcoming. In May 1897 a young conductor came to Vienna to conduct *Lohengrin*, a man who eight years before had made an arrangement of Weber's *Die drei Pintos* and had been mauled for it by the critics. His name was Gustav Mahler.

So began the Gustav Mahler decade, which has gone down in operatic history as the most brilliant period there has ever been. There has always been a certain glamour about opera houses when a composer is at the helm: Carl Maria von Weber in Dresden, Meyerbeer in Berlin, Franz Liszt in Weimar, and later Richard Strauss in Vienna. But Gustav Mahler was the only one with the genius to conjure up something completely new for eyes and ears alike. He was also gifted with the fanatical eye for detail and energy to realise his ideals in the day-to-day running of an opera house. He — and he alone — was so possessed by his conception of an Opera Director's mission that the only time he found time to compose was during the summer vacation or in the very early morning. And his strength of character and will-power were of a Herculean calibre.

The Mahler era was the earliest about which I have been able to learn a good deal from artists and habitués who were part of it, especially in the 1920s, when I started to be a 'regular customer' of the Vienna Opera. My neighbour in the standing-room was a veteran who could remember the Jahn era: in my youthful eyes he was a reincarnation of Methusaleh. When I reminisce nowadays about the Richard Strauss era, I suppose I create the same impression (only I prefer to call these 'the best years of a man's life').

The Mahler era was the big experience of my parents' lives. My father often used to describe to me how exciting it was before the curtain went up, waiting to see who was going to conduct. In those days the conductor's name was not given either on the posters or in the programme. As the house-lights dimmed the young people up in the fourth gallery used to crane their necks so as to be able to spot the conductor before anyone else, and the atmosphere became electric when the clean-shaven Mahler was seen darting toward the podium like a man possessed. The three other principal conductors at the Vienna Opera in Mahler's time, Hans Richter, Bruno Walter and Franz Schalk, all had beards. Making his way to the podium the short, lean, pale and bespectacled figure, something like E. T. A. Hoffmann's daemonic *Kapellmeister* Kreisler, would often fling out his left foot in a sort of nervous

twitch, or stamp his right foot hard down on the floor. Sometimes he would pause for a moment, almost motionless, as if lost to the world, like the title of one of his songs with orchestra, 'Ich bin der Welt abhanden gekommen'.

It was Mahler who had the conductor's podium raised and pushed close up to the strings. His predecessor Jahn still used to sit on a round cane chair in the middle of the orchestra, and before that the conductor's rostrum was right up in front of the footlights; the musicians sat behind him and he busied himself almost exclusively with the singers and with what was happening on the stage. A broad gangway, which was kept clear behind him, enabled him to turn round and attend to the orchestra as required. The present position of the rostrum, what already seems to us to be its classical, one might almost say its natural place, has only been customary since the time of Mahler's successor Felix von Weingartner.

When Mahler was conducting, the daemonic spark that emanated from him seemed to electrify the entire audience. As Director of the Opera, Mahler was swept aside after ten years by a 'smear' campaign of unprecedented venom. As a composer he remained a controversial figure right up to his premature death. But as a conductor he excited almost universal admiration. The *furioso* gestures of his early years later gave way to a calmer manner. If he liked a singer, his fascinating eyes would entreat, question, inspire. If he was in a bad temper, his baton would go scything through the air like a knife. And if the audience was misguided enough to start applauding an aria before the orchestral epilogue was finished it would be treated to one of this 'fascinating but inhuman personality's' terrifying scowls. As to whether Mahler's tempi were on the fast or slow side, the *brio* of his *Don Giovanni* Overture was positively orgiastic, whereas his *Meistersinger* took even longer than Hans Richter's. He also kept the volume of sound rather lower than the taste of the times approved of.

It was another of those proverbial 'Austrian miracles' when the Court Steward Prince Liechtenstein ventured to advise the Emperor that a man whose name was completely unknown except in exclusively musical circles should

Gustav Mahler, borne up on the clouds of incense emitted by the Press, triumphs over Director Jahn who ist holding his pension rights in his hand. Mahler has notes in the place of fingers. (Caricature by Theo Zasche, 1897.)

Opernbirigent Mahler.

Germany, and her husband was an influential music critic named Hans Paumgartner. So it is greatly to the prince's credit that he was prepared to listen to 'the right people'.

Gustav Mahler was born in 1860 at Kališt in Bohemia. He studied at the Vienna Conservatorium and soon attracted the attention of Anton Bruckner. He started as a *Kapellmeister* at the small provincial theatres of Halle, Olomouc, and Ljubljana (where he once whistled through 'The Last Rose of Summer' when the Martha suddenly lost her voice). For some weeks he was in charge of the chorus at the Carl Theatre in Vienna. Via Prague and Leipzig he made his way to the post of Director of the Imperial Opera in Budapest, where he was supposed to detach the Hungarians from their fondness for Italian and German music by building up a Magyar ensemble in readiness for the national Opera which patriotic circles had set their hearts on. After putting on *A Rajna Kincse (Rheingold)* and *A Walkür* he departed after little more than a year and a half as the result of a dispute with the somewhat dilettante Intendant, and accepted a post as *Kapellmeister* at the Hamburg Opera, where he attracted the attention of Hans von Bülow, who appointed him to be his successor as conductor of the Hamburg Symphony Concerts. Mahler would then spend the summer composing at his 'hide-out' on the shores of the Attersee. In 1896 he paid a visit to Johannes Brahms at the nearby resort of Bad Ischl, and it may be assumed that the conversation turned on the attainment of Mahler's lifelong ambition to be Director of the Vienna Opera. It was a remarkable clash of musical cross-currents: here was Brahms sponsoring the passionate Wagnerite Mahler as Director of the Vienna Opera, while away at Bayreuth Wagner's widow, the awe-inspiring Cosima, was doing her utmost to prevent the appointment of 'that Jew'. Fortunately Austria took the only proper course, and that in spite of Mahler's discordant departure from the Imperial Opera in Budapest. The announcement of Mahler's appointment as Opera *Kapellmeister* coincided with the news of Brahms's death. Mahler's début at the Vienna Opera was a triumphant performance of *Lohengrin* in May 1897. The ailing Jahn, now no more than a figurehead as Director, was faced with a *fait accompli* and more or less forced to

be appointed Director of the Vienna Opera. Mahler had already written three symphonies, but none of them had ever been performed in Vienna, though in 1889 Jahn had put on Mahler's version of Weber's comic opera *Die drei Pintos*. Mahler prepared his version at the request of Weber's grandson (whereas Meyerbeer had turned down a similar request from Weber's widow). The verdict of the critics was 'more Mahler than Weber' (mehr *gemahlt* als *gewebt,* literally 'more painted than woven'). Nevertheless, in the eyes of a few leading connoisseurs Mahler was the coming man.

Johannes Brahms was full of praise for a performance of *Don Giovanni* under Mahler in Budapest. The singer Rosa Papier had sung at a concert he had conducted in

As soon as he was appointed Director, Mahler set about assembling a team of fanatically dedicated singers with whom he could realise his intellectual concept of the theatre. The leading members of that team are seen a few pages further on. This photograph shows Mahler strolling with his wife, Alma Maria, in the Vienna Woods.

The first five years of Mahler's term were devoted to a thorough overhaul of the musical side. When Hans Richter walked out because Mahler was conducting all the Wagner operas himself, moreover — unlike Richter — without cuts, Mahler promptly took on two new young conductors: Bruno Walter, who for the time being was mainly concerned with the Italian operas, and Franz Schalk, who shared the German repertoire with Mahler. Mahler's second five years were spent refurbishing the scenery in collaboration with the painter Alfred Roller, a friend of Klimt's and a member of the Secession Group. Under the influence of the Swiss stage-designer Adolphe Appia (and long before neo-Bayreuth trends) Roller cleared the stage of all superfluous scenery and became the pioneer of modern lighting. Top left: Gustav Mahler. Top right: Bruno Walter. Below: Alfred Roller.

During his years as an operatic conductor Mahler's technique underwent a fundamental change. When he first arrived in Vienna in 1897 his excitable, almost frenetic gestures were admired, criticised — and caricatured. But by the time he left the Vienna Opera in 1907 there was a truly classical composure about his conducting.

The main feature of Mahler's and Roller's policy was a series of all the German-language operas that would do justice, musically and decoratively, to Wagner's 'Gesamtkunstwerk' ideal. In the prison-scene from *Fidelio* (top) Florestan and Leonore start climbing the steps to the opening bars of the Leonore Overture No. 3, which Mahler was the first to insert between the prison-scene and the Finale. The outstanding features of the production of *Don Giovanni* in commemoration of the 150th anniversary of Mozart's birth were Roller's much-discussed towers on either side of the stage, which remained on stage throughout but with a different function in every scene. The illustration on the right is of part of the cemetery, with the statue of the Commendatore in the centre.

Mahler's association with Roller started with *Tristan und Isolde* in 1903 in commemoration of the 20th anniversary of Wagner's death. Each Act was given its own basic colour: a flaring orange-yellow for Act One (below right), a deep violet for Act Two (above), and a uniform grey for Act Three (below left). Roller was acclaimed by the progressively-minded members of the audience, but the more conservative elements were all against him, and many people found the stage too dark for their liking (similar criticisms are being levelled at a good many modern producers). A recurring gravamen of the anti-Mahler agitation to which he succumbed in 1907 was that he 'relied too much on Roller's newfangled ideas'.

To succeed Winkelmann Mahler engaged the Danish tenor Erik Schmedes (left as Canio/Pagliaccio). Though not notable for beauty of tone, Schmedes was later (under Weingartner) the Vienna Opera's first Cavaradossi. He was a superb Wagnerian hero and a good actor who was equally at home in Italian opera. At his farewell performance in 1924 he sang the 'Evangelimann'. Marie Gutheil-Schoder (below left as Carmen), who came from Weimar, was called upon to succeed the popular favourite Marie Renard and had a difficult time at first, but her intelligence and outstanding talent soon won over her audiences. Under Mahler she sang anything that came along (Musette, Iphigénie, Frau Fluth). Leopold Demuth (below centre as Sachs) was a chemist from Brno and the possessor of one of the most beautiful voices of the Mahler era, a lyrical baritone which was heard to particular advantage in Italian operas, notably *Rigoletto*. As an actor he was no more than mediocre (what the Viennese politely term 'interessant'). Selma Kurz (below right

as Astaroth in *Die Königin von Saba*), was one of Mahler's most brilliant discoveries and became the finest coloratura prima donna Vienna had ever had. Anna Mildenburg (right page, below left as Brünnhilde) was the Isolde and Brünnhilde, usually partnered by Schmedes, in Mahler's uncut performances of Wagner. Lucy Weidt (top right as Leonore), whom Mahler brought to Vienna from Leipzig, was at first rather overshadowed by Anna Mildenburg, but came into her own in Weingartner's *Fidelio*. Mahler was '*kurz-sichtig*' (short-sighted), and Weingartner is '*weidt-sichtig*' (long-sighted) was how the wags put it. Wilhelm Hesch (below centre as Rocco), a Bohemian, was first engaged by Jahn and in Mahler's time shared the bass rôles with Richard Mayr. Hermine Kittel (below right as Brangäne), was a contralto who was first engaged by Mahler and served the Vienna Opera until well on into the Clemens Krauss era as the first choice for secondary rôles such as Magdalena in *Die Meistersinger*. She was renowned for her sense of humour.

Late-comers, or people who started applauding before the orchestral accompaniment to an aria was finished, were treated to black looks from that 'fascinating fiend' Gustav Mahler. But the same 'fascinating fiend' rewarded singers who complied with his directions with a beaming smile.

This painting (1937) by W. V. Krauss shows Strauss, who was a Mozart conductor of genius, conducting a performance of *Così fan tutte* at the Vienna Opera. It was a wonderful experience to watch Strauss, the composer of the finest operas of this century, conducting his own works, with his celebrated economy of gesture and his short baton. Before the days of organised theatre-going it was not unusual for the house to be half-empty, which was just what we Strauss fans wanted, because we had him more to ourselves.

The Idol of My Young Days, Richard Strauss

After waiting for him to emerge from the stage-door we would often be rewarded by a pat on the shoulder. I even flatter myself that he once took my hand in the same hand that had written *Der Rosenkavalier*, and of course I was in the seventh heaven. Above: Roller's scenery for Act Two of the 1911 productions of *Der Rosenkavalier* in Dresden and Vienna: the basic colour is silver. This set lasted until 1929, when Clemens Krauss and Lothar Wallerstein moved the stairs to the back to allow the audience a better view of Ochs's motley retinue chasing Faninal's maids. The one and only Richard Mayr sang Ochs no fewer than 158 times, and as he himself says in the opera . . . 'Mit mir keine Nacht dir zu lang.'

Renewing acquaintance with this original set of Roller's for *Elektra*, designed in accordance with the wishes of both Strauss and Hofmannsthal, one realises only too clearly what a criminal travesty of the work is Wieland Wagner's 1965 production. Instead of the grim blank wall of the King's palace in Mycenae, with its single opening, Wieland Wagner preferred six wretchedly irrelevant and incomprehensible blocks of stone, each surmounted by the head of an animal. Unfortunately I never heard Marie Gutheil-Schoder as Salome, as in this illustration. She alternated with Jeritza in the part beginning in 1918; previously the work had been banned from the Imperial Opera because it portrayed a Biblical character, John the Baptist. My only personal recollection of Gutheil-Schoder is as a producer — of *Elektra*.

'. . . that we two are together,' *i. e.* Strauss and Hofmannsthal, was indeed a stroke of luck for the operatic world. All together they collaborated on six operas. Above: a page in his own handwriting from Strauss's sketch-book for *Elektra*. The cutting is an amusing illustration of the two friends at work. The scene reproduced here in which Elektra recognises Orestes is for me one of the highlights of all opera, and the dissonances of the passage immediately after Elektra's cry of 'Orest!' put even the 'wildest' moderns in the shade. And afterwards? A flood of glorious melody: 'O lass deine Augen mich sehen! Traumbild, mir geschenktes . . .'

Strauss built himself a house in Vienna at Jacquingasse 10 (right).
We young people often used to stand for hours at the gate hoping
to catch a glimpse of him walking in the garden perhaps with his
family. We once heard the sound of a piano — the Waltz from
Rosenkavalier! We were very excited ... until we realised that
the wind had carried the music across to us from the house op-
posite. Actually we only saw the Strauss family once, and that
was in the opera *Intermezzo* which is about his domestic life.
Above: Richard Strauss, with Lotte Lehmann as Christine/Pauline,
Alfred Jerger as *Kapellmeister* Storch/Strauss, and the producer
Dr. Wallerstein on his right, behind him Karl Ziegler as Baron
Lummer, and on his left Margarete Krauss as the lady's maid
Anna, after the Vienna première conducted by Richard Strauss.

'Dir angetraut' sang Lotte Lehmann in *Die Frau ohne Schatten*. Memories of Lehmann in her six great Strauss rôles are still vivid. In *Ariadne auf Naxos* she was first the Composer and later Ariadne; in *Der Rosenkavalier* she was first Octavian and later the Marschallin; here is a picture of her as the Dyer's Wife in *Die Frau ohne Schatten* at the first performance (Vienna 1919); then she was Christine in *Intermezzo*, a part she studied with Pauline Strauss at Garmisch; and her last Strauss part was Arabella in the Vienna première of 1933.

'Ich will nur, dass du glücklich bist', sang Luise Helletsgruber alternating with Margit Bokor as Zdenka in the 1933 Vienna first performance of *Arabella*. Helletsgruber's voice had something of Lehmann's about it. Her most brilliant performance was as Liu in *Turandot*. She lost her life as the result of a road accident a few years ago.

'Und du wirst mein Gebieter sein', sang Viorica Ursuleac (who succeeded Lehmann as Arabella) to Alfred Jerger (his Mandryka had an entrancing 'Balkan' flavour). Strauss is seen here congratulating them both. The Vienna production of *Arabella* was conducted by Clemens Krauss, the husband of Viorica Ursuleac, who had previously been heard as the Empress in *Die Frau ohne Schatten*, as Chrysotemis in *Elektra*, and as the Marschallin in *Der Rosenkavalier*. Among other Strauss parts that Jerger excelled in were Jochanaan, Orest, the Dyer and Ochs auf Lerchenau.

resign. Mahler's official appointment as Director followed in October 1897.

There ensued in rapid succession a series of dramatic reforms, both internal and external, in the day-to-day running of the Opera. One of his innovations was having the house-lights dimmed before the curtain went up, which nowadays is a matter of course. Even before Mahler's day, the auditorium at the Vienna Opera was much less brightly lit than at the Scala in Milan, as Verdi was delighted to find during his visit to Vienna in 1875. The first to have the Scala auditorium dimmed was Toscanini, at about the same time as Mahler was initiating his reforms in Vienna.

Following the 'claque' disorders at the first Vienna performance of Smetana's *Dalibor* Mahler obliged all the singers to sign a statement to abstain from hiring a private claque. In those days the claque was a 'semi-official institution' at the Vienna Opera, and the management gave its members a daily quota of free tickets for the gallery. Mahler put a stop to this practice, but even he was unable to administer the coup-de-grâce to this time-honoured institution (which Meyerbeer regarded as an essential factor in the success of an opera!). The singers merely increased their 'subsidies' to the 'outlaws' and professed themselves powerless in the face of such 'spontaneous' outbursts of enthusiasm . . .

Mahler proceeded against late-comers with draconian ruthlessness and (except to the boxes or standing-area) they were only admitted during the intervals, so that they missed a whole act — or in the case of *Cavalleria* the whole opera. When the Emperor was told of this latest edict of Mahler's, and about the new Wagner productions without cuts, he allowed himself a smile and observed with more than a trace of dynastic superiority: 'Come come, isn't the theatre a place where people go to enjoy themselves?'

Accuracy and precision were the keynotes of Mahler's artistic credo. There is his oft-quoted remark about tradition being an excuse for slovenliness. Another failing Mahler would not tolerate was deviation, however brilliantly conceived. He also detested singers who took it easy at rehearsals, but assured him that 'it would be all

right on the night': on these unhappy creatures he would discharge the full torrent of his fury.

Mahler's reforms involved a thorough overhaul of the rehearsal system. He appointed an admirable supervisor in the person of Ferdinand Foll, in whom he had complete confidence, but nevertheless insisted on taking a great many rehearsals himself, with a piano. As he played — and also sang — he would go off into the visionary, ecstatic world of his symphonies, and gradually the piano stool would tilt farther and farther forward on its front legs until disaster seemed imminent. He was not by any means a virtuoso pianist and used to fluff through difficult passages, but when he wanted to impress a particular passage on a singer's memory he would play it with the utmost precision. At passages including two successive quarters on the same note he used to explain to the singers that each quarter was to be taken differently, that was how the composer (in Mahler's interpretation) wanted it. To the day-to-day conduct of affairs he brought all the fanaticism of his dynamic personality. Every performance was to be a high festival. His predecessor Wilhelm Jahn had always sat in one of the boxes at the back of the auditorium from which he could telephone to the stage. Mahler sat in the second box in the second tier, from which he could get down on to the stage in a flash. He installed a phone in the pit.

From his singers he demanded complete absorption in whatever rôles they were singing at the time. He even expected them to read the outpourings of his beloved Wagner. If he felt that a singer understood what he wanted, he was all smiles and jokingly explained what he wanted: 'Don't keep staring slavishly at the conductor: you might regret it if in *Siegfried* you started singing at him "Ein Ross ist's, rastend im tiefen Schlaf" ("It is a horse, wrapp'd fast in slumber").'

In nearly all the first performances during his term of office Mahler himself was the producer as well as the conductor, and people used to describe how at orchestral rehearsals he would leap down from the podium and scramble over the double-basses on to the stage with the agility of a monkey. If he was not producing, and the rehearsal was in the hands of some dreary mediocrity or

Feuilleton.

Extract from the 'Wiener Sonn- und Montagszeitung' on 8 November 1897. It is no longer possible to ascertain the identity of the author who used the pseudonym L. A. Terne (Laterne — lantern). (Translation on page 214.)

Regulativ für die Besucher der Hofoper.

(Vollzugsvorschriften zu dem Erlasse wider das Zuspätkommen.) (Auszug)

§ 1. Es wird täglich um 5 Uhr im k. k. Arsenal durch einen Kanonenschuß den Besuchern der Hofoper das Zeichen gegeben, daß sie daheim in Bereitschaft zu treten haben. An den Tagen, für welche der Beginn der Vorstellungen auf halb 7 Uhr angesetzt wurde, erfolgt der Signalschuß schon um halb 5 Uhr.

§ 2. Um 6 Uhr, beziehungsweise halb 6 Uhr, mahnt ein zweiter Kanonenschuß, daß die Opernbesucher aus den entfernteren Bezirken ihre Reise zur Hofoper antreten sollen. Es wurde mit den Wiener Hausbesitzern vereinbart, daß die Hausmeister denjenigen Parteien, welche an dem betreffenden Tage die Oper besuchen wollen, die erfolgte Abfeuerung des 6 Uhr-, beziehungsweise halb 6 Uhr-Schusses melden und sie zum Verlassen des Hauses drängen müssen.

§ 3. Da Tramway und Omnibus, zumal während der gegenwärtigen Röhrenlegung, am ehesten durch Verkehrsstockungen zu leiden haben und somit leicht ein massenweises Verspäten der Opernbesucher verschulden können, verpflichtet sich jeder Opernabonnent und Abnehmer einer Opernkarte ehrenwörtlich, nach dem zweiten Signalschusse niemals eines der obgenannten Behikel für die Fahrt zur Hofoper zu benützen.

§ 4. Das Verweilen und Plaudern in den Garderoben vor Beginn der Vorstellung wird behufs schnellerer Abwicklung des Garderobeverkehrs untersagt. Insbesondere ist es den Kritikern, welche die Generalprobe besucht haben, strenge verboten, durch Prophezeiungen vor einer Première das Publicum in den Garderoben aufzuhalten.

§ 6. Schlag 7 Uhr, beziehungsweise halb 7 Uhr, gibt eine Dampfpfeife im Opernhause das Anfangszeichen. Wer bis dahin seinen Platz noch nicht erreicht, hat alle Folgen zu tragen, welche in dem Directionserlasse vom 2. November a. c. angedroht sind.

§ 7. Nach Heben des Vorhanges hat das Publicum strenge darauf zu achten, daß ihm die Illusion nicht verloren gehe. Behufs Erhaltung der Illusion im Zuschauerraume wird wie folgt verfügt:

a) Die Thürhüter werden beauftragt, Brautleuten, welche bekanntlich durch lebhaften Meinungsaustausch die Nachbarn häufig belästigen und von den Vorgängen auf der Bühne abziehen, den Eintritt in den Zuschauerraum zu verwehren. Paarweis eintretende Personen verschiedenen Geschlechtes haben sich daher durch Vorzeigen eines Trauscheines bei den Eingängen als Ehepaar zu legitimiren.

b) Auffallend schönen Damen, welche leicht die Blicke der Herrenwelt auf sich lenken dürften, kann der Eintritt in den Zuschauerraum verweigert werden.

e) Die Operngläser dürfen nur auf die Bühne gerichtet werden. Wer sein Glas während einer Vorstellung nach dem Zuschauerraume wendet und seine Illusion damit preisgibt, hat jedesmal zu Gunsten des Pensionsfonds einen Strafbetrag von fünfzig Kreuzern zu entrichten.

f) Harte Bonbons dürfen während der Vorstellung nur in der Weise genossen werden, daß das Zuckerwerk, ohne daß die Zähne mithelfen, zwischen die Zunge und den Gaumen gelegt, dort geräuschlos vermittelst der i-Stellung der Zunge an den Gaumen gepreßt und in dieser Lage erhalten wird, bis die Süßigkeit über die Zungenwurzel sich unhörbar in den Schlund verliert.

g) Husten, Räuspern und Schneuzen kann nur während eines Fortissimo gestattet werden. Der Concertmeister ist dazu verhalten, unmittelbar vor Eintritt eines Crescendo dem Publicum mit dem Violinbogen ein Zeichen zu geben, daß das Taschentuch hervorgeholt und das Husten oder Räuspern vorbereitet werden darf.

h) Jenen Kritikern, welche gern Partituren in die Oper mitschleppen, wird das Umblättern, weil es Geräusch verursacht, strenge untersagt. Keineswegs ist das Mitlesen in Partituren gestattet, welche eine andere als die zur Aufführung gelangende Oper enthalten. Hier würde das hastige Umblättern noch störender empfunden.

i) Die Buffetdamen haben darauf zu achten, daß keinem Opernbesucher in den Zwischenacten mehr als eine Caviarsemmel oder dergleichen verabreicht werde, denn eine allzu reiche Ernährung in den Zwischenacten erzeugt leicht Congestionen, welche die Illusion in dem nächsten Act beeinträchtigen können.

§ 9. Das Rauchen außerhalb des Opernhauses vor Beginn und nach Schluß der Vorstellung wird den Opernbesuchern unbedenklich gestattet.

§ 11. Jenen Kritikern, welche noch am Abende zwei Blätter mit einer Recension zu versorgen pflegen, wird, wenn eine ungestrichene Wagner-Aufführung angekündigt ist, behufs leichterer Abwicklung des Geschäftes gerne gestattet, die eine Recension vor der Aufführung fertigzustellen.

§ 12. Die Opernbesucher werden ausdrücklich aufmerksam gemacht, daß für den Theil des Publicums, welcher wegen verspäteten Eintreffens nicht nur während der Ouverture, sondern auch während des ganzen ersten Actes vor den Einlaßthüren ausharren muß, daselbst keine wie immer geartete Separatvorstellungen veranstaltet werden.

Wien, am 8. November 1897.

Gesehen:

L. A. Terne.

other, the tremendous energy Mahler expended while conducting would alternate with an almost total withdrawal from the proceedings for several minutes at a time. Bruno Walter, who started as a *Kapellmeister* under Mahler in Hamburg at a very early age, used to recall how once at a rehearsal, when the producer indicated to Mahler that he was ready to resume, Mahler on the podium absent-mindedly shouted at the top of his voice: 'Waiter, my check!'

During Mahler's first five years several of the masterpieces in the repertoire were given a thorough overhaul. In his very first year he disentangled *Figaro* from the undergrowth of arbitrary trills and cadenzas that had accumulated over the years. In *Götterdämmerung* the 'Norns' scene had hitherto invariably been cut: Mahler restored it, and the way the players went through the motions of paying out rope (without any actual rope) excited universal admiration, though the performance lasted over an hour longer than previously. In *Così fan tutte* the new revolving stage made a rather creaking début, and Mahler himself accompanied the *secco* recitative on a piano, but went over to the harpsichord six years later. In *Freischütz* the traditional spookiness of the Wolf's Glen scene was replaced by an ultra-modern interplay of light and shade and clouds, the comment of Mahler's enemies being that he had turned the Wolf's Glen into a 'rendezvous in the Vienna Woods near Purkersdorf'.

Mahler was very fond of Slav music. He introduced Tchaikovsky (*Eugene Onegin*, *Iolanthe*, and *Pique Dame*) to the Vienna Opera, and also staged Rubinstein's *Daimon* and Smetana's *Dalibor*. Nor did he neglect works by contemporary composers. In 1898 Leoncavallo's *Bohème* was included in the repertoire after a stormy scene between Leoncavallo and Mahler during a rehearsal. Actually it was Wilhelm Jahn who first accepted the work following the success of the same composer's *Pagliacci*. Puccini's opera of the same name had been performed at the Theater an der Wien in 1897, but it was not until 1903 that Mahler introduced it to the Opera. Siegfried Wagner, Richard's talented son, scored a great but short-lived success in 1899 with his fairy-tale opera *Der Bärenhäuter*, and a contemporary pun was to the effect that the Emperor allowed Siegfried Wagner to use the title 'von' because he preferred 'Siegfried von Wagner' (which could also mean 'Siegfried by Wagner') to 'Siegfried Wagner'. Then came the memorable evening in 1902 when Richard Strauss took his first curtain-call on the stage of the Vienna Opera after the first Vienna performance of *Feuersnot*, while in her box his wife Pauline never stopped telling everyone that 'the whole of this hotchpotch of my husband's is stolen from Wagner'.

It goes without saying that the upheaval occasioned by Mahler's reforms was bound to lead to far-reaching staff changes as well. Mahler was always at pains to keep the latent conflict between him and Hans Richter from boil-

In spite of the Bohemian nose this is not, as you might think, Slezak, but the Danish Viking Erik Schmedes as Lohengrin. (Silhouette by Theo Zasche, 1912.)

The first contract with Anna von Mildenburg, in 1897, provides for a salary of 14,000 guilders per year payable in arrears in equal monthly instalments, ten duty performances per month — and no leave of absence other than 'in summer during the general theatre vacations.'

ing over too soon, but the day came when it was obvious that the house was not big enough to hold both of these staunch supporters of Wagner. Hans Richter, a Germanic Teuton type with a big blonde beard beginning to go grey, was the very incarnation of a slow-moving flow of feeling building up at a leisurely tempo, whereas the high-strung and electrifying Mahler not only saw Wagner differently but lived in an entirely different world. When Mahler announced in 1900 that in future he intended to conduct all Wagner performances himself, Hans Richter walked out. He moved to England and until the day of his death in 1918 never conducted in Vienna again. Mahler replaced him with Franz Schalk, a disciple of Bruckner's, a sound but not exactly inspiring conductor and many years later an efficient Director of the Vienna Opera. He had a mordant wit and spent much of his time in coffee-houses intriguing against Mahler, just as he did many years later against Richard Strauss.

But Mahler's most important acquisition was the young conductor Bruno Walter, a friend from his Hamburg days. Walter started by taking over most of the French and Italian repertoire (*Aida, Ernani, Ballo in Maschera, La muette de Portici* etc.). In time he became one of the world's foremost conductors (after he had shaved off his beard). He came from Berlin, and his real name was Schlesinger ('von der Vogelweide' added a Viennese wit). A year or two later Mahler imported a specialist in Italian opera, Francesco Spetrino.

The élan, tempo and uncompromising thoroughness of Mahler's intellectual concept of 'total' theatre was not to everybody's liking. Many popular favourites departed, including Marie Renard, who survived under Mahler long enough to sing a wonderful Tatiana before marrying a Count Kinsky and saying farewell to the stage with a Carmen that brought the house down; and two superb tenors, van Dyck and Franz Naval from Ljubljana, who had been Puccini's first Rodolfo at the Opera as well as at the Theater an der Wien. Mahler replaced them with his celebrated ensemble of 'Mahlersänger', who for sheer fanaticism have often been compared to a religious order or brotherhood.

Mahler never particularly liked 'lovely' voices: he

K. k. Hof-Operntheater in Wien.

VERTRAG,

welcher vorbehaltlich der Ratification durch die k. u. k. General-Intendanz der k. k. Hof-Theater zwischen der k. u. k. Direction des k. k. Hof-Operntheaters einerseits und *Fräulein Anna von Mildenburg* anderseits abgeschlossen worden ist:

Fräulein Anna von Mildenburg, wird (bleibt) in der Eigenschaft als *Opernsängerin* an dem k. k. Hof-Operntheater engagirt, und zwar auf Grund der beigefügten allgemeinen Engagements-Bedingnisse und folgender besonderer Bestimmungen:

Urkund dessen die nachstehenden eigenhändigen Unterschriften.

WIEN, den *14. März* 18*98*. *Hamburg, den 7. März 1898.*

Die k. u. k. Direction des k. k. Hof-Operntheaters.

Gustav Mahler *Anna von Mildenburg*

Ratificirt
Von der k. u. k. General-Intendanz der k. k. Hof-Theater
ad N° *457* WIEN, den *24. III.* 189*8*.

68

preferred hard, steely voices of great power, artists who could run the whole gamut of the emotions and give expression to the things of the mind in terms of singing and acting.

There was the Viennese Anna Mildenburg, a pupil of Rosa Papier and a former colleague of Mahler's in Hamburg. Mahler moulded her into a great player of tragic, imperious rôles, and with him as her mentor she became a superb Brünnhilde, Isolde and Ortrud. She was one of Mahler's most ardent disciples, and in her memoirs Mahler's widow Alma indulges in some rather indelicate innuendoes about their relations outside the theatre. Anna Mildenburg later became the wife of Hermann Bahr.

The Danish singer Erik Schmedes was a fine Siegfried and Tristan. It was to him that Mahler tried to explain how to portray Tristan, with the lapidary instruction: 'Before the love potion as a baritone, after it as a tenor!'

To replace Renard, Mahler secured Marie Gutheil-Schoder from Weimar. Whereas Renard's Carmen was a woman to whom no drawing-rooms would have been barred, Gutheil's was elemental and 'naturalistic'. At first the public showed little liking for her metallic, glassy voice but Mahler's faith in her never wavered, and in the end this highly intelligent and artistic personality became a great popular favourite. Her great triumph was as Frau Fluth (Mistress Ford) in *The Merry Wives of Windsor*, and in 1901 she sang all three soprano parts in *Tales of Hoffmann*.

Friedrich Weidemann, whose somewhat hard voice contained a great deal of warmth and humanity, superbly played Hans Sachs and Wotan.

Apart from these stars there were a number of *bel canto* exponents who under Mahler's guidance positively excelled themselves. Selma Kurz from Galicia started as a mezzo-soprano but Mahler made her right away into a coloratura prima donna. It all began at a rehearsal, when Mahler noticed that Selma Kurz could maintain an unusually long trill: he took out his watch and timed her. Together, they systematically prolonged the duration of it until it became a phenomenon of the operatic stage and, later, of the concert halls. The Kurz trill became world-famous. In Lucia's aria she attained such a wonderful

unity between her voice and the accompanying flute that, in a recording, one hardly notices where the flute ends and Selma Kurz begins ... Mahler did not restrict her to coloratura parts; she was the heroine in both the Puccini premières of the Mahler era, in *Bohème* and *Madame Butterfly*.

Among the basses there was Wilhelm Hesch, who had been taken on by Jahn, and the superb Richard Mayr from Salzburg. The finest baritone voice was Leopold Demuth, a pharmacist from Brünn (Brno), who after Theodor Reichmann's death blossomed out under Mahler with a wonderful Wolfram and Flying Dutchman.

But the most popular of all the singers Mahler engaged was beyond doubt Leo Slezak, a giant of a man from Brünn, a locksmith with a voice ranging from the most delicate pianissimo of the 'tenore amoroso' to outbursts of high dramatic intensity, and a repertoire ranging from Mozart to Meyerbeer and Wagner. He eventually became one of the world's most celebrated singers. His lively sense of humour on the stage caused more than one singer almost to miss an entry from laughing at one of his whispered asides.

The most revolutionary period of Mahler's rule was his last five years. After spending his first five years perfecting the singing and acting, he now applied his concept of something new for eyes and ears alike to perfecting all the other ingredients of a stage production. His ambition was to devise entirely new productions of all the great German operas (Gluck, Mozart, Wagner) in accordance with Wagner's *Gesamtkunstwerk* ideal. As regards scenery, Vienna could provide all he wanted, lavish and commodious settings for spectacular productions (including ballets), alongside naturalistic backcloths. So he kept his eyes open for a kindred spirit of genius who would embark with him upon a thorough reform and modernisation of operatic scenery. Many of his ideas were inspired by Adolphe Appia's book *Die Musik und die Inszenierung* (1899) in which the author postulates settings in which the scene is no more than indicated (as in some recent Bayreuth productions). Mahler's first choice was an artist from the Vienna *Hagenbund*, Heinrich Lefler, but Lefler's new scenery for *Aida* failed to

Gustav Mahler was indulgent with international stars. He let Nellie Melba die of consumption in 'La Traviata' and then immediately had her stand up and sing the mad scene from 'Lucia di Lammermoor'.

meet with Mahler's approval. Later, Hermann Bahr observed of Lefler that there was no one who could design bad scenery better. It was not until Alfred Roller appeared upon the scene that a new chapter in operatic history was written.

Roller was a painter, a friend of Gustav Klimt's and President of the Vienna *Secession*, which founded the *Jugendstil* and professed as its creed: 'Every age must have its own art.' The great collaboration between Mahler and Roller arose out of an exchange of views on the proper setting for *Tristan*. Mahler was completely fascinated by Roller. The autocrat who was accustomed to giving orders and not taking them from anybody was as shy as a child in Roller's company. For the commemoration of the twentieth anniversary of Wagner's death in 1903, the year in which Klimt completed his celebrated frescoes in Vienna University, Mahler and Roller collaborated in a stage-production for *Tristan* which, besides being regarded for many years as authoritative, proved the truth of the theory that today's experiment is tomorrow's law. Long before Bayreuth embarked on its recent course of 'uncluttering' the stage, Roller allowed the scene to dissolve in a kaleidoscope of light and colour. In Act One, for instance, Anna Mildenburg and Erik Schmedes drank the potion amid a symphony of flaring reddish-orange. In Act Two the marble palace was bathed in violet: it was symbolising night. The costumes were less fortunate: it was difficult not to laugh when Richard Mayr as King Mark came back from hunting wearing a crown over his fur-trimmed hunting cap. In Act Three the 'mournful strain' was symbolised by a symphony in grey swathing the great lime-tree on the steep hill.

There was a great deal of comment on Roller's 'painting in light' and Mahler's 'music in light'. It was as if the music were made visible. But Roller did not always equate light with brightness, and like most other scenic revolutions in the history of opera his too was criticised in many quarters as 'too dark'.

After the success of *Tristan* Roller was given a firm contract with the Vienna Opera. The next opera in which he collaborated with Mahler was *Fidelio* in 1904. It was in this production that Beethoven's great hymn to humanity was first presented in its present form. Hitherto the overture 'Leonore No. 3' had been played during the interval, though Hans Richter put it at the beginning of the opera in place of the E major Overture. It was Mahler who first played 'Leonore No. 3' where it is nearly always played nowadays, between the Prison Scene in Act Two and the Finale, as a sort of sublime recapitulation of the theme of suffering and triumph. Again, the first scenes, in accordance with the 1814 version, had previously been set in the prison. Mahler transferred them to Rocco's lodge, as in the 1806 version. The

After the turn of the century a shop selling gramophone records advertised that it could offer the most beautiful voices 'without background noises'. You are sure to have heard an old Slezak or Kurz record — but without background noises?

Wozu wir noch die großen Gagen bezahlen?!

C. Janauschek & Cie.

Wien, I., Kärntnerstraße

liefert uns viel billiger die schönsten Stimmen ohne Nebengeräusch.

prisoners came groping their way out of a dark hole with almost shocking realism; the guards were just a collection of furtive shadows. Erik Schmedes transposed Florestan's aria a whole tone lower.

It was in the much-discussed Mahler-Roller *Don Giovanni*, part of the commemorations of the 150th anniversary of Mozart's birth, that the so-called 'Roller towers' made their début; massive, greyish, angular constructions framing the scene on either side. From the beginning to the end of the opera they were never shifted,

serving in turn as the house of the Commendatore, the inside or outside of Don Giovanni's mansion, Elvira's balcony, tombstones, etc. From the point of view of quick changes of scene they were a brilliant invention. To cut down costs, Mahler used them in *Die Entführung* too.

It was certainly not Roller's fault if his successors destroyed the illusion by misusing his idea of permanent scenery. In this particular performance of *Don Giovanni* Anna Mildenburg gave a wonderful performance as Donna Anna à la E. T. A. Hoffmann: vowing vengeance, she is really only waiting for Don Ottavio's discomfiture and her own surrender to Don Giovanni. The opera ended with Don Giovanni's descent into the nether regions, and the final sextet was cut.

In the same Mozart series there was also a new *Figaro* (1906). In order to make Marcellina's law-suit clearer Mahler inserted the trial scene from Beaumarchais' comedy, given in a *recitativo secco* specially composed for the occasion, and accompanied it on the harpsichord.

Among other notable Mahler-Roller productions were *Das Rheingold* (1905), for the first time without an interval after the Nibelheim scene, and *Walküre* without cuts (1907), with a 'Ride of the Valkyries' that was full of ingenious cloud and lighting effects, and with Fricka making her entry without the two traditional cardboard rams. Their last production was *Iphigenia in Aulis* (1907) with Gutheil-Schoder as Iphigenia. The players moved across the scene as if in a classical frieze and the action was played out in front of a curtain which only at the very end rose to reveal the harbour of Aulis.

Mahler had many admirers in Vienna, but he also made many enemies, and he was too anti-social ever to be really popular. Vienna has never reacted kindly to fanatics and geniuses of Mahler's stature. There was precious little of the Viennese about him. A detail of psychological interest is that in the last four symphonies written during his term as Director, the Austrian folk-song element recedes further and further into the background. In view of his split personality, it was inevitable that he should be either loved or detested. He could be tyrannical and in the next moment yielding; one minute he was aloof and withdrawn, and the next outgoing and even genial. The only possible exception to his un-Viennese traits was his love of coffee-houses. Before and after performances he often used to frequent the Café Imperial, where he might hope to catch the Emperor's ear through Katharina Schratt's tarot partners. He always read the critics' comments ('What have our lords and masters got to say today?') and used to enjoy discussing the latest or the next performance. It was at times like this that a totally different Mahler emerged. Max Graf recalls how he once heard Mahler declare in a coffee-house: 'In forty years'

time people won't be playing Beethoven's symphonies, they'll be playing mine instead.'

In the course of a normal 'Mahler year' the Opera would put on fifty-four operas and sixteen ballets. During his term there were a number of brilliant performances of contemporary works. In 1905 Hans Pfitzner made his first appearance at the Vienna Opera with his *Rose vom Liebesgarten* and became one of Mahler's closest friends. Mahler had to overcome a lot of opposition — including that of the orchestra — before actually getting the work onto the stage. Roller's blue setting matched Pfitzner's D major perfectly. Eugen d'Albert turned up with two one-act operas, and Wolf-Ferrari with *Le donne curiose*. Among other composers who made their début at the Vienna Opera about this time were Leo Blech, Emil Nikolaus von Reznicek, Ludwig Thuille and Alexander von

Zemlinsky. The latter was an adherent of Schoenberg's, and Zemlinsky was for a short time one of the conductors at the Opera.

If in Mahler's opinion everything was not just as he wanted it, he would have no compunction about putting off a première at the last moment, as for instance in 1903, when only a day or two before the first night of his *Louise* Gustave Charpentier wanted some surrealist scenery which Mahler considered worth trying out.

Dear Sir;
The office of the Director of the Court Opera House is in receipt of an intimation that the Censor's department objects to the release of the libretto of the opera 'Salome' on 'religious and ethical grounds' and 'the General-Intendancy of the Court Theatres is not in a position to grant permission for this stage work to be performed.'

I take the liberty of communicating this decision to you, while expressing at the same time my most lively regrets that, in these circumstances, I am unfortunately compelled to refrain from performing your work.

I am, etc.

Mahler

Vienna, 22 September 1905.

The censor disclosed the reasons for his refusal in a detailed memorandum dated 31 October 1905: 'The first objection is to the repeated references in the text expressed or implied, to Christ... 'Er ist auf einem Nachen auf dem See von Galiläa'... All these passages would have to be deleted. A further difficulty consists in the fact that John the Baptist is brought on to the stage... But quite apart from these textual objections I cannot reconcile myself to the repellent nature of the whole subject-matter, and can only say once again: Events which pertain to the sphere of sexual pathology... are not suitable for presentation on the stage of our Court theatres!' The censor is cowardly enough to add: 'I should like to leave to your discretion in the interests of all concerned, the desirability of adopting the attitude towards the Press that the question whether or not the suppression of 'Salome' is final, still remains an open one...' May the story of this suppression serve to dry the tears of all those who, in every kind of connection, are forever bemoaning the death of the old Austria.

Gustav Mahler was determined to put on Richard Strauss's 'Salome' in Vienna. On 22 September 1905 he sent the composer the following telegram (left): 'Hofkapellmeister Dr. Richard Strauss, Charlottenburg. Please cause two or three piano scores of Salome to be despatched as soon as possible so that principals can commence study. Who are the publishers of the work? Greetings Mahler.'

A few moments after this telegram had been sent off the censor's veto arrived in the Director's office. Mahler informed Strauss by letter on the same day.

Das Verhältnis Mahlers zu seinen Künstlern ist, abgesehen von der Notizenwut der Zeitungen und des Publikums und von der Reklamesucht mancher Sänger und ihrer Rechtsanwalte, die immer irgend etwas zu „vertreten" haben, damit sie in einer Zeitung genannt werden, auch noch aus einem Fehler zu erklären, der allen absolutistischen Regierungen anhaftet. Es ist nicht einzusehen, warum gerade Gustav Mahler der einzige Autokrat sein sollte, der davon verschont bliebe. Je mehr er für sich allein stehen will, desto mehr mußte er sich in mancher Hinsicht auf andere verlassen, und so mag es kommen, daß Einflüsse in ihm und durch ihn tätig waren, die er selbst nicht kannte. Und dann — eine selbstherrliche Natur, wie es Mahler glücklicherweise ist, sollte niemandes Freund sein. Im Augenblick, wo es eine Partei f ü r ihn gab, mußte es auch eine g e g e n ihn geben. Wäre a l l e s gegen ihn gewesen, er wäre nicht sobald des Kampfes müde geworden. Und wie jeder Selbstherrscher, hat Mahler zu viel untertänige Geister um sich gesehen, um nicht auch ein ehrliches Urteil unberücksichtigt zu lassen. Nichts aber braucht ein Künstler mehr als R e d l i c h k e i t der Gesinnung, die man ihm entgegenbringt. Wenn der französische Minister G u i z o t einmal sagte: „Wenn ich im R e c h t e bin, brauche ich meine Freunde nicht," so gilt für den Künstler nicht das gleiche. Die Allzuvielen, die sich an Mahler herandrängten, weichen zurück, da er die Macht niederlegt; wer weiß, wie viele, die eine lächerliche Kundgebung für ihn unterschrieben, nicht auch gleichzeitig eine für seinen Nachfolger — er sei, wer er sei — bereitwilligst unterschreiben würden?

Nun geht Mahler, um wieder alle künstlerische Freiheit zurückzugewinnen, die seine ekstatische Natur braucht. Er hat im einzelnen Lob und Tadel verdient und gefunden, im ganzen sich aber den Anspruch auf Ruhm und mehr als dies, auf Liebe erworben. Und er soll nicht ohne die Versicherung scheiden, daß ihm ein guter Teil Wiens, das sich seiner Leistungen freuen durfte, dieses Gefühl in Aufrichtigkeit und Dankbarkeit bewahren wird.

Dr. D. J. Bach.

From the article by David Bach in the 'Arbeiter-Zeitung' of 7 June 1970, on the occasion of Mahler's resignation. (Translation on page 214.)

the work had been accepted and was desperately upset that the first performance was put off. In one of his fits of insanity he is said to have claimed to be the Director of the Opera himself.

On the whole, however, the new works Mahler put on were less epoch-making than his revivals, largely because of the mediocrity of the former. Of all the important works Mahler was responsible for staging, only *Tosca*, *Tiefland* and *Pelléas et Mélisande* really eluded him.

When Italian stars were appearing, the entire cast had to sing in Italian, for instance in Caruso's performances in 1906 and 1907, and also in 1900 when Gemma Bellincioni created the role of Fedora in Giordano's opera of the same name. On such occasions Mahler was unusually tolerant, even when in 1900 Dame Nellie Melba, after duly expiring in *La Traviata*, resurrected herself and gave a stirring performance of the mad-scene in *Lucia di Lammermoor*.

During the closing years of his term the campaign against Mahler mounted to a crescendo, and smouldering embers of revolution were fanned by discarded and superannuated singers. Although he conducted their concerts for three years, Mahler never really enjoyed the support of the Philharmonic Orchestra, even though its leader Arnold Rosé (the founder of the famous Rosé Quartet) was married to Mahler's sister. Press attacks were mainly concentrated on the dimness of Roller's stage-designs, the number of imported stars, and Mahler's (by modern standards ridiculously short) trips abroad to conduct his own works. German-nationalist circles demanded 'more new German works'. Coffee-houses hummed with jokes about Mahler's 'Caesar complex': it was said that he was anxious to settle down at Mödling, but only on condition that he could get there by the Northern instead of the Southern Railway, and that the Vienna Woods should be replaced by one of Roller's lighting schemes. His characteristic foibles were exaggerated — in all probability Mahler really did have a streak of sadism and masochism; it seems to be audible in his symphonies. When Schalk took over *Lohengrin* Mahler insisted that Schalk conduct an orchestral rehearsal in his presence, as if it were an audition, with Mahler standing on the stage like a State

Hugo Wolf, whom Mahler allowed free tickets for the rest of his life, died in an asylum just before the posthumous success of his *Corregidor*. Wolf had been told that

examiner and staring fixedly at Schalk, much to the annoyance of the orchestra as well as of Schalk. As a child Mahler was once asked what he was going to be and replied 'a martyr'. However, it was not until there was a persistent rise in expenditure and a corresponding drop in the takings that the anti-Mahler campaign was taken seriously by the authorities. Mahler had already offered to resign once before, in 1905, when the Court Censor banned Richard Strauss's *Salome*, which Mahler wanted to stage in Vienna on the same day as the world première in Dresden, but his resignation had not been accepted. In the summer of 1907, Mahler felt unequal to further resistance to the 'revolt of mediocrities' and offered his resignation again, this time for good. A galaxy of Austria's leading intellectuals tried to induce him to reconsider his decision: Arthur Schnitzler, Stefan Zweig, Arnold Schoenberg, Gustav Klimt, Sigmund Freud, but to no purpose. The last time Mahler conducted in the Vienna Opera *(Fidelio)* was on the fifteenth of October 1907, after which he left all his awards and distinctions in a drawer of a desk in his office ('for my successor') and departed to America to conduct cut versions of Wagner's operas at the Metropolitan as well as some of the New York Philharmonic concerts.

From 1907 on he suffered from a serious heart complaint and is said to have had a coronary thrombosis on the stage during a rehearsal of *Lohengrin*. In New York his condition deteriorated, so he came back to lay his bones in the Vienna he both loved and hated. In May 1911, on a day of wind and rain, 'the man who was fired', as he called himself, was laid to rest in the Hietzing cemetery in the presence of a 'vast concourse'. In a letter of farewell to the staff of the Vienna Opera Mahler had written: 'Instead of something complete and entire, as I had dreamed, I am leaving behind something imperfect and unfinished, as is our human lot.' But was it not E. T. A. Hoffmann who said that without a clear vision of an unattainable ideal there could be no artists?

When Mahler shook the dust of Vienna from his feet on the ninth of December 1907, Arnold Schoenberg, Alexander von Zemlinsky and about a hundred others went to the West Station to see him off. As the train pulled out

AN DIE GEEHRTEN MITGLIEDER DER HOFOPER!

Die Stunde ist gekommen, die unserer gemeinsamen Tätigkeit eine Grenze setzt. Ich scheide von der Werkstatt, die mir lieb geworden, und sage Ihnen hiemit Lebewol.

Statt eines Ganzen, Abgeschlossenen, wie ich geträumt, hinterlasse ich Stückwerk, Unvollendetes: wie es dem Menschen bestimmt ist.

Es ist nicht meine Sache, ein Urteil darüber abzugeben, was mein Wirken denjenigen geworden ist, denen es gewidmet war. Doch darf ich in solchem Augenblick von mir sagen: Ich habe es redlich gemeint, mein Ziel hochgesteckt. Nicht immer konnten meine Bemühungen von Erfolg gekrönt sein. „Dem Widerstand der Materie" — „der Tücke des Objekts" ist Niemand so überantwortet wie der ausübende Künstler. Aber immer habe ich mein Ganzes darangesetzt, meine Person der Sache, meine Neigungen der Pflicht untergeordnet. Ich habe mich nicht geschont und durfte daher auch von den Anderen die Anspannung aller Kräfte fordern.

Im Gedränge des Kampfes, in der Hitze des Augenblicks blieben Ihnen und mir nicht Wunden, nicht Irrungen erspart. Aber war ein Werk gelungen, eine Aufgabe gelöst, so vergaßen wir alle Not und Mühe, fühlten uns reich belohnt — auch ohne äußere Zeichen des Erfolges. Wir alle sind weiter gekommen und mit uns das Institut, dem unsere Bestrebungen galten.

Haben Sie nun herzlichsten Dank, die mich in meiner schwierigen, oft nicht dankbaren Aufgabe gefördert, die mitgeholfen, mitgestritten haben. Nehmen Sie meine aufrichtigsten Wünsche für Ihren ferneren Lebensweg und für das Gedeihen des Hofoperntheaters, dessen Schicksale ich auch weiterhin mit regster Anteilnahme begleiten werde.

WIEN, am 7. Dezember 1907.

GUSTAV MAHLER.

Mahler's farewell notice to the members of the Court Opera. (Translation on page 215.)

Mahler said to his wife: 'Repertory opera is finished. I'm only glad that I didn't have to stay here to preside over its demise.' — Prophetic words . . .

Felix von Weingartner
1908—1911

To find a successor to Gustav Mahler was obviously going to be no easy matter. The logical choice would have been Felix Mottl, a native of Vienna whose career as a conductor had started at the Ringtheater and who was now *Generalmusikdirektor* in Munich. But Mottl was one of that goodly company of musicians in Viennese musical history whom nothing could induce to set foot in the hornet's nest of the Vienna Opera. His name had come up for consideration as far back as 1897, when Jahn departed, but the almighty Hanslick had lodged a vehement protest against having a Wagnerian as Director of the Vienna Opera, and so the choice fell on Mahler, who was just as much of a Wagnerian as Mottl, only Hanslick didn't know it at the time. So Mottl seemed the obvious choice to succeed Mahler, and approaches were made to him in Munich. But Mottl declined.

It is of course common knowledge that whenever the Director's chair at the Vienna Opera is vacant a number of aspirants, or people who think they are in the running, just happen to be in Vienna at the time, visiting friends and relations or keeping sudden and urgent appointments with their dentists. Among the crowd converging on the Austrian capital in the summer of 1907 was Felix von Weingartner, Edler von Münzberg. He put in an appearance at a couple of fashionable performances, was asked to call on Prince Liechtenstein, was duly offered the post of Director of the Vienna Opera, and accepted on the spot.

On the face of it the choice was by no means an unhappy one, for although Weingartner too was a well-known conductor, he was a completely different type of musician from Mahler, and it seemed better to entrust the Directorship to a diametrically opposite personality than to some colourless imitator of Mahler.

A greater contrast than between Mahler and Weingartner can hardly be imagined. Weingartner was of Austrian aristocratic descent and was the first Director to take office as a member of the nobility: the others were not ennobled until after their appointment, Dingelstedt for example, for services rendered, or Jauner as compensation for his dismissal.

Weingartner was born at Zara in Dalmatia and studied in Graz and at the Leipzig Conservatorium. He had been a conductor in several German cities (Königsberg, Danzig, Hamburg), had been a pupil and close associate of Liszt's at Weimar, and in 1882, at the age of nineteen, had enjoyed a long conversation with Richard Wagner, which he never forgot. Later he was appointed *Kapellmeister* at the Royal Opera in Berlin as well as conducting the Berlin Chapel Royal. In short, towards the turn of the century he was regarded as one of the leading conductors in the German-speaking world. In 1897 he cancelled his Berlin contracts (his successor being Richard Strauss, whom he could not abide) and moved to Munich to be the conductor of the 'New Orchestra' founded by Dr. Kaim. In this capacity he invited Gustav Mahler to visit Munich, and it was with Kaim's orchestra, under Weingartner's supervision, that Mahler conducted the first performance of his Fourth Symphony.

By and large, then, the omens for Weingartner's term at the helm of the Vienna Opera were distinctly favourable.

He duly took up office on the first of January 1908, and he would have done well to give immediate and careful consideration to the problem of how to make the best use of Mahler's heritage. If he had done so, he would have concluded that it was a question of preserving its best elements and enlarging it by devoting particular attention to the aspects over which Mahler had taken too little trouble (or so the critics unanimously maintained), and notably to the cultivation of *bel canto*. On the other hand, Mahler had trained up a select ensemble of highly intelligent Wagner singers who probably had no equals anywhere in the world.

Instead, what did Weingartner do? Today it can be said without fear of contradiction that he harboured a completely mistaken idea of his duties and of the possibilities they opened up. He allowed himself to be hailed as the champion of the anti-Mahler clique (whose numbers he grossly overestimated) and saw himself as the 'avenger' of his predecessor's 'sins'.

He had the unfortunate idea, for instance, of hastily putting on a new *Fidelio* in the very first month of his term of office, whereas it was precisely Mahler's *Fidelio*

76

Siegmunð! Sieh' auf mich! Ich bin's, der balð ðu folgst.
Nur Toðgeweihten taugt mein Anblick; wer mich
erschaut, ðer scheiðet vom Lebenslicht.

Siegmund! Look on me! I come to call thee hence.
Death-doomed is he who looks upon me;
who meets my glance must turn from the light of life.

that was universally regarded as one of his most superb productions. In Weingartner's new production all Mahler's brilliant ideas were simply mutilated. In Act One there was a reversion to the old practice of using the same scenery for the whole Act, and the Overture 'Leonore No. 3', which Mahler had introduced with such tremendous effect between the Prison Scene and the Finale, was dropped altogether. So was the shorter 'Fidelio' Overture: Weingartner preferred 'Leonore No. 2'. Roller's scenery for the Finale was left to languish in the store-room.

Weingartner defended himself with passionate conviction against the charge of having been 'destructive': Mahler had only played 'Leonore No. 3' after the Prison Scene to give Roller the good ten minutes he needed for the scene-shifters, etc., etc. Whereas he, Weingartner, considered 'Leonore No. 3' too good to be used as a 'fill-in'. So from the very first Weingartner's 'reforms' were controversial, to say the least.

It was not long before he started getting anonymous letters uttering dire threats as to what would happen if he dared to conduct in person, and amid the applause with which he was greeted there was an unmistakably counter-demonstrative undertone. It was only thanks to strong police reinforcements that his *Fidelio* passed off without undue incident.

There was also severe criticism of the cast: it looked as if the new Director had little sense of the theatre. It was the general opinion that compared with Anna Mildenburg the new Leonore, Lucy Weidt, lacked the mental equipment for the part, and that Don Pizarro was not nearly ruthless enough.

This Don Pizarro was Leopold Demuth, a lyrical baritone with a superb voice who unfortunately looked like a secondary-school teacher, for all his geniality and bonhomie. Mahler had thought little of him, but Weingartner adored him. The new Pizarro's costume was also against him: he was given a wig with a pigtail which merely enhanced the incongruity of his appearance, and even the Governor's soldiers wore rococo get-ups instead of the usual severe military uniforms. Weingartner was as much criticised for his passion for pigtails in *Fidelio* as he was later on for depriving Gounod's Marguerite of the

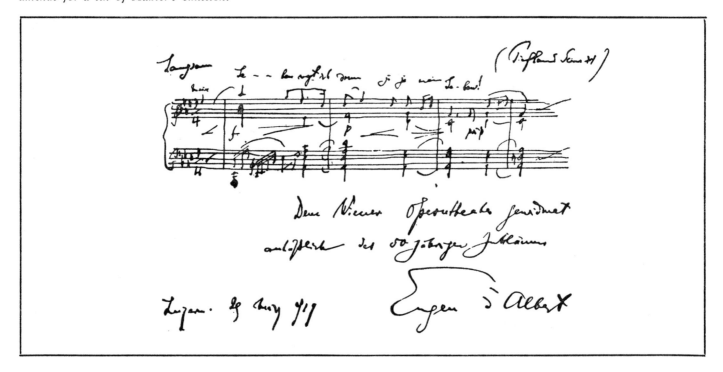

attractive pigtail she had worn so becomingly and for so long.

It was the new production of *Fidelio* that started off the antagonism between Weingartner und Alfred Roller, who was in charge of scenery and now had to watch the work of years being consigned to oblivion. Roller left the Opera in high dudgeon in 1909. Weingartner subsequently modified the *Fidelio* scenery to some extent in collaboration with a former theatrical producer named Wilhelm von Wymetal, whom he had summoned to Vienna from Cologne and who later exchanged Vienna for the New York 'Met'. For the change of scene after the Prison Scene Wymetal thought up a process that took so little time that it was possible to restore Roller's scenery for the Finale without having recourse to the 'Leonore No. 3' Overture. In January all Weingartner used for this scene were two huge towers rising straight out of the ground, so that there was no need of a break between the Prison Scene and the Finale.

Weingartner was just as heavy-handed with Wagner as

he had been with *Fidelio*. In the Mahler era all Wagner's operas had been performed without cuts, yet within a few months of Weingartner's taking over there was a heavily cut *Walküre*.

To the question of cuts in Wagner (like everything else) Weingartner had devoted a good deal of thought. In Berlin there had been experiments in the form of alternating cut and uncut performances. But Vienna audiences had been so well trained by Mahler that by now they were not only sitting through uncut performances but were applauding them more and more enthusiastically. It was therefore a serious tactical error on Weingartner's part to break almost overnight (out of pure animosity towards Mahler) with what had become a tradition and to put on a production of *Walküre* with cuts, especially as Mahler's production of the *Ring* had only got as far as *Walküre*. The new production of *Walküre* with cuts, and *Siegfried* and *Götterdämmerung* to come, meant that all Mahler's work on a complete *Ring* without cuts was being undone. Fortunately, however, Weingartner eventually bowed to the chorus of protest from all sides and performed *Siegfried* and *Götterdämmerung* without cuts, but the cuts in *Walküre* remained.

Weingartner was particularly ruthless in his treatment of Roller's scenery for *Siegfried,* which was so complicated that it needed a whole day to set up and another whole day to dismantle, a loss of two whole days of rehearsal time. What made Roller furiously angry was Weingartner's insistence on the stage's being less dark. Perhaps Weingartner had Possart's injunction in mind: 'My good Weingartner, remember that a night at the theatre should not be a night of utter darkness.' The wall of fire which Siegfried has to pass through in Act Three and which dies down behind him to reveal the Valkyries' rock was one of Wilhelm von Wymetal's most ingenious sets.

There were distinctly rowdy scenes at Weingartner's first *Walküre.* Once again he was deluged with anonymous letters, and the standing-area denizens followed the opera in pocket scores, setting up a chorus of catcalls and whistling whenever there were cuts. The applause that greeted Weingartner as he made his way to the rostrum at the beginning of each act was also liberally laced with booing. To make matters worse, the cuts violated the sense and continuity of the tetralogy. In Act Two, for instance, one of the most vital moments in the whole of the *Ring,* the passage where Wotan cries out in despair '. . . eines will ich noch, das Ende — das Ende!' was left out.

During his last years in office Mahler had incurred some disapproval for not bringing to administrative matters the same burning zeal as had characterised his first five years, his time of greatness. Details of leave and engagements were no longer subjected to the same searching scrutiny. It was Weingartner who reaped the consequences. Within four months of his taking over, the customary Wagner cycle fell due in May (in accordance with a hard and fast tradition). But Mahler had allowed so many Wagner singers to be on leave at the same time that it was only after desperate efforts and the most far-reaching concessions that Weingartner's first complete Wagner cycle ever found its way to the stage at all.

It was the custom in Vienna to put on three complete Wagner cycles a year. Mahler raised it to four, and in 1909 Weingartner too gave four complete performances of the *Ring.*

Among the singers whom Mahler bequeathed to Weingartner, there was plenty of room for replenishment and refurbishing; replenishment in the *bel canto* ensemble which Mahler had rather neglected, and refurbishing among the Wagner ensemble. The tenor Erik Schmedes was still at his peak, but the dramatic soprano Anna Mildenburg was well past her best by the time Weingartner took over. So were Marie Gutheil-Schoder and the superb Wotan and Sachs, Friedrich Weidemann. Mahler was alleged to have so overstrained their voices that their careers ended earlier than they need have done.

The lyrical stars were Leo Slezak, the celebrated coloratura soprano Selma Kurz, and the baritone Leopold Demuth, who was at his best in Italian opera (he died in Weingartner's third year). Wilhelm Hesch, the bass from the palmy days of the Jahn era, died in 1908, and almost the whole of his repertoire was taken over by the incomparable Richard Mayr of Salzburg.

With Slezak and Selma Kurz, Weingartner had a great deal of trouble over contracts. At the time he took over neither of them had any ties with Vienna, so they were in a position to state their own terms. Slezak refused point-blank to sign a new contract with the Vienna Opera; he wanted to be an Austrian Caruso with engagements all over the world. It was more or less the same with Kurz, but in the end Weingartner succeeded in securing her for Vienna, whereas Slezak never sang under Weingartner in Vienna except as a guest artist.

Weingartner had nothing but trouble with his singers from the very first. The name-part in *Elektra* for instance, which was to be given for the first time in Vienna in March 1909, and was to prove the most epoch-making event of Weingartner's entire term, was still going begging in December 1908, mainly because Weingartner was not convinced that Gutheil-Schoder was up to such an immensely difficult rôle. She actually acquitted herself wonderfully well as Elektra in later years, despite her vocal shortcomings.

On the very last day of 1908 a certain Lucille Marcel, an American who had studied with Jean de Reszke in Paris, presented herself for an audition. She came, sang, and conquered. The full extent of how she conquered is related by Weingartner in his peculiar Courths-Mahler style in his Memoirs.

'Deeply impressed, I made my way on to the stage by the bridge over the orchestra-pit and introduced myself. Was it those strange, deep eyes that had sung to me? I tried to blot out of my memory the hideous cacophonies of *Elektra*. I could feel those great shining eyes following me around. O, this duality of the sexes! The dim interior of the Opera House seemed suddenly brighter. Lucille said she could see an aureole round my head that she had never seen in any other conductor.' (A good many other ladies have said the same to a conductor or a Director after an audition.)

Weingartner goes on to relate how some time later, when the two of them were standing in front of the Beethoven statue, a bird alighted on the composer's bronze head 'and twittered away upon the spring air. I knew then that this was the singer I wanted.'

Lucille Marcel eventually became Weingartner's wife. She scored a spectacular success as Elektra: people said that she invested the hysterics of this difficult part with a kind of elegance. 'The voice of an exotic Siren' enthused the critics, 'an odalisque of *bel canto*.' Richard Strauss supervised the rehearsals in person but did not conduct. The conductor was Hugo Reichenberger, Weingartner's *Kapellmeister* who replaced the Schoenberg disciple Alexander von Zemlinsky, who had been engaged by Mahler.

Although *Elektra* was the outstanding event of Weingartner's term, it was nothing more or less than a windfall, as he never took any trouble over it and was not even interested in it. He was jealous of Strauss for using the same material as he had for an opera entitled *Orestes*. He said he just wanted to take one close look at this new opera of Strauss, this monstrosity about which there had been such an elaborate publicity campaign. Another thing that particularly annoyed him was the considerable sum he had to pay out in performing rights.

The scenery, one of Roller's most brilliant inspirations, is still vividly imprinted on my memory and made a lasting impression on more than one generation of Viennese operagoers. In the middle of the massive city-wall of Mycenae was the fateful gateway through which all the figures involved in the tragedy had to pass. I remember particularly clearly Clytaemnestra's superb entrance, craving for something to dispel her bad dreams as she consigned the slaves and victims to their sacrificial doom. *Elektra* is the stage realisation of one of the Strauss-Hofmannsthal partnership's greatest conceptions.

At the first-night the part of Clytaemnestra, tired of life and love, was sung by Anna Mildenburg, who was unanimously acclaimed. There are still stories of how the ashen sheen of her robe made her look the very personification of a bad dream. Shortly afterwards she married the author and playwright Hermann Bahr, and an ungallant jest went the rounds. 'Which is the oldest bar in Vienna? The Mildenburg.'

Richard Strauss's 'modern' music went down very well with the audience, but the critics castigated 'the sublime vulgarity of the melody', 'the appalling cacophony', 'the elemental din', 'the lamentable impotence of the musical invention' and 'the artistic nadir of our time'. Dr. Julius Korngold, the father of the composer E. W. Korngold and Hanslick's successor as music critic of the *Neue Freie Presse*, wrote that 'in Strauss's *Elektra* that very precious fluid known as blood is dispensed like drinking-water', and ended with the words: 'How beautiful was the Princess Salome!' Yet at the time Korngold had not found *Salome* so marvellous either.

Another critic voiced that '*Electra* was like the trumpeting, bellowing, neighing and squealing of a whole lot of elephants, cattle, horses and pigs — especially pigs — being rounded up with atrocious cruelty'.

About a year later, when Strauss conducted *Elektra* himself at the Vienna Opera, Weingartner caused a good deal of ill-feeling by being 'away'.

However, the affection that Weingartner conspicuously failed to feel for Richard Strauss was lavished on Johann. In 1910 he added *Der Zigeunerbaron* to the Opera's repertoire and conducted the première himself. And one

Der Rosenkavalier

'Ist wie ein Gruss vom Himmel . . .'

After *Elektra* Richard Strauss said he would 'like to write a Mozart opera'. The result was *Der Rosenkavalier*, the last opera in German to be a 'best-seller' all over the world. It is a delightful blend of tragedy and comedy. 'You know how I am — half gay and half grave.' The emotional appeal of many operas lies in a striking central situation: in *Lohengrin* it is the entry of the knight by swan, in *Der Rosenkavalier* the offering of a silver rose. This 'custom among the nobility' was an invention of Hofmannsthal. The town residence of the Counts Rofrano is the present-day Palais Auersperg. The scenery for the first performance in Dresden and for the first Vienna performance in 1911 was designed by Alfred Roller of Vienna, and it is his figurines in this photograph that have characterised *Rosenkavalier* performances everywhere. Among the famous names who have sung the part of Octavian in Vienna are Jeritza, Lehmann, Jarmila Novotna, Sena Jurinac, Wanda Achsel, Margit Schenker, Irmgard Seefried, Gwyneth Jones, Christa Ludwig, etc.

'Da muss ma weinen, weil's gar so schön is'

To start with, the libretto was castigated by the critics as an 'anti-musical comedy', but now it is beloved above all others. The scene is a baroque Vienna that there never was — but how lovely it would have been! The language the characters use is also largely a product of Hofmannsthal's imagination. The actors in the comedy are by now old friends: the titled nouveau-riche Herr von Faninal with his 'twelve houses in Wieden and a mansion on Am Hof,' Baron Ochs and his retinue ('straight from the turnip-fields into livery'), the three poor aristocratic orphans who importune the Marschallin in a minor key but modulate to the major to express their gratitude, and the landlord of the 'shady inn' where 'personages of distinction' carry on their furtive affairs.

'*Jetzt wird gefrühstückt. Jedes Ding hat seine Zeit*'

The whole of the Marschallin's part is one long farewell to youth; yet Strauss saw her as a woman of 32 who never feels too old for her 17-year-old lover except when she is in poor spirits. Whether or not Octavian will be her last lover, he certainly is not her first. And how much does 'the little Moor in yellow' know, the one who serves the chocolate in Act One, and in Act Three picks up the handkerchief and waves it to the audience? The Marschallin has a lot to sing, the little Moor nothing at all, though he seems to understand German all right, and he must have had plenty to think about. Among Vienna's greatest Marschallins have been Lotte Lehmann, Anni and Hilde Konetzni, Reining, Zadek, della Casa, Rysanek, Ludwig, Schwarzkopf.

'Ein Kavalier lässt alles, was ihm nicht konveniert, da draussen vor der Tür . . .'

Sometimes he forgets his wig too. The Marschallin learns something that Ochs will never learn, how to grow old; and that is the tragedy of both of them. Strauss once said to Richard Mayr, the greatest Ochs there has ever been: 'When I was working on Ochs I kept thinking of you'; to which Mayr replied: 'Am I to take that as an insult or a compliment?' Other popular singers of the part of Ochs in Vienna: Krenn, Weber, Czerwenka, Edelmann, Böhme, and Berry.

In 1888 Josef Hassreiter, first solo-dancer and later producer of the Opera Ballet, in collaboration with Franz Gaul, 'scenery-painter and stage technical supervisor of the Imperial Opera', produced one of the most successful ballets in theatrical history: *Die Puppenfee*. The music was by the 'Conductor of the Imperial Opera Ballet' Josef Bayer, who had already composed a number of other ballets including *Sonne und Erde* and *Wiener Walzer*. During Weingartner's term he also concocted a ballet entitled *Aschenbrödel* out of some posthumous works by Johann Strauss.

It became a Viennese tradition, both under the Monarchy and during the First Republic, that every Christmas the Opera should put on *Die Puppenfee* as well as *Hänsel und Gretel*, and parents used to be almost as delighted as their children when on the stroke of midnight the inhabitants of the toyshop came to life and started dancing.

It was a domestic occasion in the Vienna Opera House at which even the Wagnerites and the anti-Wagnerites agreed to bury their differences and enjoy the delightful 'Puppenfee' Waltz.

An extract from a contemporary account of the first performance of *Die Puppenfee* in 1888 describes how 'the front rows are occupied by gentlemen, mostly of distinction, on whom their hairdressers have conferred eternal youth. They know every one of the *drum-bunnies* in the first quadrille, and all the little dolls in the last one. They are quick to spot budding talent yet remain courteously faithful to the worthy veterans still serving in the ranks. The ballet Maecenas gazes at the stage with loving eyes that have seen generations of ballet-dancers come and go: only he survives while all around him changes, and he transfers his affections from the departing to the up-and-coming generation. Can there be any more delightful scene than this original *Puppenfee* in the splendid environment of our Imperial Opera House?'

Left: Josef Bayer (1852—1913), the godfather of *Die Puppenfee* on the musical side.
Below: 'Mama — Papa', sings the big doll (*Die Puppenfee* in 1956).

From a performance of *Die Puppenfee* in 1937 directed by Willy Fränzl.
The decoration of the toyshop. A woodcut by J. E. Scheurer.

Die Puppenfee

The traditions of baroque fairy-tale theatre, 'Kasperl' shows, marionette theatre and the great classical ballet combined — this is the *Puppenfee*.

From Willy Fränzl's 1956 *Puppenfee*.

day Frau Adele Strauss presented herself in his office: her diligence in the matter of her late husband's performing rights and royalties had earned her the title of 'The Importunate Widow'. She handed him a posthumous score of a ballet entitled *Aschenbrödel* (Cinderella). Weingartner instructed Josef Bayer, the composer of *Puppenfee*, to prepare it for performance, and it was a great success.

In fact, Weingartner always had a soft spot for 'lighter' music. On one occasion, after he had resigned from the Opera, he conducted music by Johann Strauss at a gala concert given by the 'Concordia' journalists' club in the Main Hall of the *Musikverein*. Lehár and Leo Fall conducted at the same concert.

Like Mahler, who was always interested in new operas, Weingartner was constantly on the lookout for contemporary works. In Mahler's day there was no chance that Debussy's *Pelléas et Mélisande*, Eugen d'Albert's *Tiefland* (the outstanding example of German *verismo*), and Puccini's *Tosca* might be performed at the Vienna Opera. In fact, *Tosca* was one of Mahler's pet aversions. But in 1908 Weingartner performed *Tiefland*, which had started on its successful career in Berlin, and in 1910 *Tosca*. *Tiefland*, with Erik Schmedes as Pedro and Marie Gutheil-Schoder as Martha, caught on at once and was enthusiastically received, but *Tosca*, which had previously been put on at the Vienna Volksoper, was not at first a success at the Imperial Opera. People found it far too brutal, and Weingartner was bitterly reproached for putting it on at all. 'Instruments of torture wrapped in scented cotton — steel spikes with harmless horn buttons — an insult to the intelligence for which a diseased mind is no excuse' (Robert Hirschfeld in the *Wiener Zeitung*); 'protestations in unison of ecstatic love with sobbing appogiature — intolerable harmonic violations — a horror-comic for backwoodsmen — a dramatised penny dreadful'; ' "it is revolting" says the idiotic sacristan in Act One in a moment of sanity' — these were some of the Press comments. Max Kalbeck wrote, 'One laughs so as not to weep, and it is only one's healthy merriment that prevents one's stomach from turning over'.

With her great big childlike eyes, her dimples, her smile and her artless gestures Lucille Marcel was enthusiastically applauded after her prayer in Act Two, but otherwise the reception was distinctly cool. For this the cast was partly to blame. Leo Slezak had always given Weingartner a lot of trouble; so Erik Schmedes, a Wagner tenor, had to take over the part of Cavaradossi, which did not suit him at all, apart from the 'Vittoria' in Act Two, which he brought off to perfection. And Leopold Demuth was much too kind-hearted for the diabolical Scarpia. In short, Act One was a moderate success, in Act Two there was applause after the prayer but some booing at the end, and Act Three was received with perfunctory applause which was also meant for Weingartner's conducting. Yet a few years later *Tosca* was setting the Danube on fire, especially when Maria Jeritza was giving her incomparable and unforgettable performance in the title rôle.

The commemorations Weingartner was obliged to celebrate always annoyed him intensely. 1909 was the centenary of Haydn's death, so very much against Weingartner's wishes a minor opera of Haydn's, *L'isola disabitata* (sung in German), was dutifully trotted out. That was not so bad. What gave Weingartner much more trouble was the sixtieth anniversary of the Emperor's accession in December 1908. The gala performance was to open with 'an Austrian ballet' designed by the ballet-master Hassreiter with music by Josef Bayer, the composer of *Puppenfee*. Then there was to be a pageant entitled *The Emperor's Dream* written by Countess Christiane Thun-Salm with music by Anton Rückauf. It was a terribly difficult piece to prepare, required almost the entire staff of the Burgtheater, presented almost insoluble rehearsal problems, and completely disorganised the repertoire.

Then someone had a brilliant idea: while the Burgtheater company was rehearsing *The Emperor's Dream* in the Opera, why shouldn't the Opera do *The Barber of Seville* at the Burgtheater? In the event the opera scored such a success at the Burgtheater that Weingartner approached Prince Montenuovo about rescinding the respective 'terms of reference' of the Burgtheater and the Opera which had been agreed upon in 1810. After all, a century or so previously straight plays had been performed at the Kärntnertor Theatre, and a little later the Burgtheater had been used for opera as well. So why not from now on put on comic operas in the Burgtheater and invite the Burgtheater to use the Opera House for plays with big casts such as *Wilhelm Tell* or *Julius Caesar*? Montenuovo turned the idea down.

Like his predecessor Jahn, Weingartner had a predilection for comic opera and took every opportunity of pandering to it. He put on old French operas such as *Joseph et ses frères*, *Le postillon de Longjumeau*, *Fra Diavolo*, *Djamileh*, *Le domino noir* as well as Flotow's *Stradella* and Lortzing's brilliant triad *Der Waffenschmied*, *Der Wildschütz* and *Zar und Zimmermann;* not to mention *The Bartered Bride* and Peter Cornelius's *Barbier von Bagdad* with its delightful final chorus 'Salaam aleicum' and with Richard Mayr in the title rôle. He also introduced two operas by Goldmark, *Wintermärchen* (after Shakespeare's *A Winter's Tale)* and in celebration of Goldmark's eightieth birthday in 1910 *Götz von Berlichingen*. The latter was one of the last premières of the Weingartner era.

In 1909 there were three performances by the Imperial Russian Ballet from the Marinsky Theatre in Saint Petersburg, including Anna Pavlova in *Swan Lake*.

But all this activity was permanently clouded by the undeniable fact that Weingartner had no success where he needed it most, in obtaining new singers. His one real success was the engagement of Lucille Marcel, and her one real success was in *Elektra*, though she also gave quite a good account of herself as Eva and Marguerite.

In order to put a stop to the flood of gossip about the romance between her and the Director of the Imperial Opera, Weingartner prevailed upon her to put an early end to her association with the Opera, which only lasted one year. She then married him and died prematurely in 1912.

Hedwig Francillo-Kaufmann, Viennese born and bred, returned to her native city from the Komische Oper and the Hofoper in Berlin. She enjoyed a fair measure of success in coloratura parts for a number of years; later she moved on to Rio de Janeiro, where she died.

Josef Schwarz, a fine lyric baritone from Riga, moved from Graz to the Vienna Volksoper and from there, on the strength of a previous contract agreed to by Mahler, to the Imperial Opera. Unfortunately his stage presence was unimpressive.

The brightest stars of the Italian *stagione* were Alessandro Bonci and Mattia Battistini. There was also *Rigoletto* with Battistini and a certain Alfredo Piccaver, a tenor from England, though it was not until the days of Weingartner's successor Gregor that Piccaver blossomed out into one of the most popular favourites the Vienna Opera has ever known.

To succeed Leo Slezak in Wagner parts (Lohengrin, Tannhäuser, Stolzing) Weingartner engaged an American tenor named William Miller, who enjoyed considerable success for a few years.

Weingartner's lack of success in his search for new singers was to some extent compensated for by his efforts on behalf of two Austrian composers, Julius Bittner and E. W. Korngold.

Bittner was a judge by profession. He was one of the most lovable characters in the history of Austrian Opera, with a great sense of humour and a real flair for the theatre. He was also gifted with a fund of melody of the colourful, popular kind. He presented himself to Mahler with a somewhat exuberant early work in North-German neo-Wagner style, and Mahler spotted straight away that Bittner's real talent lay in a totally different field. He accordingly advised Bittner to have a word with the Opera's First *Kapellmeister*, Bruno Walter. It was under Walter's influence that Bittner wrote *Die rote Gred*, which was first performed in Vienna in 1908 with Bruno Walter conducting (its actual first performance was in Germany). It is a medieval tale of a seductive female with flaming red hair, a mixture of Carmen and Salome, superbly played in Vienna by Marie Gutheil-Schoder. It was a great success for Bittner, and he followed it up in 1910 with a work which became even more popular, *Der Musikant*, in which Erik Schmedes played the part of a strolling minstrel and Richard Mayr that of a bassoon-player named Oberstierberger who gets himself entangled with two women, one of whom, a violinist named Frie-

K. K. Hof- Operntheater.

Im Jahres-Abonnement 1. Viertel — **Donnerstag den 3. Dezember 1908** — Bei aufgehobenem Saison-Abonnement

Des Kaisers Traum

Festspiel in einem Aufzuge von Christiane Gräfin Thun-Salm.

Musik von Anton Rückauf.

Kaiser Rudolf von Habsburg	Hr. Sonnenthal
Herzog Albrecht } seine Söhne	Hr. Reimers
Herzog Rudolf }	Hr. Zeska
Hugo von Tausers, Vorsitzender im Rat	Hr. Baumeister
Der Hofmarschall	Hr. Loewe
Ein Baumeister	Hr. Hartmann
Ein Wiener Bürger	Hr. Thimig
Eine Bürgersfrau	Fr. Witt
Ein Bürgermädchen	Fr. Albach-Retty

Edelleute der österreichischen Länder; mehrere Baumeister; Bürger, Frauen, Mädchen und Kinder; Gefolge, Pagen, Knappen, Volk, Musikanten.

Die Zukunft	Fr. Römpler-Bleibtreu
Die Liebe	Hr. Hohenfels
Die Treue	Fr. Medelsky

Traumbilder:

I. Die Doppelhochzeit in der Stephanskirche 1515. Unter Mitwirkung der Fr. Tressler, Fr. Wittels, Frl. Schulz, Frl. Wilke, Fr. Liesenberg, Fr. Danegger, des Hrn. Bittikau und Hrn. Zenbach.

II. Die Begegnung Kaiser Leopold I. und König Sobieski nach dem Entsatz von Wien 1683. Unter Mitwirkung des Hrn. Gehri und Hrn. Guttenberger.

III. Kaiser Karl VI. proklamiert in Gegenwart der achtjährigen Erzherzogin Maria Theresia die pragmatische Sanktion 1725. Unter Mitwirkung der Fr. Devrient-Reinhold, der Herren Moser und Heller und der kl. Eisner.

IV. Kaiserin Maria Theresia und Kaiser Franz I. mit ihren Kindern lauschen dem Spiel des kleinen Mozart 1763. Während dieses Bildes wird ein Menuett gespielt, das Mozart in seinem fünften Lebensjahre komponiert hat. Unter Mitwirkung der Frau Lewinsky, der Frls. Mell, Müller, Rub und Schopf, der Herren Sommer, Gregori, Walter, Danegger, der kl. Erzhofer und der kl. Liebel.

V. Der Wiener Kongreß 1814. (Nach Isabey) Unter Mitwirkung der Herren Devrient, Römpler, Gimnig, Kainz, Tressler, Frank, Paulsen, Brechter, Elmhorst, Rub, Baumgartner, Basch, Strebinger, Muratori, Geraich, Sendelmann und Wiesner.

Pause.

Freitag den 4. Carmen. „Don José" Hr. Hermann Jadlowker vom großh. Hoftheater in Karlsruhe als Gast. (Anfang 7 Uhr).

Samstag den 5. Des Kaisers Traum. Hierauf: Aus der Heimat. (Anfang halb 8 Uhr). Bei aufgehobenem Saison-Abonnement.

Sonntag den 6. Des Kaisers Traum. Hierauf: Aus der Heimat. (Anfang halb 8 Uhr) Bei aufgehobenem Saison-Abonnement.

Zum Dienstgebrauche.

Aus der Heimat

Nationales Tanzspiel mit Gesang in fünf Bildern.

Choreographie von Josef Haßreiter. — Musik von Josef Bayer.

1. Bild: Kirchweihfest in den Alpen.

Tänze:

Ländler. Frl. Fleischinger, Hr. Godlewski und das Ballettkorps.
Oberösterreichisches Lied. Fr. Pohlner.
Schuhplattler mit Gesang. Hr. Maikl, Frls. Berger C., Kohler, Berger L., Pentel, Windbeck, die Herren Bauer, Buttula, Kammel, Reuber.
Koschat-Quintett. Fr. Elizza, Frl. Paalen, die Herren Koschat, Trazler, Tournes, Fochler, Haan.
Meranertanz. Frls. Wopalenski, Spuller, die Herren Rathner F., Dubois und das Ballettkorps.

2. Bild: Südslavische Hochzeit.

Tänze:

Kroatien-Slavonien. Frls. Wasserbauer, Katlein, die Herren Cjadill und Scotti.
Dalmatien. Frls. Kohler, Berger L., Pentel, Windbeck, die Herren Bauer, Buttula, Reuber und Kammel.
Herzegowina. Frl. v. Strohlendorf und Hr. Raimund.
Slavisches Lied. Fr. Weidt.
Bosnien. Frls. Wasserbauer, Katlein, Kohler, Berger L., Pentel, Windbeck, v. Strohlendorf, die Herren Cjadill, Scotti, Bauer, Buttula, Reuber, Kammel, Raimund und das Ballettkorps.

Walzer (1836—1908).

3. Bild: Erntefest in Böhmen.

Lied. Fr. Förster-Lauterer.

Tänze:

Mähren und Schlesien. Frls. Preinersdorfer, Arnoldt, Reingruber, v. Strohlendorf II., die Herren Mytteis Winter R., Kopetly und Meier.
Böhmen. Frls. Wopalenski, Peterka, Berger L., die Herren Godlewski, Rathner F. und Dubois.
Hanna. Frls. Pentel, Fleischinger und Herr Scotti.
Slowaken. Frl. Spuller und Hr. Raimund.
Bukowina. Frl. Gerri und Hr. Raimund.
Polen. Frls. Berger O., Kohler, Berger E., Biringer, Luftig, Pohl, Nowak und Jusl.

4. Bild: In der Csárda.

Ungarische Tänze. Frls. Windbeck, Wasserbauer, Katlein, Kaar, Pohl, Popper, die Herren Cjadill, Rathner F., Dubois, Buttula, Bauer, Reuber, Kammel und das Ballettkorps.

Nationale Märsche.

5. Bild: Allegorisches Tableau.

Das Gesamtpersonale der k. k. Hofoper.

Der freie Eintritt ist heute ohne Ausnahme aufgehoben.

Der Beginn der Vorstellung sowie jedes Aktes wird durch ein Glockenzeichen bekanntgegeben

Abendkassen-Eröffnung vor 7 Uhr. Anfang halb 8 Uhr. Ende um 10 Uhr.

Weingartner was very distressed about the great gala evening which he had to rehearse in honour of the Emperor Franz Joseph I's Diamond Jubilee in 1908. The cast of the festival play by Countess Christiane Thun-Salm included practically every member of the Burgtheater ensemble, and Adolf Sonnenthal appeared as Rudolf von Habsburg. The two

'Puppenfee' authors Hassreiter and Bayer created 'Aus der Heimat', a 'national festival of dance' in which Georg Maikl could be heard dancing the schuhplattler, and Elise Elizza and Bella Paalen sang in a quintet with Thomas Koschat. (The Carinthian song composer — 'Verlassen bin i' — was a member of the Vienna Opera chorus. Second bass!)

derike, provided an enchanting rôle for Gutheil-Schoder. Bruno Walter was again the conductor.

The name of Korngold, a composer who later became world-famous, is associated with one of the most unusual incidents not only in the history of Weingartner's term, but in the whole history of the Vienna Opera. On the fourth of October 1910 the thirteen-year-old Erich Wolfgang Korngold, son of the above-mentioned and all-powerful music critic of the *Neue Freie Presse*, Dr. Julius

Korngold, came on to the stage of the Vienna Opera to acknowledge the enthusiastic applause for the first performance of his ballet *Der Schneemann*.

The events leading to this incident make a remarkable story from every point of view. Young Erich Wolfgang started composing at the age of six or seven, and when his father took the boy to see Mahler, for whom Korngold *père* had the highest regard, Mahler made no secret of his high opinion of the young composer's talent. A

It was with mixed feelings that Weingartner experienced the triumph of the hated Richard Strauss and of his beloved Lucille Marcel at the première of 'Elektra'.

year later Universal Edition distributed some compositions by Erich Wolfgang, including a piano score of *Der Schneemann,* to some of the leading musicians of the day, requesting their opinion. No details were given of the composer except that he was a boy of eleven. All the opinions were more than favourable.

In the following year the wife of the Austrian Prime Minister Bienerth gave a party at which young Korngold played some of his own piano works and some dancers

from the Opera danced to them. It all went very well and was brought to the ears of Felix von Weingartner, whereupon the Director of Universal Edition, Alfred Hertzka, offered the première of the ballet *Der Schneemann* to the Opera. Weingartner accepted it, although father Korngold is known to have been against the idea as he was afraid it was a bit premature. But Weingartner adhered to his decision.

It was now of course that tongues began to wag, and the scoring of the work was alleged to be by *Kapellmeister* Alexander von Zemlinsky. There was even a malicious rumour that Zemlinsky had composed the whole thing. Everyone was asking why on earth Weingartner had accepted it. The answer was simple and plausible enough: if it was a fiasco it would be one in the eye for Weingartner's arch-enemy Dr. Korngold, who had sworn to obliterate Mahler's successor. If on the other hand it went down well, it would be a great feather in Weingartner's cap and old Dr. Korngold would have to come crawling in gratitude.

In the event *Der Schneemann,* contrary to everyone's expectations, was a really tremendous success. There was enthusiastic applause after the A major Serenade, and the leader of the orchestra (Arnold Rosé) performed his solos superbly. At the end, a boy of thirteen took his bow in front of the huge curtain, shambling like a bear, and looking (so the story goes) as if he were more interested in the snowman on the stage than in the sensational success of his two-year-old composition; behaving just like a child, in fact. He said himself that the best thing about the whole evening was the lovely white snowman, which is pummelled to pieces at the end.

The prodigy eventually developed into one of the leading operatic composers of the first half of the present century (*Die tote Stadt, Das Wunder der Heliane*).

Papa Korngold, the dreaded critic, bullied and suppressed his son just as unmercifully as he bullied the rest of the world when it was a matter of furthering his gifted son's career. A week or two after the success of *Der Schneemann* there was a performance of a piano trio by young Erich Wolfgang, with Bruno Walter at the piano. During a rehearsal the boy was sitting between

K. K. Hof= Operntheater.

Dienstag den 4. Oktober 1910

Im Jahres-Abonnement | 4 Viertel | 122. Vorstellung im Saison-Abonnement

Zum erstenmale:

Susannens Geheimnis

Intermezzo in einem Akt nach dem Französischen von Enrico Golisciana, deutsch von Max Kalbeck
Regie: Hr. v. Wymetal — Musik von Ermanno Wolf-Ferrari — Dirigent: Hr. Schalk

Graf Gil .... Hr. Rittmann | Sante, Diener .... Hr. Goblewski
Gräfin Susanne, seine Gemahlin Fr. Gutheil-Schoder | Ort der Handlung: Piemont — Zeit: Gegenwart

Das Textbuch ist an der Kassa für 80 Heller erhältlich

Hierauf zum erstenmale:

Der Schneemann

Pantomime in zwei Bildern von Erich Wolfgang Korngold. Choreographie und Inszenierung von Karl Godlewski
Regie: Hr. Hassreiter — Instrumentierung von A. v. Zemlinsky — Dirigent: Hr. Schalk

Pierrot .... Hr. Godlewski | | Frl. Spuller
Pantalon .... Hr. van Hamme | | Frl. Fleischinger
Colombine .... Frl. Wopalensky | | Frl. Windbek
Diener } bei Pantalon .... Hr. Bauer | Colombinens Freundinnen | Frl. Katlein
Dienerin } .... Hr. Haumayer | | Frl. Wasserbauer
Ein Schornsteinfeger .... Hr. Gadill | | Frl. Zulta
Ein Bauer .... Hr. Fränzl J. | | Frl. Pohl
Eine Bäuerin .... Hr. Schimanel

Käufer, Verkäufer, Wachleute, Gassenjungen, Bauernburschen

Vorkommende Tänze:

1. Akt. 1. Walzer. Die Damen Wopalensky, Spuller, Fleischinger, Windbek, Katlein, Kaar, Wasserbauer, Zulta und Pohl.
2. Schneemann-Walzer. Die Kleinimen.
2. Akt. 1. Valse lente. Frl. Wopalensky und Hr. van Hamme.
2. Tanz der Schneemänner. Die Herren vom Balletkorps.

Zum Schluß:

Mondweibchen

Ballett-Féerie in zwei Abteilungen (fünf Bildern) von H. Regel. Musik von Richard Goldberger. Choreographie
von J. Hassreiter.
Regie: Hr. Hassreiter — Dirigent: Hr. Lehnert

Die Tochter der Wellen .... Frl. v. Stroblendorf | Ein Glaser .... Hr. Gadill
Der Mann im Mond .... Frl. Kohler | Schiffer .... Hr. Bauer
Ein Wasserbold .... Hr. Godlewski | | Hr. Batula
Ein Wanderbursch .... Hr. Dubois | Erstes } .... Frl. Wopalensky
Fee Morgana .... Frl. Cerri | Zweites } Mädchen .... Frl. Fleischinger
Ein Mondstrahl .... Frl. Wopalensky | Drittes } .... Frl. Kaar
Ein Bagant .... Hr. Rathner | Eine Kellnerin .... Frl. Jamrich
Ein Dauffeerei .... Hr. van Hamme | Schiffermädchen und Burschen, Mondstrahlen, Wellen-
Erste } .... Frl. Berger L. | töchter, Perlen, Libellen, Morganas Garden
Zweite } Bretonin .... Frl. Wasserbauer | An der bretonischen Küste

Tänze:

Erste Abteilung:

Libellen-Polka: Frl. v. Stroblendorf und die Kleininen. | Zigeunerweise: Frls. v. Stroblendorf, Wopalensky,
Sehnsuchts-Walzer: Frls. v. Stroblendorf, Kohler | Windbek, Fleischinger, Jamrich, u. d. Herren God-
und Herr Godlewski. | lewski, Dubois, van Hamme, Rathner, Gadill.
Mondzauber: Frls. v. Stroblendorf, Kohler, Wopalensky, | Wellenwalzer: Frls. v. Stroblendorf, Kaar, Biringer,
Peterla, Spuller, Fleischinger, Windbek, Kaar, | Pohl, Berger C., die Herren Godlewski, van Hamme,
Zulta, Katlein, Pohl, Biringer, Popper, Lustig | Rathner, Gadill und die Damen vom Ballett.
u. d. Damen v. Ballett. | Marsch der Garde: Die Kleininen.
| Morgana-Gavotte: Frls. Cerri und Hr. v. Stroblendorf.
Zweite Abteilung: | Perlenwalzer: Frls. Cerri, v. Stroblendorf, Wopalensky,
Schiffertanz: Frls. Berger L., Wasserbauer, Herren Bauer, | Peterla, Spuller, Fleischinger, Windbek, Wasser-
Batula und die Damen und Herren vom Ballett. | bauer, Zulta, Kaar, Katlein, Berger C., Popper
| Pohl, Lustig und die Damen vom Ballett.

Der freie Eintritt ist ohne Ausnahme aufgehoben.

Der Beginn der Vorstellung sowie jedes Aktes wird durch ein Glockenzeichen bekanntgegeben.

Abendkassen-Eröffnung vor halb 7 Uhr. Anfang 7 Uhr. Ende 10 Uhr.

Der Kartenverkauf findet heute statt für obige Vorstellung und für:

Mittwoch den 5. Violetta (La Traviata). (Anfang halb 8 Uhr.)
Donnerstag den 6. Czaar und Zimmermann. (Anfang halb 8 Uhr.)

Weiterer Spielplan:

Freitag den 7. Der fliegende Holländer. (Anfang halb 8 Uhr.)
Samstag den 8. Die Jüdin. (Anfang 7 Uhr.)
Sonntag den 9. Tannhäuser. (Anfang 7 Uhr.)

On this evening Vienna became the richer by two local characters: the elder and the younger Korngold. It was the first time that a thirteen-year-old composer had acknowledged the applause of the audience in the Opera.

his parents (his mother was nicknamed 'the Salzgrisette' because her family lived in a street in Vienna called Salzgries). The moment Bruno Walter started the first movement old Korngold muttered, 'too fast'. 'Too slow' riposted the 'Salzgrisette'. 'I say it's too fast,' repeated father Korngold. 'And I say it's too slow,' insisted his wife. The boy, who after all was the composer, interrupted to say that in his opinion Walter's tempo was quite all right. He was promptly squashed by both his parents who shouted in unison: 'You shut up!'

Weingartner lost interest in running the Opera House at a very early stage. The Press kept up its remorseless campaign, and even Mahler's opponents were soon agreeing that Weingartner's term of office was the best justification of Mahler's.

Even after his son's success Dr. Korngold remained Weingartner's most implacable opponent: it was not in jest that in 1907, according to Johann Strauss's brother-in-law, when Mahler resigned, Dr. Korngold observed at the top of his voice outside the Café Museum: 'Whoever succeeds him had better look out!' To make matters worse, Richard Batka, the music critic of the semi-official *Fremdenblatt* which was very popular in Court circles, took sides against Weingartner and turned the Court against him as well.

On the first of March 1911, after exactly three years and two months in office, Weingartner tendered his resignation. His last première the evening before he left Vienna for a holiday at Semmering was one of the most interesting of his entire term, Berlioz's *Benvenuto Cellini* with William Miller and the new baritone Rudolf Hofbauer.

Although always on the defensive, Weingartner was fundamentally a kind-hearted character, an aristocrat and a man of the world. But he was not an easy person to get on with, and made as many enemies in Vienna as he had in Berlin, where he had always been at daggers drawn with the *Generalintendant* von Hülsen and had stirred up trouble on all sides. He would have had fewer enemies if he had not been so riddled with complexes, especially his aversion to Mahler as a Director (he stoutly denied having inherited from Mahler a splendid ensemble of singers and a comprehensive repertoire), and his aversion to Richard Strauss as a composer.

When he first came to Vienna, so much was expected of a Director of the Vienna Opera that the Press complained that Weingartner had not the proper qualifications for the post, that 'he only conducted instead of being a producer as well, like Herbeck, Jahn and Mahler'. (How little is expected of a Director nowadays in comparison!) After his resignation doubts were voiced from the opposite side: whether it was a good thing to have a Director who was a practising musician, whether it would not be better, at the Opera as in politics, to keep the executive and the administrative sides apart, etc.

Weingartner had an almost pathological addiction to sentimentality and *Kitsch*. 'I myself am a child of light', he once wrote of himself. In order not to be tarred with the same brush as Mahler and his friends he anticipated phraseology that became notorious a quarter of a century later, such as, 'I've got Aryan written all over me', and in contempt of his critics, 'These grovelling worms! My domain is the pure upper air'. He referred to the intrigues against him as if they were poisoned drinks concocted in a Borgia kitchen. He also had recourse to all sorts of occult books about how to ward off the attacks of his enemies by magic arts.

He was particularly irritated by the *Generalintendant's* Office, 'that hotbed of intrigue' as he called it. He used to maintain that opera-singers were spoken of there as 'those layabouts'. On one occasion he was trying to secure a higher fee for one of his singers, but the official concerned was adamant. So Weingartner asked him why. 'My good Weingartner', replied the official, 'I'm not listened to by my superiors, and I'm not listened to by my inferiors, so if I want to amount to anything I've got to be close-fisted sometimes.' By 'my inferiors' he meant of course Weingartner.

This typically Austrian encounter recalls another scarcely less typical incident from the early days of his term. The new Director wanted a certain phrase in his terms of reference altered, so he approached Baron Wetschl, a senior Civil Servant in the *Generalintendant's* Office. The latter merely shook his head and said: 'My dear fellow, don't you know Vienna? Surely you know there's not a word of truth in the whole document anyway?'

During the whole of his term Weingartner also suffered from indifferent health. He had a bicycle accident one summer holiday at Tegernsee, and the after-effects kept him in bed for weeks. And the following autumn a piece of scenery in the Opera House fell on him and broke his leg. Julius Korngold's comment, in rather bad taste, was that even the scenery in the Opera House was lining up against Mahler's enemy Felix Weingartner. The accident left Weingartner with his left leg shorter than his right, and from then on he had to conduct from a specially constructed chair.

His conducting was unostentatious and precise, and his elegant gestures were a household word, like those of Hans Knappertsbusch a generation later. One of his most characteristic attitudes was a fully extended left arm with the fifth finger up against the fourth and the third up against the second, leaving a big gap between the two pairs. Weingartner was the first conductor who was said to practise his gestures in front of a mirror.

As a composer — of operas, incidental music to *Faust* Part Two and symphonies — Weingartner is virtually forgotten nowadays. His Third Symphony, *Le sermon d'amour*, is in E major, the letter E being a combination of F for Felix and L for Lucille (Marcel). The Finale consists of variations on a theme from *Die Fledermaus*. Now and again his effective setting of Lenau's poem *Frühlingsfeier* crops up at Lieder recitals, and his orchestration of Weber's *Invitation to the Dance* is frequently performed. A female critic summed him up in the *Neues Wiener Journal* as 'golden mediocrity'. But as a conductor of Beethoven he is far from forgotten: his reputation was world-wide and is supported by gramophone records that are still in circulation. He conducted the Vienna Philharmonic concerts from 1908 until 1927, and even returned for a second term as Director of the Vienna Opera.

For all his shortcomings, Weingartner took his duties at the Opera very seriously and left at least one indelible mark on orchestral procedure: he was the first to conduct from the position we know today, before the railing which separates the pit from the audience. There he could see and be seen.

Another innovation during Weingartner's term was the appearance of the conductor's name on the posters. Weingartner liked seeing his name in print, so he could hardly object to the names of Bruno Walter and Franz Schalk appearing too.

His Majesty's new Court Chamberlain was Prince Alfred Montenuovo (1909—1917); his name was an Italianised form of the German name Neipperg. He administered the Imperial palaces, the museums, the Court gardens and the Court Theatre — but nothing gave him as many worries as the Opera.

Once again there had to be a hunt for someone to sit at the Director's desk, and the Court Chamberlain reviewed the experiences of the last decades. In the person of Gustav Mahler an unruly genius had been conjured up who had supplied some notable triumphs, but on the whole the Court Chamberlain had had nothing but trouble with him. After Mahler, Liechtenstein had appointed an unruly non-genius, Felix von Weingartner, who also left in his wake a strong tide of discontent. It was therefore quite understandable that this time the Court Chamberlain resolved to strike out in an entirely new direction. Mahler was Jewish; Weingartner Catholic; now came the Protestant.

The circumstances under which contact was first established with the new Director were certainly unorthodox: his name was put forward by an agency. Agencies of the present-day kind were already an established feature of European musical life; they were ambitious, they were enterprising, and they had a finger in nearly every pie. Apart from collecting their percentages (as agents have always done) they had a say in the wording of contracts, encouraged the 'star' system, and acquired clients just in time for contract renewal.

It was one of these agencies that recommended a certain Hans Gregor, of whom little was known in Vienna. He was a native of Dresden, born 1866, had been an actor at the Deutsches Theater in Berlin, and theatre-manager in various German towns, including Barmen-Elberfeld, where he was said to have built up an extremely interesting operatic repertoire. In Berlin he had founded and managed the Komische Oper, where he had shown plenty of discernment in his choice of opers. The house on the corner of the Friedrichstrasse and the Weidendamm had 1,250 seats, far too little space for the orchestra, small offices, but was cleverly run by Gregor with a very small administrative staff with a view to

make money. He had scored at least one world-wide 'scoop' with Eugen d'Albert's *Tiefland* and had been the first to stage *Tales of Hoffmann* in the form in which it fills so many houses today (it had been first performed in Paris in a woefully inadequate version, Offenbach having left only a few scraps and jottings for certain scenes at his death). There were no less than 600 performances before full houses within five years! The agency's cry, 'Grab him quick!' was listened to with attention by the authorities.

He was preceded by a barrage of propaganda that hailed him as 'the Max Reinhardt of Opera', on the strength of one or two productions of his in Germany that had attracted some attention. A man of his type was something quite new to Vienna, and Prince Montenuovo was under no illusions as to the chance he was taking. When receiving the new Director in audience, Montenuovo assured Gregor that 'I have my reasons for wishing to break with the present system, and instead of a celebrated conductor I have now come round to the idea of appointing a man with practical experience of the theatre'. In other words, the appointment was a deliberate experiment.

Gregor's term of office lasted seven years (a long time in those days) and exhibited all the advantages and disadvantages of having a 'manager' at the helm. It is particularly interesting in that it saw the beginning of many phenomena that are now part of the operatic world.

The authorities were well aware that it was not going to be easy to foist on to the good people of Vienna an Opera Director of the 'manager' type in succession to Jahn, Mahler and Weingartner. Accordingly, official announcements concentrated on playing up his artistic qualifications, and he was introduced for the time being as a producer. In fact, the Court had deliberately chosen a business-man. Once Gregor is said to have stopped in front of the entrance of the Hoftheater in Dresden, stretching out his arm, hat in hand, saying: 'With all their throwing money out of the window, perhaps I may catch some.' Apart from that, he shared the opinion of Heinrich Laube, Director of the Burgtheater, that a theatre director needs power equal to that of a gang leader.

Gregor promised to 'buy cheap' — singers, conductors, wood for the decorations. Those firms who heretofore had supplied the Opera, found themselves suddenly cut off from their prestigious client: Gregor made a principle of having almost everything produced in the Opera's own workshops. Nobody would have thought it possible that an opera could be produced as cheaply as Gregor's runaway hit, *Le jongleur de Notre Dame* by Massenet.

Very soon Gregor managed to create a stir. He was a bull-necked North German type with a barrack-square voice and manner — tall, fat, bald and bespectacled. He had a robust, arrogant Prussian sense of humour which did not always go down very well, though in his own way he was 'a jolly good fellow'. During his very first days in office he sent for the two musical directors, (*i. e.*, the two 'first conductors'), Bruno Walter and Franz Schalk, and gave them a lecture on modern methods of producing opera, which (he said) was far more than just a matter of good singing (as if Mahler had not been harping on the same point all along). It was his intention, Gregor announced, to introduce Vienna to the very latest up-to-date methods. 'For instance,' he went on, 'a really modern producer will want more than just three Rhine Maidens in *Rheingold*.' To which Bruno Walter replied: 'But you can't turn the whole stage into an aquarium.' 'Why not?' retorted Gregor. 'Well, for one thing,' explained Walter patiently, 'Wagner only wrote for three Rhine Maidens.' But Gregor was unabashed. 'I'm going to change all that,' he challenged. 'I'll have three singing and the fourth swimming.'

This was only the first of several harangues he delivered in the course of his first few weeks. Bruno Walter used to relate for instance how Gregor once said to him: 'You know, Wagner didn't know so much about the theatre as many people think he did. *The Flying Dutchman* is a very poor piece — two ships on the stage at the same time! Absurd. If Wagner had only let me have a look at it, I'd have told him to go home and change it.' When Bruno Walter ventured to point out that the composer's wishes must always come first, Gregor rejoined: 'My good Walter, you've far too great a respect for the composer. As far as I'm concerned the composer has no further say in the matter once he has handed in his score at the porter's lodge.'

The one thing a manager really needs in business matters is luck, and Gregor certainly had plenty. His very first première, on the eighth of April 1911, was *Der Rosenkavalier*, which meant that Strauss's wonderful Op. 59 was first heard at the Vienna Opera within five weeks of Weingartner's departure. Actually Weingartner had accepted it, though half-heartedly of course, before leaving. He had even tried to secure the first performance for Vienna, and Richard Strauss was all in favour too; but as all his other works had been first performed in Dresden, it was in Dresden too that *Der Rosenkavalier* was born. Strauss of course knew as well as anyone else that Richard Mayr would be the perfect Ochs. Attempts were accordingly made to secure Mayr for the Dresden performance, but to no purpose, and Strauss had to wait another three months before hearing the incomparable Mayr in the part.

By and large it was in its original Dresden form that *Der Rosenkavalier* reached Vienna. But the Dresden producer was not exactly a genius and Strauss, who was a personal friend of Max Reinhardt's, managed to persuade him to take over the production, but anonymously, so as not to offend the Dresden producer. So it was really Reinhardt who launched *Der Rosenkavalier* in its present version. Hofmannsthal and Strauss returned the favour to Max Reinhardt by creating *Ariadne auf Naxos* for him; it was first performed in Stuttgart in 1912, produced by Reinhardt.

At the Vienna rehearsals for *Der Rosenkavalier* nobody had any idea how much the work was to become a part of Viennese life. Gregor's barrack-square manner did not exactly help the rehearsals along; yet all went well except for one unfortunate incident. In those days there was no audience at dress-rehearsals, and very few people were allowed in unless they had something to do with the Opera. Selma Kurz, the Sophie, asked Gregor if she could invite her sister to the dress-rehearsal; Gregor turned her request down very abruptly, and Kurz promptly walked out. Her part was taken by Gertrude Förstel, who scored a great success.

This opera had already been accepted by Felix von Weingartner. It just fell into Gregor's lap — a 'Morgengabe', to speak with Ochs.

K. K. Hof- Operntheater

Samstag den 8. April 1911

n Jahres-Abonnement 4. Viertel   Bei aufgehobenem Saison-Abonnement

Zum erstenmale:

Der Rosenkavalier

Komödie für Musik in drei Aufzügen von Hugo von Hofmannsthal

Regie: Hr. v. Wymetal   **Musik von Richard Strauß**   Dirigent: Hr. Schalk

Der freie Eintritt ist ohne Ausnahme aufgehoben

Der Beginn der Vorstellung sowie jedes Aktes wird durch ein Glockenzeichen bekanntgegeben.

Abendkassen-Eröffnung vor ½7 Uhr.   Anfang 7 Uhr.   Ende nach 11 Uhr.

Der Kartenverkauf findet heute statt für obige Vorstellung und für:

Sonntag   den 9. Lohengrin. Für das Pensions-Institut dieses Hoftheaters. (Anfang 7 Uhr.)
Montag   den 10. Der Rosenkavalier. Bei aufgehobenem Saison-Abonnement. Für das Pensions-Institut dieses Hoftheaters. (Anfang 7 Uhr).

Von Dienstag den 11. bis einschließlich Samstag den 15. April geschlossen.

Preise der Plätze:

modernstem Gepräge zu kontrollieren ist. Und da darf man nun ein bißchen protestieren, ja dieser Protest muß gegen den „Rosenkavalier" aus Wien kommen: Wenn Wien wirklich die Stadt der Walzer ist, so ist es keineswegs die Stadt der gegenwärtig herrschenden, ausdrucksleeren, schablonenhaften, banalen Operettenwalzer. Walzer solcher Art vertragen wirklich nicht die Standeserhebung, die ihnen Richard Strauß, obendrein in tiefer Verkennung der Kunst Johann Strauß', zugedacht hat. Nicht um die Verwendung des Walzers überhaupt würde es sich handeln, der heiterer Opernmusik nie ganz fremd blieb, sondern um Verwendung dieser Walzer, vollends um Verwendung in geradezu unwahrscheinlicher Menge. Wenn der erste und zweite Walzer auftauchen, mag man vergnügt schmunzeln, zum dritten und vierten noch lächeln; wenn aber der fünfte und sechste heranrücken, stutzt man und ist gründlich verstimmt, wenn dann noch im dritten Akt eine unaufhörliche Folge von zum Teil unbegreiflich schalen Walzern — an fünfzig Seiten des Klavier-

„Der Rosenkavalier."

Komödie für Musik in drei Aufzügen von Hugo v. Hofmannsthal, Musik von Richard Strauß. — Zur Erstaufführung im k. k. Hofoperntheater am 8. April 1911.

Es ist eine Komödie, tatsächlich eine Komödie: wie Richard Strauß nämlich es sofort gespürt hat, als die sexuell-neuropathische Hausse vorüber war. Unversehens waren Salome und Elektra ins gefährliche Alter geraten: vergebens buhlte das Tierchen Salome um die Gunst des Publikums, umsonst wand sich die Bestie Klytämnestra in halbleeren Häusern in hysterischen Zuckungen. Inzwischen stieg die Operette hoch im Kurs; die Operette mit ihren „süßlichen Wiener Glissandi", ihren klebrigen Sentimentalitäten und ihrer so ganz unkomplizierten, daher gemeinverständlichen Erotik. Die Leute, sie hören es gerne ... So ist nun diese Komödie für Musik entstanden, von den heulenden Derwischen, die seit einigen Jahren Strauß verzückt umtanzen, als die heiß ersehnte „komische Oper" proklamiert; diese Komödie, die wiederum mehr eine Komödie mit dem Publikum ist, als für das Publikum. „Das Ganze war halt eine Farce, weiter nichts," wie die Feldmarschallin sagt. Eine Farce, die stellenweise zur Operette herabsinkt, stellenweise noch tiefer, zur Posse mit Musik.

...of the most modern description. And here a mild protest is permissible; indeed this protest against 'Rosenkavalier' must come from Vienna. If Vienna is truly the city of waltzes, it is by no means the city of the hollow, stereotyped, banal operettish waltzes which prevail at the present time. Waltzes of this kind really cannot support the strain of such a steep social ascent as Richard Strauss — who moreover lacks all understanding of the art of Johann Strauss — has conferred upon them. We are not disputing, as such, the use of the waltz which was never wholly a stranger to the lighter forms of opera; we are objecting to the use of these waltzes, and above all to their use in such incredible quantity. When the first and second waltzes are heard, our faces may light up, we may still smile at the third and fourth, but when the fifth and sixth come into view it is more than can be endured; when, in Act Three, an unending sequence of often inconceivably shallow waltzes, about fifty pages of the score ...

'DER ROSENKAVALIER'

A comedy for music in three acts by Hugo v. Hofmannsthal, music by Richard Strauss. — On the occasion of the première in the Court Opera on 8 April 1911.

It is a comedy, in truth highly comical, the way in which Richard Strauss instantly realised that the boom in sexual neuropathology was over. Imperceptibly, Salome and Elektra had arrived at a dangerous age: the little animal Salome solicited the favours of the public to no avail, it was in vain that the beast Klytaemnestra indulged in paroxysms of hysteria before half-empty houses. In the meantime the stocks of operetta had risen steeply; operetta with its 'sickly Viennese glissandi', its sticky sentimentalities and its so utterly uncomplicated and thus perfectly understandable eroticism. The audience lapped it up ... So now this comedy for music has been written, proclaimed by the howling dervishes who have danced ecstatically round Richard Strauss for years, as the longed-for 'comic opera'; this comedy which is more of a joke against the public than with it. 'It was all just a farce, nothing more', as the Marschallin put it. A farce, which sometimes sinks to the level of operetta, sometimes deeper still, to a burlesque set to music.

Court Opera. For the first time, 'Der Rosenkavalier', a comedy for music by Hugo Hofmannsthal. Music by Richard Strauss. The disturbances of the Richard Strauss Week in Vienna reached their happy climax last night. Elsewhere in this paper, on page 15, the reader will find a detailed report on the libretto and the music, with which the present writer became acquainted at a performance in Munich. Unhappily, the Vienna première has done nothing to cast a more cheerful light upon the impressions gained on that occasion.

In spite of their intricate instrumentation the widely acclaimed waltzes in 'Rosenkavalier' are very little to our taste; and their banal tunes are directly reminiscent of operetta. Ready as we are to acknowledge Richard Strauss's enormous talent, we are unable to say that 'Rosenkavalier' marks an advance in his creative work, nor do we believe that this 'comedy for music' will retain a place for long in the repertoire of our Court Opera.

Hofoperntheater. Zum ersten Male „Der Rosenkavalier", Komödie für Musik von Hugo Hofmannsthal. Musik von Richard Strauß. Die Ruhestörungen der Wiener Richard Strauß-Woche haben gestern glücklich ihren Höhepunkt erreicht. An einer anderen Stelle dieses Blattes, auf Seite 15, findet der Leser ausführlichen Bericht über Dichtung und Musik, die dem Schreiber dieser Zeilen schon von einer Münchener Aufführung her bekannt waren und die ihm die Wiener Première leider in kein froheres Licht zu rücken vermocht hat.

Die vielgepriesenen Walzer im „Rosenkavalier" haben uns trotz ihrer raffinierten Instrumentation wenig Geschmack abgewinnen können und ihre banalen Melodien gemahnen direkt an die Operette. So sehr wir das enorme Talent Richard Strauß' zu schätzen geneigt sind, so können wir seinen „Rosenkavalier" nicht als einen Fortschritt seines Schaffens bezeichnen und wir glauben auch nicht, daß sich diese „Komödie für Musik" im Repertoire unserer Hofoper lange erhalten wird.

Hans Liebstöckl in the 'Illustriertes Wiener Extrablatt' on 9 April 1911.

Alfred Angermayer in the 'Neuigkeits-Weltblatt' of 9 April 1911.

Theresias, der die Ausstatter der Hofmannsthalschen Stilkomödie peinlich getreue Formen entnahmen, der Wiener Walzer noch gar nicht geboren war und daß der Walzer nicht das Tempo jener Zeit gewesen ist. Er mutet in dieser Umgebung so unecht an wie das fürchterliche Hofmannsthalsche Wienerisch im „Rosenkavalier", das nicht allein mit „Führa (!) g'fahr'n" eine bedenkliche Orthographie aufzuweisen hat.

Die Gründe des Mißvergnügens, das sich um den „Rosenkavalier" verbreitet, liegen aber tiefer. Hugo von Hofmannsthal und Richard Strauß, die sich für eine musikalische Komödie befähigt hielten, sind gänzlich von H u m o r verlassen; sie bringen nicht mehr als kleinen, niedrigen W i t z in ihr Werk. Die

Leiblied erkoren. Für Wiener Ohren klingt der Walzer zu normalwienerisch, um das Auffälligste, Merkwürdigste, Besondere zu sein — daß Richard Strauß Walzer schreibt, kann vor der Aufführung die Neugier reizen, aber mit dem Ablauf der Musik wird auch die Erwartung entspannt. Für das Merkantilische, um mit Nestroy zu sprechen, ist allerdings, wie es scheint, der Walzer ·die Hauptsache. In dem großen Berliner Kaufhaus Wertheim, in dem man schlechterdings alles erhält, wird auch der neueste Strauß verschleißt, und zwar ein Potpourri, das heißt ein Gemengsel der hübschesten Walzerthemen aus dem „Rosenkavalier" — der Unterschied von dem rührigen Vertrieb irgend eines kolossalen Operettenschlagers, wie die Verleger und sonstige Interessenten zu sagen pflegen, ist wahrhaftig nicht sehr bedeutend.

...of Maria Theresia, to which the stage designers of Hofmannsthal's comedy of style were so scrupulously faithful, the Vienna waltz was not yet born and that the waltz was not the rhythm of that era. The impression it makes in these surroundings is as spurious as Hofmannsthal's dreadful Viennese dialect in 'Rosenkavalier' which is spattered with errors.
The reasons for the general discontent with 'Rosenkavalier', however, lie at a deeper level. Hugo von Hofmannsthal and Richard Strauss, who believed themselves capable of writing a musical comedy, are wholly devoid of all humour; all that they offer in their work is cheap, low-class wit.

In Viennese ears the waltz sounds too normal too everyday-Viennese to be able to express that which is most striking, remarkable and exceptional. That Richard Strauss should write waltzes excites curiosity before the performance, but while listening to the music expectancy slackens. In commercial matters, on the other hand, to quote Nestroy, the waltz appears to reign supreme. At Wertheim, the large department store in Berlin where positively everything can be obtained, the latest Strauss is also for sale in the shape of a potpourri called 'A Medley of the Prettiest Waltz Tunes' out of the 'Rosenkavalier' — the difference from the busy sales management of some colossal hit as the publishers and other interested parties are pleased to term it, in the world of operetta, is certainly rather insignificant.

The house which was packed to overflowing at all levels did not greet the new work with quite the enthusiasm which is usual at a Strauss première. The applause after the first act was lukewarm, and a few dissident voices were heard. After the second act with Herr Mayr's drastic performance, Herr Strauss also appeared before the curtain and once brought Kapellmeister Schalk with him. The third act was followed by the noisy and persistent applause of the determined few, to which Herr Strauss responded repeatedly, but the audience went home with mixed feelings.
Balduin Bricht

Das in allen Rängen geradezu überfüllte Haus bereitete dem neuen Werke nicht ganz den straußüblichen Premierenerfolg. Der erste Aufzug wurde mit zurückhaltendem Applaus aufgenommen, auch einige Opposition ließ sich hören. Nach dem zweiten Akte mit der drastischen Leistung des Herrn M a y r erschien auch Herr S t r a u ß wiederholt an der Rampe und brachte einmal auch Kapellmeister Schalk mit. Auf den dritten Akt folgte der überlaute und zähe Beifall der Unbedingten, dem Herr Strauß wiederholt Folge leistete, das Publikum aber ging mit gemischten Gefühlen nach Hause.

Balduin Bricht.

This is how 'Der Rosenkavalier' was received by the critics. Extracts from the Vienna newspapers.

K. K. Hof Operntheater

Samstag den 16. März 1912

Im Jahres-Abonnement   2. Viertel   66. Vorstellung im Saison-Abonnement

Zum ersten Male:

Aphrodite

Oper in einem Aufzug. Dichtung nach Pierre Louÿs von Hans Liebstoeckl

Regie: Hr. v. Wymétal   Musik von Max Oberleithner   Dirigent: Hr. Schalk

Chrysis	*	Myrtokleia } Freundinnen	Frl. Jovanovic
Königin Berenice	Fr. Hilgermann	Melitta } der Chrysis	Frl. Luna
Demetrios, Bildhauer	Hr. Weidemann	Aphrodysia	Fr. Cahil
Der erste Priester der Göttin	Hr. Gaudier	Djala, eine Sklavin der Chrysis	Frl. Moravetz
Timon, ein Fremder	Hr. Beuer	Sefo, eine Sklavin der Bacchis	Frl. Pohl
Nautrates, sein Gastfreund	Hr. Betetto	Der Haushofmeister der Königin	Hr. Fränzl J.
Bacchis	Frl. Paalen	Ein Neger	Hr. Schreitter

Junge Mädchen im Dienste der Göttin Aphrodite, Wächter des Tempels, Trabanten im Gefolge der Königin, Volk etc.

Ort der Handlung: Alexandria. Zeit: Um das Jahr 200 vor Christi Geburt

Syrischer Tanz: Frl. Jamrich, Fleischinger, Katlein, Kaar, Piringer, Pohl, die Koryphäen und das Ballettkorps.

Das Textbuch ist an der Kassa für 80 Heller erhältlich

* * * „Chrysis" Fr. **Mizzi Jeritza** als Gast

Maria was still 'Mizzi' in those days. Jeritza's first evening at the Vienna Opera.

The conductor was Franz Schalk. Lucie Weidt, a popular favourite in Wagner and as Fidelio, was a superb Marschallin, Gutheil-Schoder was Octavian, and Richard Mayr's Ochs has never been surpassed. The bed scene was played in the discreet form requested by the censor in Dresden (Otto Schenk's production in 1968 restored the original realistic form intended by the authors) and Gutheil stood up bravely to the Viennese authorities by playing the first scene in shirt and knee-breeches only, without a waistcoat.

The audience's enthusiasm was unbounded: even more unbounded was the ferocity with which the Press tore the new work to pieces. Reading the Press notices of the first night one can hardly believe one's eyes. 'A farce which in places degenerates to the level of operetta . . . wobbling uncertainly between two entirely incompatible varieties of asthmatic melody . . . an import from the nethermost regions of operetta, an artifice but not a work of art . . . a final duet of the utmost banality . . . an orgiastic bunch of galleryites and their henchmen applauded vigorously . . . Richard Mayr's Ochs was a mixture of sly cunning and self-satisfied complacency, vulgar to the last degree' (Moritz Scheyer in the *Wiener Allgemeine Zeitung.*) — 'Der Rosenkavalier will enjoy as brief a homunculus existence as other pieces whose appeal is based solely on their curiosity value . . . The whole thing was like a village fair . . . It should be called a "Comedy *against* music" . . . Richard Strauss is one of those people who always make themselves heard when they have nothing to say' (Balduin Bricht in the *Österreichische Volkszeitung*). — 'The work is totally devoid of humour . . . a Field-Marshal's wife indulging in erotic amusements at retirement age' (*Wiener Abendpost*). — 'The opera ought to be called "The Swine of Lerchenau". The music is in the highest degree morbid and unnatural . . . a hullabaloo that is enough to melt the marrow of one's bones . . . How can such a piece possibly be deemed worthy of the Imperial Opera?' (Hans Buchstein). In the *Neue Freie Presse* Dr. Julius Korngold wrote: 'Ochs is just a dunghill Falstaff, a cesspool Don Juan . . .' And Lehár: 'Richard Strauss has stolen motifs from *Fatinitza*.'

It only remains to add that there were innumerable curtain-calls, and the following year Richard Strauss himself conducted a repeat performance.

So one of the greatest operas of all time, and one which was destined to become a particular favourite with Viennese audiences, fell into Gregor's lap like a ripe plum at the very beginning of his term of office. The new Director lost no time in exploiting his success. He was a marvellous judge of expediency, of what to include in his programme. He never for one moment subscribed to the modern practice of drawing up the programme as far ahead as possible and slavishly adhering to it. Nowadays it is impossible to exploit an outstanding success because the programme has been arranged at least a year in advance and improvisation is out of the question. For the same reason a fiasco no longer matters so much. Everything is pre-arranged to death. However, Gregor had no scruples in re-arranging the whole future programme at a moment's notice. Operas that had not caught on were dropped without hesitation, but during the remaining nine months of 1911 *Der Rosenkavalier* was put on no fewer than thirty-seven times, an impossibility by today's standards.

Gregor applied the same ruthless methods when it came to the outstanding success of his first Christmas première (1911), Massenet's *Le jongleur de Notre Dame*, which altogether he put on fifty-two times in 1912. If a work was not an immediate success it was immediately removed from the repertoire. Hans Pfitzner, then already regarded as a great composer, found this out at his own expense: his *Der arme Heinrich* had such a lukewarm reception that it ran for only two nights. Gregor showed no respect whatsoever towards music which only emptied his Opera.

In 1913 Gregor put on the Paris version of *Tannhäuser* with the lavish Venusberg ballet, and he was also particularly keen on giving Wagner's swan from the 1875 production (it had provoked Daniel Spitzer's caustic comment quoted in the chapter on Franz Jauner) another outing. The 1913 swan led Max Springer to write in the *Reichspost:* 'A splendid swan with a wonderfully flexible neck and magnificent plumage swims up to the lady resting on the bank, and his gestures leave little to the imagination...' After the swan came the forest at the foot of the Wartburg teeming with thoroughbred horses and baying hounds (it was not so very long ago that Karajan employed real hounds and falcons for his production of *Tannhäuser*).

Another stroke of luck for Gregor was the expiration of the thirty-year copyright of *Parsifal* on the first of January 1914. Wagner had stipulated that until then the work could only be performed at Bayreuth, though in America an 'illegal' version had been staged, complete with a well-trained dove in the last act. Gregor lost no time in offering *Parsifal* to his Viennese audience in 1914, yet even so he was beaten to the post by the Grande Opéra in Paris (to which special trains were run from London!).

Parsifal at the Vienna Opera was a great success, with Erik Schmedes as Parsifal, Richard Mayr as Gurnemanz, and Anna Mildenburg as Kundry. It was Mildenburg's last rôle under Gregor: she had found Gregor exceedingly difficult to get on with from the very first, and eventually she retired from the stage and worked as a nurse during the First World War.

In view of its popularity Gregor repeated *Parsifal* twenty-seven times in its first year. Before the first night he passed the word round among all the restaurants in the neighbourhood warning them to be on their toes to minister to the hundreds of fugitives from the Opera who would probably be descending on them during the long intervals. For one performance Gregor actually experimented with the idea of auctioning gallery tickets.

Gregor's pride and joy was the Transformation Scene at the end of Act Two where Klingsor's magic garden withers away. The transportation of the scenery and props from the workshops to the stage and back needed thirty large trucks and was such a complicated business that three whole days' valuable rehearsal time were lost. And some idea of how strenuous the rehearsals for *Parsifal* were can be gathered from what Gregor had to say at a press conference about the Opera's antiquated technical installations which dated back to 1869. The scene-shifters could communicate with each other across the stage only by megaphone (imagine the noise!). It took eight strong men to get the massive plush curtain up: they were posted in relays at varying heights and at a given signal had to heave on the ropes with all their might. No wonder that even the dress-rehearsal was dogged by one mishap after another. The mechanism for the transformation from the Good Friday morning landscape to the Temple of the Holy Grail refused to budge and, as if all this were not enough, Gregor was criticised in the house for not having allowed as many rehearsals for *Parsifal* as he had for Puccini's *La fanciulla del West*.

In March 1914, two months after his triumphant success with *Parsifal*, Gregor put on Casper's *The Aunt Slept*. But she only slept for one night: the audience's hostility amounted almost to a public demonstration against the Director. The malicous assertion that the fiasco of *The Aunt Slept* caused the outbreak of the First World War is, however, an exaggeration.

Later on Hans Gregor told very amusing stories about the attacks on him in Vienna. The eighty-year-old Princess Metternich requested that the auditorium — as in bygone days — should be lit up so that one could see the dresses of the ladies in the audience. And when Gregor wanted to break with the tradition whereby Holy Week was kept free of performances and rehearsals, a group of ballerinas submitted a complaint to the heir to the throne, Franz Ferdinand: Gregor, the wicked Protestant, wanted to prevent them from going on a pilgrimage...

K. K. Hof- Operntheater

Samstag den 7. März 1914

Im Jahres-Abonnement   3. Viertel   56. Vorstellung im Saison-Abonnement

Die Tante schläft

Singspiel in einem Akt von Hector Crémieux — Deutsch von M. Oscar

Regie: Hr. v. Wymétal   Musik von **Henri Calvert**   Dirigent: Hr. Reichenberger

Die Marquise d'Ambert . . . . Fr. Hilgermann   Scapin, Kammerdiener des Chevalier Hr. Preuß
Gabriele, ihre Nichte . . . . . Frl. Jovanovic   Martine, Gabrielens Kammer-
Der Chevalier de Kerpry . . . . Dr. Rittmann   mädchen . . . . Fr. Kiurina

Das Stück spielt im französischen Städtchen Pau, Gasthof zur Sonne; 18. Jahrhundert

In his search for box-office hits Director Gregor was not choosy. This time he blundered. One performance.

The main charge against him was his obsession with the financial side of things. In other countries Directors are criticised for being too little concerned with the box-office: in Vienna the gravamen of the charge against Gregor was that he always put the box-office first.

People found it difficult to understand why all at once they had been given a Director who not only tried to save the Emperor money but actually tried to make ends meet in the running of the Imperial Opera, whereas the generally accepted recipe for success in the operatic world was a spendthrift in the Director's office and courtesans on the stage. And anyway it was all so undignified. Dr. Julius Korngold demanded: 'Give culture more space in your mind than the box-office!' Gregor: 'Why does your paper carry ten pages of advertisements and only one on culture?'

As a producer Gregor went from strength to strength, notably with Debussy's *Pelléas et Mélisande* which he had already produced at Barmen-Elberfeld. He really was a brilliantly imaginative producer, particularly as regards lighting, and he collaborated rather well with Bruno Walter, who conducted the first Vienna performance. In its first year *Pelléas* was performed nine times, and in its second, three times; nothing out of the way admittedly, but still a good deal more often than any other Vienna Director has managed since. Gutheil sang Mélisande.

Second in importance to the box-office in Gregor's view came the appeal to the eye: the music came a bad third. He was all for spectacular productions with plenty of crowd-scenes, and if it was a question of only being able to make an opera pay its way by giving it a lavish production, he could be the very reverse of a cheap opportunist. He would work like a demon, insisting on the utmost precision down to the minutest details, and on such occasions his exorbitant rehearsal schedule had the entire staff cowed. For both *Pelléas* and *Bohème* there were no fewer than forty rehearsals, which is still a record. But for operas in which he was less interested, or which were being put on by other producers, he often permitted only five rehearsals.

Gregor's term saw the emergence of a number of phenomena that are all too familiar features of the present despotism of the producer. For instance, producers began to take exception to new singers without rehearsal participation before the première. Gregor, for instance, refused point-blank to allow Caruso to sing Rodolfo because he had not found time to attend the rehearsals for Gregor's new *Bohème*. Gregor was responsible for no more productions after 1915.

As for the music, the bad third, Gregor was quite content to leave it to the experts. His enemies said that whereas Weingartner put on productions without music, Gregor was putting on productions against music; but as the productions in question are no more, this and similar judgements can be neither refuted nor upheld.

Despite his somewhat unenthusiastic attitude toward music, Gregor did do his best to secure some of the most popular conductors of the day for the Vienna Opera. He invited Arthur Nikisch and Ernst von Schuch, but both declined. But the Italian Antonio Guarnieri came. In time he became one of Italy's greatest Wagner conductors, despite the towering figure of Toscanini. Unfortunately he found himself at loggerheads with Gregor from the very first over the latter's lack of interest in musical considerations, and after only four or five months he broke his contract and left Vienna overnight. The same thing happened in the case of Gregor Fitelberg, Poland's leading conductor, who had actually been discovered by Gregor. He was an attractive figure, in appearance not unlike Gustav Mahler; pale, clean-shaven, with black eyes and

In 1912 Siegfried Wagner conducted his 'Banadietrich' at the Vienna Opera. (Silhouette by Otto Böhler.)

Vienna Opera for many years. Reichwein is said to have been a somewhat erratic performer: on his good nights he really scaled the heights, especially in the first production of *Parsifal*, which he conducted alternately with Schalk. At other times he was not nearly so good. Another acquisition was Bernhard Tittel, a workmanlike conductor from the Volksoper. In this respect Gregor was less successful: Directors' departments are often hampered by a conducting Director's jealousy towards other conductors, but a managerial direction should really make it possible for a number of prominent musicians to appear on the rostrum.

Scanning the heated invective against Gregor in the Press and other publications of the time, one wonders whether Gregor can really have been such a bad Director after all. A man who never had fewer than sixty or seventy works in the repertoire, and never fewer than thirty-five even when it was reduced during the war, cannot have been all bad. Although he put on enough new works almost to qualify for the epithet avant-garde, the most frequently performed composers during his term were still Wagner, Richard Strauss, Verdi and Puccini, just as they always have been and still are. Whether a Director professes to be artistically minded and progressive or to have a careful eye on the box-office, Wagner, Richard Strauss, Verdi and Puccini will still be the backbone of his repertoire (and nowadays Mozart).

Can Gregor really have been so bad? He was, after all, the Director who revived Mahler's production of *Fidelio*, insisted that Verdi be sung in Italian whenever possible, and while stoutly maintaining that the only one of the moderns who would survive was Richard Strauss, continued to put on mediocre contemporary works because he thought he owed it to the public.

During the seven years his opponents called the 'seven fat years for the box-office and seven lean years for art' this 'lowbrow vandal', this 'Philistine' put on five complete series of all Wagner's works and fourteen cycles of the *Ring* (except in 1917). In seven years he launched three big Richard Strauss premières *(Rosenkavalier, Ariadne* and *Salome)* all of which were frequently repeated! Just as Jauner had made Vienna a Wagner

a daemonic look about him reminiscent of E. T. A. Hoffmann. But Gregor gave him the wrong job: Fitelberg was an excellent *Kapellmeister* in modern operas, Richard Strauss for instance; in an opera like Marschner's *Hans Heiling* he was bound to be all at sea.

Eventually even Bruno Walter failed to hit it off with Gregor and departed for Munich. Schalk stayed on, an act of mercy for Gregor, who would have been lost without him. In place of Walter came Leopold Reichwein, who was first engaged by Gregor and remained with the centre, so Gregor made it a Strauss centre. And incidentally this same Hans Gregor who was said not to have an ounce of artistic feeling in his make-up also introduced Vienna to three of the most popular stage idols it has ever known: Lotte Lehmann, Alfred Piccaver and Maria Jeritza. Even in the business of engaging artists his luck still held.

Which brings us to the great Maria Jeritza. Gregor had quite a tussle to get hold of this star of the Volksoper. Mizzi Jeritza, as she was billed in those days, was a native of Brünn, had made her dèbut at Olomouc and had sung in operetta at the Imperial summer theatre at Bad Ischl before finding her way to the Vienna Volksoper when Rainer Simons was in charge. Later she caused a sensation as 'la belle Hélène' in Reinhardt's production in Munich and in the same brilliant producer's *Ariadne* in Stuttgart. At the Vienna Volksoper she presented its Director with the greatest triumphs in its history as Elsa, as Elisabeth in *Tannhäuser*, as the slavegirl in *Quo vadis?* by Nougès, as Agathe in *Der Freischütz* and in Wilhelm Kienzl's *Kuhreigen*. It was only after infiniteley complicated negotiations that Gregor managed to secure her for the Imperial Opera, where she made her debut in 1912 in Oberleitner's *Aphrodite*, in a degree of nudity that the house had never seen before. Here as everywhere she took the audience by storm.

The second big Jeritza première was Puccini's *La Fanciulla del West* on the twenty-fourth of October 1913. By the end of the year it had been given fourteen times, and in the following year it was repeated twenty-seven times. For Gregor, success was all that mattered, and he had no compunction in putting on Puccini's melodious 'gangster story' on Christmas Day! It had been first performed under Toscanini in New York in 1910 with a cast headed by Caruso and Emmy Destinn: it was a moderate success that only became a sensation when it arrived at the 'Met' with Jeritza. Without Jeritza the opera has never really established itself in the repertoire.

Gregor was doubly fortunate in being able to present as Jeritza's partner in the first Vienna performance of *La Fanciulla* a young English tenor named Alfred Piccaver in the rôle of Ramerrez. Vienna had waited a long time for such a popular pair of opera singers. As Alfredo Piccaver he had already substituted for a tenor who was taken ill during the Italian *stagione* of 1910, and more will be heard of him in the next chapter. For the present, suffice it to say that he had a glorious voice with a nasal timbre of extraordinary tenderness and beauty in its upper-middle register; that he made very many appearances as Jeritza's partner, but unlike her he was a wooden and conventional actor. If, instead of standing riveted to the stage, he actually by some miracle took two paces forward and raised his left hand, it was a positively intoxicating experience for us young galleryites. 'Did you see that? Who said Piccaver couldn't act?' His lack of imagination sometimes made things rather difficult for Jeritza, whose elemental vitality and instinct for making an effect often depended on her partner's co-operation. In *Cavalleria Rusticana* for instance, when she is pushed down the steps of the church by the furious Turiddu, Santuzza is unable to fall down the steps convincingly unless Turiddu really does give her a push. Piccaver was a man of moods and whenever he was having a tiff with Jeritza he would refrain from giving her a push and excuse himself after the show by saying that on this particular occasion he had taken a less violent view of his part.

Puccini was in Vienna for the first night of *La Fanciulla*. He was enthusiastic about Jeritza and always referred to her thereafter as his greatest interpreter. Another of her brilliant rôles at the Vienna Opera was Tosca, with Piccaver as Cavaradossi.

It is very difficult to describe what Jeritza was like to a generation that never saw her in her great days with her tremendously erotic aura and her positively volcanic voice. I have the great good fortune of being a personal friend of hers, and whenever, as in the summer of 1969, from the garden of her villa near New York I hear her 'sung' call for her beloved secretary 'Liiiieeeeslllll' wafting from the house, her 'Liesl' becomes a Valkyrie call, a resplendent 'Hojotoho' — and even this call for Liesl still has more volume than many Valkyrie calls today.

In Vienna as well as in America, if any member of the older generation mentions the legendary name Jeritza, the faces of all present seem to light up. I wonder

My Years
as a Standing-area Habitué

This is how Lotte Lehmann in Korngold's one-act opera *Das Wunder der Heliane* (1927) described 'The Stranger' — Jan Kiepura, the young tenor from Poland. The year before he had made a sensational Vienna debut as Calaf in *Turandot*. From then on we teenagers could get no sense out of our girl-friends — they had eyes only for Kiepura.

The Complete Star

Jan Kiepura (above, in the rôle of the Duke in *Rigoletto*) really was a 'schöne Knabe'. There was a boyish look about him all his life. He was a superb purveyor of top C's or even C sharps, and the sex-appeal in his voice was as irresist-ible as his charming smile. He was the complete all-round star. Apart from his fantastic successes in operetta and in the recording studios he was one of the greatest box-office magnets in the film world. For the film *Zauber der Bohème* which he made in Vienna with his wife Marta Eggerth his advance

on future takings amounted to 150,000 dollars. He was the only singer in the history of the Vienna Opera to be paid a percentage of the takings at his appearances. He used to get on an average 1,000 old dollars a performance, the equivalent of 2,000 dollars nowadays. He was also the first nomadic star: during the 1930s he was always on the move from one European or American opera house or film studio to another. Through films he enjoyed a world-wide popularity that no opera-singer had ever dreamed of until then. He had only to put his head out of the window in Vienna, Paris, London, Milan or Warsaw and a crowd would collect in no time. He anticipated the modern practice of singing only a very limited repertoire: Calaf, Cavaradossi, Don José (see left), Rodolfo, Manrico, the Duke of Mantua in *Rigoletto,* and 'The Stranger' in *Das Wunder der Heliane.* Now of course singers have to wear the costumes the producer has decided on, but Kiepura used to travel with his own. If the word 'star' had never existed it would have had to be coined for Jan Kiepura.

Right: Emil Schipper was a baritone from the Volksoper. Personally I preferred him in Italian parts. He is seen here as Renato in *Un ballo in Maschera.* I can still hear his dazzling top G in this rôle, as well as his top A flat in *Rigoletto.* His best German rôle was probably Borromeo in *Palestrina.* For Hans Sachs he was in my view not intellectual enough. He had a voice of positively elemental volume but he was not an out-and-out bel canto singer. Further down the scale his voice lost a lot of its volume, and if he could not quite manage a low note he would point downwards instead with his index finger. — Below: Josef Kalenberg, originally an electrical engineer, was the Vienna Opera's most reliable repertoire tenor. He sang anything that came along — Wagner, Verdi, Mozart, Puccini — everything. He was celebrated for the number of times he deputised at short notice, especially for Piccaver, who was celebrated for the number of times he cried off at short notice. Kalenberg would probably have been more appreciated if he had sung less. He is seen here as Walther Stolzing with Erich Zimmermann, a fine tenor, as David. Zimmermann was exceptionally short, and whenever Slezak as Alfred in *Die Fledermaus* took his dressing-gown he would ask Rosalinde if her husband was from Lilliput.

I remember clearly how in 1930 we standing-room habitués whipped up the audience's enthusiasm at the first night of *Wozzeck*. It was a memorable occasion, the first performance of a highly dramatic opera by a brilliant young contemporary who enriched the whole vocabulary of music. Furthermore I was very keen on Rose Pauly at the time (she is seen here as Marie). She was a pupil of Rosa Papier's and a superb Strauss singer — Salome, Elektra, or the Dyer's Wife. I used to be terribly pleased with myself whenever I was permitted to escort her home after the performance to her apartment in the Petersplatz. Curiously enough politics intruded into her private life, because her husband was the owner of the notorious Hotel Dreesen at Bad Godesberg on the Rhine where Hitler received Neville Chamberlain. The other illustration is of Alban Berg sitting in front of Georg Maikl (an admirable Mozart tenor who had been taken on by Mahler) as the Captain, Josef von Manowarda (another import from the Volksoper who was probably at his best as King Philip in *Don Carlos*) as Wozzeck, and Hermann Wiedemann, the regular Beckmesser and Alberich of those days, as the Doctor.

Giuditta was not the first operetta to find its way to the Vienna Opera (1934): Jahn had promoted *Die Fledermaus*, Weingartner *Der Zigeunerbaron*, and Clemens Krauss *Der Opernball;* but it was the first operetta to be given its first performance there.

Richard Tauber was at his zenith, and once again Lehár wrote the arias with the particular qualities of his voice in mind. Nearly all of them are in D flat, D, or E flat so that Tauber could end on a thrilling A flat, A, or B flat, his best notes. On the first night Jarmila Novotna made 'Meine Lippen, die küssen so heiss' a smash-hit virtually overnight. As a pair, Tauber and Novotna were an even greater success than the operetta itself, and shortly afterwards they were together again in *The Bartered Bride.*

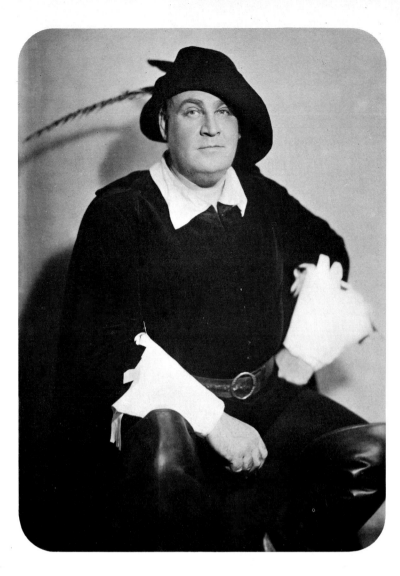

I was also an ardent admirer of Elisabeth Schumann (right), and my spies were very often successful in finding out when she would be taking her two terriers for a walk in the Burggarten, where I used to lie in wait for her and ask for her autograph. Nowadays of course singers of her class have no time to take dogs for walks in gardens, they are hurrying to the Airport. Elisabeth Schumann was world-famous as a Mozart singer and as Sophie in *Der Rosenkavalier*, but personally I enjoyed her perhaps most of all in rôles that in theory were outside her voice, Eva or Mimi for instance. The way her silvery soprano blended with other sopranos in, say, the trios in *Der Rosenkavalier* or *Ariadne* was unforgettable. She is seen here as Susanne in *Figaro* (1927). — With the wonderful Alfred Piccaver (above) I could never really come to terms because I was a militant Kiepura fan, but I always knew how very good he was. All too often we are disappointed when we try to revive youthful memories with the help of gramophone records, but not in the case of Piccaver: to listen again to some of his Puccini arias, or the dream from *Manon*, or some of his favourite sentimental English ballads is still to wonder how on earth it was that this English tenor who made Vienna his home was never really a celebrity outside Vienna apart from one or two isolated successes on tour. 'Pikki' was very attached to his home in the Brahmsplatz and detested travelling. He is seen here as Babinsky the bandit in Jaromir Weinberger's *Schwanda, the Bagpiper* (1930).

Margit Schenker-Angerer was one of the Vienna Opera's best-looking singers. Her lyrical soprano was of medium volume but with brilliant top notes. She invested every rôle the sang — Octavian, the Composer, Elsa, or Elisabeth — with the charm of her personality. Unfortunately her technique was not what it should have been and her career was correspondingly brief. She is seen here with Franz Völker in a new production of Tchaikovsky's *Pique Dame* (1931) conducted by Clemens Krauss. Normally Franz Völker's stage presence was far from inspiring, but the producer Lothar Wallerstein worked wonders with him. Völker was gifted with a wonderfully flexible and powerful tenor voice that was unsur-

passed in the 'Winterstürme' scene in Act One of *Die Walküre*, for instance, or in the Prize Song in *Die Meistersinger* or the Grail Narration in *Parsifal*. In *Pique Dame* he and Margit Schenker-Angerer sounded glorious together. — I have heard a good many wonderful contraltos — Maria Olczewska, Kerstin Thorborg, and later Giulietta Simionato — but there were certain passages that nobody could sing more beautifully than Rosette Anday (below). Particularly lovely were her chest-notes in, say, 'Ich lieb' ihn ja noch immer' (in those days *Aida* was sung in German), or 'Er gedachte, Brünnhilde, dein' from *Götterdämmerung*. She is seen here in Saint-Saëns' *Samson et Dalila*.

Maria Jeritza

'Du schönes Wesen!
Bist du die Göttin dieser Insel?'
(Richard Strauss, *Ariadne auf Naxos*.)

Top left: 'Ihr habt bei einem edlen, guten und reinen Herzen ein engelschönes Angesicht' sang Alfred Piccaver as the robber Ramerrez to Maria Jeritza in the German version of Puccini's *La Fanciulla del West* ('As well as a noble, good and pure heart you have the face of an angel'). — Top right: Jeritza's face, with the golden-blond hair, charming dimples, and radiant smile of a Moravian peasant girl. — Below: Jeritza twice played the most beautiful woman in the world: in Richard Strauss's *Die Ägyptische Helena* and (in this illustration) a long time earlier in Max Reinhardt's Munich production of Offenbach's *La belle Hélène*. — Right page: As Tosca she became Puccini's favourite diva. She sang the prayer in Act Two lying on the ground — a classical interpretation of a naturalistic operatic scene which is still often imitated today.

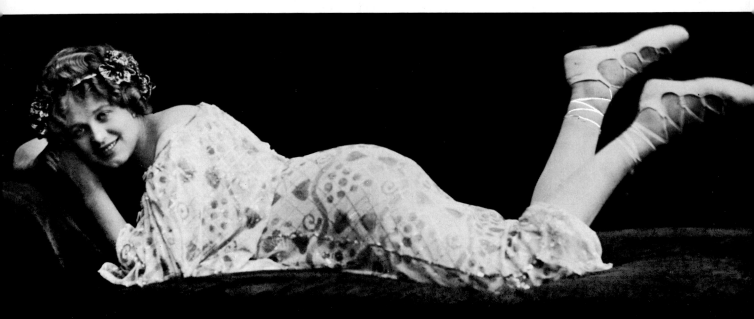

She was called 'the Duse of
Opera', and the Vienna
Burgtheater (and later Broad-
way) were all for featuring her
in straight plays. There was
an extraordinary radiance
about her voice, and her acting
was like a volcanic outburst of
pent-up emotions. She seemed
to project her top notes into
the audience with every muscle
in her body. There was a release
of emotion in every note.
The 'Jeritza cry' was as
famous as the 'Jeritza twist'
with which she threw herself
into the tenor's arms and
yielded to his kiss. Jeritza was
versatile — she was coquette,
diva, and soubrette all in one.
She is seen here as Manon
Lescaut.

Left: Maria Jeritza as Elisabeth in *Tannhäuser*. One day Alfred
Roller, who was responsible for the scenery, said to Franz Schalk:
'Herr Direktor, the tree in Act Three of Tannhäuser is beginning
to look a bit tired, it won't last much longer'; to which Schalk
replied: 'It looks all right when Jeritza stands in front of it.' —
Right: Her first part at the Vienna Opera was Aphrodite in
Oberleithner's opera of that name. Many operas were written
expressly for Jeritza: with her they were a success, without her
they flopped. The fascination of her stage presence made the most
outrageous scenery acceptable, and even invested *kitsch* with a
sort of glamour.

As Turandot (right) she used to make her entrance in Act Two from below instead of the top of the stairs as most other singers did. She would slowly mount the great stairway, the huge train fanning out behind her, and by the time she turned to face the audience at the top the train was spread out in front of her almost to the edge of the stage. With each riddle she came further down the stairs: by the second riddle her eyes were already gazing into Calaf's and the ice was beginning to melt. — Below: a caricature by L. Unger.

Jeritza was the first star of the Vienna Opera to be engaged by the New York 'Met', and from 1921 on she was at the 'Met's' disposal every autumn and winter. There was a good deal of comment about her commuting between Vienna and New York: two long ocean voyages a year won't do her voice any good, etc., etc., warned the crystal-gazers in what might be termed the Stone Age of the itinerant star.

unseren lieben
Prowijku
den besten und liebsten
Freund der ganzen Welt.
Maria Jeritza Seery
September 1951
The best friend of all —
Winfield Seery

There is a photograph of Jeritza on Puccini's desk at Torre del Lago, and at her home in the United States Jeritza has a photograph of Richard Strauss with a wonderful dedication by the grateful composer. This photograph is of the well-known portrait by Arthur Halmi. (I am proud of the dedication, in which she calls me her most faithful friend. This I am and shall always remain.) In *Die tote Stadt* she doubled the rôles of a living girl and a dead woman; or as one of her admirers put it, she played the part of a girl who looks exactly like a certain dead woman, which was a clever idea on the part of the librettist, because there is no woman alive who looks like Jeritza.

Hoch Slezak!

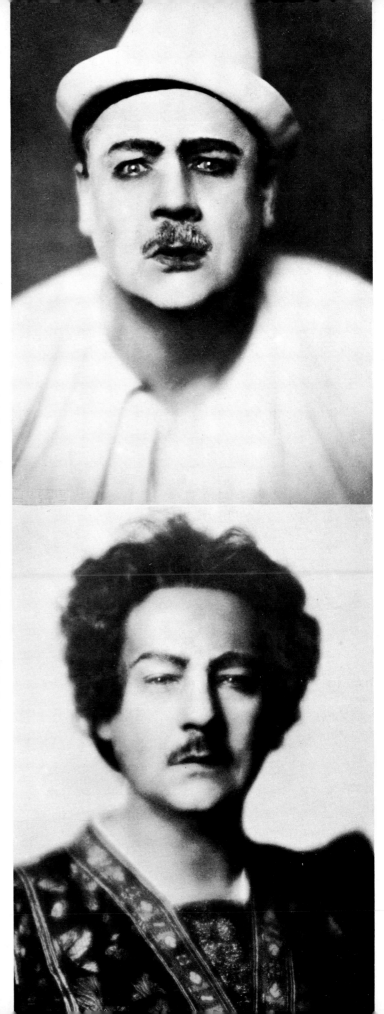

The last time this shout was heard was after a performance of *Pagliacci* in 1934 when Slezak was 61. It was 33 years since he had made his debut at the Vienna Opera, but his voice was still impressive. We could hardly believe our ears when we heard that this had been his farewell performance. It was typical of Slezak that there was no fuss, no ceremony. When the one-time apprentice locksmith from Mährisch-Schönberg with the enormous voice sang 'Otello' it sent shivers down one's spine. Compared with him, the volume of Caruso's voice was for the Viennese a disappointment. Pictures of Slezak in his younger days show him to have been remarkably slim, but in later years he as well as everyone else used to make jokes about his girth. 'Hier in den Stuhl?' he sang as Walther Stolzing in *Die Meistersinger*, looking incredulously at the narrow seat he would have to squeeze himself into. Perhaps he was no great actor, but the profound sincerity of his playing often moved audiences to tears. His voice was uncommonly flexible, and he had a wide variety of the subtlest nuances imaginable at his command. It was impossible to forget the scorn and disappointment with which as Tannhäuser he invested the words: 'Wolfram bist du, der wohlgeübte Sänger...' He was also the last of the Meyerbeer operatic heroes, and after his retirement they were heard no more. He was a great favourite at the New York 'Met', and was as popular as a man as he was as a singer. His lively sense of humour (particularly on stage) has become a legend and was the terror of his colleagues. After his retirement he wrote very amusing books and embarked on a new career as a comedian in the films. He died in 1946 at his Tegernsee home in Bavaria, where he and his friends Ganghofer and Ludwig Thoma were the local celebrities; and by the Tegernsee he is buried alongside his dearly beloved wife Elsa. The pictures on the following pages are of him as Canio in *Pagliacci* and as Vienna's first Calaf in *Turandot*.

'Wie sah meine Mutter wohl
aus?' sang Slezak as Siegfried,
but only in his younger days.
His mother was an embroidress
and seamstress, the Mimi of
Mährisch-Schönberg.

'Hohldeee aiidoh' sang Slezak
as Radames in the days when
Aida was still sung in German.
His Bohemian accent was
irresistible, and he never lost it.

'O Mathilde' sang Slezak as Arnold von Melchthal in the German version of *William Tell*, perhaps not to Schiller's satisfaction, but very much to Rossini's.

'Lodern zum Himmel' sang Slezak in the German version of *Il Trovatore*. He once admitted that he had not the foggiest idea of what this opera was about.

'Gegrüsst sei mir, du teure Stätte' sang Slezak as Faust (in German) with the finest falsetto top C in his repertoire.

'Dir, Göttin der Liebe, soll mein Lied ertönen' sang Slezak as Tannhäuser, which was always his most brilliant rôle. Partnered by Lehmann or Jeritza, he sang it right up to his last years.

Verl. Herm. Leiser, Berlin-Wilm.

'Magische Töne, berauschender Duft' sang Slezak in *Die Königin von Saba*, his soft voice sweetly caressing the Oriental night air. This was one of the operas that failed to hold its place in the repertoire after Slezak's retirement. This illustration of him in the part of Assad shows how adroitly he used to swathe his cloaks to hide his corpulence.

'Hast du zur Nacht gebetet, Desdemona?' asks Slezak as Otello in the German version of *Otello*. 'Beloved, take my life, but be careful of my corns,' Desdemona would sigh as the giant Slezak set about throttling her.

Left: Leo Slezak
as Walther Stolzing
in *Die Meistersinger*
('Hier in den Stuhl?').
See caption on page XV/1.

Caricature of Leo Slezak by L. Unger.

'Der
Le-he-he-he-henz
ist da!!'

Slezak was also an
excellent singer of
Lieder by
Schubert,
Schumann, Hugo
Wolf, or Richard
Strauss. One of
his encores that
always brought
the house down
was 'Der Lenz'
by Eugen Hildach.
'I'm absolutely
fed up with the
thing,' Slezak used
to grumble. Like
most other artists
of his time Slezak
did not sing by
heart at recitals, as
can be seen from
this unsigned
drawing.

whether mention of a present-day singer's name forty or fifty years from now will have the same effect?

The Jeritza legend was born before the advent of 'canned' music. She was by no means a stickler for accuracy and often sang an eighth too few or too many, sometimes even three or four. Nor was she always dead in tune, and many a répétiteur would try to put her right, but Puccini and Richard Strauss were among those who protested: 'For Heaven's sake don't alter a note of it.' On the stage she was the radiant, unchallenged queen. She was the greatest prima donna of the century, the symbol of everything worthy of the name of the theatre. When Alfred Roller — after 1924 — went to Franz Schalk and said, 'Herr Direktor, the tree in the third act of *Tannhäuser* is getting pretty shabby', Schalk replied, 'The tree's fine as long as Jeritza stands in front of it.'

Jeritza had an immediate, instinctive grasp of the essence of stage-acting. In 1966 she invited me to her permanent box at the 'Met', just after the new house had been opened, to see *Elektra*, a fantastic performance with the finest cast imaginable for this particular opera, an indescribably brilliant galaxy of singers. After every particularly lovely phrase Jeritza leaned over to me and, in her unique compound of English, German and Czech, which no one has ever changed or ever will, whispered: 'Prawyček, schön, beautiful — ach, singen die schön!' But after the curtain had fallen she suddenly grew pensive and said: 'You know, Prawyček, Gutheil-Schoder and Mildenburg may not have sung so beautifully (in *Elektra*) but they did inspire terror.' Of course she hit the nail on the head: in a modern performance of *Elektra* you can hear some of the finest voices in the world, an ocean of lovely sound, but you can't imagine anyone being afraid of them.

Among Gregor's premières was to be *Ariadne*, which had been first performed in Stuttgart in 1912 — with Jeritza. But as an experienced man of the theatre Gregor was not happy about the Stuttgart version, which united Molière's *Le bourgeois gentilhomme* with the opera: it would not do for Vienna. He therefore allied himself with certain circles who were pressing for a revi-

sion. Always offering a ready ear to criticism on purely dramatic grounds, Hofmannsthal and Strauss produced the so-called Vienna version in which *Ariadne* duly made its Vienna début in 1916. Divorced from the play the work soon established itself all over the world.

The première was a great occasion, with Jeritza as Ariadne, Franz Schalk conducting, and Strauss in the proscenium box. The part of the Composer was sung by Lotte Lehmann, a native of Berlin who had settled in Vienna and was to remain there until moving to America.

This was her début in Vienna, and along with *Die Frau ohne Schatten* and *Die Walküre*, *Ariadne* was one of the few operas in which she and Jeritza appeared in the same cast. In *Die Frau ohne Schatten* (abbreviated to 'Frosch' in the correspondence between Hofmannsthal and Strauss) she sang the Dyer's Wife, and in *Walküre* Sieglinde.

Relations between the two stars were never exactly cordial, and the feuds between their two 'fan-clubs' were correspondingly bitter. When the rival gangs clashed at the stage-door there used to be pitched battles. In those days there were two stage-doors, in the Kärntner Strasse for men and in the Operngasse for women. Jeritza and Lehmann, however, managed to use two different doors on the Operngasse side.

Lotte Lehmann was by birth a Prussian. In her glorious, warm voice there was always the exultation of youth, but as the Marschallin in *Der Rosenkavalier* no one has ever portrayed more movingly the process of growing old. She infused Hofmannsthal's 'language of old Baroque Vienna' with an unmistakable Prussian timbre and so created the 'Rosenkavalier German' with which we have all been familiar from the day we first saw this wonderful opera. She came to Vienna from Hamburg, where Otto Klemperer discovered her. With her kind-hearted and eminently feminine nature she was at home as Elsa, Elisabeth, the Marschallin, Manon (as Piccaver's partner), Sieglinde, Eva, the Countess in *Figaro*, Desdemona, Korngold's Heliane, and nearly all of Puccini's heroines. But first and foremost she was a superb Fidelio. She and Piccaver were Vienna's leading lyrical partnership during their long years together; Manon and Des Grieux, Lotte and Werther . . .

Another artist who made his début at this *Ariadne* première was a tenor named Béla Környey, one of Gregor's most recent acquisitions. He was a giant of a man from Hungary with a tremendous voice, what the Viennese call 'a voice like an organ-pipe'. But he was hideous, anything but the beautiful young god that Hofmannsthal had conceived in Bacchus. The Zerbinetta of this memorable première was Selma Kurz, with whom there was trouble once again: her fee per performance was 2,800 crowns (guaranteed forty times), a full house brought her in 6,000 to 7,000 crowns. 'Zerbinetta', argued Gregor, 'sings for twenty-eight minutes. A hundred crowns a minute. Too much!'

Apart from these stars, Gregor signed up a large number of first-class singers. He was particularly adroit in luring talent away from the Volksoper: the baritone Emil Schipper (an excellent Hans Sachs and a brilliant Rigoletto), a bass-baritone named Josef von Manowarda (also a wonderful Hans Sachs and later, in Clemens Krauss's day, the first Wozzeck, and a very good one too), and a lyrical baritone named Hans Duhan, who took on two parts at the première of *Ariadne* (Harlequin and the Music-master). Later he was the first Morone in Pfitzner's *Palestrina* and he was also a brilliant Papageno. In addition he was a competent producer and even a conductor: I myself remember seeing *Gianni Schicchi* conducted by him, as well as *Tosca*, with Jan Kiepura as Cavaradossi.

Other singers engaged by Gregor who are still fresh in our memories were: Georges Baklanoff, the impressive Russian Mephisto (he remained for only a short time); the charming and vivacious Rose Ader, the soubrette Carola Jovanovic, the brilliant Mozart singer Lotte Schöne, the baritone Hermann Wiedemann (equally daemonic as Alberich or Beckmesser), the tenor Hermann Gallos (an unforgettable David), Olga Bauer-Pilecka, Bela Alten, Nicola Zec, Charlotte Dahmen, etc.

Leo Slezak was re-engaged and as well as singing superbly in *La Juive*, *Otello*, *Meistersinger* and *Le Prophète*, kept his stage partners off balance with his witty asides, but not until after he had surmounted all the most difficult hurdles of his own part. As soon as Stolzing ends the song contest in *Die Meistersinger* with 'Parnass und Paradies', he has little more to do, so at this point Slezak would move over to where Hans Sachs was standing and start telling him the latest joke about little Audrey. Some of his improvised asides would have done credit to the best cabaret compère in the business. Rosette Anday relates how once when she was singing Azucena in *Il Trovatore* and he Manrico, while the chorus were shuffling off the stage after the chorus of gypsies, Slezak came over to her and whispered: 'They just asked me to give you their kindest regards.'

Gregor's zeal in signing on good singers was matched by his alertness in keeping an eye open for new operas. He accepted works from nearly all the leading composers of the day, even if in some cases it was only too evident that their reputations would be short-lived: such cases included the Dutch composer Brandt-Buys, with an opera called *Die Schneider von Schönau* (three tailors wooing Lotte Lehmann), and Heinrich Schreker. Born in Monaco, Schrecker grew up in Vienna and worked in Berlin, a poet-composer gifted with great musical imagination, in whose life's work fairy-tale, dream and reality are happily united. *Das Spielwerk und die Prinzessin* scored a moderate success, though the action — a mixture of symbolism and metaphysics — was beyond most of the audience. At the end the minstrel gets to his feet again after dying and with his deathly cold hands strikes up a dance tune. The people drop to their knees in prayer chanting, 'Lord, we know not what to do', which was what the audience felt too. The producer Gregor also did not know what to do.

Felix Weingartner made his Vienna début as an operatic composer with *Kain und Abel* in 1914, and Jeritza appeared in Max von Schillings' *Mona Lisa* in 1915. Gregor put on d'Albert's *Die verschenkte Frau*, with which, however, he failed to repeat the success of *Tiefland*, and, with Walter conducting, the *Bergsee* by

Richard Strauss personally intervened in the highest quarters to have the ban on 'Salome' lifted at last. The première was the last in the history of the Empire.

Julius Bittner. His lake has all the Wagnerian enchantment of unleashed nature and revolutionary peasants; a most effective work by this talented Austrian lawyer.

Gregor was all for having composers conducting their own works. In the past Wagner, Brahms, Verdi, Rubinstein, Delibes and Massenet had all conducted the Imperial Opera Orchestra in their own works: so now Siegfried Wagner conducted *Banadietrich*, d'Albert *Tiefland*, Kienzl *Der Evangelimann*, Max von Schillings his *Mona Lisa*, Franz Schmidt *Notre Dame*, and Oskar Nedbal (the composer of the operetta *Polenblut*) his ballet *Der faule Hans*. Richard Strauss frequently conducted his own works.

At his second première at the Vienna Opera in 1916 Erich Wolfgang Korngold was eighteen years old. The two one-act operas, *Violanta* and *Der Ring des Poly-*

krates, which he also conducted himself in due course, were his first operas and gave astonishing evidence of his talent. *Violanta* was a brilliant part for Maria Jeritza — Korngold's music held a whole spectrum of sensual and passionate colours with which to tell Hans Müller's story of a lady of the Renaissance who plans to punish the seducer of her sister but herself falls a victim to his wiles. In *Der Ring des Polykrates* Selma Kurz and Alfred Piccaver were a delightful little petit bourgeois married couple living in 1797. Kurz was adorable in the diary scene as she sang Korngold's first great aria to celesta accompaniment: 'Kann's heut' nicht fassen, nicht verstehn . . .'

Young Korngold and his all-powerful critic father, old Korngold, were an inexhaustible source of gossip in Vienna. There was a matinée in the house of a wealthy Viennese industrialist, where young Korngold played his own works, and as usual the old man acted his rôle as 'the boss'. When it was suggested to the industrialist that, next time, he might have a Pergolesi matinée, he answered: 'All right, but only on one condition — papa Pergolesi stays at home!'

A high spot of the Gregor era was the guest performance of Diaghilev's Russian Ballet (1912 and 1913), which, for the Vienna public, threw an entirely new light on the art of dancing. It was the first time Stravinsky's *Petrouchka* was heard here, and one could admire Nijinsky and Karsavina in *Scheherazade*.

During the war Frenchmen and Italians had to be dead for their works to be played; no living foreigners were allowed. This pained Gregor very much indeed, and Verdi's first name had to be converted from Giuseppe to Josef. No *Bohème*, no *Cavalleria*, no *Pagliacci* — how could one hope to fill the box office without them?

In 1914 the summer holidays were prolonged until October, and from then until the end of 1915 there were on an average not more than four performances a week. Yet Gregor managed to put on two new works in 1915, Pfitzner's *Der arme Heinrich* and von Schillings' *Mona Lisa*. In 1916 life went back to normal, in fact as far as the Opera was concerned it was a case

99

of full speed ahead. Prices were sky-high but the house was sold out night after night. The 1916 audience consisted mainly of war profiteers to whom high prices meant nothing. 'People go to the Opera without even looking to see what's on,' as somebody put it. From the death of the Emperor Franz Joseph in November 1916 until the end of the year the Opera was closed, but in 1917 the normal routine was resumed.

During the second half of Gregor's term the curtailment of the repertoire and certain modifications in the running of the Opera reflected only too clearly the death throes of the Dual Monarchy. It was interesting to observe how the Imperial Government's attempts to patch up the differences between Vienna and the various nationalities comprising the Monarchy were reflected in the Opera's programmes. The first Vienna performance of Janáček's *Jenufa* in February 1918 was construed as a political move to woo the Czechs, as the work was nearly twenty years old and nothing much was expected of it. As things turned out, the music made a great impression, and Jeritza made a noble contribution to Janáček's first success outside his native land. Nowadays of course Janáček is accepted as one of the foremost twentieth century composers. No wonder Jeritza, who was a native of Brünn and always looked like a village beauty from Moravia, was in her element. Demonstrations were expected but never materialised. The posters announced '*Jenufa,* by All-Highest command. Special prices.' The stage-designer Püringer was actually despatched to Bohemia to study local conditions. What more could one do? Not that it made much difference. Janáček was in the audience and took his curtain-calls. The German-nationalist Press wrote: 'The only people who applauded him were his compatriots, who were present in force.' This was quite untrue; the enthusiasm was genuine and unanimous.

Political motives were also attached to the performance of *Ferdinand und Luise* by a Slav composer named Zaiczek-Blankenau in 1917. The libretto was from Schiller's *Kabale und Liebe* and Luise was sung by Jeritza. Gregor told the story later on that he had put on the wretched *Kabale und Liebe* opera, composed by the piano teacher to the Imperial family, in order to soften up the Court and get them to lift the censorship ban on *Salome*. But that succeeded only just before the end of the war — Richard Strauss had even intervened with the Cardinal Archbishop — and now the censorship regulations (again too late) were relaxed. Suddenly, the ban which had been imposed on *Salome* because of its portrayal of a Biblical figure, John the Baptist, was lifted. There were jokes about an 'Imperial and Royal *Salome*' because the première on 14 October 1918 was billed as 'By Imperial command for the benefit of the Royal Austrian War-Widows' and Orphans' Fund'. The conductor was Franz Schalk and Salome was played alternately by Jeritza and Gutheil-Schoder. The *Deutsches Volksblatt* wrote: 'Jeritza displayed all the ferocity of a beast of prey and looked ravishing in an ingenious garment that revealed her charms long before the Dance of the Seven Veils.' The bass-baritone Weidemann gave a somewhat indistinct account of Jokanaan, the Press observing that a prophet who could not make himself understood was unlikely to go far in his profession. The scenery was much admired, apart from a minor astronomical detail: the moon moved from right to left. There was some surprise at the idea of an artist who sang the part of Salome doing the Dance of the Seven Veils herself, which is the normal practice nowadays, and there was also disappointment over the lighting: 'The stage was so dark that it was impossible to distinguish the upper part of Frau Jeritza's body from the lower.' Apart from his poor singing, the prophet was faulted for appearing in a robe that looked as if it had just come from the laundry. Finally, the *Arbeiter-Zeitung* got exited about Salome reappearing in her original costume after discarding seven veils, 'presumably normal etiquette in our Imperial Opera'.

During 1918 one or two interesting concerts were given in the Opera House. Mahler's Eighth Symphony was performed in April 1918, and Richard Strauss conducted some of his orchestral works during a 'Strauss Week' (*Elektra, Der Rosenkavalier* and *Ariadne.)*

By this time Gregor was showing signs of having had enough. Money was losing its value, and the amount in the till was a matter of minor importance. The whole atmosphere was quite different from that when he had taken over. He had always been criticised for being too materialistic, and long before he resigned people had almost forgotten about him. In November 1918 the Emperor renounced all participation in state affairs and a Republic was proclaimed, but the contract Gregor had insisted upon so shrewdly in 1911 was extremely difficult to dissolve, and it was not until towards the end of November that a solution was found. Gregor departed, never to return to theatre-management, and wrote a book called *Die Oper der Welt — die Welt der Oper*, an extremely interesting account of the problems he had encountered in running an Opera House. For several years he lived in the United States and died in 1945 in Germany.

The last Intendant appointed by His Majesty the Emperor, Leopold Freiherr von Andrian-Werburg, held office from July to November 1918. One day he asked Richard Strauss, who was often in Vienna for the frequent 'Strauss Weeks', to call on him in his office and asked him: 'Would you be prepared to be appointed Director of the Vienna Opera?' Strauss said he would.

As far as the Opera was concerned, the Monarchy certainly made a graceful exit.

Richard Strauss at the Helm
(with Franz Schalk)
1919—1924

'Hab' mir's gelobt, ihn lieb zu haben'
(From 'Der Rosenkavalier')

I think I owe it to my readers to state here and now that there can be nobody in the world who is a greater admirer of Richard Strauss than I am. In my young days he was my God, and for me and my friends everything he did was perfect. Our admiration was unconditional and we allowed no criticism. If anyone were to ask me when the Richard Strauss 'era' in the Vienna Opera was, I should reply: 'Always.' There were from time to time changes in the actual technical designation of Strauss's association with the Vienna Opera — his first appearance was as a guest conductor, and from the first of January 1920 until 1924 he was co-Director with Franz Schalk; after 1924 Schalk was in sole charge, but we were always waiting impatiently for Strauss and wondering when he would be coming back, and then one day he did come back as a guest conductor during Schalk's term. But all these subtle distinctions left us cold; for us, the wonderful Richard Strauss era lasted well on into Clemens Krauss's term of office.

The last *Generalintendant* under the Monarchy, Leopold Freiherr von Andrian-Werburg, a close friend of Hofmannsthal's and himself an amateur writer, had already offered Strauss the post of Director, and Strauss now submitted a masterly plan for a complete overhaul (on the artistic side) of the Vienna Opera. The entire repertoire was to be revised and expanded and was to range from Baroque opera to the end of the nineteenth century, irrespective of nationality. The plan was obviously going to cost a great deal of money, but Strauss had made a profound impression on Baron Andrian, and the two men arrived at an agreement by which Strauss was morally (and in fact legally) 99 per cent under contract to the Vienna Opera.

On the tenth of November 1918, the last day of the Monarchy, Franz Schalk was appointed Director, but even then Andrian had every intention of finding a place alongside him for Strauss too. As yet there was no friction between Strauss and Schalk, and in his plan Strauss had explicitly stated that he would be glad to work with Schalk. Strauss suggested leaving Schalk as Director and putting Roller in charge of scenery.

He also let it be known that he had nothing against Gregor's remaining as Administrative Director.

Indeed, Strauss seems to have had a finger in a good many Viennese pies at that time. He suggested entrusting the running of the Burgtheater to Max Reinhardt, and a year or two later he proposed taking the Volksoper away from his arch-enemy Felix von Weingartner and running it as a subsidised appendage of the State Opera for trying out new works and new talent; very much the same sort of policy, in fact, as is being pursued by the Volksoper's present Director, Albert Moser.

Now that the Dual Monarchy had disintegrated, the double-headed eagle and the designation '*k. k.*' (Imperial and Royal) disappeared from the Opera's posters, and the Court Opera itself was thereafter to be known as the 'Vienna State Opera'. The question therefore arose whether the Republic would confirm or annul the agreement reached between Strauss and Baron Andrian. In the event, the new state authorities stated unequivocally that they wanted Strauss, and the agreement was officially approved on the first of March 1919.

There followed one of the most lamentable and grotesque episodes in Vienna's history. After showing its nobler side in appointing a composer of world stature as Director of the Opera at one of the darkest periods in Austria's history, Vienna then proceeded to show her other face and act with a meanness, now charmingly veiled, now openly unveiled, for which she has been notorious from time immemorial. 'The Viennese admire the talents of a dead man; they forgive the living their talents only if they starve,' says Richard Specht.

The ink was hardly dry on the state's official appointment of Strauss before almost the entire staff of the Opera delivered an ultimatum to the authorities demanding the withdrawal of Strauss, adding that the ultimatum had been approved at a plenary-meeting of 800 members of the State Opera. It later transpired that this meeting never took place at all. What actually happened was, if possible, even more grotesque. Four organised bodies — the singers, the ballet, the orchestra and the chorus — held separate meetings. Those attending were shown by 'delegates' of these bodies into separate rooms, and each group in turn was told that the other three groups had already voted in favour of the ultimatum and had passed an anti-Strauss 'resolution'; all that remained was for them to support it. In other words, all four groups were tricked into lodging a protest against the appointment of the new Director.

The attack on Strauss was mounted on three fronts. First, was it not incorrect and wrong for the Republic to start by confirming an appointment made under the Monarchy? Second, the 'delegates' were incensed by the colossal salary being offered to Strauss, 80,000 crowns for seven months as Director, plus 1,200 crowns a night for conducting — 'an impoverished country like the new Austria cannot afford the luxury of such an expensive genius' was the attitude. It later transpired that a number of other officials at the State Opera were being paid exactly the same amount, and even the conductor Hugo Reichenberger, who was by no stretch of the imagination a leading light, was being paid two-thirds of Strauss's salary. In Germany at this time Richard Strauss was earning incomparably more. However, in the end, thank goodness, the anti-Strauss campaign fizzled out, and the agreement was confirmed and adhered to. Strauss was required to be at Vienna's disposal for five consecutive months a year and to conduct forty performances a year for a salary of 60,000 crowns.

The third front in the assault on Strauss was stage-managed by Felix von Weingartner, who hated the idea of Strauss at the Opera worse than the devil. He persuaded the Vienna Philharmonic Orchestra that Strauss was intending to sabotage their subscription concerts by putting on concerts at the Opera. From what we know today, there was not a word of truth in the allegation. Equally untrue was the assertion that Strauss intended to run the Berlin and Vienna Operas at the same time, much to the disadvantage of Vienna. The truth is that after Germany's collapse in 1918,

The first and only world première of a Richard Strauss opera in Vienna.

Operntheater

Freitag den 10. Oktober 1919

Bei aufgehobenem Jahres-, Saison- und Stammsitzabonnement

Für das Pensions-Institut des Operntheaters

Bei erhöhten Preisen

Zum ersten Male:

Die Frau ohne Schatten

Oper in drei Akten von Hugo Hofmannsthal — Musik von Richard Strauß

Spielleitung: Hr. Breuer — Musikalische Leitung: Hr. Schalk

Der Kaiser	Hr. Oestvig
Die Kaiserin	Fr. Jeritza
Die Amme	Fr. Weidt
Geisterbote	Hr. Manowarda
Die Erscheinung eines Jünglings	Frl. Blei
Die Stimme des Falken	Frl. Mihacsek
Barak, der Färber	Hr. Mayr
Sein Weib	Frl. Lehmann
Der Einäugige	
Der Einarmige } des Färbers Brüder	Hr. Betetto
Der Bucklige	Hr. Arnold

Kaiserliche Diener, fremde Kinder, dienende Geister, die Stimmen der Wächter, Geisterstimmen

Entwürfe: Alfred Roller

Schauplätze der Handlung: I. Aufzug: Auf einer Terrasse über den kaiserlichen Gärten. — Färberhaus. — II. Aufzug: Färberhaus. — Wald vor dem Pavillon des Falkners. — Färberhaus. — Schlafgemach der Kaiserin. — III. Aufzug: Unterirdischer Kerker. — Geistertempel: Eingang. — Geistertempel: Inneres. — Landschaft im Geisterreich.

Das Textbuch ist zum Preise von 3 Kronen, "Die Blätter des Operntheaters" zum Preise von 3 Kronen an der Kassa erhältlich.

Nach dem zweiten Akt eine größere Pause

Der Beginn der Vorstellung sowie jedes Aktes wird durch ein Glockenzeichen bekanntgegeben

Kassen-Eröffnung vor ½5 Uhr   Anfang 5 Uhr   Ende 9 Uhr

Der Kartenverkauf findet heute statt für obige Vorstellung und für:

Samstag den 11. Die Frau ohne Schatten. Bei aufgehobenem Saison-Abonnement. Zu erhöhten Preisen. Für das Pensions-Institut des Operntheaters.
Sonntag den 12. Violetta (La Traviata) Für das Pensions-Institut des Operntheaters. Zu erhöhten Preisen (Anfang 6½ Uhr)

Weiterer Spielplan

Montag den 13. Die Königin von Saba (Anfang 5 Uhr)
Dienstag den 14. Die Frau ohne Schatten. Zu erhöhten Preisen. Für das Pensions-Institut des Operntheaters (Anfang 5 Uhr)

Preis 50 Heller

Strauss acceded to the Berlin Opera's request that he should take it over for the time being, but only for the time being and without any written contract, because he was already counting on the Vienna appointment. He had been a guest conductor of the Berlin Opera for over twenty years and he could not bring himself to leave it in the lurch in its hour of need.

There were of course a few members of the State Opera who had no part in the egregious 'resolution'. The signatures of, for instance, Maria Jeritza, Selma Kurz and Franz Schalk, who at that time were all in favour of Strauss's appointment, were conspicuous by their absence. One amusing and very human aftermath

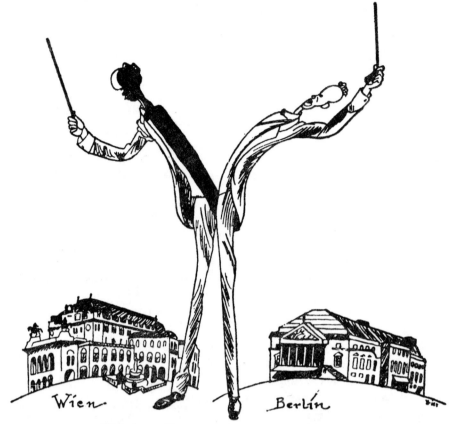

Geteilter Strauß ist — doppelte Freude.

*During the course of intrigues in 1919, intended
to prevent Richard Strauss from becoming
Director of the Vienna Opera, a rumour went
round that Strauss wanted to run the Vienna and
Berlin opera houses simultaneously.*

of the whole affair was that many artists who had
been tricked into supporting the 'resolution' got in
touch with the Press after it was all over: 'Yes, I
admit I was there, but I never meant to support
anything, it just slipped out, I was coerced.' And in
May 1919 the well-known musicologist Richard Specht,
who was an ardent admirer of both Johann and
Richard Strauss, gave a lecture in the Vienna Opera
on the occasion of its fiftieth birthday, and after
describing the revolt against Richard Strauss, ended
with the words: 'Anyway, if there were any more
Strausses about we should bring them all to Vienna!'

All this time Strauss was not in Vienna but at his
villa in Garmisch; and it was to Garmisch that a telegram was sent by personages such as Arthur Schnitzler, Stefan Zweig, Hugo von Hofmannsthal, George
Szell, Josef Marx, Julius Bittner, Alfred Roller and
others — the intellectual cream of Vienna, urging
Strauss to ignore the incivility of the 'resolution' and

come at once to Vienna. So the operetta revolution
dwindled down and he came, and by doing so gave
Vienna's cultural morale a much-needed boost. People
were sure that with such an experienced and proverbially
successful man of the theatre at the helm things couldn't
possibly go wrong. All this took place in the spring of
1919, against a background of industrial unrest, com-
munist risings and hunger strikes, not to mention the
wildest rumours about plans to close both the State
Theatres and hand them over to private management, to
auction both the State Museums, to tear up the asphalt
of the Ringstrasse and plough up the whole street, to
convert the Burgtheater into a cinema, etc.

Such was the atmosphere in which Richard Strauss
was confirmed as Schalk's co-Director in December 1919.
But even before then, in May 1919, he conducted several
performances during the Opera's fiftieth anniversary
celebrations: *Tristan, Die Zauberflöte, Der Rosenkavalier,
Ariadne* and *Fidelio*. During this festival, which was the

big social and artistic occasion of the year, the State Opera paraded its entire repertoire. Among the composers who came to Vienna to conduct their own operas were Franz Schmidt *(Notre Dame),* Wilhelm Kienzl *(Der Evangelimann),* and Korngold (his one-act operas). But the brunt of the Festival — Mozart, Beethoven and Wagner — was borne by Franz Schalk.

The failure to define legally the two Directors' exact terms of reference was to have fateful consequences in a year or two. Schalk's contract described him as 'Head of the Opera House', whereas Richard Strauss, who appeared on the scene a little later, was designated as 'artistic supervisor'. This vagueness was to lead to a good deal of friction later on, because Strauss was very often away, and it became a question of who was responsible during his absence. There was nothing in the co-Directors' contracts to provide for such a contingency. Strauss, as we have seen, was committed to Vienna for five consecutive months a year, *i. e.,* from the fifteenth of December to the fifteenth of May every year. For the rest of the year Schalk was in charge *de facto,* but not *de jure.* Later, when tension mounted between the two co-Directors, Strauss launched a violent attack on what was, on the whole, the obvious arrangement, much to Schalk's annoyance. Schalk was beginning to realise that he was in fact less than half a co-Director, though he had to shoulder the full responsibility. Although he and Strauss were *de jure* of equal rank, in actual fact whenever an important decision had to be taken people often used to say: 'Why go to the boss's mate, why not go straight to the boss?' The boss, of course, being Strauss.

But to start with, everything went smoothly. Those were wonderful days, even if in after years it was often said that Strauss had only accepted the post of Director so as to get his own works performed as often as possible. To be quite honest one must admit, *post festum,* that there was a good deal of truth in the allegation that 'Richard Strauss's programme was Richard Strauss'. But that's just what we liked.

The Viennese, always glad of something to grumble about, complained that one Strauss theatre was enough (the Johann Strauss Theatre in the Favoritenstrasse, later the Scala, and now demolished); why should they have to put up with a 'Richard Strauss Theatre' at the Opera as well?

Strauss was not one to take criticism of this kind lying down. Before taking over, he stated that if there was any suspicion that he was plugging his own works he was perfectly prepared to withdraw the première of *Die Frau ohne Schatten,* which had been put down for October 1919. This particular première did not in fact fall within his official period as Director.

Apart from the première of *Die Frau ohne Schatten,* the first year after the First World War saw another notable first performance at the State Opera; Pfitzner's *Palestrina* was put on in March (it was first performed in Munich under Bruno Walter). Erik Schmedes was Palestrina ('Hans Sachs in the tenor clef', as the rôle was then described), and the work was an immediate success. The general verdict was that just as J. S. Bach had written a High Mass, so Pfitzner had written a High Opera. *Palestrina* was loved by a large group of connoisseurs who admired Pfitzner's original music and his text.

Both *Palestrina* and *Die Frau ohne Schatten* were played out against a background of hunger, unemployment, lack of fuel for heating, and the most daunting difficulties in keeping the Opera on its feet. Every performance was dogged by the virtual impossibility of procuring the necessary material. *Die Frau ohne Schatten* was the first and last time a Strauss opera had its world première in Vienna, The conductor was Franz Schalk, the scenery was by Alfred Roller, and the producer was Hans Breuer, a character-tenor who had been taken on by Mahler. He was best known as Mime in *Siegfried,* his favourite opera. He always regretted that he had never been able to sing the part of Siegfried, so it was perhaps to console himself that he named his eldest son Siegfried. The son eventually became one of Vienna's leading film actors. Breuer did not succeed in solving the biggest staging problem in *Die Frau ohne Schatten.* How does one lose or get a shadow on the stage? (Admission was ten times the price of Caruso's last guest performance.)

Die Frau ohne Schatten led to the formation in Vienna

of an informal but fanatically enthusiastic 'fan club'. Though *Die Frau ohne Schatten* was never such a great favourite as *Der Rosenkavalier* or *Ariadne,* it was warmly acclaimed by Strauss's admirers. For us young people it was the most important work Strauss had written up till then, a work that showed his inspiration at its zenith. A good many people found Hofmannsthal's libretto almost if not quite beyond them, though personally I must say I had no difficulty in grasping it from the very first. What I could not grasp were the introductory notes we were offered, and it was this experience that, later on, prompted me to write my own 'opera guides' for television.

A brilliant cast was assembled around the central figure of Jeritza as the Empress, the transformation from a white gazelle that after purification becomes a human being. Lotte Lehmann gave a superb performance as the Dyer's Wife, and as the Dyer Barak, her husband, Richard Mayr was as splendid as ever.

In the part of the Emperor, Vienna welcomed for the first time a Scandinavian tenor named Karl Aagard-Oestvig who later became a great popular favourite. He was exceptionally good-looking and had as effective a stage presence as his countrymen Set Svanholm and Helge Roswaenge in later years. He was an excellent Wagner tenor, whose view of Wagner was first and foremost a lyrical one, which was why he was such a brilliant Lohengrin. The Nurse was Lucy Weidt, who took over many Wagner parts after Anna Mildenburg's departure. Intellectually of course she was not a patch on Mildenburg, and whenever she indulged in her stereotyped gesture of raising both arms above her head, we used to say to each other: 'There she goes again, hanging out the washing!'

We Strauss enthusiasts were absolutely convinced that *Die Frau ohne Schatten* would come into its own one day, and we were delighted to find our conviction substantiated when in the autumn of 1966, staged by Nathaniel Merrill, it proved a real 'smash-hit' at the opening of the New Metropolitan Opera in New York, and the first thing New York fans used to say to each other was: 'Have you seen the "Frau"?'

But to return to Strauss and December 1919, when he officially took up his appointment. He made his début as an active Director by conducting *Lohengrin* on the first of January 1920 with Jeritza as Elsa and Oestvig as Lohengrin. By a curious coincidence it was also *Lohengrin* with which Mahler had made his active début in 1897, and it was to be *Lohengrin* with which Franz Schalk introduced himself later on. The performance was uncut — including Lohengrin's aria after the grail narrative.

During his term of office Strauss frequently conducted repertoire as well as gala performances. He was an adept at taking over other people's productions with the minimum of fuss. 'We know this bit, gentlemen,' he used to say, 'we understand all that.' — Just a few short rehearsals, and everything went perfectly. He conducted a lot of Mozart and Wagner, a famous performance of *Der Freischütz* with Michael Bohnen as Kaspar, *Hänsel und Gretel, Der Barbier von Bagdad,* and *Carmen* (the first time Vienna had ever seen a blonde Carmen — Jeritza!). In short, Strauss had as much time for routine, everyday performances as he had for brilliant, gala occasions.

At this point, if things are to be seen in their proper historical perspective, it might be well to make a brief excursion into the realms of social history. Shortly before the end of the war there had begun to emerge the kind of audience that Gregor had enjoyed exploiting, the *nouveaux-riches* and war-profiteers (the Viennese call them *Schieber,* smooth operators) who could afford to pay through the nose for the best seats while the populace was half-starving. The stabilisation of the Austrian currency was followed by a new crisis: the profiteers had made off, the middle-classes had lost all their savings in the War Loan, and even the better-off classes thought twice before reaching down into their pockets. The result: rows upon rows of empty seats at the State Theatres. To counter this slump in the theatre world, and to bring a visit to the theatre within the reach of those who were finding it beyond their means, various cultural organisations were formed which from the mid-1920s onwards entirely changed the constitution of the average audience. I can well remember how at a performance of, say, *Ariadne* with Strauss conducting we could be standing

jammed like sardines, while between us and the stage yawned a half-empty auditorium. The new organisations set up by the political parties, the Ministry of Education and the Vienna Municipality soon changed all that. The days when the box-office ruled the roost were over. It was no longer possible to tell whether a new production was successful or a flop just by counting the audience. In our young days we often used to say: 'There mustn't be a full house for *Elektra;* the real enthusiasts only half fill it.' In those days there was no such thing as a 'casual' audience, going to the opera on the 'fourth Tuesday in the month'.

To understand what the Strauss era meant, one must have some idea of the sort of man Strauss was. He was a totally different person from Gustav Mahler. Mahler was a dervish, a priest, a fanatic, whose gaze was permanently fixed on the life beyond, whereas Strauss had his feet firmly in this world. He was the last great composer who wrote simply to give pleasure. There was his habit, for instance, of sitting down at the piano and regaling close friends who came to see him at Garmisch with extracts from his most recent work: after a while he would break off and with a quizzical look at the company ask them what they thought. 'That's real music, isn't it? Easy to listen to.'

Strauss was so much a creature of this world that we had the feeling that when Salome, Ariadne, or Elektra died, they would merely be transported to an extension of this world and not to the next. His music for the theatre is the loveliest this century has produced. He liked listening to it himself, and he was happy if other people enjoyed it too.

His term of office as Director was an accurate reflection of his personal character, and that is saying a good deal. It may be that his period in office lacked the consistency and dedication of the Mahler era, and he certainly had no intention of offering a complete new series of the whole gamut of German opera: he simply put on the operas he enjoyed most, and as he enjoyed his own operas very much, he put them on very often (not that any of his successors have been able to afford to put them on less often).

I find it impossible to describe what we young people felt as Strauss made his way to the podium. This is the man, we thought to ourselves, who wrote *Elektra.* As a conductor he made an indelible impression on us. His gestures were minimal and there was no theatricality of any kind, and this was perhaps why he was such a fascinating conductor to watch. By the late 1920s, of which I have a particularly vivid recollection, his hair had gone white. He was still tall and slim but had a slight stoop as he stood there like a *grand seigneur*. The players under him used to relate how he had only to bend his knees for a sort of electric charge to run through the entire orchestra. Sometimes he would allow himself a slight jerk of the elbow; now and again he would half rise from his seat; sometimes his mouth was half open, as though he were asleep. For the most part, he conducted with a glance of the eyes and with the magic of his personality; with the simple fact that he was Richard Strauss, which alone was enough to spur the forces under his command to scale the heights of musical expression. I can still recall nuances in *Elektra* that only he could bring out. Maybe they were improvised on the spur of the moment; at all events, it was impossible to define exactly how he got the results he did.

He was no stickler for accuracy, far less so than any other composer about whom we have detailed knowledge. All he wanted was that his work should come to life, here and now, in the glamour of an evening at the theatre, and any deviation from the score that enhanced the brilliance of the occasion was not only tolerated but welcomed. It has been said that when Strauss was rehearsing a work of his in which Jeritza was singing, she used to compose as she went along, sometimes for pages on end, and when the others tried to put her right Strauss used to stop them: 'No, leave her alone, she knows what she's doing.' One could quote hundreds of observations of this kind at rehearsals of his own works, for instance: 'If you can't hit that note, sing another. Whatever's easiest, it doesn't matter.'

Those were the days before the present insistence on accuracy, before the advent of the gramophone record exerted its deadening effect on opera houses. In those days there was no *eminence grise* subjecting works and their interpretation to remorseless scrutiny, no recording supervisor (armed with a score) interrupting the proceedings every two minutes because of some minute inaccuracy that neither the interpreter nor the audience nor even the composer would ever have noticed.

During the Strauss-Schalk era, the cessation of hostilities was reflected in the programmes as clearly as the war had been in the last days of Gregor's administration. As an 'enemy alien' Puccini had been banned for four years; now he was back again, and Vienna positively wallowed in Puccini. The first post-war Puccini première was of the three one-act operas *Il Tabarro, Suor Angelica* and *Gianni Schicchi* in October 1920. The composer made a personal appearance and was full of praise for the performance. In *Il Tabarro*, Alfred Piccaver was joined by Jeritza, one of the very few occasions on which she deputised for Lotte Lehmann, taking over the part of Georgette at very short notice. Lehmann's performance as Angelica was deeply moving, all the more so as word had got round in Vienna that Puccini's own sister Romilda had become a nun and that he once played the opera over on the piano for the assembled nuns in her convent. In 1923, a year before his death, Puccini paid another long visit to Vienna and there were some glorious performances of his works, notably *Manon Lescaut* with Jeritza and Piccaver, which took thirty years to make its way to the Vienna Opera. There were of course the inevitable comparisons with Massenet's *Manon*, which had been a popular favourite in Vienna for many years and was still in the repertoire. On the whole Puccini's opera stood the test quite well, but it has never really established itself in Vienna.

Alfred Piccaver was now at the zenith of his career and was far and away the State Opera's most popular tenor. To his adoring public he was 'Pikki', but his closest friends called him 'Teddy'. He was a most extraordinary person, with a voice like satin that could manage anything, no matter how high, but his top notes were never really brilliant. He could get up to top C with effortless ease, but he never aspired to membership of the top-C club. His real forte was his melting middle register with a slight nasal tinge, quite natural and unforced. When he was singing one felt as if one were being stroked. He was notorious for the number of times he cancelled a performance, sometimes at very short notice, and some wag once observed 'Piccaver has already arranged all his indispositions a year ahead'. His readiness to cancel a performance was really due to his extreme conscientiousness, a morbid terror of marring his reputation with his public.

An opera performance in 1920. Strauss is conducting, Slezak and Jeritza are singing, the leaders of the orchestra are Professor Arnold Rosé and Franz Mairecker. In the house, the audience is sitting, standing, lounging, talking, necking, playing cards, guzzling and sozzling: the era of the black marketeers. (Caricature by Theo Zasche.)

There were stories of how every morning in his apartment in the Brahmsplatz he would sit down at the piano and start singing, and if a single note in his middle register was not 100 per cent to his satisfaction he would immediately ask his wife Ria to cancel for that night.

His manner of singing was as remarkable as his singing itself. Like Caruso, he very often sang with his eyes shut (like Karajan conducting). His pronunciation was a trifle wayward too, especially his vowels. I have also been told that he used diphthongs for vocalising, whereas most singers vocalise, *i. e.*, sing scales, arpeggios, etc., on ordinary vowels like A, E, or O. Piccaver, English by

birth und brought up in America, used English diphthongs for his scales, preferably the last syllable of the word father-in-law-aw-aw. Hence his peculiarly nasal 'diphthong' pronunciation.

Richard Strauss knew every opera. When a singer had chosen whatever aria it might be for an audition, Strauss sat down at the piano and accompanied him. He did this for the buffo and character tenor William Wernigk, who sang 'Selig sind, die Verfolgung leiden' at his audition. (How magnificent he was as Wenzel in *The Bartered Bride!*)

Unless there were some special reason for holding auditions on the stage, they took place in the first-floor Grosse Salon of the Opera House, where the Gobelin Saal is now, on the corner of the Ringstrasse and the Kärntner Strasse, just above where the arcade begins. This room was the nerve-centre of the Opera. It had a piano and a table big enough for a peace conference, with a wine-coloured tablecloth and wine-coloured chairs. It was used for minor meetings and rehearsals as well as for auditions. The next time you stroll through the Gobelin Saal during the interval, besides thinking of the next act you are looking forward to (or of the sandwiches at the buffet), you might like to think of Jauner, Jahn, Mahler, Strauss, Schalk and Weingartner running the Opera from this very room.

Running an unprejudiced eye over the novelties introduced by the Strauss-Schalk regime, one cannot help being amazed at the number of living composers who managed to get a hearing besides Strauss. Apart from Puccini and Korngold there were Schreker, Bittner and Schmidt and many other lesser composers. In one of his letters Strauss maintained that in his view a composer should not be admitted to the Vienna Opera until he had proved himself elsewhere: the Vienna Opera was no place for experiments. But he was prepared to give the contemporary Austrian composers a hearing even if they had had no successes outside Vienna or Austria to point to. (Strauss repeatedly — but without success — tried to obtain additional subsidies, from the Vienna Municipal Council for instance, for particular productions.)

After his resignation Strauss maintained that he had played everything but had been unable to prevent the failure of numerous contemporary operas. He would, he said, even have 'played Schoenberg and Křenek', because he wasn't obliged to like everything he played. Strauss let it be known later on that Schalk had been opposed to all modern premières, 'except for Korngold' he added spitefully . . .

In the second year of the Strauss-Schalk administration Franz Schreker introduced himself with *Die Gezeichneten*, a lavish, tuneful but somewhat too richly scored opera of Renaissance times. The protagonists are a cripple and a woman artist with a heart ailment who, like Isolde, meets her 'Liebestod'; in other words, she dies at the height of her love. Schreker followed this up in 1922 with *Der Schatzgräber*, a medieval affair containing the one melody — Alice's cradlesong — on which his tenuous reputation rested for so long.

By far the most successful contemporary opera during this period was Korngold's *Die tote Stadt* in 1921. The leading rôles were sung by Jeritza and Aargard-Oestvig, the Emperor in *Die Frau ohne Schatten*. The opera afforded Jeritza ample scope for displaying the full range of her phenomenal genius: she had two completely different parts to play, the happy-go-lucky dancer Marietta and the serious-minded Marie, who had died a short time before and looked exactly like her. There was an unfor-

That evening, Maria Jeritza made 'Glück, das mir verblieb' into the last hit song in German opera.

Staatsoper

Montag den 10. Jänner 1921

Bei aufgehobenem Jahres- und Stammsitz-Abonnement

Zu besonderen Preisen

Zum ersten Male

Die tote Stadt

Oper in drei Bildern, frei nach G. Rodenbachs Schauspiel „Das Trugbild" von Paul Schott — Musik von **Erich Wolfgang Korngold**

Inszenierung: Hr. Wymetal   Musikalische Leitung: Hr. Schalk

Paul	Hr. Oestvig
Marietta, Tänzerin	} Fr. Jeritza
Die Erscheinung Mariens, Pauls verstorbener Gattin	
Frank, Pauls Freund	Hr. Wiedmann
Brigitta, bei Paul	Fr. Kittel
Juliette, Tänzerin	Frl. Rajdl
Lucienne, Tänzerin	Fr. Hussa
Gaston, Tänzer in Mariettas Truppe	Hr. Nemeth
Victorin, der Regisseur	Hr. Maikl
Fritz, der Pierrot	Hr. Mayr
Graf Albert	Hr. Gallos

Beginnen, die Erscheinung der Prozession, Tänzer und Tänzerinnen
Spielt in Brügge, Ende des 19. Jahrhunderts; die Vorgänge der Vision (2. und zum Teil 3. Bild) sind mehrere Wochen später nach jenen des 1. Bildes zu denken

Die dekorative Ausstattung ist im Atelier Kautsky hergestellt

Die modernen Toiletten und Anzüge wurden im Atelier der Firma Heinrich Grünbaum hergestellt

Der im Orchester zur Verwendung gelangende Flügel ist von der Firma Bösendorfer beigestellt

Die „Blätter des Operntheaters", Heft 9, Sonderheft „Die tote Stadt", sowie Textbücher zum Original-preise sind an der Kasse erhältlich

Das offizielle Programm nur bei den Billeteuren erhältlich

Nach jedem Bild eine größere Pause

Der Beginn der Vorstellung sowie jedes Aktes wird durch ein Glockenzeichen bekanntgegeben.

Kassen-Eröffnung vor 6 Uhr   Anfang 6½ Uhr   Ende 10 Uhr

gettable moment in the first act when Jeritza stepped out of a picture frame and modulated her voice, which up till then had had all Marietta's youthful radiance, to the muffled, hollow timbre of a voice from another world. Another unforgettable scene was when Marietta gave vent to her jealousy of the portrait by going into a wild dance and attacking it with a switch of the dead woman's hair!

There was also another reason for the success of *Die tote Stadt*. Every really successful opera has at least one 'hit-tune' in it, a tune that accompanies you home after the theatre, turns up again at breakfast time and keeps running through your head the whole morning at the office, one of those tunes that make the world seem a better place, that you keep humming or whistling. The history of the opera 'hit-tune' in German music dates from Gluck's *Orfeo ed Euridice* ('Che faro') up to Korngold's *Die tote Stadt*. Today Korngold's tune is still sung all over the world, and no melody from a German opera has since achieved anything like its popularity.

Even Richard Strauss himself sometimes pulled strings a bit alongside Erich Wolfgang and his father, who, as a critic, was anything but an ally: 'Now in December, Erich my dear, we *might* put on *Violanta* again, *if* your father would kindly ...'

The father's support did his son more harm than good, but Erich knew when to exploit the situation. In 1921 Maria Jeritza sang *Die tote Stadt* (*The Dead City*) at the 'Met' with a few cuts, and she wanted to make the same cuts in Vienna. Erich was in despair and whispered in the goddess's ear: 'Exactly these three pages are the ones my father likes so much!' Maria kept the cuts nevertheless ...

The next première after *Die tote Stadt* was Julius Bittner's *Die Kohlhaymerin*. The piece was set in the old Austrian Empire and contained a number of waltzes that made it sound rather like an operetta or even *Der Rosenkavalier*, so much so that Franz Schalk, never at a loss for a joke with a sting in it, told Bittner that his opera ought really to be called *Die tote Vorstadt* (*The Dead Suburb*). Like Korngold, Bittner managed to get a second opera accepted, *Das Rosengärtlein*, based on legends about the dreaded open-air prison at Aggstein Castle on the Danube.

Another opera that was given its first performance during the Strauss-Schalk regime was Franz Schmidt's *Fredigundis* based on a novel by Felix Dahn. It provided the female lead with yet another opportunity of showing what she could do as a dancer, a talent that since *Salome* and *Elektra* seemed by now to have become virtually *de rigeur* in the operatic world. The action is set in Merovingian times and tells of a maiden named Fredigundis who becomes a queen by murdering her way through the whole piece, not only men but even robins (much to the disgust of nature-lovers). During her wild dance round her lover's coffin her flaming-red hair turns snow-white. The rôle was a great personal success for Wanda Achsel-Clemens, who was later an excellent Composer in *Ariadne* and an extremely vivacious Rosalinde in a Salzburg Festival *Fledermaus*.

The première was conducted by Clemens Krauss, whom Richard Strauss summoned to Vienna from Graz for a two year term as *Kapellmeister*. He was an outstandingly talented conductor, especially of Strauss, and more will be heard of him when we come to the year 1929. For the present, after his two years as *Kapellmeister* he was appointed to take charge of the Opera House in Frankfurt. Before the première of *Fredigundis*, Strauss said to Franz Schmidt: 'It's very good, but out of so much music I could make four operas.'

There were many stories about Strauss's relationship with other composers. Strauss ran into Hans Pfitzner one day in a passage in the Opera House and they started talking, the tall and typically easy-going Bavarian and the small, somewhat fidgety and querulous Pfitzner. Pfitzner obviously regarded himself as the profounder composer of the two, because he suddenly said: 'You mustn't forget, my good Strauss, that I spent ten years over *Palestrina* alone.' After Pfitzner had departed Strauss turned to a couple of friends standing by and said in his broadest Bavarian: 'If the poor fellow finds it so difficult to compose, why does he do it?'

Among other contemporary operas selected by Strauss and Schalk were Alexander von Zemlinsky's *Der Zwerg* and two one-acters by Felix von Weingartner, *Meister Andrea* and *Die Dorfschule*. The fact that Weingartner had stirred up such anti-Strauss agitation when Strauss was appointed Director did not deter the latter from furthering Weingartner, just as he would any other composer.

There is no denying, however, that the backbone of Strauss's programme was Strauss. 'How nice of Director Strauss to play Strauss so often,' was the usual refrain in the Press. 'So what?' retorted we young people. And the fact remains that during his whole time as a Director there was not one world première of a Strauss opera. *Die Frau ohne Schatten* made its, or her, appearance in October 1919, *i. e.* two months before Strauss officially took over, and the two other Strauss premières during his term with Schalk were both ballets: *Josephslegende* and *Schlagobers*.

Yet although his duties at the Opera left him less time for composition than he would have liked, nearly the whole of his new opera *Intermezzo* was written in Vienna. But it is a small-scale work of almost chamber-music proportions, and he was not keen on launching it in the Vienna Opera House, which he was afraid would be too big for it, not intimate enough. He thought of the Theater an der Wien, but nothing came of these plans.

The ballet *Josephslegende* was based on a book by Hofmannsthal and Count Harry Kessler and was produced by the new ballet-master Heinrich Kröller. (The world première was in Paris in 1914, under Diaghilev.) The scenery for this baroque version of the Old Testament episode of Joseph and Potiphar was to be in the style of Veronese. It was a very expensive production, and the costume of the archangel who appears near the end and conducts the valiant Joseph to Heaven was said to have cost about a million crowns. A sensational amount even in the year 1922 when the inflation was at its peak, when the price of food was soaring to astronomical heights and a stamp for a letter abroad cost 5,000 crowns.

The attitude of the Press towards this 'danced Scripture lesson' was sceptical. It was an original (and successful) idea to have the part of Potiphar's wife not danced but acted by Marie Gutheil-Schoder. Without singing a note she gave a portrayal of the character's cupidity and lasciviousness which is said to have been tremendously impressive. *Josephslegende* was billed with one of Strauss's earliest works, *Feuersnot*. 'These dancers could even turn the head of St. Francis,' said Giacomo Puccini after one of the performances of the Vienna *Josephslegende*.

In May 1924, the year of the first 'Opera Redoute' since 1894, of Strauss's sixtieth birthday and of the first signs that differences between the two co-Directors were blowing up, the ballet *Schlagobers* was given its first performance during a gala 'Strauss Week'. The cast included all the tastiest delicacies of a Viennese confectioner: plum fairies and gingerbread figures were dancing on the stage, Marzipan with Prince Coffee (Hedy Pfundmayr) and Prince Cocoa, Mademoiselle Chartreuse (Adele Krausenecker) and Princess Praline (Gusti Pichler), Tea Blossom (Tilly Losch), Don Sugarro (Willy Fränzl) and of course such Viennese specialities as 'Schmalznudeln', various forms of 'Gugelhupf', and a 'Baumkuchen'. One or two frivolous observers maintained that the ballet had been written only because none of the delicious confections it featured were to be had in the immediate post-war years. Cost of scenery and costumes: 5,000 million crowns ...

It was written as a present for Strauss's son Franz, whom he adored. Another fine portrait of Franz is the small boy in *Intermezzo*. Shortly before the première, Dr. Franz Strauss had married Alice Grab, whereupon the word immediately went round Vienna that Strauss had now buried ('zu Grab getragen') his anti-Semitism in the Schottenkirche.

In this same year (1924), the great Wagner tenor Erik Schmedes said farewell to the stage in a performance of *Der Evangelimann*. He had been a faithful servant of the Vienna Opera ever since he was first engaged by Mahler. When such a popular favourite says farewell to his adoring public it is a painful occasion for both. Schmedes's departure meant that Slezak now had no rival at the State Opera, just at the very time when his voice was at its best, so that he had no difficulty in appropriating the applause that had once been lavished on Schmedes.

There can hardly ever have been a tenor with such a brilliant fortissimo and such an infinitely delicate

This was our view of the Opera in our young days, listening to 'O schöne Jugendtage' or 'Glück, das mir verblieb', or 'Che farò...' or seeing Valhalla go up in flames.

The Opera House after the air-raid on 12 March 1945.

The Theater an der Wien in 1945: the people on the roof are the fire-watchers. This historic theatre, in which *Fidelio*, *Die Fledermaus* and *The Merry Widow* were heard for the first time, had been closed and without a manager since 1938 and was in grave danger of dilapidation. During the war it had been used as an army clothing depot. In 1945 it shared with the Volksoper the privilege of being the provisional home of the Vienna State Opera.

'O Gott! O welch ein Augenblick!
O unaussprechlich süsses Glück!
Gerecht, o Gott! ist dein Gericht,
Du prüfest, du verlässt uns nicht.'

On 6 October 1945 the Vienna Opera gave its first performance in its new home, the Theater an der Wien: *Fidelio*, conducted by Joseph Krips. Nobody who was present will ever forget the occasion. The scenery could only be described as primitive: even the bare walls of the theatre itself were roped in, and many of the sets were from the Volksoper's *Aida*. Seen here (foreground, left to right) are Herbert Alsen (Rocco), Willy Franter (Florestan), Anni Konetzni (Leonore), and Paul Schöffler (Pizarro). The Marzelline was Irmgard Seefried, the Jaquino Anton Dermota, and the Don Fernando Fritz Krenn. The producer was Oscar Fritz Schuh, and the scenery was by Robert Kautsky.

The big scene... this is really what we go to the theatre for and carry home in our memories after the show is over. It may be a murder or a prayer, a flashing knife or an embrace, a venomous glance or a kiss or a smile; it can involve hundreds or just one still small voice from the shadows; it can be worked out by the producer in meticulous detail, or it can be born of one of those spontaneous inspirations that are beyond any producer's ken. — Left: 'Ha, welch ein Mut! Begeisterungsglut!' from *Die Meistersinger* with Paul Schöffler as Hans Sachs and Wolfgang Windgassen as Walther Stolzing. — Above: 'Du missverstehst die Tatsachen, das Urteil kommt nicht mit einemmal, das Verfahren geht allmählich ins Urteil über', from Gottfried von Einem's *Der Prozess*, with Max Lorenz as Josef K. and Ludwig Hofmann as the priest. — Right: 'You have the honour to speak to Nika Magadoff, conjurer and telepathist . . . I need a visa', from Menotti's *The Consul*, with Laszlo Szemere as the magician, (left) Polly Batic as Vera Boronel, and (foreground) Martha Rohs as the Secretary.

'War ich gestern ein Tor,
Weil ich hundert verlor,
Macht mich klug heut' das
                    Glück,
Hol' ich tausend zurück!'
From Tchaikovsky's *Pique
Dame* with Peter Klein as
Czekalinsky.

Below left: 'Ist Sie ein rechter Kapricenschädel. Steigt Ihr das Blut gar in die Wangen, dass man sich die Hand verbrennt?' from Richard Strauss's *Der Rosenkavalier,* with Hilde Güden as Sophie, Kurt Böhme as Ochs, Alfred Poell as Faninal, and Judith Hellwig as Leitmetzerin.

'Mori!'
From Puccini's *Tosca,* with Carla Martinis as Tosca and George London as Scarpia.

From Offenbach's *Contes d'Hoffmann*
George London as Dr. Mirakel. 'Pour conjurer le danger il faut le reconnaître... A mon pouvoir vainqueur cède de bonne grâce!'

During the preparations for the reopening of the Opera House, in the late autumn of 1955. On the new safety curtain by Rudolf Hermann Eisenmenger is a portrayal of the scene from Act Three of Gluck's *Orfeo ed Euridice* in which Orfeo is leading his beloved wife back to earth out of Hades. In the old house, Karl Rahl also used scenes from the Orpheus myth for the curtain used for tragic operas.

'Dich, teure Halle, grüss' ich wieder!'

The reopening in 1955 (Henri Cartier-Bresson, Magnum)

If it was symbolic that the last opera performed before the Opera House went up in flames in 1945 was *Götterdämmerung*, it was equally symbolic that the house should reopen in 1955, the year the Austrian State Treaty was signed.

The curtain goes up again after ten years of reconstruction. Since 5 p.m. thousands of people have been gathering outside the floodlit house, and not just to see the big names that have foregathered in Vienna from the four corners of the earth, after paying through the nose for their seats months in advance. They want to take part in a ceremony that touches their hearts just as keenly as the flames on that March evening ten years before.

Left: Ministerialrat (now Sektionschef) Dr. Fritz Meznik, Head of the Federal Press Service, arranging the seating for the opening performance, a task that was one long headache. The question 'who sits where' was almost as vital as 'to be or not to be'. All had to pay.

Right: The ushers and box-keepers had to attend just as many rehearsals (including of course, the dress-rehearsal) as the orchestra and singers. — Right page: As the great moment drew near the great staircase was resplendent with illustrious personages from all over the world. There were also a great many people who had only come to 'stand and stare'. The surge of press photographers was at times positively alarming.

Left page top: The President of Austria, Dr. Theodor Körner, was warmly acclaimed as he entered his box. — Left page below: The standing-area was as packed as ever, and there was not even anything to lean against (just like the old days!). In 1962 however rails were installed, so that nowadays it is more of a 'leaning-area' than a standing-area. — Below, both pages: Lists of all the celebrities were available in the Director's office, but the man in the street had to be content with just staring at the bemedalled personages and their bejewelled ladies making their way to their seats.

Right: Among the many celebrities from abroad were Henry Ford II and his wife, and among the Austrian notables was Dr. Bernhard Paumgartner (below), son of the great contralto Rosa Papier and the critic Dr. Hans Paumgartner, both of whom had a hand in securing Gustav Mahler's appointment as Director of the Vienna Opera.

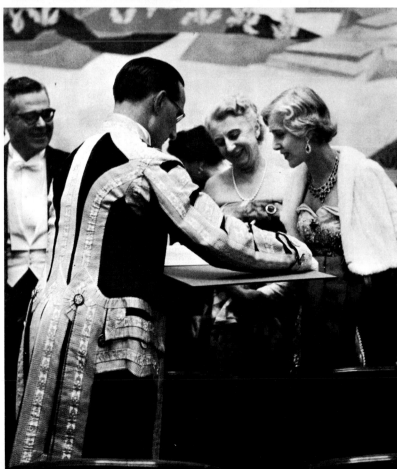

Above: In the boxes as well as in the house as a whole a glance at the audience was enough to confirm that the ten years of austerity since the end of the war were now really over. — Right: Mrs. Clare Boothe Luce, then U.S. Ambassador in Rome.

After all the 'pomp and circumstance' came *Fidelio,* a work which was particularly appropriate to the occasion, especially passages such as 'Wir wollen mit Vertrauen auf Gottes Hilfe bauen, wir werden frei, wir finden Ruh' ('Trusting in God we shall count on his help and we shall find peace'). Musically, however, the performance left a good deal to be desired.

pianissimo as Slezak, and none of his contemporaries could touch his top C. His great rôle in those days was Otello, and memories are still vivid of his entrance clad in a dark satin cloak and a purple satin cap with blue and white feathers, and of his 'Freut euch alle' (the opera was sung in German in those days), which he fairly hurled into the auditorium. The jealousy between Slezak and Schmedes before the latter departed was responsible for more than one incident. On one occasion Schmedes's little daughter Dagmar went up to Slezak and said: 'Uncle Leo, Papa says he is an artist, but you are only a tenor,' whereupon Slezak bent down to the child and replied with a smile: 'And you tell your Papa that if he had my top C he would only be a tenor too.'

Another milestone in the Strauss-Schalk era was the incorporation of the lovely Redoutensaal in the domains of the State Opera. Maria Theresia and Joseph II had both wanted to have operas performed in these ceremonial but still intimate Hofburg apartments above the Spanish Riding School, but it was not until 1921 that the step was taken with a performance of *Figaro* conducted by Franz Schalk. This was followed by Donizetti's *Don Pasquale*, with the part of Norina alternately sung by Maria Ivogün, the great coloratura diva from Munich, and Elisabeth Schumann. Next came a little opera that everyone had forgotten, Boieldieu's *Jean de Paris*. It was one of Strauss's particular favorites because it was the first opera he had been allowed to hear when still little more than a child. He had conducted it often in Germany; now he conducted it again in a highly skillful arrangement for Selma Kurz.

As regards ballet, full-length ones like Gluck's *Don Juan* were given in the Opera House, and the Redoutensaal was kept for smaller pieces such as a 'Couperin Suite', arranged by Strauss from music by Couperin. On the same evening, one could watch Richard Strauss conducting Johann Strauss — the dancers did the 'Tritsch-Tratsch Polka'.

The conversion of the Redoutensaal into an operatic stage was entrusted to Alfred Roller and the new stage-designer, Robert Kautsky. Before taking over the

Theater in der Josefstadt Max Reinhardt, who was a great friend of Strauss's, had staged Goethe's *Clavigo* and *Stella* and Calderón's *Dame Kobold* (in German) at the Redoutensaal. And as a joint production of the State Opera and the Burgtheater Richard Strauss put on Molière's *Le Bourgeois Gentilhomme* with incidental music of his own, taken from the original version of *Ariadne*. He conducted himself, and the leading rôles were played by Willi Thaller and Alma Seidler. It was the swan song of the Strauss era.

The very last première in the Opera House during the Strauss-Schalk regime was *Die Ruinen von Athen* in an arrangement by Hugo von Hofmannsthal. The result was as delightful as it was original. What Hofmannsthal concocted was a blend of play and ballet, with songs and choruses, revolving round a figure resembling Goethe, a Hellenist of the late eighteenth and early nineteenth centuries who, amid the ruins, has a vision of the glory of classical Athens. The music was by Beethoven, partly from *Die Ruinen von Athen* and partly from *Prometheus*.

Looking back, one finds it hard to understand how such a profoundly human and harmonious blend of all the constituents of opera — aria, chorus, acting, dancing and scenery — should have been the immediate prelude to the discordant termination of a close collaboration between two great personalities.

Throughout 1922 the rift between Strauss and Schalk became wider and wider, though unlike later differences involving Directors of the Vienna Opera, the staff noticed nothing. The quarrel was enacted behind the scenes, and it was not until the final year that it came to the ears of the general public. Even the closest friends of the protagonists involved were almost unaware of it; in those days differences were not aired in public.

The root cause of the squabble has already been indicated; the failure to delineate at the outset the precise terms of reference of the two Directors. There was also Schalk's quite understandable envy of Strauss, who seemed to turn to gold everything he touched, without spending more than a modicum of his time in

Where the Tapestry Hall is today (corner of Ringstrasse and Kärntner Strasse next to the entrance hall) used to be the nerve centre of the Vienna Opera. Director Dr. Heinrich Reif-Gintl, who began here as a very young man during the Schalk era, drew a sketch to show me what it used to look like. The corner room was where discussions and minor auditions used to be held. Next door was Franz Schalk's room, then Strauss's room and then a third which was taken over later by Dr. Kerber. Next door sat Dr. Manker of the Federal Theatre Administration (later Dr. Reif-Gintl), then came the secretaries and the room of the secretary for Administration (Dr. Reif-Gintl's first post). Dr. Lothar Wallerstein sat in the end room. All these rooms were interconnected by the corridor of the Director's Department. The spiral staircase which led up from the stage door ended near Dr. Wallerstein's room.

Vienna. It seemed he could do what he pleased, yet whenever a decision had to be made Strauss was the boss and Schalk was number two. Everyone spoke of Strauss as Director, not of Strauss and Schalk as co-Directors. And Schalk insisted on the terms of his appointment in 1918 in which there was no mention of a co-Director. He wanted the artistic direction of Richard Strauss to be confined to 'rostrum and rehearsal', but to have nothing whatever to do with the sphere of planning and administration. Schalk did all he could to cancel certain concessions Strauss had made to particular artists in the interests of his own works. Lotte Lehmann's guest performances at Richard Strauss performances abroad, for example, were not counted against her annual leave.

In April 1924 Strauss signed a new contract — it committed him to five months out of twelve in Vienna — in which he stipulated that Schalk should be retired at the end of the 1924/25 season. The Minister of Education, Dr. Schneider, is said to have hesitated to give Strauss an assurance on this point, and to have put him off until Christmas. Yet Strauss cherished what in his opinion were justifiable hopes that his stipulation would be agreed to.

But Strauss was not the only member of the partnership working towards its demise. Not unnaturally, Schalk was not letting the grass grow under his feet either. After all, he was a well-educated man, artistically-minded through and through, but he also had a brilliant capacity for maintaining excellent contacts with the authorities and for making good use of them when the occasion arose. In any subsidised and state-controlled theatre there are always latent elements of conflict between the government and the artistic sides, and when this particular conflict came to a head, Schalk ranged himself whole-heartedly and deliberately on the side of the government authorities and against Strauss, until eventually, unable to rid himself of the spirits he had conjured up, he was toppled by them in the very same way that Strauss was.

Having signed his contract Strauss left Vienna in April and did not return until mid-December. During

After the resignation of Richard Strauss the leading Viennese writer on music Dr. Heinrich Kralik wrote a resounding appeal in the 'Neues Wiener Tagblatt' on 3 November 1924, saying that Strauss must be kept in Vienna at all costs. It was, he said, a second 'Mahler case'. The concluding paragraph of his article is given below.

his absence Schalk contrived an extension of his own contract and obtained new instructions whereby in Strauss's absence he, Schalk, bore sole power of decision. It was for the Ministry of Education to try to persuade Strauss to swallow all this. If he refused, Vienna was already prepared to face the consequences. In December an official named Ludwig Karpath, a good friend of Strauss, was despatched to Dresden, where Strauss was busy with the last rehearsals for the first performance of *Intermezzo*. Nearly all his operas had been given their first performance in Dresden, and the rather small and intimate Dresden Opera House was just what he wanted for *Intermezzo*, especially as Fritz Busch was now in charge. Suddenly, in the middle of the dress rehearsal, Karpath arrived with the news that Schalk's contract had been renewed. He showed Strauss Schalk's instructions about responsibility, and asked him to agree to them. Strauss rejoined that it was simply and solely Schalk's personality that made acceptance impossible. Strauss was perfectly prepared to accept the 'responsibility' clause in theory, but not if it was Schalk who was to be entrusted with it.

Strauss accordingly tendered his resignation the very same day, and it was accepted, though there were one or two half-hearted attempts by Vienna to induce him to withdraw it. The anti-Strauss campaign now rose to a crescendo, with such devices as: 'No more Richard Strauss Theatre' and 'Strauss muss 'raus aus dem Haus' (in other words, 'Strauss go home!'). Most critics, including Dr. Julius Korngold, described the dual directorship as a failure. Heinrich von Kralik was the only one who saw in the loss of Richard Strauss a new 'Mahler case' ... But compared with the campaign against Mahler, the opposition to Strauss included an additional nuance: envy. 'The Viennese forgive the living their talents only if they fail to make the grade' ... and Strauss was doing fine.

As a popular *bon mot* put it, less brusquely: 'If it must be Richard, then Wagner, and if it must be Strauss, then Johann; if there must be an Intermezzo, then the one from *Cavalleria Rusticana*, and if there must be 'Schlagobers', then at Demel's.'

Wo ist der Mann, der uns mehr zu bieten hätte, wo ist das große theatralische Ingenium mit den großzügigen Plänen und Ideen, meinetwegen auch mit dem unfehlbaren „System", von dem wir einen nennenswerten künstlerischen Gewinn erhoffen dürfen? Wohin man sieht, nichts als Mittelmäßigkeiten; bestenfalls Phantasten mit strohfeuerartigen Augenblickserfolgen. Die Genies sind eben spärlich gesät. Wir aber sind in der glücklichen Lage, eines zu haben. Und wollen es ziehen lassen? Wegen opernpolitischer Kanapeefragen? Man möge „höheren Orts" einmal weniger auf die Meinung der Beamten, Diplomaten und sonstigen unverantwortlichen Berater hören, sondern sozusagen auf die Stimme des Volkes, dessen Begeisterung, Liebe und Anhänglichkeit jedesmal, wenn Richard Strauß am Dirigentenpult erscheint, in überwältigender Weise zum Ausdruck kommt. Seit Gustav Mahler hat kein Dirigent das Wiener Publikum auf die Dauer so stark zu packen gewußt. Der Jubel, der dem Meister gilt, zeigt deutlich an, daß dem naiven Hörer, der keine Vorurteile, keine Programme und keine Opernpolitik kennt, die Magie des auserwählten Genius tausendmal wertvoller ist als die noch so systematische Bewährung des bloß Berufenen. Diese junge oder weniger junge, aber immer empfängliche und immer begeisterungsfähige Hörerschaft stellt das wunderbare Medium dar, das dem Opernhaus Wärme, der Kunst Leben verleiht; sie repräsentiert zugleich die höchste demokratische Instanz, die in Kunstdingen entscheidet; ihr tausendmal abgegebenes Votum lautet: daß man Richard Strauß nicht ziehen lassen darf.

Dr. Heinrich Kralik.

Where is the man who would have more to offer us, where is the great genius of the theatre with inspiration and a grand design, even perhaps with an 'infallible system', from whom we might be able to expect any artistic gains worth mentioning? Look where we will, nothing but mediocrity; at best a few fantasts whose achievements flare up like burning straw and are gone. Genius is a rare plant. But we are in the happy position of possessing one. And shall we let him go? For reasons of internal politics of the lowest description? 'The authorities' should, for once, listen less to the counsel of civil servants, diplomats and other irresponsible advisers, and more to the voice of the people whose enthusiasm, affection and loyalty are overwhelmingly displayed each time Richard Strauss appears on the conductor's rostrum. In the long run no other conductor has been able to seize the imagination of the Viennese public since the days of Gustav Mahler. This acclamation shows distinctly that to the naive listener, knowing nothing of prejudices, programme planning, or operatic policy, the magic of genius is a thousand times more valuable than the most systematic conservation policy of capable men. It is these listeners, be they young or old, who being receptive and capable of such enormous enthusiasm, give warmth to the Vienna Opera, breathe life into art. At the same time they represent the highest democratic court of appeal which can pronounce on artistic matters. Its vote has been cast a thousand times over: Richard Strauss must not be allowed to go. Dr. Heinrich Kralik

Franz Schalk in Sole Charge
1924—1929

'*Wer nun dem Gral
zu dienen ist erkoren*'
(From '*Lohengrin*')

Thus one Richard Strauss era came to an end and another one started — the years of waiting for his return.

The fact that it was Strauss as Director, and not Strauss as a composer, that the senior Korngold objected to, caused my youthful conscience considerable qualms. One of Schalk's first actions as sole Director was to engage young Korngold to conduct his *Violanta*, whereupon the Strauss faction, to which I naturally belonged, took concerted action to hiss the performance. Every member was told to attend the opera and boo Korngold because of his father's complicity in the compaign against Strauss. On the other hand, as well as being a personal friend of young Korngold's I liked his music very much. I therefore compromised by putting in an appearance at the Opera, as instructed by the ringleaders of the faction, but I took no part in the anti-Korngold booing.

There was a terrific uproar, and after a while Korngold left the rostrum. It must have been fully seven minutes before he came back to start the performance.

Strauss's resignation was followed by all sorts of bizarre episodes, some of them totally unconnected with it. There was, for instance, the notorious incident involving Maria Olczewska, a native of Bavaria and a superb Amneris and Carmen. On one occasion she was singing Fricka in *Die Walküre*, and Wotan was being played by her husband Emil Schipper. Waiting in the wings for their next entrance were Maria Jeritza (Sieglinde) and the contralto, Hermine Kittel, and their 'whispered' conversation must have been rather too loud. Anyway, during Wotan's angry tirade Olczewska kept telling them in good Bavarian invective (and louder each time) to shut up. At last she could stand it no longer and after her great outburst 'Wann ward es erlebt, dass leiblich Geschwister sich liebten?' she suddenly moved to the wings and spat straight at Jeritza. She missed Jeritza but scored a direct hit on Hermine Kittel. 'Symbolic of the tiny new Austrian Republic,' people said, 'the big powers quarrel and the small ones get it in the neck.' Olczewska was dismissed from the Opera after the incident. Some

time later, during one of her Lieder programmes on the radio, she announced the next item with the words: 'I'm now going to sing two Lieder by Richard Strauss, who shared my fate in this lovely city.'

Schalk was now in sole charge at last, and he acquitted himself admirably. Under his guidance the Opera took on a new lease of life, as can be gathered from the sheer extent of the repertoire. In the 1926/27 season, which can be taken as fairly representative of Schalk's term as a whole, it comprised eighty-four different works (66 operas and 18 ballets), a record which, as far as I know, has never been approached since.

Born and bred in Vienna, Schalk was a pupil of Bruckner and, by the time he embarked on his career at the Vienna Opera, could already point to a successful career as a conductor, including an appearance at the New York 'Met'. It was Mahler who brought him to the Vienna Opera as a *Kapellmeister*. From that day on Schalk never severed his connection with it (he conducted *Die Meistersinger* no fewer than 149 times in Vienna alone!). He was also on the teaching staff of the Vienna Academy and was for many years the conductor of the concerts organised by the 'Gesellschaft der Musikfreunde'. He was of medium height, and very thin, had a small beard and wore a pince-nez. He looked more like a professor than an Opera Director. He was extremely well educated, an out-and-out humanist, and was gifted with a cynical, even macabre, sense of humour. But behind the facade was a heart of gold, as his friends well knew. And last, but by no means least, he loved the Opera above everything in the world.

Until the crisis over the dual directorship developed, Schalk was on terms of something approaching friendship with Strauss and had put on the premières of *Der Rosenkavalier* and *Ariadne* with the greatest enthusiasm. Now that he was in sole charge he still found room in his programme for a great deal of Strauss, deliberately demonstrating that his quarrel was with Strauss the co-Director and not with Strauss the composer. He also lost no time in restoring *Die Frau ohne Schatten* to the repertoire and was eager to put on *Intermezzo* and *Die ägyptische Helena* as soon as possible.

Although we had to admit that we were being given wonderful entertainment night after night, we young people still could not take kindly to Schalk as sole Director. We were waiting impatiently for the return of Strauss and devoured the newspapers for odd scraps of information about what he was doing, where he was, what he was composing. Looking back, I cannot help feeling rather ashamed of our treatment of Schalk. We found out that he used to spend the summer at Edlach near Reichenau, so I and one or two friends of mine got into the same train with him. When he got out at Reichenau, our little band of hooligans lined up on the platform as if on parade and shouted at Schalk as he passed by: 'Long live Strauss — down with Schalk' — just to spoil his summer holiday. After which we took the next train back to Vienna feeling very pleased with ourselves.

Nevertheless, whether we liked it or not we had to admit that Schalk was making an excellent Director. For one thing, he was well aware of the gaps in the repertoire left by Strauss, and he set about filling them with a number of interesting works that Strauss either didn't like or for some reason or other was unable to do justice to. The first was *Boris Godunov* in 1925, in which Boris was sung by Emil Schipper, a doctor who had been taken on by Gregor from the Volksoper and given his first big rôle by Strauss in a new production of *Der fliegende Holländer,* in which he scored a great success.

The scenery for *Boris* presented all sorts of problems. Alfred Roller, who had left the Opera during Weingartner's term but had been coaxed back by Schalk in 1919 (like Anna Mildenburg, who had been unable to hit it off with Gregor), was once again in charge of scenery and had made a number of sketches of a naturalistic, three-dimensional late-sixteenth-century Russian city. But in those hard times they would have cost far too much. 'We must find something less expensive,' insisted Schalk, so the experiment was made of entrusting a young Viennese artist named Emil Pirchan

with the scenery for *Boris.* Pirchan had already attracted considerable attention in the expressionist school of the Berlin producer Leopold Jessner. He succeeded in making relatively inexpensive material look like gorgeous hangings and carpets by the sheer cleverness of his colours and designs. Instead of using a whole cathedral, which would have cost far too much, he conjured up a marvellous vision of sixteenth-century Moscow with a mere sprinkling of onion towers. Nothing like it had ever been seen in Vienna, and the success was sensational — rather too much so for Roller, who though agreeing to Pirchan's engagement was said to be a bit put out by his rival's success.

At a performance three years later (May 1927) Boris was sung by the world-famous Chaliapin. He was engaged by the Vienna Opera for three performances, one as Boris and two as Mephistopheles in Gounod's *Faust.* His voice was by that time slightly on the wane, but his portrayal of Boris's pangs of conscience and metaphysical introspection was phenomenal. Some of the words he sang were not in the libretto, nor was he above improvising the music, especially in his mad scene with the clocks. For some reason he was not on the best of terms with the Vienna Opera, and it was suggested in some quarters that what he was singing in Russian was 'to hell with the Vienna Opera' or words to that effect. During the duet at the end of Act One in *Faust* there was an angry scene between Chaliapin and the conductor Alwin, whose tempi were too slow for Chaliapin's liking (they had to be slow because the tenor refused to speed up). Suddenly Chaliapin strode to the front of the stage shouting 'faster, faster', and kept clapping his hands to indicate the tempo he wanted, virtually 'conducting' the entire scene until the end of the Act. Such behaviour was (and still is) unheard of in the Vienna Opera. One critic wrote that 'it was at best a dress-rehearsal in public; one could hardly describe the proceedings as a performance'.

I can well remember how at a song recital he gave, instead of programmes he had little booklets distributed, containing his entire repertoire with a number against each item. Armed with a copy himself, he would announce the next item like the vicar announcing the next hymn — in French: '*Numéro trente-et-un, s'il vous plait — Et maintenant numéro cinquante-deux*' meant and so on.

The success of *Boris Godunov* meant that one of the biggest gaps in the repertoire was filled. Schalk next set about reinforcing the Italian repertoire, which Strauss had sadly neglected.

The first new Italian première was of Umberto Giordano's *André Chénier,* the realistic predecessor of *Tosca* that had not been given during the Monarchy because of its revolutionary slant. It had not been officially banned, but the Intendant had invariably turned a deaf ear whenever there was talk of putting it on. Mahler had been very anxious to stage it but had had to be content with *Fedora,* a vastly inferior work. The première, in January 1926, with Trajan Grosavescu as Chénier and Lotte Lehmann as Madeleine de Coigny, was a pronounced success. Later, the rôle of the poet sentenced to be guillotined was one of Alfred Piccaver's favourite and most successful parts.

In October of the same year — 1926 was a vintage 'Italian year' — there followed the legendary first Vienna performance of Puccini's last (and unfinished) opera *Turandot,* which had first been performed at the Milan Scala in the previous spring, Toscanini conducting. Nobody who was not present can possibly imagine the transports of enthusiasm at its first Vienna performance. As well as being introduced to one of the masterpieces of twentieth century opera, the audience was presented by Schalk with a staging of the utmost brilliance. There were two alternate casts: on the first night Lotte Lehmann was Turandot, Leo Slezak was Calaf ('a Chinese Tamino' as the part was christened), and Berta Kiurina the loving, suffering Liu. On the second night the Turandot was Maria Nemeth, a Hungarian with one of the most natural voices of her day, the Liu was Luise Helletsgruber, and the Calaf was Jan Kiepura (he had previously scored a triumphant success as Cavaradossi in a mixture of Italian, German and Polish, with Jeritza

as Tosca). From now on he had Viennese audiences eating out of his hand.

He was twenty-four at the time, had studied law in Warsaw, and originally had come to Vienna for an audition. After the very first notes Schalk exclaimed 'An unconscionable voice,' but Kiepura's behaviour was even more unconscionable. 'You want a top C? You can have it.' His top C was as good as his word. 'Another one? Here.' 'And again?' Schalk could only stand and stare as Kiepura let loose a stream of top Cs, one after the other.

He was exceptionally good-looking too, as striking a figure as the one Strauss envisaged for Bacchus in *Ariadne.* His acting was full of poetry and perfectly natural, and his romantic appearance held audiences spellbound. There has been nothing like him since. Another of his unique achievements was that besides being a tenor over whom the world's greatest Opera Houses fought, he soon became a film star of the first magnitude and effectively combined the two careers.

Kiepura's connection with the Vienna Opera lasted till 1938. He was a splendid Rodolfo and Des Grieux, a captivating Duke of Mantua in *Rigoletto,* and of course the ideal Calaf in *Turandot.* He and Jeritza made a marvellous pair in *Tosca, Turandot* and *Manon.*

In one of his films in which he played the part of a famous singer, there was a scene in which he was being fêted at the stage-door and suddenly jumped onto the roof of his car and delivered one encore after another. His Viennese fans (female) naturally wanted to see this performance repeated live, so from then on every time Kiepura emerged from the stage door he had to clamber on to the roof of his car and sing 'Tonight or Never'. As time went on it was usually a taxi, because he didn't want his own car to suffer. Nowadays, of course, with Vienna's traffic what it is and parking an impossibility, the whole performance would be out of the question, especially as the car was invariably surrounded not only by a couple of dozen teenagers and opera fans but also by what looked like the entire audience, not to mention casual passers-by. Traffic on the Ringstrasse ground to a standstill, and from the Opera House to well up the

Franz Schalk conducting.
(Silhouette by Hans Schliess-
mann, 1900.)

Kärntner Strasse there was a sea of humanity listening enraptured to the 'unconscionable' voice of their beloved 'Janek'.

On one occasion, the audience clapped and cheered for so long after a performance of *Rigoletto*, that as he stood on the stage in front of the curtain, Kiepura decided on the spur of the moment to sing one or two of his most popular songs as encores. There was a piano in the orchestra pit, and as luck would have it there always happened to be someone in the audience to accompany him ('Would any lady or gentleman kindly oblige?'). Heinrich Reif-Gintl, then an official at the Opera and now its Director, told him that this practice of singing popular songs with piano accompaniment as encores must cease forthwith, so the next time his fans started chanting 'Songs, songs, songs' after the performance, Kiepura made a short speech à la Till Eulenspiegel: 'Unfortunately I have been informed I must not sing on the stage with a piano accompaniment. So I will sing without a piano.' And he did — two songs by Robert Stolz: 'Ob blond, ob braun, ich liebe alle Frau'n', and 'Mein Herz ruft immer nur nach dir'.

After the première of *Turandot* Dr. Lothar Wallerstein took over as senior producer and stamped his personality on everything he touched until the end of Clemens Krauss's term. Wallerstein's talents as a producer lay not so much in directing individual singers as in his handling of crowd scenes, notably the chanting throng in Act One of *Turandot*.

A word or two about *Turandot* which made such a profound impression on me when, as a child, I was lucky enough to see the Vienna première, and on the countless other occasions I saw it during the 1920s and 1930s. In present-day performances we are usually given a horribly hard and positively evil Princess who amuses herself by having people's heads cut off, never utters a friendly word, and never vouchsafes anyone a semblance of

Vienna rejoiced over this new opera and the new discovery Jan Kiepura. He sang in German; at his first guest perform-ance in 'Tosca' the brilliance of his voice atracted as much attention as his curious mixture of Polish and Italian.

119

warmth or humanity; one actually hopes this Calaf, who sings so nicely, will manage to avoid being saddled with such an unattractive creature. The reason is that the rôle is wrongly interpreted. As Jeritza played her, Turandot was a woman who falls in love with Calaf even before he answers the riddles. For the first time in her life she is overcome with real emotion and longs to have to surrender to Calaf. Along with capitulation, she desires victory, a feminine victory in which Calaf is vanquished by love. When Jeritza was Turandot, we all knew exactly when she fell in love with Calaf — during the second riddle. All at once the Princess changed from an iceberg into a woman, a woman in love, ready to surrender. We were also well aware that at the second of this opera's great climaxes, when Turandot is lying on the ground like a piece of dirt, submissive because Calaf has guessed all three riddles, her surrender is the fulfilment of her most cherished dream, and that Turandot can now at last feel that through her love for Calaf she has conquered her own nature. The great aria 'Del primo pianto' towards the end of Act Three is often cut nowadays because it is so exacting. But without this aria it is impossible to unterstand Turandot's character, for in it she confesses, while lying prostrate at Calaf's feet, that tears came into her eyes for the first time in her life when she saw him. This is the only aria in which Turandot is portrayed as a woman in love.

As soon as 'the right man comes along' the ice melts and the riddles have a purely symbolic function, like the love potion in *Tristan*, which only puts the seal on a process that has already started: 'Ich sah ihm in die Augen . . .'

With Jeritza as Turandot and Kiepura as Calaf, the currents of love and hate, of domination and surrender, that the two protagonists managed to convey on that immense staircase purely by their singing and acting would defy even the 'super-producer' of today. Today's producers misunderstand this scene. Even on the second night there were obscurities: one Vienna newspaper asked how Calaf could possibly solve the riddles in view of Maria Nemeth's incomprehensible German and Kiepura's terrific Polish accent!

Verdi's renaissance in German was launched by Werfel's version of 'La forza del destino'.

The third great event of the 'Italian year', 1926, was the Vienna première of Verdi's *La forza del destino*. It inaugurated a Verdi revival that lasted for years. Schalk himself conducted, and Franz Werfel, whose reputation as a writer was already world-wide, turned out a German libretto that had far more dignity and poetry than the Italian original. It was the first time a Verdi opera had been given in a German version that was worthy of it. This sensational première was also the début of the ethereal and charming Margit Schenker-Angerer, a prominent figure of Viennese society, who was also extremely good-looking, with the smile and figure

Operntheater

Samstag den 21. Mai 1927

Bei aufgehobenem Abonnement   Zu außerordentlichen Preisen

Margarethe
(Faust)

Oper in vier Akten, Text nach Goethe von J. Barbier und M. Carré, übersetzt von
Gollmick — Musik von Ch. Gounod

Regie: Hr. Runge   Dirigent: Hr. Alwin

Faust . . . .
Mephistopheles . . . .
Valentin . . . . Hr. Schipper
Brander . . . . Hr. Muzzarelli
Margarethe . . . .
Siebel . . . . Frl. Helletsgruber
Marthe . . . . Fr. Kittel

Studenten, Soldaten, Bürger, Mädchen und Frauen, Volk, Hexen und Gespenster, Schutz-
geister

Vorkommende Tänze: Lais: Frl. Pichler, Alpasia: Frl. Krausenecker, Cleopatra:
Frl. Pfundmayr, weiters die Damen Horvath, Fränzl F., Dirtl, Weinrich, Steinlein H.,
Hurm, Knöpfler, Fränzl H., Maninger, Köcher und das Ballettkorps

* * „Faust" Hr. **Paul Marion** a. G.
* * * „Mephistopheles" Hr. **Fedor Schaljapin** a. G.
* * „Margarethe" Fr. **Margit Angerer** a. G.

Das offizielle Programm nur bei den Billetteuren erhältlich. Preis 40 Groschen

Nach dem zweiten Akt eine größere Pause

Der Beginn der Vorstellung sowie jedes Aktes wird durch ein Glockenzeichen bekanntgegeben

Kassen-Eröffnung nach 6 Uhr   Anfang 7 Uhr   Ende nach 10 Uhr
Während der Vorspiele und der Akte bleiben die Saaltüren zum Parkett, Parterre und den Galerien
geschlossen. Zuspätkommende können daher nur während der Pausen Einlaß finden

Der Kartenverkauf findet statt für obige Vorstellung

Sonntag den 22. **Die Meistersinger von Nürnberg** (Anfang 6 Uhr) 4. Viertel
Montag den 23. Aïda, Anläßlich der Anna elenheit dänischer Pflegeeltern. Bei aufgehobenem Jahres- und
Stammlitz-Abonnement. Kein Kartenverkauf (Anfang 7 Uhr)

Weiterer Spielplan:

Dienstag den 24. Margarethe (Faust). „Margarethe" Fr. **Margit Angerer** a. G. „Faust" Hr. **Paul
Marion** a. G. „Mephistopheles" Hr. **Fedor Schaljapin** a. G. Bei aufgehobenem
Abonnement. Zu außerordentlichen Preisen (Anfang 7 Uhr)
Mittwoch den 25. Tannhäuser (Anfang 7 Uhr) 3. Viertel
Donnerstag den 26. Der Rosenkavalier. „Sophie" Fr. **Adele Kern** vom Opernhaus in Frankfurt am
Main als Gast (Anfang 7 Uhr) 4. Viertel
Freitag den 27. Palestrina (Anfang 6½ Uhr) 1. Viertel
Samstag den 28. Madame Butterfly (Anfang ¼ Uhr) 2. Viertel
Sonntag den 29. Othello (Anfang 7 Uhr) 3. Viertel

The tenor in this performance was dragging his notes far too much in the final duet in Scene 1, and the conductor Alwin was giving way to him, when Chaliapin came to the front of the stage and beat time by clapping his hands.

of a Botticelli nymph. She was the wife of an import and export merchant named Schenker, who eventually left her and went into a monastery. To her friends and acquaintances she was known as 'Manzi', and with the cattiness that is not unusual in social circles, the aforesaid friends and acquaintances were just waiting for the merchant's wife to come a cropper and disgrace the entire opera as well as herself. Was it not a clear case of a stage-struck amateur aspiring to make a career as a singer with her husband's money and position behind her? But as the première took its course it became increasingly obvious that 'Manzi' was a professional to

her finger-tips, and as Leonora she went from strength to strength, while the faces of the friends and acquaintances grew redder and redder.

Margit Schenker-Angerer was a wonderful Octavian and created in Vienna the rôle of Dorota in Jaromir Weinberger's *Schwanda the Bagpiper*. She was also much admired as Elsa, Elisabeth, and the Composer in *Ariadne*. Unfortunately her career lasted only five or six years: she had never really worked hard enough when she first took up singing and managed to get by with her lovely natural voice; but her lower notes were somewhat insubstantial and it was a grave mistake to let her sing the part of Octavian, which is written very low, before she was ready.

Franz Schalk now tried his luck with modern opera, which he seemed determined to make a success of at all costs. To understand his tenacity of purpose, we must go back a bit. It all started with a letter from Richard Strauss to one of his most loyal admirers, the music critic Heinrich Kralik, in which he listed all the modern operas he had put on while co-Director, adding that it was hardly his fault if not one of them had made the slightest impact. Strauss also alleged that all these modern works had been put on against Schalk's wishes, except of course the operas of Erich Wolfgang Korngold. For who would have dared to turn down Korngold junior, whose father was the awe-inspiring critic?

That letter really got under Schalk's skin, and he was determined to show that as sole Director he possessed a keener flair for picking out modern operas that stood a good chance of establishing themselves than Strauss ever had; to pay Strauss back in his own coin, in fact. His first experiment was Paul Hindemith's *Cardillac*, based on a tale by E. T. A. Hoffmann. Hindemith was one of the most serious composers of the day, but much as connoisseurs of his music admired the way he set about tackling the complicated problems of form, the opera was just as much of a flop as most of the modern works Strauss had put on. After attending some of the rehearsals, Hindemith left Vienna before the actual performance.

In the same year, 1927, came another opera by E. W. Korngold, *Das Wunder der Heliane*. It was the last Korn-

Operntheater

Samstag den 31. Dezember 1927

Bei aufgehobenem Abonnement   Besondere Preise mit Zuschlag

Zum ersten Male:

Jonny spielt auf

Oper in zwei Teilen von **Ernst Křenek**

Regie: Hr. Dr. Wallerstein   Musikalische Leitung: Hr. Heger

Der Komponist Max . . . Hr. Pataky	Der Manager . . . . . Hr. Norbert
Die Sängerin Anita . . . Frl. Schwarz	Der Hoteldirektor . . . Hr. Breuer
Der Neger Jonny, Jazz- band-Geiger . . . . . Hr. Jerger	Ein Bahnangestellter . . Hr. Wolken Erster . . . . Hr. Arnold
Der Violinvirtuose Daniello Hr. Duhan	Zweiter Polizist . . . . Hr. Madin
Das Stubenmädchen Yvonne Fr. Schumann	Dritter . . . . Hr. Gitt

Ein Stubenmädchen, ein Groom, ein Nachtwächter im Hotel, ein Polizeibeamter, ein Chauffeur ein Ladenmädchen, ein Gepäckträger, Hotelgäste, Reisende und Publikum

Vorkommende Tänze einstudiert von Leo Dubois, ausgeführt von Frl. Berka, Ranninger, Steinlein H., Szakal, Steinlein J., Wuttera, Graf, den Herren Fränzl R., Bauer, Casson, Nemeth, Buttula, Binder und dem Ballettkorps

Die Handlung spielt teils in einer mitteleuropäischen Großstadt, teils in Paris und teils an einem Gletscher in den Hochalpen, in der Gegenwart

In Szene gesetzt von Dr. Lothar Wallerstein

Entwürfe der Bühnenbilder und Kostüme von Dr. Oskar Strnad

Die Toiletten der Damen Schwarz und Schumann wurden im Atelier der Firma Heinrich Grünbaum hergestellt — Damenhüte: Modehaus „Susanne" — Schuhe: Haus der Schuhmoden H. Bauer, I., Fleisch- markt 10 — Schmuckgegenstände: „Brillantenkönigin", I., Kärntnerstraße 51 — Das Auto wurde von den Steyr-Werken A. G. beigestellt — Staubsauger: „Rib-Nat" von der Firma F. Wießer

Das offizielle Programm nur bei den Billetteuren erhältlich. Preis 50 Groschen

Nach dem ersten Teil eine größere Pause

Der Beginn der Vorstellung sowie jedes Aktes wird durch ein Glockenzeichen bekanntgegeben

Kassen-Eröffnung nach 6½ Uhr   Anfang 7½ Uhr   Ende nach 10 Uhr

Während der Vorspiele und der Akte bleiben die Saaltüren zum Parkett, Parterre und den Galerien geschlossen. Zuspätkommende können daher nur während der Pausen Einlaß finden

Der Kartenverkauf findet heute statt für obige Vorstellung und für

Sonntag den 1. Jänner 1928. Jonny spielt auf. Besondere Preise mit Zuschlag (Anfang 7½ Uhr)
Montag den 2. Die Zauberflöte (Anfang 7 Uhr)

Weiterer Spielplan:

Dienstag den 3. Ariadne auf Naxos. Dirigent: Hr. Dr. Richard Strauß a. G. Im Abonnement (Anfang 7½ Uhr)
Mittwoch den 4. Jonny spielt auf. Bei aufgehobenem Abonnement. Besondere Preise mit Zuschlag (Anfang 7½ Uhr)

Die tote Stadt substituted. E. W. Korngold was present on both nights and was very unhappy at Schalk's tempi in *Das Wunder der Heliane* (Schalk was notorious for his slow tempi). As he sat in his box in a state of utter despair Korngold started beating time, as he always did. In the middle of Act Three, half an hour before the opera was due to end, he suddenly stopped and said, 'I've already come to the end.' At the performance of *Die tote Stadt* the next day the conductor was Karl Alwin, who was notorious for his quick tempi. After it was over Korngold observed: 'Thank God, Alwin made up the time Schalk lost yesterday.'

Meanwhile Schalk had got wind of a new opera that was breaking all box-office records in Germany whenever it was put on, *Jonny spielt auf* by Ernst Křenek, Mahler's son-in-law. It was the first jazz opera and was first performed in Leipzig in 1927. Although Schalk had absolutely no use for works of this kind, he secured it anyway. He was motivated first by box-office considerations and secondly by his determination to refute that letter of Strauss by scoring a success with a modern opera. And this time he did the trick — at last. *Jonny spielt auf* was a terrific success. As Schalk himself cynically put it, 'The takings exceeded my direst forebodings.'

The première on New Year's Eve 1927 created a sensation. It was conducted by Robert Heger, a native of Alsace who was on the staff of the Opera and who found the work as repugnant as Schalk did. One of the figures in the opera was a Negro band-leader who steals a European virtuoso's violin. A story of this kind was something quite new to the Vienna Opera, and was meant to symbolise the shift of musical hegemony from Europe to America, home of jazz. In the Vienna production there was a very effective scene in which Alfred Jerger as Jonny jumped on top of a huge globe and played his stolen violin. There was no end to the novelties the opera featured: a motor-car, a radio set, a train, spotlights, telephones — not to mention the music, which seemed enormously daring at the time. To-day of course we take it in our stride and we certainly do not regard it as typically American. In fact it was not even genuine jazz, but an exceedingly clever distillation of the kind of music

---

gold première at the Vienna Opera, and perhaps the most interesting as well. But it too was a flop, and not only in Vienna. Jeritza declined the part of Heliane, and it was given to Lotte Lehmann. Alfred Jerger sang the part of the daemonic tyrant with a lonely heart, while the contrasting figure of The Stranger was Jan Kiepura. The setting was a fairy-tale realm, the somewhat abstruse story based on a mystery-play by Hans Kaltenecker. I can still remember the very effective Trial Scene in which Heliane, accused of adultery, protests her innocence in an aria which is put together in such a way as to make it quite clear that she is really guilty. And in fact she is found guilty.

But even a brilliant cast could not save it — or rather two casts, as there had been for the première of *Turandot*, though this time the second cast never even faced an audience, because the second première was cancelled and

Poster encouraging a protest demonstration against the performance of 'Jonny spielt auf!'

Wiener und Wienerinnen!

Die Zersetzung und Vergiftung unserer bodenständigen Bevölkerung durch das östliche Gesindel nimmt einen gefahrdrohenden Umfang an. Nicht genug, daß unser Volk durch die Geldentwertung einer durchgreifenden Ausplünderung zugeführt wurde, sollen nun auch alle sittlich-kulturellen Grundfesten unseres Volkstumes zerstört werden.

Unsere Staatsoper,

die erste Kunst- und Bildungsstätte der Welt, der Stolz aller Wiener,

ist einer frechen jüdisch-negerischen Besudelung zum Opfer gefallen.

Das Schandwerk eines tschechischen Halbjuden

„Jonny spielt auf!"

in welchem Volk und Heimat, Sitte, Moral und Kultur brutal zertreten werden soll, wurde der Staatsoper aufgezwungen. Eine volksfremde Meute von Geschäftsjuden und Freimaurern setzt alles daran, unsere Staatsoper zu einer Bedürfnisanstalt ihrer jüdisch-negerischen Perversitäten herabzuwürdigen. **Der Kunst-Bolschewismus erhebt frech** sein Haupt. Die Schamröte muß jedem anständigen Wiener ins Gesicht steigen, wenn er hört, welch ungeheuerliche Schmach und Demütigung der berühmten Musikstadt Wien durch volksfremdes Gesindel angetan wurde

Da die christlich-großdeutsche Regierung diesem schamlosen Treiben untätig zusieht und von keiner Seite eine Abwehr versucht wird, so rufen wir alle Wiener zu einer

Riesen-
Protest-Kundgebung

auf, in welcher über die Wahrheit der jüdischen Verseuchung unseres Kunstlebens und über die der Staatsoper angetane Schmach gesprochen werden wird.

Christliche Wiener und Wienerinnen, Künstler, Musiker, Sänger und Antisemiten erscheint in Massen und protestiert mit uns gegen diese unerhörten Schandzustände in Oesterreich.

Ort: Lembachers Saal, Wien, III., Landstraße Hauptstraße.

Zeitpunkt: Freitag, den 13. Jänner 1928, 8 Uhr abends.

Kostenbeitrag: 20 Groschen. / Juden haben keinen Zutritt!

Nationalsozialistische deutsche Arbeiterpartei
Großdeutschlands.

purveyed by night-club dance-bands in the 1920s. Later, when I was studying at the University, Egon Wellesz analysed *Jonny* for us in one of his lectures. A lot of it came from operas we had never heard, from Dukas' *Ariane et Barbe-bleu* for instance, and from other obscure sources. Other passages we managed to track down ourselves. We had prepared ourselves for what we called 'a hot evening', for tensions that would be resolved in the end. But when Alfred Jerger leaped with his stolen violin on to the piano and sang his big aria, 'Now the violin is

---

A dangerous threat

One morning, the 'divine' Leo Slezak came to a rehearsal, bore heavily down upon the old stage-manager Franz Blümel wo was standing in the wings. Eyes rolling and in unexceptionable Bohemian dialect, Slezak hissed: 'I dreamed about you last night! If ever that happens again I shall box both your ears!'

---

mine', we identified a passage of it as 'Aus meiner Truhe stehlen' from the German-language version of *La Bohème*. The spell was broken; the rest of the evening passed agreeably enough and we applauded enthusiastically. There was some booing, but it was soon drowned out. Alfred Jerger and Elisabeth Schumann were paid more than the whole of their month's salaries by the millionaire Castiglioni to sing their blues-duet 'Leb wohl mein Schatz' at a fancy-dress ball at his villa. The press notices mentioned 'Fidelio-girls' and suggested brightening up the Vienna Opera by engaging the popular, but sometimes very vulgar, cabaret star Gisela Werbezirk with Karl Farkas to top the bill.

Though sensational at first, *Jonny's* success was short-lived. In 1928 it was put on twenty-two times, in 1929 eight times, in 1930 four times, and in 1931 once. And that was the end of *Jonny*.

Even before the first performances there were noisy demonstrations in front of the Opera by German Nationalists, and I well remember a Member of Parliament exclaiming: 'Who ever heard of a nigger at an Opera House?' whereupon he was asked by another member whether he had ever been to *Otello*.

A performance in Munich had to be stopped halfway through because of the resentment against coloured men after the French occupation of the Rhineland involving Colonial troops and because the audience thought the actor playing Jonny really was a Negro. In reality it was our old friend Alfred Jerger from Brünn. His fans gave him a great welcome at the stage-door after the performance was abandoned.

In fact this was Jerger's big year. Both as Jonny and in *Cardillac* he was superb. A fellow-countryman of Slezak's, he was originally summoned by Richard Strauss to Vienna from Zurich, where he was working in a three-fold capacity as *Kapellmeister*, singer and actor. Under Strauss he took over the part of Ochs at very short notice and thereafter sang no fewer than 130 parts at the Vienna Opera, six in *Die Meistersinger* alone: Sachs, Pogner, Beckmesser, two Meistersingers and the Night-watchman. Later he tried his hand at producing too, and on one occasion he actually conducted a lively performance of *Die Fledermaus*. He was one of the most interesting and versatile personalities at the Vienna Opera's disposal.

Scanning the list of prominent artists engaged by Schalk, one is struck by the preponderance of foreigners. Jeritza, like Slezak and Jerger, came from Brünn, Kiepura came from Poland, Piccaver was British, Grosavescu Rumanian, Koloman von Pataky and Rosette Anday were Hungarians and Lotte Lehmann and Elisabeth Schumann came from Germany. Austria was represented by Richard Tauber, Richard Mayr, Hans Duhan and Hermann Gallos.

Rosette Anday was a discovery of Schalk's. After hearing her in Budapest when she was still very young, he introduced her to Vienna as Carmen in 1921. Her voice had a peculiarly romantic timbre, which is perhaps why she liked singing Hungarian and gipsy songs at receptions and gala parties. With her exquisitely slim figure and the erotic glint of her great big eyes she captured all hearts in her very first Vienna appearance. During here forty years at the Vienna Opera she sang all the big contralto parts: Delila, Amneris, Azucena, Fricka,

Brangäne, and the Messenger in *Das Wunder der Heliane*, until in 1961, still in full possession of her vocal qualities, she retired from the stage. Her farewell appearance was as Klytaemnestra in *Elektra*. The ringing tones of her chest-notes were unforgettable, and I can still hear her 'Und wenn ich liebe, nimm dich in acht' in *Carmen* (German version). Equally unforgettable for all who heard her were her appearances on the concert platform, especially the profound poignancy of the alto solo 'O Röslein rot, der Mensch liegt in tiefster Not' in Mahler's Second Symphony, or her 'Ewig, ewig' in *Das Lied von der Erde*.

Elisabeth Schumann, a native of Thuringia, was the wife of Karl Alwin, a fine pianist whom Richard Strauss engaged as a conductor. She too came to the Vienna Opera during Strauss's term, and very soon became one of the most brilliant soubrettes and the loveliest Sophie we have ever heard. She had a gossamer pianissimo, yet oddly enough, and paradoxically, she could sing the softest note so distinctly that for all its tenuousness her top B when Octavian hands her the silver rose 'Wie himmlische, nicht irdische' filled every corner of the house. There has never been anyone like her in this rôle.

Richard Tauber, a native of Linz on the Danube, an incomparable Mozart singer before he defected to operetta (but without abandoning opera altogether), and one of the idols of my younger days, was a classic example of how, by sheer intelligence, it is possible to make the most of a voice with limited top notes, and become world-famous. His main assets were his unique and quite wonderful middle notes, but in forte passages anything above B flat always gave him trouble. Yet in passages that spelt danger his phrasing and disposition of emphasis were so clever that even when he just missed a top note you could have sworn he had hit it. His pianissimo and falsetto had to be heard to be believed. Perhaps his finest moment was the crescendo on the long F in Don Ottavio's 'Il mio tesoro' in *Don Giovanni*. It was Tauber's voice that enabled Franz Lehár to give operetta a new lease on life. As for gramophone records, there was hardly a salon or a bar that did not serve up 'Ich küsse Ihre Hand, Madame'.

The list of celebrated singers at Schalk's disposal is by no means exhausted, and since recollecting the great names of old is a favourite pastime among opera-goers, to recall a few more may not be out of place. There was the heroic tenor Laurenz Hofer, for instance; the character-player William Wernigk, a marvellous Monostatos in *The Magic Flute;* Viktor Madin, who made over 4,000 appearances and whose real name was Madincea, cut down to Madin by Mahler, when he engaged him; Maria Gerhart, a great coloratura soprano to whom so many have cause to be grateful; Luise Helletsgruber, a lovely Liu who was killed in a road accident; Felice Hüni-Mihacsek, an admirable Mozart singer; Maria Rajdl, Oestvig's wife; Lotte Schöne; Claire Born, who was cast in the same sort of parts as Lotte Lehmann; the charming Aenne Michalsky; and Richard Schubert, a heroic tenor with beautiful legs whose career was so tragically short: before losing his voice he was a wonderful Siegfried and Walter Stolzing. Then there were Helene Wildbrunn, a brilliant Brünnhilde, Leonore and Isolde who had been engaged by Strauss, and Gertrude Kappel, an outstanding Elektra who later emigrated to America. One of the house's most loyal and reliable singers who could be trusted to deputise in heroic tenor parts at the shortest notice was Josef Kalenberg, who was also Honorary President of the 'Rapid' football club, which has frequently won the Austrian championship. Whenever Kalenberg was singing at a Sunday afternoon performance and 'Rapid' had a match, between appearances on the stage he would rush to the telephone to find out the score. The fact that I only mention the great Vera Schwarz towards the end has nothing to do with her status. A great star, she came to the Vienna Opera from Zagreb and had the whole of Jeritza's repertoire at her finger-tips. Nor should Bella Paalen be forgotten, a contralto engaged by Mahler; her great part was the mother in Meyerbeer's *Le Prophète*. Karl Norbert was an accomplished bass who excelled as Kezal in *The Bartered Bride* and was a great friend and admirer of Richard Mayr's. Mayr died in 1935 and is buried in St. Peter's churchyard in Salzburg. And Norbert is buried at his feet, in accordance with a clause in his will.

It was a magnificent era for tenors. In 1927 for instance we had Slezak, Piccaver, Kiepura, Tauber, Grosavescu, Schubert, Hofer and the excellent Mozart and Verdi singer Koloman von Pataky.

But all this did not suffice. We had set our hearts on the return of Richard Strauss. And at long last, here he was, not as Director but as a visiting conductor, as an artist, a man and a citizen of Vienna, which was far more important.

What really brought Strauss back to Vienna was his house in the Jacquingasse. On the occasion of his sixtieth birthday in 1924 he had been made an honorary citizen of Vienna and had been presented with a plot of leasehold land near the Botanic Gardens, out by the Belvedere. One of the terms of the lease was that he should present the Austrian National Library with the score of *Der Rosenkavalier*. At the time quite a number of people got worked up about a whole plot of land being traded for a few pages of music, but we young fans maintained that for the score of *Rosenkavalier* the free gift of Schönbrunn Palace would not be enough. We were of the opinion that Strauss had been shabbily treated. Anyway, on this plot of land he built a house known as the 'Strauss-Schlössl', in which he and his wife Pauline occupied the top floor, and his son Dr. Franz lived below with his wife, Alice.

Richard Strauss was too much a practical man of the world to harbour animosity for very long, so there was no very great difficulty in coaxing him back to Vienna two years after his dismissal from the Vienna Opera. The new Director-General of the Federal Theatres regarded getting Strauss back as one of the cardinal points in his policy. The negotiations proved to be not nearly so embarrassing as they might have been with a man of less common-sense, and eventually Strauss signed a new contract in which he undertook to conduct 100 performances and present the score of his *Ägyptische Helena* to the Austrian National Library. In return he was guaranteed sole ownership of the Jacquingasse property. So he returned to Vienna, the quarrel was patched up, and a grateful audience received as a dowry, so to speak, a superb performance of *Elektra*.

In the following year, 1927, came the long overdue Vienna première of *Intermezzo*, written in 1924, a 'comedia domestica' which is the operatic counterpart of the *Sinfonia domestica* (1904), the symphonic portrayal of his domestic life. The protagonist is Strauss himself (*Kapellmeister* Storch), and his dearly beloved wife, Pauline, his 'good companion' as he called her, appears as Christine Storch. There is also a part for their small son. The work is highly original and a unique phenomenon in the history of music. It consists of a sequence of scenes (domestic episodes, sleigh-riding, a country dance, etc.) sung in a sort of parlando style that Strauss called *parlandissimo*. In the foreword to *Intermezzo* Strauss gives detailed instructions as to how this parlando style is to be managed. The foreword also contains valuable advice on singing in general. Strauss points out for instance that the main thing in singing is to pronounce the consonants clearly, so that the singer is not drowned out by even the loudest orchestra. If the consonants are not pronounced distinctly it only needs a mezzo-forte to drown out the singer completely.

On the top notes the parlando blossoms out into normal singing. Between the various scenes of *Intermezzo* there is a string of wonderful orchestral interludes in homage to the 'good companion'. In one of the parlando scenes Strauss also pays homage to the game of skat. (He was a skat fiend all his life.) He even used to get in a quick game or two between acts when he was conducting in the Opera. Whenever the programme had to be changed and a longer opera substituted for a short one, people say he used to speed up the tempi so as not to miss a minute of his precious skat.

The libretto of *Intermezzo* is by Strauss himself. His domestic life is presented in such detail that the audience is actually informed about what Strauss's favourite jam was (it was called *Hagebuttenmark* in Germany). We young people were such slavish admirers of Strauss that we had nothing better to do than scour half of Vienna to get hold of a jar of *Hagebuttenmark*. We finally ran one to earth in a shop in the Neue Markt, where we were told that the reason we had had such difficulty in getting hold of it was that it was known in Vienna as *Hetschepetsch Marmelade*.

'I want the head of ... Minister Prochnik', says Maria Jeritza in this caricature by Ludwig Unger (1929). The Austrian Minister in Washington had failed to appear at a reception given in her honour. Right: Franz Schneiderhan, Director-General of the State Theatres, and Federal Chancellor Dr. Ignaz Seipel.

In my view, *Intermezzo* is as important for an understanding of Richard Strauss's personality as *Tristan* is for an understanding of Wagner's. The tiff and reconciliation are merely the dramatic frame: the essence of the opera is to provide a portrayal for posterity of Pauline Strauss and of her profound influence on his creative activity. As the 'Hero's companion', the rôle in which she is portrayed in *Ein Heldenleben*, she was not to everyone's taste and in real life she could be just as bloody-minded as she could be all smiles. As an opera-singer she had been good enough for Bayreuth. Strauss adored her, but others regarded her as the most unpleasant affliction an opera house could suffer from. There are hundreds of stories about her. During Schalk's term, for instance, she is supposed to have haunted the auditorium during rehearsals, and if she didn't like the way things were going she would let out a shrill whistle and there had to be changes. In the end the head producer, Wilhelm von Wymetal, got so fed up with Pauline Strauss's antics that he cancelled his contract and threw in his lot with the New York 'Met', where he scored a great success with a production of Korngold's *Die tote Stadt* in which Jeritza made her New York début. So at the 'Met' he stayed.

During a rehearsal of *Intermezzo* Alfred Jerger, who was singing the part of *Kapellmeister* Storch, suddenly banged on the table with his fist; whereupon Strauss walked on to the stage and said: 'That was fine, Jerger, that's exactly the way I bang on the table — do it just like that on the night.' Two minutes later Pauline appeared in Jerger's dressing-room and said: 'Well done, Jerger, very good, singing, acting, everything. But banging your fist down on the table like that! You must cut that out — my husband would never dare to behave like that.' Still, she was a great woman. Manfred Mautner Markhof, the President of the Vienna Konzerthaus, once told me how she burst into tears when showing a singer how to play the recognition scene in *Elektra*.

Some time after the Vienna première of *Arabella*, in which Jerger was Mandryka, Strauss and Jerger and one or two friends were travelling from Genoa to Rapallo to visit Gerhart Hauptmann. During the journey Strauss started reading a letter from his wife which had arrived just before they started, and after finishing it said to the others: 'Another lovely letter from Pauline: just listen to this,' and he started reading it aloud. 'Ass', 'Fool', 'Idiot' were only the milder names the writer called her husband. The others naturally asked what was so 'lovely' about the letter. 'Ah, you don't understand,' replied Strauss. 'The lovely part is between the lines.'

Schalk was tireless in his pursuit of novelties to get back at Strauss for saying that he, Schalk, had no use for contemporary works. To make matters even more hectic, another letter from Strauss, one of the last he had written to Schalk during their partnership, just before the final break, was also keeping him on his toes. In the letter Strauss tried to enlist Schalk's support for a united front against the economies the authorities were threatening; unless they took active measures, Strauss argued, they would soon both be out of the job and might as well spend their time playing chess. Even more important, however, was a paragraph in which Strauss enjoined Schalk to have a good look at Ravel's operas, particularly *L'heure espagnole*, and Stravinsky's works for the stage, in particular *Pulcinella*. So Schalk put on Ravel's *L'enfant et les sortilèges* and took *Pulcinella* and *Oedipus Rex* into the repertoire, the latter much to the audience's consternation, as the libretto was in Latin. A dozen or so Viennese school-children had good cause to rue *Oedipus*, because one or two masters who were opera fans included parts of its libretto in the Latin examination papers.

With a characteristic sense of duty Schalk continued to do all he could for contemporary Austrian operas. Within two years of becoming sole Director he accepted Bittner's successful *Höllisch Gold* which had brilliant parts for Rosette Anday and the bass-baritone Josef von Manowarda from the Volksoper. The opera is about the Devil, who visits the earth with bags of gold in search of a soul to buy. But in his unaccustomed human environment he takes on human attributes. In the end he is content with the soul of an evil old witch.

A ballet, *Das lockende Phantom*, was the first work by the highly talented Franz Salmhofer to be accepted by the Vienna Opera. The phantom was danced by Tilly Losch.

The conductor apart, on the contemporary operatic stage the producer is king. In former times the composers were often their own producers, alternatively it might be the *Kapellmeister* or retired singers. Production was not an end in itself. Peak performances or total theatre may have meant nothing to them, but they were not so presumptuous as to alter or distort a work of art in order to satisfy their self-esteem, conceit, or an impulse for originality for its own sake. In Wieland Wagner's *Lohengrin* (1965) the hero was made to come on much too soon and at an entirely wrong moment in the score where-upon, bored stiff, he had to listen to the whole chorus which describes Lohengrin's arrival. (The whole thing felt like a performance of the St. Matthew Passion.) In this way one of the most dramatic moments in operatic literature was turned into a dreary anti-climax, with the result that the great theme in A major which is meant to accompany Lohengrin's entrance, becomes quite incomprehensible. At this point in the score Lohengrin has been on the stage, where he has no business being, for a considerable time. The scene below shows Elsa's entrance in Act One, beneath a kind of plastic roof reminiscent of a church window — just in case anyone should suppose that the action is taking place where Wagner intended, in 'a meadow on the banks of the Scheld'. Some find this scenery beautiful. Perhaps it is. But it is certainly incorrect. (Ortrud: Christa Ludwig; Telramund: Walter Berry; Herald: Robert Kerns; King: Marti Talvela; Elsa: Claire Watson.)

As a producer, Otto Schenk is a fanatic for absolute fidelity to the original work; his style can be summarised as heightened realism. He prepares himself for his productions by long and intensive work, studying all the existing books, pictures and recordings to assimilate the atmosphere of the opera. He exudes a power of suggestion which is so compelling that stage and costume designers often adopt his concepts at the expense of their own. Schenk's precise instructions for the decor go into the most minute detail and he draws innumerable sketches for

each scene. His theory runs: 'Imagination does not work in a vacuum — we cannot invent anything that does not already exist.' Schenk comes to the first stage rehearsal with a comprehensive knowledge of the work but with no fixed plan for the individual positions, movements, groupings or gestures. He improvises all this on the spot, the ideas pour from him in an unending flood. The singers love him because they can laugh with him and also learn from him how to behave in their rôles like genuine people. In the *Rosenkavalier* which he produced

in 1968 Roller's blueprint was abandoned for the first time. Together with the brilliant stage designer Rudolf Heinrich he designed a set for Faninal's Palace in three sections (below). Hall and staircase formed one large area which could be partitioned off with screens for the intimate scenes. (Stage design: Rudolf Heinrich, costumes: Ernie Kniepert, from left to right — Octavian: Gwyneth Jones; Ochs: Walter Berry; Faninal: Erich Kunz; Sophie: Reri Grist; Leitmetzerin: Emmy Loose.)

Herbert von Karajan was the only director of the Vienna Opera to create a new production of the entire Wagner tetralogy and then to conduct it himself. *Walküre* (1957) — (*Rheingold* followed in 1958) introduced a very interesting lighting system (there were 25 lighting rehearsals), and the stage designs and costumes by Emil Preetorius attempted to maintain a happy medium between the old Wagnerian style and neo-Bayreuth. Later, Karajan disassociated himself from this Vienna *Ring* and at his Easter Festivals in Salzburg (jointly with Günther Schneider-Siemssen) he found a much more original, more abstract solution. (Picture: Act Three, cliffs of the Valkyries. Production: Herbert von Karajan; scenery and costumes: Emil Preetorius; the Valkyries from left to right, above: Margarethe Sjöstedt, Christa Ludwig (!), Hilde Rössl-Majdan, Marta Rohs, Rosette Anday, Ljuba Welitsch (!), below: Gerda Scheyrer, Judith Hellwig.) Above right: Zeffirelli, like Schenk, is a realist. In the first and fourth acts of his *Bohème* one could positively inhale the smells of the atelier, in the second and third acts the crowd pushed and elbowed their way in front of the Café Momus (a live pony drew the toyseller's cart), and one shivered during the farewell scene in Act Three: A wintry landscape, winter in the hearts of men. (Production and scenery: Franco Zeffirelli; costumes: M. Escoffier; Mimi: Mirella Freni; Rudolf: Gianni Raimondi.)

Below: *Jenufa* by Leoš Janáček was Otto Schenk's first production at the Vienna Opera (1964). In collaboration with the highly distinguished stage designer from Augsburg, Günther Schneider-Siemssen, he created a shatteringly authentic picture of life among the people of Moravia. (Producer: Otto Schenk; scenery: Günther Schneider-Siemssen; costumes: Hill Reihs-Gromes; Jenufa: Sena Jurinac; Grandmother Buryja: Elisabeth Höngen; Laca: Waldemar Kmentt.)

Die Frau ohne Schatten, produced and conducted by Herbert von Karajan, was the last première of his era (June 1964). He was in magnificent form, and the way he staged this fantasy in all its dreamlike transcendence was deeply impressive. The transformations aided by the under-stage machinery were fascinating. However, perhaps for the first time in the history of modern operatic stage-craft, this *Frau ohne Schatten* suffered not only significant cuts but also fundamental structural innovations. The first, third and fifth scenes in Act Two take place in the Dyer's house, the fourth shows the vision in which the Emperor turns to stone. This fourth scene was now placed before the third, and the third and fifth scenes were merged into one large, uninterrupted sequence. The producer saw this as an effective simplification, but it distorted the inner meaning of the whole series. The guilty Empress should not see the vision of the petrifying Emperor (Scene 4) until her growing compassion for the Dyer Barak (Scene 3) has almost transformed her into a human being. But here the Empress's reaction was shown in advance of the event which caused it. (Pro-

duction: Herbert von Karajan; scenery: Günther Schneider-Siemssen; costumes: Ronny Reiter; Empress: Leonie Rysanek; Dyer's Wife: Christa Ludwig; Nurse: Grace Hoffman.) Above right: the most expensive stars, the most costly materials, much ado and little imagination — scenic production on the level of window-dressing: that was the new *Turandot* in 1961. (Production: Margarete Wallman; scenery: Nicola Benois; costumes: Chou Ling; Turandot: Birgit Nilsson; Calaf: Giuseppe di Stefano.) — Below: Günther Rennert is one of the most distinguished opera producers of our time, his range extends from the modern era back to Wagner and beyond to Mozart and Rossini. In 1966 he staged a *Barber of Seville* in a playful, almost choreographic style. The unified stage setting is a house seen lengthwise, its rooms open and close alternately. Rosina lives on the first floor to the left. (Production: Günther Rennert; scenery and costumes: Alfred Siercke; Basilio: Oskar Czerwenka; Rosina: Reri Grist; Marzelline: Hilde Konetzni; Figaro: Eberhard Wächter; Bartolo: Erich Kunz; Almaviva: Fritz Wunderlich.)

To Oscar Fritz Schuh, theatre is a product of the mind and preparation is all. Before he begins on the work of production, months are spent in research in libraries and galleries. In contrast to Schenk whose real work of stage production only begins with inspired improvisation during rehearsals, Schuh comes to the first stage rehearsal with a concept which is complete down to the last detail. The sequel is a realisation of what had been born in his mind long before. Schuh insists on first-class cooperators and the best of casts, and he possesses a superb talent for getting what he wants. His Vienna *Orpheus* (1959) was put on in partnership with Casper Neher — the team which created so many magnificent productions of Mozart. Schuh cut *Orpheus* down to one-and-a-half hours and played it straight through without an interval; this met with some criticism. The decor was rather reminiscent of *art nouveau* with its curious geometrical shapes and alternating pillars forming the scene of action (the scene below shows the two rings in Elysium), the stage was enclosed by revolving screens which presented a different colour scheme at each rotation. (Production: Oscar Fritz Schuh; scenery and costumes: Caspar Neher; Orpheus in the centre of our picture: Giulietta Simionato.)

In a modern Opera House it is the conductors and the producers who rule the roost. In Vienna, up to the end of Mahler's term, it was not customary to give the name of the conductor, but Weingartner liked seeing his name in print, so from his time on the conductor's name was duly displayed. Before the advent of the star conductor the *Kapellmeister* had a threefold job: to mark time, to give the singers their cues, and to indicate to members of the orchestra who had had nothing to do for some time when they were to come in. Verdi used to grumble about the fuss being made of the *Kapellmeister*. Now that the star conductor is almost part of the scenery in any first-class Opera House, the question often arises as to which kind of conductor is the 'proper' one; the dancing dervish, the cynosure of all eyes, or the almost motionless figure with a minimum of gestures. Surely what matters is the result; how it is achieved is less important. Clemens Krauss (below) conducted like a grand seigneur, but not a showman. He was exceedingly thorough at rehearsals, often requesting not only individual groups to play a passage alone but also individual players, or unusual combinations of players. ('They can never hear themselves at a performance, so now is their chance'). From anyone else the players would have taken offence, but not from him.

'... und zwingt uns,
ihm noch Gröss'res zuzutraun.'
(Franz Werfel: 'Der Dirigent')

During his 68 years as a conductor Toscanini appeared at the Vienna Opera on four occasions. In 1929 he conducted the Milan Scala; in 1930 he conducted concerts by the New York Philharmonic Orchestra; in 1934 he conducted Verdi's Requiem in memory of the Austrian Chancellor Dollfuss, who had just been assassinated; and in 1936 he conducted *Fidelio* with a cast including his favourite singer Lotte Lehmann. The son of a poor Parma tailor, he was for the Scala what Mahler was for Vienna. He was recognised as one of the world's greatest conductors and the very antithesis of Furtwängler. He was one of the first to conduct practically everything by heart — he had to, because of his poor eyesight. He was also the first to give priority to absolute precision. It was therefore hardly surprising that he was the gramophone's first star conductor.

My good friend Karl Alwin was engaged by Richard Strauss as a repertoire conductor at the Vienna Opera. I am well aware that he was certainly not world class, but he had great talent and an enormous repertoire. He was also a brilliant accompanist at his wife Elisabeth Schumann's Lieder recitals. I remember many pleasant evenings together when, if asked, he would sit down at the piano and play any opera in the repertoire, including *Elektra*, right through by heart.

Unlike Toscanini's ideal of absolute accuracy, what Wilhelm Furtwängler (right) strove for was a sort of romantic surge of sound. Toscanini was admired for being able to maintain a positively metronomic regularity of tempo for pages on end, whereas Furtwängler was admired for the looseness of his phrasing at any given moment. When he was conducting, his head wagged as busily as his flickering baton. Members of first-class orchestras who were used to him divined their entrances intuitively, but newcomers had a difficult time. With a technique that was all his own he created the so-called 'Furtwängler sound' that was his life-long ambition. He did not want a chord involving the whole orchestra, say the opening of the *Meistersinger* Overture, to be produced by every single member of the orchestra playing with absolute precision down to the tiniest fraction of a second: the flickering of his baton ensured a deliberate imprecision almost like an arpeggio. From his first *Rheingold* in 1928 Furtwängler maintained a desultory connection with the Vienna Opera right up to the Theater an der Wien era.

Hans Knappertsbusch was not so reluctant to rehearse as the many stories about him would suggest, but it was only difficult key passages that he worked at in detail. With Knappertsbusch one always had the feeling that the whole performance was a brilliant improvisation. He was very tall, and when he suddenly drew himself up and lunged at the orchestra with his baton one could imagine that it was at this very moment that the music of Wagner or Strauss was being born. Knappertsbusch was most intimately connected with the Vienna Opera from the mid-1930s until after the reopening in 1955.

Right: Conductors of international reputation and experience have contributed to making the Vienna Opera what it is. So have all those lesser figures of the type described by Julius Korngold as 'conductors of authoritative craftsmanship' who selflessly devoted themselves to the repertoire, to the singers, and to routine work. In their hands, everything was sure to be all right. A typical example was Rudolf Moralt, a nephew of Richard Strauss, who was much in demand during and immediately after World War II.

Bruno Walter was all kindness and courtesy at rehearsals, and never lost his temper. His favourite injunction to the orchestra: 'Make it sing, gentlemen, sing!' If he was really unhappy about the results he was getting he would whisper abjectly: 'You know, I'm still not quite happy about this.' That was the nearest he ever got to losing his temper! Gustav Mahler left most of the Italian operas to Walter, but what I remember him best by are his wonderful *Eugene Onegin* (1934), *Orfeo* (1935), and a new production of *Carmen* (1937). From 1925 Bruno Walter was intimately associated with the Salzburg Festival. Although a native of Berlin he felt much more at home in Vienna, and it was a thousand pities that circumstances prevented his association with the Vienna Opera from being as close as he would have wished. As a disciple of Mahler's he could not endure the regimes of Weingartner and Gregor and departed in 1912 after conducting over 500 performances. As Artistic Adviser during Kerber's term he lasted only 18 months until the German occupation of Austria in 1938.

Karl Böhm (right) started at the Vienna Opera with *Tristan* in 1933. He was appointed Director shortly before the reopening in 1955 but after two years he resigned in the summer of 1956 following adverse criticism of the amount of time he was spending abroad. He was succeeded by Herbert von Karajan (left) with the title of Artistic Adviser. Karajan also started at the Vienna Opera with *Tristan* and spent even more time abroad than Böhm did. Karajan resigned in 1964: like Weingartner in 1911, Strauss in 1924, Schalk in 1928, and Clemens Krauss in 1934, he had had enough. Karajan is a native of Salzburg and Böhm of Graz. Both rose from the ranks, but whereas Karajan's international reputation was made first in the concert-hall and later at the Opera, with Böhm it was the other way round. At the New York 'Met' the two manage to 'coexist', but their activities are usually at different times of the year.

Joseph Krips is one of the steadily dwindling number of conductors who personally preside over a new production from the very first piano rehearsal to the actual first night. It was Krips who rescued his adored Mozart from being little more than a stop-gap in the repertoire. On everything he does, repertoire performances no less than first nights, Krips concentrates the full force of his boundless enthusiasm. For him, a first night is a page of musical history.

Leonard Bernstein began *Falstaff* in 1966 and *Der Rosen-kavalier* in 1968 with a leap into the air. Opera-goers found themselves wondering what effect such a dynamic upheat would have on the first chord of *Lohengrin*. Bernstein became a popular favourite in Vienna literally overnight. As he makes his way slowly to the rostrum he looks not unlike Karajan, but actually they are two very different personalities. Fanatical admirers of Bernstein call him 'Lennie'; fanatical admirers of Karajan call him 'Herr von Karajan'. The secret of Bernstein's popularity is his unconcealed enjoyment of all forms of music, an enjoyment that he transmits to the audience. All forms of music come alike to him: in 1967 he conducted a thrilling performance of Mahler's Second Symphony in the Opera House, yet nobody found it strange that the same man was the composer of *West Side Story*, or that he could sit down at the piano and throw off a trifling piece such as a Mozart Concerto with the Vienna Philharmonic, not to mention explaining Beethoven to American TV audiences. Or even jazz.

An outstanding success for Schalk was a fairy-tale that must still be in a good many people's memories, *Peterchens Mondfahrt* by Clemens Schmalstich.

There was also a new operetta by Johann Strauss: after *Fledermaus* and *Der Zigeunerbaron* Schalk took *Eine Nacht in Venedig* into the repertoire, with Jeritza as Annina. Korngold produced an ingenious arrangement, which he conducted himself, and the 'King of the operetta revival', Hubert Marischka, made his début at the Vienna Opera in the part of Caramello.

Another feather in Schalk's cap was the Vienna Opera's first full-scale foreign tours, at the Paris Grande Opéra in May 1928 with *Tosca, Don Giovanni, Der Rosenkavalier, Fidelio* and *Die Walküre,* and at the Royal Opera, Stockholm in 1929 with *Fidelio* and *Don Giovanni.* Simultaneously, the Paris Grande Opéra delighted Vienna with *Manon, Faust, Carmen* and *Werther.*

The *Fidelio* that Schalk took on tours was the new production devised for the Beethoven Centenary in 1927. It was one of the highlights of Schalk's term and included for the first time the experiment of having the two main rôles sung by lyric instead of dramatic voices. From then on, Lotte Lehmann and Alfred Piccaver in *Fidelio* were a staple.

Another company to visit Vienna was the Cologne Opera with *Pelléas et Mélisande* and Handel. There were also some magnificent performances in 1929 by the entire company of the Milan Scala conducted by Arturo Toscanini. Toti dal Monte was Lucia and Mariano Stabile was superb as Falstaff. Toti dal Monte was partnered by Aureliano Pertile. The quality of the ensemble and Toscanini's conducting were eye-openers, and the visit made a vital contribution to our understanding of what Italian opera really was.

The year 1927 was clouded almost at the start by a terrible tragedy. On the fifteenth of February Trajan Grosavescu, a young and highly promising Rumanian tenor with a lovely natural voice but no great pretensions as an actor, possibly because he was on the corpulent side, was shot dead by his wife Nelly in their Lerchenfelder Strasse apartment. The motive was jealousy. The fact that his last appearance was in *Rigoletto* was played up with due sentimentality by the Press. He had been scheduled to go to Berlin, where he had a rendezvous. Suddenly his wife said she had changed her mind and would like to come too. There was a scene, and then came the shot. In view of the fact that Nelly had just had a miscarriage and was in a state of extreme hypertension, she was acquitted as having acted while the balance of her mind was disturbed.

In June 1928 Schalk's contribution to Strauss's sixty-fourth birthday took the form of the first Vienna performance of *Die ägyptische Helena,* Strauss himself conducting.

Based on Herodotus and Euripides, Hofmannsthal's libretto is a departure from the usual Helen story: after the Trojan War Menelaus is sailing for home with Helen when they are wrecked on a desert island, where Aithra, a daughter of the King of Egypt, tells Menelaus that the Helen he has brought from Troy is only a phantom: the real Helen had been spirited away to Egypt by the gods ten years before and never set foot on Trojan soil. The work was not received with the same enthusiasm as earlier Strauss operas. There was one unforgettable moment when at the beginning of the interlude Jeritza as Helen rose from the great divan on which she had been reclining and slowly made her way down a huge flight of stairs. Memorable also was the fact that for the first time in the history of the Vienna Opera an amplifier was used, for the part of the singing shell.

Among many interesting operatic stars who appeared at the Vienna Opera during Schalk's term were Gitta Alpar, who later became an operetta diva, as Aithra; the Spanish tenor Miguel Fleta in *Carmen* (with Georges Baklanoff); Lauri-Volpi in *Rigoletto;* and Benjamino Gigli as Rodolfo, a memorable evening because in his big aria in Act One his famous top C didn't come off, and there were shouts from the gallery of 'Good old Piccaver!' It was not until Act Three that Gigli's triumph was assured.

To commemorate the centenary of Schubert's death there were performances of three of his Singspiele on the same evening: *Rosamunde, Der Zwillingsbruder,* and *Der häusliche Krieg,* a remarkable experience if only for the variety of the fare provided.

Barely a year later Franz Schalk was no longer Director. He was toppled by the same authorities he had successfully invoked to get rid of Strauss. In 1928 the General Intendant's office brought out a new list of instructions which granted the General Intendant special powers in the matter of selecting premières, engaging singers, casting, etc. This meant such a severe curtailment of the Director's prerogatives that Schalk had no option but to oppose them tooth and nail. As unequivocally as possible he maintained that in running a theatre there must be one authority, and one only, that has the last word. However, there was no weakening on the other side, so Schalk had no choice but to hand in his resignation, effective as of the thirty-first of August 1929.

He still retained his connection with the Opera as a guest conductor, but at the time of his resignation he was already a fairly sick man. The last performance he conducted was of *Tristan* in June 1931. People who were there said that he was 'all mind and no body'. He died during the following August and was buried in Edlach near Payerbach. He was honoured posthumously with the title of 'Österreichischer Generalmusikdirektor' which was invented for him. The only musician to have been awarded the title since is Karl Böhm.

Schalk, a sarcastic humanist who looked as if he were completely detached from this world, was unsurpassed at intrigue and at getting round officials; there was also a sentimental streak in his make-up, but it was genuine and therefore unexceptionable. 'I have done my duty,' were his farewell words to the Opera which he had served like a ministrant of the Holy Grail. When the time came for him to take over, he rose to the occasion magnificently. And his farewell message to the staff contained the noble injunction: 'See to it that you enrich the storehouse of what in the language of civilised humanity we call tradition.'

In October 1928 Furtwängler had conducted a new production of *Das Rheingold*, and Opera patrons were as enthusiastic about him as were the Philharmonic audiences. Vienna felt sure that the new Director of the Opera would be Furtwängler.

But things were to turn out rather differently.

Beneath the surface of the crisis that culminated in Schalk's resignation lurked a positive maze of intrigues and personal jealousies, the *éminence grise* being the *Generalintendant* Franz Schneiderhan, Viennese by birth and a hatter by profession. The Ministry of Education had had him transferred back to Vienna from Breslau, his terms of reference being to restore some semblance of stability to the Federal Theatres' finances.

Schneiderhan's immediate aim was to appoint Wilhelm Furtwängler Director of the Vienna Opera. Furtwängler had succeeded Felix von Weingartner as permanent conductor of the Philharmonic Concerts and during the 1927/28 season had scored a series of sensational successes. After protracted negotiations in the spring of 1928 a contract was agreed committing Furtwängler to the Vienna Opera for a limited period during the 1928/29 season, and in October 1928 Furtwängler did in fact conduct a new production of *Das Rheingold*, which was enthusiastically applauded. This production was the Vienna Opera's prelude to its third presentation of the whole of the *Ring*. The first had been put on by Jauner, and the second had been started by Mahler (*Rheingold* and *Walküre*) and finished off by Weingartner (*Siegfried* and *Götterdämmerung*). In view of the enormous success of Furtwängler's *Rheingold* he seemed the obvious choice for Director, in due course.

Schneiderhan, however, went a step further and behind Schalk's back definitely offered Furtwängler the post as of 1930, the year Schalk's contract was due to expire. Schalk got wind of what was going on, and it was said at the time that it was this secret offer to Furtwängler, rather than the General Intendant's new instructions of 1928, that really led Schalk to tender his resignation. What form Furtwängler's acceptance took will never be known for certain; but in official circles there was no doubt that Furtwängler was now as good as committed to Vienna, and it was generally assumed that he would be the new Director. Accordingly, Schneiderhan went to Berlin to draft the final contract with Furtwängler in person, but just as the two men were about to shake hands on it, Furtwängler's secretary, Beate Geismar (to quote her own account of the incident), suddenly parted the two outstretched hands and thus averted the handshake that would have sealed the bargain.

What Schneiderhan did not know at the time was that in Furtwängler's office there was another contract committing him to the Berlin Philharmonic: in fact, he had already been invested with the specially invented title of 'Generalmusikdirektor der Stadt Berlin'. In the event, Furtwängler signed the Berlin contract, and that was the end of Vienna's hopes.

Meanwhile, however, Schalk had resigned and there was no successor in sight. Schalk was not in such good odour with the authorities as he used to be, and they had no compunction in accepting his resignation. But a successor had to be found quickly, if possible in time for the 1928/29 season.

Among the names that were bandied about in the Vienna Press (Erich Kleiber, Bruno Walter, etc.) was that of the one-time Intendant of the Frankfurt am Main Opera, Clemens Krauss. In December 1928, shortly after the debacle with Furtwängler, Krauss was offered a contract, which after some hesitation he signed. Krauss agreed to accept the post of Director of the Vienna Opera for five years from the first of September 1929, and the appointment was made public forthwith.

The obvious haste with which Krauss was approached led to persistent rumours that certain circles had never wanted Furtwängler in the first place, and that secret negotiations with Clemens Krauss had been going on for a long time, in order to keep Furtwängler out. There was even talk to the effect that Schalk had been roped in to invite Krauss back to Vienna, if not as Director, at any rate as *Kapellmeister* with special authority. The critics, particularly Julius Korngold in the *Neue Freie Presse*, had been clamouring over and over again for what Korngold called 'an authoritative working conductor to help out the present Director'.

Be that as it may, Clemens Krauss was now Director and (Vienna being what it is) was immediately acclaimed as 'Frankfurtwängler', and Hermann Leopoldi, famous comedian of the Vienna cabaret, whetted his wit upon him:

Melodie: 'O Tannenbaum, o Tannenbaum'
O Furtwängler, o Furtwängler,
wie hoch sind deine Gagen!
Du gabest uns dein Ehrenwurt,
dann gingst du nach Berlin uns furt,
doch wir, wir holten flugs uns her
aus Frankfurt den Frankfurtwängler.

(To the tune of 'My Maryland, My Maryland'
Dear Furtwängler, dear Furtwängler,
thou art a money grabber,
thou promis'd us and cross'd your heart
and then for Berlin you did part
which made us rush to Frankfurt, where
we got a new Frankfurtwängler.)

Melodie: 'Da geh' ich ins Maxim'
Der schöne Clemens Krauss,
der passt fürs Opernhaus,
die Damen rufen: Nehmen S'
doch nur den schönen Clemens!
Der Künstlerhut rutscht schief,
die Locke sitzt ihm tief,
was immer er auch leistet,
er wirkt dekorativ.

(To the tune of 'I'm Off to Chez Maxim'
Our darling Clemens Krauss
fits in our Opera House,
the ladies are enraptured
their hearts in storm you captured;
your artist's cap gives way,
your hair in disarray,
whatever your endeavour,
oh, handsome lad, do stay!)

Of all the personages who have at one time or another been Director of the Vienna Opera, Krauss was perhaps the one with the best qualifications for the post. He had the necessary experience, and his *curriculum vitae* told very much in his favour. He was Viennese born and bred, had been a member of the Vienna Boys Choir, was without question an outstanding musician and an excellent conductor, and had completed his studies in Vienna. After a year or two in Brünn he had gone on via Nuremberg, Prague, Stettin, etc., to Graz. There he attracted the attention of Schalk and Strauss, who eventually appointed him *Kapellmeister* of the Vienna Opera, a post he occupied from 1922 to 1924, his finest hour being the first performance of Franz Schmidt's *Fredigundis*. He also succeeded Furtwängler as the conductor of the Vienna Tonkünstler Orchestra's more important concerts. Subsequently, Krauss had the ill luck to succeed Furtwängler twice again, once as conductor of the Vienna Philharmonic concerts and then as Director of the Berlin Opera.

In 1924 he transferred his activities from Vienna to Frankfurt, first as Director and later as Intendant of the Opera and simultaneously as permanent conductor of the 'Museum Concerts'. As Director he was highly successful and offered a programme that was an attractive blend of standard repertoire and ultra-modern novelties. He was the first, for instance, to stage Janáček's opera *The Makropoulos Affair* in Frankfurt. He put on operas by Busoni and Hindemith and also attempted to realise his lofty ideal of making the Frankfurt Opera the home of 'spectacles with music', *i. e.* productions that appealed to the eye and the ear alike. His principal assistants were Lothar Wallerstein as Chief Producer (in 1927 he moved to Vienna, where Krauss him joined later), and as stage-designer Ludwig Sievert, who also worked with Krauss in Vienna for a time.

Lother Wallerstein was one of the most outstanding producers who ever worked for the Vienna Opera in a long-term capacity. He was extraordinarily gifted, and his professional knowledge of the theatre was far greater than his counterparts who run modern opera houses can boast of today. A native of Prague, he was a doctor of medicine as well as a pianist and had been a *Kapellmeister* at the Poznán Opera for some years. I well remember in the years after the First World War how during a rehearsal at the Volksoper he would suddenly jump up and sit at the piano; he often knew the music better than the *Kapellmeister*.

This then was the team that was running the Vienna Opera from December 1929 on. Krauss was also on the teaching staff of the Vienna Academy of Music and Dramatic Art, just as he had been during his earlier period in Vienna. He never completely severed his connection with the Vienna Academy, not even during his spell in Frankfurt.

Thus began the reign of Clemens Krauss.

Clemens Krauss was an outstanding musician whose personal appearance, his whole career in fact, was like something out of an operetta. Wearing his short coat that looked like an opera cloak, his wide-brimmed hat and his remarkable scarf, he looked for all the world like Danilo in *The Merry Widow* when he makes his first entrance in Act One. One half expected him to start singing 'Dann geh' ich ins Maxim'. The Viennese were constantly thinking up something or somebody new to compare him with. 'He has the head of a Roman and looks like a classical bust.' 'On the contrary, he looks like a Torero.' 'Not at all, he looks like a Habsburg.' And so on.

In fact, though not actually a Habsburg he was not far from being one. Even about Clemens Krauss's origin there is an element of operetta, halfway between Johann Strauss and Emmerich Kálmán. His mother, Clementine Krauss (hence the name Clemens), was a dancer at the Opera. When he came into the world illegitimately in 1893 his mother, in obedience to the moral code then prevailing, had to leave the *corps de ballet* forthwith. His father, it transpired, was Count Baltazzi, who had a position at the Court of the Emperor Franz Joseph I. To complete the operetta scenario there was even a connection with Mayerling, for Count Baltazzi was an uncle of Mary Vetsera. Like Hubert Marischka in Kálmán's *Teufelsreiter* at the Theater an der Wien, Baltazzi was a keen horseman and show-jumper with a good collection of cups and other trophies. After being appointed Director of the Vienna Opera, there was nothing that Clemens Krauss in his turn used to enjoy more than a morning canter in the Prater on a white Irish gelding. Count Baltazzi's father, *i.e.* Clemens Krauss's grandfather, was a Secretary at the Austrian Embassy in Paris, and when the Prussians besieged Paris in 1870/71, it was he who was said to have got the Empress Eugénie safely away to England.

Clementine Krauss also was by no means an uninteresting personality. After being dismissed from the Opera she embarked on a career as a singer at the Volksoper. As 'Clemy' Krauss she sang substantial rôles like Selica in Meyerbeer's *L'Africaine*, and when Rainer Simons took over the Volksoper she became Vienna's first female operatic producer.

Besides proving himself the most individual Director since Mahler, Krauss also demonstrated that he had the best possible qualifications for the post. By the time he took office he had decided on a definite policy, whether people liked it or not, and astonishingly enough he succeeded in adhering to it throughout his five year term, which came to an abrupt and dramatic conclusion that again smacked of operetta.

In brief, his policy was ensemble pushed to its logical extreme. An adequate chronicle of Krauss's term must therefore start by saying something about how he staged his repertoire, before passing to what it consisted of. He assembled round himself a group of artists who were unconditionally at his disposal and retained them under contract as long as he possibly could. To all intents and purposes it was with this group alone that he built up his repertoire and put on his premières. To singers outside the group his attitude was often distinctly aloof.

Conflicts with the 'old guard' are of course inevitable when a new broom gets to work with new material. In Mahler's day it was Renard and van Dyck who left the Opera in a huff; now it was Lotte Lehmann and Elisabeth Schumann, the two bright particular stars of the Schalk era who felt themselves slighted by Krauss's importation of new blood. For his part, Krauss maintained that the older singers were not what they had been (he was wrong), and that they would not want to take part in the laborious and meticulous rehearsals that he would insist upon. 'What they are trying to do,' he alleged, 'is to cut down the number of their rôles and slip in a foreign tour or two.' And there was something in what he said.

I cannot believe that he had no appreciation of the older singers; I think that by relying too much on youthful memories we do Krauss an injustice. We young people kept complaining about how Krauss never let Lehmann sing the Marschallin in *Rosenkavalier* and always preferred Viorica Ursuleac. Yet statistics show that during Krauss's regime Lehmann sang the Marschallin far more often than Ursuleac (who later became Krauss's wife). It was just that for us Lehmann was incomparably the better, warmer and more charming Marschallin of the two, and it annoyed us when she wasn't singing. Prejudice distorts, but statistics can always put the record straight.

Krauss proceeded to blend his new imports, who were all first-class material, with the singers from the previous regime whom he could rely on to offer their willing cooperation; Josef von Manowarda and Richard Mayr, for instance, and especially Alfred Jerger, who was given much to do. Krauss particularly enjoyed working with these three.

This 'Krauss group' were given a virtual monopoly of the repertoire. They sang in all the operas in which they could appear to the best advantage, and they sang in all the operas they did not exactly shine in. The casts remained unchanged, if humanly possible, from the première to the final performance. Krauss hated having to change a cast. A new production was built up round a definite group of singers, and that was how it had to stay. All Krauss's new productions were characterised by the most meticulous precision, even if opinions often differed about his casting. Of all the Directors I have known, it was Krauss who kept the first-night standards going longest.

To a great extent this was because Krauss conducted everything himself. On the musical side, his idea was to make the Vienna Opera a one-man band, and the one man was Clemens Krauss. This ambition had its negative as well as its positive aspects. As far as production was concerned, the lord and master was Lothar Wallerstein. This *l'etat c'est moi* spirit pervaded the entire house; one had the impression that the singers were under contract to Krauss personally, not to the Vienna Opera. Their

No. 546/1932   *Gen. Int. No. 1313/1932*

Budget Year 1932

Savings:

Nemeth	60 evenings at 1,026 S . . .	61,560 S
Piccaver	60 evenings at 1,026 S . . .	61,560 S
Lehmann	12 evenings at 1,026 S . . .	12,312 S
Rode	17 and 8 evenings at 1,026 S . . .	25,650 S
Slezak	18 evenings at 900 S . . .	16,200 S
Kern option on 2 months' leave at 3,064 S . . .		6,128 S
	Total	183,410 S

of which respecting new engagements, further commitments and rises in salary (Michalsky) already received:

Zika from 1. 9. to 31. 12.		10,000 S
Michalsky from 1. 9. to 31. 12. . . .		1,600 S
Jerger	18 evenings at 600 S	10,800 S
Pauly	5 evenings at 1,026 S	5,130 S
Trundt	8 evenings at 1,026 S	8,208 S
Ursuleac	15 evenings at 900 S	
by acceptance of 12 appearances between 1. 9. and 31. 12.		13,500 S
Nemeth	4 evenings at 1,026 S	4,104 S
Extension Pataky	8 evenings at 900 S	7,200 S
Extension Angerer	7 evenings at 700 S	4,900 S
		65,442 S

a number of already performed and projected replacement and conducted guest performances to a total amount of		38,919 S
	remainder	79,049 S
Roswaenge	24 evenings at 950 S	22,800 S
	remainder	56,249 S
Nemeth	14 evenings at 1,026 S	14,364 S
	remainder	41,885 S

5. 6. 1932

The top fees of the members of the Vienna Opera after the budget cuts in 1932.

personal allegiance to Krauss was demonstrated with brutal clarity when most of the company departed with him for Berlin in 1934, right in the middle of the season. The Opera was a state within a state, the Principality of Clemens Krauss; the singers were 'his' singers, and not only in the musical sense. It seemed that the Opera and its entire staff were almost his personal property.

An excellent illustration of Krauss's policy with his singers was the case of Viorica Ursuleac, a German-speaking soprano from Chernovitsy and the daughter of an Orthodox priest. She started at the Vienna Volksoper; she was the first Mimi I ever heard there (the Rodolfo was Trajan Grosavescu, who was to come to such a tragic end later on). From the Volksoper she moved to Frankfurt, where she eventually married Clemens Krauss. He brought her to Vienna with him and she soon became one of the pillars of the Vienna Opera's repertoire. She was at her best (and that was very, very good) in parts that suited the explosive radiance of her rather cold voice, Chrysothemis in *Elektra* for instance, or the Empress in *Die Frau ohne Schatten*. She also excelled in minor parts such as Penelope in Robert Heger's *Bettler Namenlos*. On the other hand, she was not at all good as Fiordiligi in *Così fan tutte*: Mozart's charm and delicacy were beyond her ken. Her Eva in *Die Meistersinger* too was only average, without a vestige of the warmth and humanity of Lehmann or Elisabeth Schumann. But not unnaturally she was Krauss's favourite singer and she was very seldom displaced even from the rôles in which she was mediocre.

The same applied to Wilhelm Rode, one of my favourite singers despite certain shortcomings. If I were asked to name the three best Hans Sachses I had ever heard, I should give pride of place to Paul Schöffler; then would come Wilhelm Rode, and I should have to ponder a while over the third. Rode, a bass-baritone from Hanover, was on the small side, and his voice was not big either, but it had a wonderful timbre, and his interpretations were essentially intelligent, which is why he was such a good Sachs and Wotan. Italian parts did not suit his voice at all: his Scarpia was decidedly mediocre, and his Dapertutto in *Tales of Hoffmann*, though original, was

certainly not first-class. As Almaviva he could only be described as poor. Nevertheless, even in these rôles it was always Rode whose name appeared on the programme. Last come, first served.

In addition to conducting virtually all the big premières, Krauss conducted nearly all the subsequent performances too. Outside conductors had no place in his plans. Now and again repertoire performances were entrusted to Robert Heger, a pupil of Pfitzner who had been engaged by Schalk and by a quirk of fate had achieved popularity in Vienna through (of all operas) *Jonny spielt auf;* or to Hugo Reichenberger, who had been engaged as a conductor by Weingartner; or to my good friend Karl Alwin, who had been taken on by Strauss and could play the whole of *Elektra* by heart on the piano. But to the star conductors of the day the Vienna Opera was 'off limits' during Krauss's regime, except of course to Richard Strauss, his great friend and mainstay. Strauss still had to finish his 100 performances in return for the Jacquingasse property. So even the Krauss regime was not the end of the Richard Strauss era.

Strauss had had a big hand in securing Krauss's appointment as Director. The whole affair amounted to a conspiracy between Strauss and Schneiderhan. Strauss was now living in Vienna for a good part of the year and was anxious that there should be a Director at the Opera who would see that Strauss figured prominently in the programme. He therefore set about ensuring that his young friend should be offered the post, and he kept pressing Krauss to make up his mind and accept, because Krauss was reluctant to take on such an important job at this stage: after all, he was only 36 (Mahler had been 37 when he became Director). But Strauss kept bombarding Krauss with letters to the effect that he must make up his mind *now*, because if he didn't the 'other fellow' would get the job. By the 'other fellow' he meant Felix von Weingartner who, as always when a change of Director was in the wind, was lurking at a point of vantage not far from Vienna (in actual fact Weingartner did succeed Krauss five years later).

The very first year of Krauss's reign — we always spoke of Krauss's term as his reign, though as a man

Krauss was not at all an autocrat — foreshadowed what the rest of it was to be like: Mozart, Wagner, Verdi, Richard Strauss and the moderns. Each of these five was represented by an interesting new production. First came *Die Meistersinger,* doubly welcome because the *Meistersinger* we had been given till then had not been produced by anybody in particular. It was a nineteenth century presentation that had found its way by accretion into the twentieth century. Even the scenery was by three different artists, so it was time for a new production.

It was an outstanding success for the 'Frankfurt Trio' of Krauss, Sievert and Wallerstein. The Walther Stolzing was Max Lorenz, a Wagner tenor from Düsseldorf who became a special favourite in Vienna and succeeded to the great heritage of Winkelmann, Schmedes and Schubert. Lorenz was the last great Wagner tenor to assume the mantle in Vienna: Set Svanholm was already a celebrity by the time he first sang here. The Eva was Lotte Lehmann and the Sachs was Wilhelm Rode.

This was the first time a Viennese audience heard Krauss's quick tempi. Accustomed to the traditional leisurely *Meistersinger* handed down by Richter and Franz Schalk, people were taken completely by surprise. From the very first bars of the Overture there was much catching of breath.

In a broadcast I once compared all the versions of the first three bars of the *Meistersinger* Overture I could lay my hands on. The results were remarkable. Knappertsbusch, notorious for his leisurely tempi, emerged as one of the quickest conductors, whilst the slowest tempo of all was set by Richard Strauss, who had a reputation for taking everything so fast.

As well as waxing indignant over these 'modern' quick tempi, the more conservative elements, as I well remember, were outraged that Walther Stolzing sang the Prize Song from a neat little two-wheeled cart with a rail at the back, rather like a pulpit, instead of from the little green mound traditionally brought on in a basket and solemnly decanted by two apprentices. It was considered almost worse than sacrilege. The interplay of the various chorus groups in the difficult Finale of Act Two was brilliantly managed.

The new *Meistersinger* was only the first of a series of interesting new Wagner productions. I remember particularly clearly *Rienzi* and the partially renovated *Parsifal* in 1933 in commemoration of the fiftieth anniversary of Wagner's death. But Krauss's most controversial new Wagner production was his completion of the *Ring* that Furtwängler had inaugurated with *Rheingold* in Schalk's time.

The new *Ring* made many friends, but many enemies too. Looking back, one must admit that it was admirably conducted by Krauss, but there was not perhaps the uniformity of style that one would have expected of a production of this calibre. The producer was Wallerstein, and the scenery was by the trusty Roller, but in his old age he started to blend his natural romanticism with modern elements verging on cubism, and the result was not always satisfactory. I recall a wonderful design for Hunding's house in *Die Walküre,* with a somewhat austere ash tree and exaggeratedly jagged, abstract rocks in Act Two (the same rocks had done duty in *Rheingold),* and a magic-fire scene in which the tongues of flame were simply long strips of red material fanned from underneath by a wind machine. One thing this new willingness to experiment with the *Ring* did show was that the theory of intellectualisation and simplification propounded by Adolphe Appia and Edward Gordon Craig, and developed by Roller, was being taken seriously long before the days of neo-Bayreuth. In practice, however, the consequences were sometimes grotesque.

I remember for instance that in the new *Walküre* the fir tree beneath which Wotan puts Brünnhilde into her deep sleep was suddenly no more. In view of the storm of criticism from audiences and critics alike, the director's staff decided to allow it to grow again by Act Three of *Siegfried,* and during the last scene there it was again; young Siegfried found his aunt fast asleep beneath it.

In *Rheingold* Wotan wore a dark-blue cloak, Loge was fiery red from top to toe, and Alberich was a sickly green. In *Walküre* there were some wonderful lighting effects and colours too.

The highlight of this new *Ring* was Maria Jeritza as

Brünnhilde. Shorn of time-hallowed Wagnerian clichés, her 'Hojotoho' was almost incredible. In some of the other parts the casting was less fortunate. Josef Kalenberg, the worthy all-round tenor who was equally at home in Italian, French and German rôles (and would have been equally at home in Russian or Chinese rôles if required) did not measure up to Siegfried either in *Siegfried* or in *Götterdämmerung*. Lotte Lehmann was a Sieglinde who irradiated the whole of Act One with her tenderness and warmth.

One of Krauss's most successful experiments in his endeavour to bring the Wagner productions up to date was his casting of Maria Nemeth in the part of Brünnhilde. Maria Nemeth was a Hungarian with a commanding, radiant voice, who had hitherto appeared almost exclusively in Italian operas.

As time went by Krauss acquired some valuable new recruits to his Wagner ensemble. There was Erich Zimmermann, for instance, one of the best buffo tenors in Europe, who is still remembered with gratitude, especially as Mime or David. Krauss's best catch, however, was the tenor Franz Völker, of Frankfurt, who had been working in a bank there before starting his career as a singer by winning a radio competition. To his dying day Völker looked exactly like the popular conception of a bank clerk, with spectacles and a homely round face. In Frankfurt he gave a brilliant account of Florestan, and in Vienna he was at his best as Lohengrin and Siegmund. His voice had enormous power and a typically German timbre, yet he was also a very good *bel canto* exponent, equally good as Canio or Don Carlos. His acting left something to be desired, and his sense of humour was more in evidence in real life than on the stage. Yet on one occasion he brought off an extempore that would have done even Nestroy credit. He was appearing in Lehár's *Land des Lächelns* in some middle-sized town in Germany, and the local paper was getting very excited over the high fee he was being paid as Sou-Chong. So during his opening aria 'Doch wie's drin aussieht geht niemand was an' ('What it looks like inside is nobody's business,' referring to the state of his heart), he held up his purse for the startled audience to see.

Krauss's first Mozart première was *Così fan tutte*, with delightful new scenery by Ludwig Sievert. The producer was Wallerstein, and the Despina was Adele Kern, a charming coloratura soubrette, though we were naturally annoyed that her success prevented our beloved Elisabeth Schumann from appearing so often. Adele Kern was a great friend of Wallerstein's. Viorica Ursuleac and Eva Hadrabova, a Czech, were Fiordiligi and Dorabella respectively, and I can still see in my mind's eye the wide expanse of sea in the background as they disported themselves on their swings. The dominating colours were those of the two sisters, pale blue for Dorabella and pink for Fiordiligi, if I remember correctly.

Two other outstanding new Mozart productions were *Idomeneo* (1931), in a new version by Richard Strauss that he conducted himself, and a new *Zauberflöte*, conducted by Krauss.

Clemens Krauss was a lifelong friend of Richard Strauss and actually wrote the libretto for his opera *Capriccio*. It was therefore hardly surprising that Strauss figured prominently in Krauss's repertoire. First came a partially renovated *Rosenkavalier* with an innovation in Act Two: for the first time there was an uninterrupted view of the passage and stairway through the great double doors of the salon, so that the audience could see Faninal's servants being chased by Ochs's uncouth louts ('straight from the turnip fields') and not just hear their screams.

Next came a partially revised production of *Die Frau ohne Schatten* with some drastic alterations in Roller's original scenery. In addition to the outside of the Dyer's house there was a new set for the courtyard, so there was no longer any need for the last scene of Act One and the first scene of Act Two to be played with the same scenery. Clemens Krauss's justification of this procedure has become a maxim in theatrical circles: 'The curtain must never, never rise on the same scene as it came down on, or people will think we can't run to any more scenery.'

But the most important Strauss première was naturally the first Vienna performance of *Arabella* in October 1933. On the opening night Arabella was sung by Lotte

Lehmann under tragic circumstances, her mother having died the same morning. Nevertheless she was determined not to let the performance down, and it was not till later that she asked for, and was granted, time off to recover from the shock. Richard Strauss came on to the stage in person to express his gratitude to her. The alternative (and alternating) Arabella was Viorica Ursuleac, who had sung the part at the first performance in Dresden. There was great applause for the duet 'Aber der Richtige', but the 'Fiakerball' ('cab-drivers ball') scene was considered totally devoid of any genuinely Austrian atmosphere. Adele Kern (coloratura) trilled and yodelled her way through her part like a filigree doll instead of a strapping 'Fiakermilli'. In order to economise, the scenery for Act Two was borrowed from the sets for Heuberger's operetta *Ein Opernball* which had proved a fiasco in 1931. The audience included Arturo Toscanini. The Zdenka on the opening night was Luise Helletsgruber, and on the second a charming new Hungarian soprano named Margit Bokor, who had been obliged by the racial laws of the Third Reich to leave Germany earlier in the year (1933). Clemens Krauss enabled her to start her career afresh at the Vienna Opera. In his personal relationships Krauss harboured no prejudices. For all his close contact with the National-Socialist regime he took under contract any number of refugees, and even in 1934, when he and his wife appeared to have come out in their true colours, one could not really see through him. The part of Waldner senior was sung by Richard Mayr, who was a great favourite with Clemens Krauss (as with everyone else). It was almost the last new part he sang. As Mandryka, Alfred Jerger imbued the part with all the romantic atmosphere of the Balkans (not to mention a wonderfully authentic Balkan accent).

Verdi was one of Krauss's particular predilections, and along with his introduction of *Wozzeck*, the consolidation of the Verdi renaissance was perhaps his most important achievement during his term of office. He went about the task with the utmost application and thoroughness, and regaled Vienna with three virtually unknown Verdi operas: *Simone Boccanegra*, *Don Carlos*, and *Macbeth*.

Franz Werfel, who had compiled such a wonderful libretto for *La forza del destino,* was again called upon to concoct new German libretti for *Don Carlos* and *Simone Boccanegra,* and once again his versions far surpassed the originals. Unfortunately Werfel was not able to complete a German libretto for *Macbeth,* because as a Jew he was no longer 'tolerable' in the Third Reich and no Opera House in Germany would have been in a position to accept his work. For not standing by Werfel and insisting on his making a libretto for *Macbeth,* Clemens Krauss laid himself open to a good deal of adverse comment in more than one quarter.

However, the Verdi evenings were superb. The title-rôle in *Simone Boccanegra* was sung alternately by Wilhelm Rode and Dr. Emil Schipper, though there was no love lost between Krauss and Schipper. Schipper boasted a voluminous baritone voice with brilliant top notes, but he knew little about the technique of singing. He sang, so to speak, 'in erratic blocks'. But his stage presence was magnificent. He was a bit too addicted to alcohol for Krauss's liking: there were evenings when he was (not to put too fine a point upon it) completely sozzled. Once when he was singing in *The Flying Dutchman* in Graz he had to hold on to the rigging of the ship like grim death to keep from falling while singing his big aria. Graz was suitably shocked.

Personally, I found *Don Carlos* the best of the three new Verdi productions. The Viennese have taken this opera to their hearts as affectionately as they took *Turandot,* and it is assured of a permanent place in the Viennese repertoire. In other musical centres *Turandot* and *Don Carlos* are not nearly as well-known or popular as they are in Vienna. That Krauss and Wallerstein succeeded in getting a German-speaking audience to accept another opera based on Schiller, which was no easy matter, was due to their superb sense of theatre and the genius of Franz Werfel.

There are two versions of *Don Carlos*: in the first (1867) version the opera opens with Don Carlos at Fontainebleau in love with Elisabeth, who later married his father, King Philip. In the later version, the one usually performed nowadays, this act is omitted and by the time the opera begins Elisabeth is already Don Carlos's step-mother.

What Krauss, Wallerstein and Werfel did was to merge the First Act of 1867 with the First Act of the later version in the form of a dream. We see Don Carlos, miserably unhappy that his beloved is his father's wife, sitting in the Royal Palace in Madrid in front of a huge tapestry depicting Fontainebleau. The tapestry revives in Don Carlos's mind happy memories of those happy days at Fontainebleau when he first met Elisabeth. To do away with Werfel's brilliant idea of the dream is in my opinion nothing short of mutilating the entire opera, for the simple reason that the love motif from Act One of the first version runs through the whole of the second version as a sort of musical flash-back, and it becomes utterly pointless if nobody can understand what it refers to because the First Act is cut out.

The blame for the disappearance, even from Vienna, of the masterly Krauss-Wallerstein-Werfel version must unfortunately rest squarely on one of the immortals, Bruno Walter, who restored Act One in the old-established form in his revival of *Don Carlos* when he was Artistic Adviser just before the German occupation. It meant the disappearance of a brilliant dramaturgical inspiration that made the opera far more intelligible from a musical point of view than it is in its present form.

At the first night 'Maestro' Clemens Krauss excelled himself, the auto-da-fé scene was a triumph for Wallerstein, and the cast was the finest Vienna could muster. The blind Grand Inquisitor was sung by Alfred Jerger, Manowarda was King Philip, and Gertrude Rünger, a new acquisition from Nuremberg, scored the triumph of her life as Princess Eboli. Rünger's mezzo-soprano was on the light side, and in later years she sang soprano parts. Under Clemens Krauss she sang Klytaemnestra, but in later years she reverted to Elektra. She was one of the singers who followed Krauss when he decamped to Berlin in 1934.

The fourth and last of Krauss's new Verdi productions was *Falstaff* in 1934, the year of his departure to Berlin. The Falstaff was Jaro Prohaska, a Viennese who later became one of the foremost Wagner baritones in Germany. This production involved the use of a revolving stage that could be dismantled in twenty minutes and stored under the stage. Originally Krauss had it constructed for a new production of *Carmen* that never materialised: it was turned down every time by the Intendant's Office as being far too costly in view of the general economic depression. The Carmen was to have been the beautiful Czech mezzo-soprano Jarmila Novotna. Instead, she sang in the performance in the Opera House of Lehár's 'Carmen operetta' *Guiditta*. And that is the story of how a revolving stage designed for *Carmen* ended up in *Falstaff*!

Krauss was irked by the authorities' constant harping on the need for economies, and the singers, especially the leading ones, were upset by having their fees cut. The sale of tickets was hampered by the absurdly high prices and by the unhealthy discrepancy between the most expensive seats (which were almost impossible to sell) and the positive deluge of free seats. The State Theatres' deficit was running at six million Schillings, or one Schilling per head of the population. And the pegging of the star performers' fees involved the Director in all sorts of difficulties. Alfred Piccaver and one or two others left the Opera for a time under protest, and Piccaver frequently transferred his services to the Volksoper. To make matters even worse a voluminous pamphlet appeared attacking Krauss, who by this time was beset with disputes on all sides. For the publication of the pamphlet he had only himself to blame, because he ill-advisedly followed the example of some of his predecessors in attempting to do away with the claque. At the time there was a schism in the ranks of the claque. The gallery was occupied by the relatively harmless claqueurs under the leadership of the veteran Josef Schostal, who had a veritable army of musical subordinates at his disposal. They were not paid, and very often they did not even get free seats; at best they were given seats at half-price in return for applauding at a given signal. These enthusiasts were deployed by Schostal as the occasion demanded. He would say: 'So-and-so is an excellent Puccini claqueur, but not hearty enough for Wagner. So I shan't need him for *Die Meistersinger*.' There were of course Verdi claqueurs and Mozart

Operntheater

Sonntag den 30. März 1930
Besondere Preise
Zum 1. Male:

WOZZECK

Oper in drei Akten (15 Szenen) nach Georg Büchners Drama von Alban Berg

Spielleitung: Hr. Dr. Wallerstein — Musikalische Leitung: Hr. Clemens Krauß

Wozzeck	Hr. Manowarda
Tambourmajor	Hr. Graarud
Andres	Hr. Gallos
Hauptmann	Hr. Maikl
Doktor	Hr. Wiedemann
Erster } Handwerksbursch	Hr. Norbert
Zweiter }	Hr. Madin
Der Narr	Hr. Wernigk
Marie	Fr. Pauly
Margret	Fr. With
Mariens Knabe	Kl. Katz
Ein Soldat	Hr. Maiwald

Soldaten und Burschen, Mägde und Dirnen, Kinder

Ort der Handlung:

1. Akt: I. Zimmer des Hauptmannes   2. Akt: I. Mariens Stube
II. Freies Feld, die Stadt in der Ferne   II. Straße in der Stadt
III. Mariens Stube   III. Toreinfahrt bei Mariens Wohnung
IV. Studierstube des Doktors   IV. Wirtshausgarten
V. Toreinfahrt bei Mariens Wohnung   V. Wachstube der Kaserne

3. Akt: I. Mariens Stube
II. Waldweg am Teich
III. Schenke
IV. Waldweg am Teich
V. Toreinfahrt bei Mariens Wohnung

In Szene gesetzt von Dr. Lothar Wallerstein

Entwürfe der Dekorationen und Kostüme: Prof. Oskar Strnad

Das offizielle Programm nur bei den Billetteuren erhältlich. Preis 50 Groschen

Nach dem zweiten Akt (zehnten Bild) eine größere Pause

Der Beginn der Vorstellung sowie jedes Aktes wird durch ein Glockenzeichen bekanntgegeben

Kassen-Eröffnung nach 6½ Uhr   Anfang 7½ Uhr   Ende nach 10 Uhr

Während der Vorspiele und der Akte bleiben die Saaltüren zum Parkett, Parterre und den Galerien geschlossen. Zuspätkommende können daher nur während der Pausen Einlaß finden

Der Kartenverkauf findet heute statt für obige Vorstellung und für

Montag   den 31. Der Evangelimann. Theatergemeinde Serie E, gelbe Mitgliedskarten. Beschränkter Kartenverkauf (Anfang 7 Uhr)
Dienstag den 1. April. Ariadne auf Naxos, Dirigent: Hr. Dr. Richard Strauß. Im Abonnement. Erhöhte Preise (Anfang 7½ Uhr)

Weiterer Spielplan:
Mittwoch den 2. Die Bohème. Im Abonnement (Anfang 7½ Uhr)
Donnerstag den 3. Carmen. Zu besonderen Preisen (Anfang 7 Uhr)

read, whispered to him: 'My name is so-and-so and I promise you I'll do the job just as well as Schostal did.'

The other faction of the claque, opposed to Schostal's, occupied the standing-area and was organised by Otto Stieglitz. It was a shrill and militant group that even negotiated with the Director's office direct, interfered imperiously in the running of the Opera and regarded itself as an élite phalanx of cultural experts — in short, it made a thorough nuisance of itself.

So Clemens Krauss did away with both the claques, but there were persistent rumours that his own friends continued to finance the claques on his behalf to ensure that there was no falling-off in the applause that greeted the Herr Direktor as he made his way to the rostrum.

The man who issued the anti-Krauss pamphlet after the abolition of the claque was Otto Stieglitz. He came to a tragic end. After the Nazi occupation of Vienna he had a foot in both camps and was even said to have been seen in a brown uniform, though he was also known to have helped a number of people whom the Nazis were pursuing. Be that as it may, he was eventually 'liquidated' by the Nazis in obscure circumstances. But to return to Clemens Krauss: Stieglitz's pamphlet took the form of the first number of a publication entitled *Forum*, of which other numbers were to follow in due course. This first number, sub-titled 'Corruption at the Opera', launched a bitter attack on Krauss for never letting other conductors get a look in (which had been common knowledge for years), for sanctioning exorbitant fees for his friends and for insisting on letting an agency run by Hugo Gruder-Guntram, a former Director of the Volksoper, enjoy a monopoly of all engagements and contracts. Between the lines, *Forum* implied rather clearly that Krauss shared the commissions with Gruder-Guntram. This was never proved, but there was a libel action, which as far as I remember was eventually settled out of court; at all events, Krauss was vindicated.

The fifth plank in Krauss's policy, re-invigorating the contemporary repertoire, produced some interesting novelties, notably Alban Berg's *Wozzeck* in March 1930. It was given fourteen performances, all conducted (excellently) by Krauss. The scenery was by Oskar Strnad, a

claqueurs too, and how Schostal sorted them all out was a mystery. He was an eminently lovable figure: if a singer was hard up, Schostal would tide him over out of his own pocket, and often enough he was never paid back. Later he emigrated to the New York 'Met', and I attended his funeral in New York. Although he had been one of the most popular claque leaders in the business, at his death he was disowned by all the singers but one, the tenor Kurt Baum, who came to Vienna from Prague and appeared in *L'Africaine,* amongst other operas. Now in New York we went to Schostal's funeral together, and as we were standing at the graveside an individual who obviously hoped to take over Schostal's 'business' sidled up to Baum, and, even while the funeral service was being

new designer for whom Krauss did a great deal. This highly unusual opera was the talk of the town, and it is greatly to Vienna audiences' credit that they took to *Wozzeck* so readily. The atmosphere of the first night was electric: the standing-area was under police supervision, and we habitués contributed to the opera's success by silencing the booers. The press notices were mixed: Kralik welcomed the work as a triumph of modern radicalism, while Julius Korngold said there ought to be a law against terrorist activities conducted from the standing-area. Other critics had recourse to phrases such as 'musical nihilism' and 'questionable art'. But the actual performance was extolled unanimously. The Wozzeck was Manowarda, and all the brutal ruthlessness of the Drum Major was brought out by Gunnar Graarud, a six-foot-tall Danish tenor who curiously enough was never entirely satisfactory in the Wagner rôles in which he was frequently cast. The Marie was Rose Pauly, one of the greatest operatic exponents of *verismo* acting I have ever known, and perhaps the best Elektra there has ever been, with a voice that positively glowed with passion. Another brilliant performance was that of Georg Maikl, Vienna's first Pinkerton in Mahler's production of *Butterfly*, as the Captain.

Wozzeck reminds me of a characteristic episode that took place in the Director's office. Alban Berg was the only one of the twelve-tone exponents to score an appreciable success, and although *Wozzeck* could hardly be said to constitute a threat to the popularity of *Cavalleria*, Berg was once called 'the Mascagni of twelve-tone music'. Berg was one of those composers who had music in his blood, and in his younger days he wrote some excellent 'normal' music. Perhaps in his heart of hearts he was loath to apply the twelve-tone theory quite as rigidly as some of Schoenberg's other disciples. This, anyway, was the opinion of Richard Strauss, who one day came into Krauss's office and noticed the score of *Wozzeck* lying on the table. 'I've heard so much about this work,' he said, 'I should like to have a look at the score for a moment, if I may.' Krauss handed it to him, and Strauss started to read it through, 'conducting' with the characteristic turn of the right wrist and the jerk of the elbow,

treating it in fact like any other work he was used to conducting. Somewhat taken aback, Krauss said: 'But take a good look at the score, all those complicated changes of time-signatur from one bar to the next — did you ever see anything like it?' Strauss, however, just went on quietly 'conducting' as was his wont; all he said was, 'Oh well, if that's the way he prefers to write it ...'

Krauss's other excursions into the domain were far less successful than *Wozzeck*. Pfitzner's opera *Das Herz* with a libretto by Hans Mahner-Mons, a hack writer of illustrated novels and film scripts, was an interesting novelty. The libretto is set in 'about 1700' and tells the story of Athanasius, medical adviser to his prince, who calls up the powers of black magic to restore to life his master, who has just died. He invokes the spirit Asmodi and promises him that, after a year has passed, the heart of a particular human being among those who are lying asleep nearby will belong to him. When the time is up Athanasius realises that his choice had fallen on the heart of his own beloved wife, Helge von Laudenheim. Helge collapses and dies, the prince dies for the second time, this time finally, and the magician (who in the meantime had been awarded an earldom) is cast into jail. He repents, the soul of his wife carries him away to freedom, and the executioner's men are left with his dead body. One remarkable feature of the predominantly late-romantic music was a melody that sounded almost like a *Ländler*; it is the only thing I can remember about this rather strange work.

A striking though short-lived success was that of *Schwanda the Bagpiper* by Jaromir Weinberger — easy-on-the-ear Czech folklore for export, full of good tunes and attractively presented. The protagonist, a Czech musician named Schwanda, plays up to the dance — not only in this world but also in the realm below. With his bagpipes he soothes the devil, wins the heart of the ice-princess and in the end saves himself from death. Under the gallows he plays the 'Höllenpolka' (hell-polka) — a tune which soon became popular — to which everybody, mortals and denizens of the nether-world alike, are compelled to dance. The part of Schwanda was a wonderful opportunity for one of

Krauss's favourite singers, the baritone Karl Hammes, who was killed in the war. The part of the devil was sung by Richard Mayr.

In the 1930s there was more variety to the fare provided on New Year's Eve than there is nowadays, with *Fledermaus* being served up year after year. Schalk even put on *Jonny spielt auf* one year, and Clemens Krauss followed suit with *Spuk im Schloß* by Jaroslav Křička, a modern Czech ghost opera in which Rosette Anday did the Charleston and Margit Schenker-Angerer, still looking as attractive as ever, sang the part of the Patience-addicted daughter of an American envoy. The ghost was Hermann Gallos, a genial and highly versatile tenor.

In Bittner's *Veilchen* Richard Mayr appeared on horseback; it was his last new part.

Another interesting opera that ran for only a few performances was *Die Bacchantinnen* by Egon Wellesz, one of Schoenberg's most prominent disciples; the libretto was based on Euripides. And out of deference to the Opera's 'own' talented conductor Robert Heger, Krauss put on his *Bettler Namenlos*, an opera based on the *Odyssey* with Viorica Ursuleac as Penelope, Max Lorenz as the beggar, and Richard Mayr as the shepherd.

Apart from Krauss's five principal projects there were Wolf-Ferrari's delightful *Vier Grobiane*, a wonderful new production of Tchaikovsky's *Pique Dame* with Gertrude Rünger in the part of the old lady who had once been a passionate gambler and the most beautiful woman in Paris, and *Eugene Onegin* (1934), conducted by Bruno Walter. Walter had lost his job as Artistic Director of the Berlin Opera as soon as Hitler came to power but had been summoned to Vienna on the instigation of the Austrian Government. He took a house on the edge of the Vienna Woods, became a great friend of Franz Werfel and was on the friendliest of terms with the Austrian Chancellor, Kurt von Schuschnigg. Besides *Eugene Onegin* he also conducted *Un Ballo in Maschera* and eventually took over the artistic direction of the Vienna Opera in 1936. *Eugene Onegin* was the first opera he conducted in Vienna since his rift with Gregor and his departure to Munich in 1912.

There was also a plan to put on *Anna Karenina* by the Hungarian composer Jenö von Hubay, but it never materialised. Clemens Krauss once said he intended to write a book called 'The collected excuses of a theatre director'. Excuse No. 1: 'We can't do it at the Opera because there's a play on at the Burgtheater called *Anna Karenina*.' Excuse No. 2: 'We can't do it at the Opera because it was such a flop at the Burgtheater.' Excuse No. 3: 'We can't do it at the Opera because everyone has read the book by Tolstoy.' Excuse No. 4: 'Who has ever heard of Tolstoy anyway?' In the end he accepted *Anna Karenina* but left it to his successor Felix von Weingartner to stage. When it did at last reach the stage, with Maria Nemeth as Anna, it was a dismal fiasco.

Minor episodes during Krauss's term were one or two operettas. Heuberger's *Opernball* was given a rather wooden performance, and curiously enough Lotte Lehmann and Margit Schenker-Angerer were all at sea in operetta and, unlike Jeritza, conspicuously failed to shine in this unaccustomed world. More successful was Suppé's *Boccaccio*, in which Maria Jeritza in a male rôle reverted with all her old élan to the operetta world she had first started in. In January 1934 came the first performance of Lehár's *Giuditta*, which was as repugnant to Krauss as *Jonny spielt auf* had been to Schalk. But at the première and at practically every subsequent performance the house was sold out; Lehár himself conducted ('doing his utmost to make it sound serious,' as one critic observed); and the cast included Richard Tauber and the highly attractive Jarmila Novotna, who lures the infatuated officer to desert from his regiment and in the end ruins him. There were innumerable encores for the two big hits of the evening, 'Freunde, das Leben ist lebenswert' and 'Meine Lippen, die küssen so heiss'. If Lehár had not been repressed by his boundless respect for the State Opera, *Giuditta* would have been a real Lehár operetta and therefore a better one. As it is, between the 'hits' there are vast expanses of sentimental third-hand Puccini. But it was a social occasion of the first magnitude, and Novotna showed off with the utmost panache what the costumier had 'created' for her. Tauber in the part of a bar-pianist actually played the piano, and

Was alles unter einen Hut geht

Caricature of Clemens Krauss riding on the boom years, which appeared in the 'Wiener Sonn- und Montags-Zeitung' on 17 December 1934, only a few days before his departure for Berlin. Beneath the sombrero of the ex-Director of the Vienna Opera: on the left 'Duce' Mussolini and 'non-arian' Dr. Wallerstein, on the right Richard Strauss and Hermann Göring.

143

for a moment or two 'Aristotle' the donkey stole the show from both of them. In short, it was a huge success, and the box-office takings were prodigious. It was the same thing all over again in 1938 when Lehár conducted *Land des Lächelns* in the Opera House.

The activities of the 'Principality of Clemens Krauss' were spread over a number of theatres. At the Redoutensaal Rossini's *Cenerentola* was performed in a version entitled *Angelina* with a brilliant soprano (instead of the usual mezzo-soprano) rôle for Adele Kern. *Der Waffenschmied* was played at the Akademietheater and Pergolesi's *La serva padrona* at the Schönbrunn Schlosstheater. But one of Krauss's pet schemes unfortunately never materialised: he wanted to do Gluck's *Iphigenie auf Tauris* in two different versions concurrently, in the original version of 1778 and in a modern version.

Krauss and his cohorts advanced to their Waterloo (one instinctively speaks of him as a military commander) by stages which became more and more dramatic as the end loomed nearer. The first intimation Krauss had that his fortunes were on the wane was a resolution adopted by the Vienna Philharmonic Orchestra, authorising its Chairman, Hugo Burghauser, to relieve him of his post as permanent conductor of its subscription concerts. Burghauser, who was an admirable bassoon player, had a number of interesting and original schemes for the orchestra. In dismissing Krauss, he broke once and for all with the tradition of a 'permanent' conductor. Until then the Director of the Opera had usually been automatically in charge of the Philharmonic concerts, because the Philharmonic was also the Opera orchestra. From now on Burghauser intended to invite only guest conductors. This was by no means the first time such an idea had been mooted, and it had even been put into practice between the Mahler and Weingartner eras. The first to be invited was to be Arturo Toscanini, who had gone into voluntary exile from fascist Italy and had also refused to conduct in Hitler's Germany. So he was available. Of all conductors, he was the one whom Krauss most feared as a rival.

Krauss was furious but could do nothing. He had been at dagger points with Burghauser for some time, because Burghauser had supplied Stieglitz, the leader of one of the claques, with material for his pamphlet. In his capacity as Director of the State Opera Krauss wanted to institute proceedings against Burghauser but his application was turned down by the Government and by the *Heimwehr*, who were not at all on his side. The reason Burghauser wanted to dismiss Krauss was that he was far less of a success with Philharmonic audiences than he was at the Opera, possibly because of his 'modern' programmes, and audiences were dwindling alarmingly. Krauss's opponents also forced him to change his mind about staging the first performance of Křenek's exceedingly interesting opera *Karl V*, although piano rehearsals had already started.

And all this time an invasion of Austria by the Third Reich was expected almost daily. That Austrian apprehensions were far from unfounded was to be proved only too clearly four years later. So far Krauss had steered his way through the political intricacies of the time extremely adroitly, and had even exploited them. He was never at a loss as to which button to press, and when. But in the present situation he pressed two — alternately. He took on a great number of Jewish artists who had been forced to leave Germany, and on the other hand he furthered singers who were *personae gratae* with the new masters in Germany. He engaged the former *Generalmusikdirektor* of Hamburg, Egon Pollak, as a conductor, but also maintained his close contacts with Berlin, where much bigger plans for him were afoot.

Just how close Krauss's contacts with Berlin already were was revealed at the 1934 Salzburg Festival. After the Nazi putsch in Vienna in July and the assassination of the Austrian Chancellor, Dr. Dollfuss, Richard Strauss suddenly and most uncharacteristically cancelled his participation in the Festival. It was the year of Strauss's seventieth birthday, and Krauss wanted him for Salzburg at all costs. He therefore got his wife Viorica Ursuleac, who was a Prussian 'Kammersängerin' and a member of the Berlin Opera, to ring up Hermann Göring in Berlin from a telephone-box in the Hotel Bristol (Göring was in charge of all German State Theatres). She succeeded in getting through to him, and in the course of the conversation it became clear to her that it was only on instruc-

The Opera House Today

The magnificent main stairway

One of the most attractive features of old opera house was the main stairway leading up from the main entrance, with its chandeliers and candelabra, its landings and vaulting, and its wealth of gilt ornamentation and frescoes. People come in from the street just to watch the audience making their way to their seats, which is one way of savouring the atmosphere of the opera, a memory to take home, without having to buy a ticket. It is all part of the glamour. Very few modern opera houses can boast magnificent stairways such as the old ones had.

The auditorium, from the stage. The total area of stage available for Rodolfo's attic, or Florestan's cell, or the meadow outside 16th century Nuremberg, or the ship in *Tristan*, is 16,200 square feet. (In the final scene of *Fidelio* the back row of the chorus are practically standing in the Hotel Sacher.) The man in the street is hardly ever vouchsafed a glimpse of the side and back stages except on conducted tours or at the Opera Ball. From the bottom of the below-stage to the grid with its 105 flies is a span of 135 feet, or one-third the height of the spire of St. Stephen's Cathedral. One of the provisos of the tenders that were invited for the projected new Opera House in 1860 was that the auditorium should have five tiers. A seating capacity of about 2,500 was also stipulated. The present house holds 2,209 (including 551 standing), 115 fewer than the house that was destroyed in 1944 because of today's insistence on wider gangways and more leg room between the rows of seats. Although the capacity of the Vienna Opera House is rather below average, it is a good deal more comfortable than most.

The official regulations of 1860 insisted that 'the auditorium is to consist of a ground floor flanked by tiers of boxes on either side'. This was the general rule in those days, and the decision to retain the boxes when the work of rebuilding started in 1945 was a fortunate one. Operas in general can only be properly enjoyed when audience, orchestra and stage form a compact community. The bare walls of so many mid-twentieth-century opera houses make them look like super-cinemas, and curiously enough the applause in a modern house is invariably less generous than in the old-style houses with boxes. Too many architects have never grasped one of the most important secrets of an opera house: there must be some seats from which people can look each other over. Which is why in even the best-built houses there are always seats that offer an indifferent view of the stage. People who insist on a house where every seat has a perfect view would be better off in the cinema.

The Foyer is at the centre of a U-shaped suite of rooms round the central stairway. It contains busts of Gustav Mahler (by Rodin) and Richard Strauss.

For distinguished personages and guests of honour there is a small salon behind the centre first-tier box — the former Imperial box — where they can mingle during the intervals. Over the years the Vienna Opera has been instrumental in forming many close friendships despite the barriers of nationality and language.

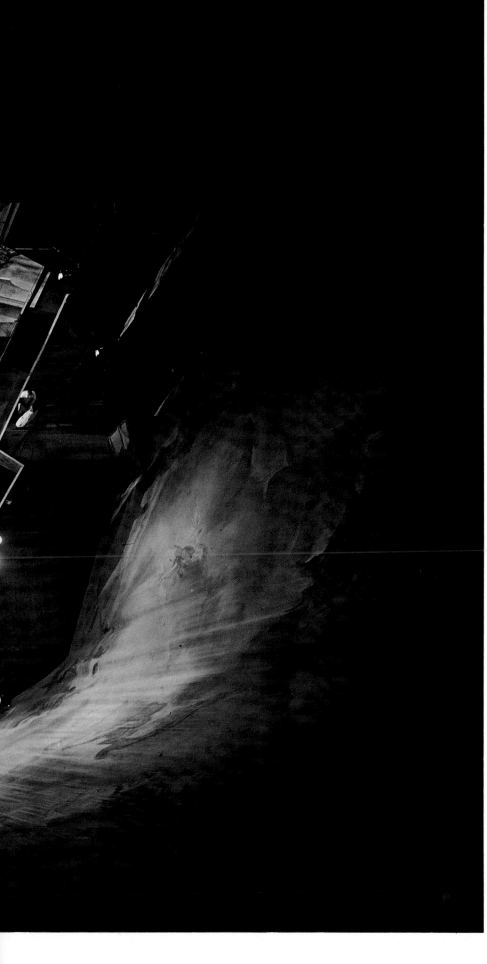

The Vienna Opera occasionally affords momentary glimpses that neither the librettist nor the composer nor the producer ever bargained for, glimpses that even the opera-going public would never have been able to enjoy without the marvels of modern photography and its exponents. Here for instance is an astronaut's view of the presentation of the silver rose in Act Two of *Der Rosenkavalier*, taken from the top of the cyclorama and looking down on to the main stage just as Octavian presents the silver rose with the words 'Mir ist die Ehre widerfahren . . .'. On either side can be seen the ramps leading up to the stage, and Octavian's retinue. This production of Otto Schenk's was the first to make a successful departure from Roller's general concept of 1911. The first-night audience in April 1968 saw a surprisingly unorthodox *Rosenkavalier* conducted by Leonard Bernstein, with Gwyneth Jones as Octavian and the coloured singer Reri Grist as Sophie. In the performance in this photograph, conducted by Joseph Krips, Sophie is Lucia Popp, and Octavian is Irmgard Seefried, the celebrated Lieder singer with a brilliant operatic repertoire ranging from Mozart to Marie in *Wozzeck*.

An anonymous army of highly skilled and hard-working individuals whose labours go totally unapplauded is hard at it in the workshops and paintshops (right), or setting up the next scene on the stage (below), so that as soon as the curtain goes up the audience can be transported back to the world of make-believe. Left, the switchboard controlling the raising or lowering of the adjustable parts of the stage.

On the last page: When an illustrious figure connected with the Vienna Opera dies, the coffin is placed on the bottom step of this section of the stairway for the funeral ceremony. It was here that the writer took his last farewell of Egon Hilbert and Anni Konetzni.

tions from Berlin that Strauss had cancelled. Moreover, it would be highly embarrassing for Göring if the true facts were to leak out. Göring therefore withdrew the instruction and Strauss was permitted to go to Salzburg. Unfortunately for Krauss the telephone-call was tapped by the Austrian police, who were left in no doubt about the excellent relations between the Krausses and the Nazi authorities in Germany. From that day Krauss's fate was sealed.

The authorities were well aware of Krauss's double dealing, and, to be on the safe side, when his contract expired in the spring of 1934 they inserted in its renewal a clause stipulating cancellation with one year's notice, but left him in the dark as to whether they would avail themselves of this clause in the spring of 1935. But no opera director can run his theatre without being able to see more than a year ahead, and this was another factor that drove Krauss into the welcoming arms of Berlin.

He was by no means the only one to take this course. Quite a lot of people in Austria acted or felt as he did, only we did not know it at the time. We did not know that many people who were so profuse in their protestations of Austrian patriotism when they were in Austria lost no time in flaunting swastika badges the moment they were over the frontier. At this terrible time few conductors had the moral courage of their convictions that Arturo Toscanini had.

The trouble over the 1934 Salzburg Festival was patched up but not completely cured. Richard Strauss came to Salzburg but did not conduct. He was present at *Elektra*, but *Die Frau ohne Schatten* was cancelled. The Austrian Chancellor, Kurt von Schuschnigg, toyed for a time with the idea of banning all works by Strauss and Pfitzner on political grounds.

At the beginning of the Krauss regime the terrifying Arturo Toscanini had conducted some concerts by the New York Philharmonic in the Opera House. In November 1934 he came to Vienna again, this time to conduct a performance of Verdi's *Requiem* in the Opera House in memory of the late Austrian Chancellor Dollfuss, who had been assassinated by the Nazis in July. At the very first rehearsal there was a typical Toscanini incident. The soprano Maria Nemeth had sung no more than a bar or two of her part when the Maestro stopped the rehearsal with an ominous frown and barked: 'Un altro soprano, Direttore!' The wretched Nemeth was replaced by Anna Bathy of Budapest.

Early in December Furtwängler resigned from the Berlin Opera in protest against the ostracism of Hindemith in Germany. By the tenth of December Krauss had signed his new Berlin contract.

On the next evening, the eleventh of December 1934, Krauss conducted *Falstaff* at the Opera. The Vienna audience was disgusted that a Director of the Vienna Opera for the sake of his career could come to terms with a regime in Germany that, quite apart from the assassination of Dollfuss, had made no effort to conceal its open hostility to Austria. To many people his action was just inconceivable. As he made his way to the rostrum he was greeted with a chorus of boos and catcalls and I still have no regrets at having joined in, though nowadays I am disposed to view Krauss's blatant opportunism more leniently than I did at the time.

Krauss submitted a proposal to the Austrian Government that he should stay on until the first of January 1935, but he was given to understand that the best thing he could do was to clear out immediately. A good proportion of the ensemble defected to Berlin with him: Ursuleac, Rünger, Völker, Manowarda, Hammes and Zimmermann. Some returned later, but in the days immediately following his departure the authorities at the Vienna Opera often had their work cut out to muster a cast at all. On the seventeenth of December there appeared in the *Wiener Sonn- und Montags-Zeitung* a caricature of Krauss wearing a huge sombrero and hobnobbing with Lothar Wallerstein and Hermann Göring over the caption 'strange bedfellows'.

So Krauss cheerfully went on making music in Germany amid all the bestial atrocities of the Third Reich. This did not prevent him from blandly paying a visit to a Jewish dentist, Dr. Schorr, in Vienna and putting in an application to the Berlin authorities for Lothar Wallerstein, a 'non-Aryan', to be allowed to produce anonymously at the Berlin Opera.

'Neues Wiener Journal' of 12 December 1934

Polizei in der Staatsoper.

„Falstaff" unter Clemens Krauß. Der Operndirektor ist also doch aus Berlin zurückgekehrt. Für 19 Uhr 30 ist der Beginn der Vorstellung angesetzt. Es vergehen Minuten, doch das Dirigentenpult bleibt unbesetzt. Plötzlich teilt sich der Vorhang: der diensthabende Regisseur Herr D u h a n erscheint. Man wittert eine Sensation. Herr Duhan lächelt, macht eine Verbeugung. Dann teilt er mit, daß in der Pause für die Winterhilfe gesammelt werden wird...

Die Lichter im Zuschauerraum werden abgedreht. Clemens Krauß zwängt sich durch die Reihen der Philharmoniker: P f e i f e n u n d Z i s c h e n v o n a l l e n S e i t e n. Gleich darauf wildes Beifallsklatschen. Seine Anhänger lassen ihn nicht im Stich. In dem Sturm wird eine hohe Trillerpfeife deutlich vernehmbar. Der Operndirektor kann das Zeichen zum Beginn nicht geben. Erst als der Beifall die Zischer übertönt, hebt er den Taktstock. Der „Falstaff" nimmt seinen Anfang.

Auf der vierten Galerie, wo das Pfeifkonzert am lautesten war, sieht man einen Wachmann neben dem anderen. So viel Polizei hat es bisher wohl noch in keiner Opernvorstellung gegeben. Und die Demonstranten, die so heftig gegen Clemens Krauß Stellung genommen hatten, müssen das wohl oder übel zur Kenntnis nehmen.

POLICE IN THE OPERA

'Falstaff' conducted by Clemens Krauss. So the Director of the Opera has returned from Berlin after all. The performance is fixed to begin at 7.30 p.m. Minutes pass, but the conductor's desk is still unoccupied. Suddenly, the curtains part: the producer on duty, Herr Duhan, appears. A sensation seems to be imminent. Herr Duhan smiles, bows. Then he says that there will be a collection for winter charities during the interval...

The lights in the auditorium go down. Clemens Krauss forces his way between the ranks of the Philharmonic: whistling and hissing from all sides. And at once a wild storm of applause. His supporters have not let him down. In the midst of the hubbub an alarm-whistle is distinctly audible. The Director is unable to give the signal to begin. Not until the applause outweighs the hissing does he raise his baton. 'Falstaff' begins.

In the fourth gallery where the whistling was loudest, police are standing one next to the other. Surely there have never been so many policemen at a performance in the Opera. And the demonstrators, who have shown their violent hostility to Clemens Krauss, have to accept the fact for good or ill.

Along with being Director of the Berlin Opera until 1937, Krauss became one of the Hitler regime's right-hand men in artistic affairs. Later, he ran the Munich Opera, and Hitler intended to entrust him with the running of the new Munich Festival Theatre that was being planned. During the war, Krauss also ran the Salzburg Festival and the Salzburg Mozarteum.

Clemens Krauss had everything. As a musician he was gifted with a touch of genius, and as a professional opera director he was thoroughly up-to-date. His natural diffidence and repressions were cloaked by a show of arrogance that made it difficult to get through to him. Yet he could be uncommonly genial and even charming once the barriers were down. He also had a marvellous fund of stories. But first and last he was, as we have seen, a careerist and an opportunist. There was in truth something of the torero in him. But it was his feckless opportunism that toppled him in the end.

As at previous times of crisis in the Directorship of the Vienna Opera, Felix Weingartner was once again waiting in the wings for the summons to fill the breach. He was working in Basle at the time and must have been sitting by the telephone day and night. One day it rang: Clemens Krauss's defection to Berlin was officially announced on the eleventh of December, and Weingartner's appointment on the thirteenth of December, the interregnum having lasted exactly twenty-four hours. If world politics were crazy at that time, so apparently were we Strauss fans: we were so disgusted by the behaviour of Krauss, Strauss's bosom friend, that we accorded an enthusiastic welcome to Felix Weingartner, Strauss's arch-enemy.

Yet again, as so often before, it was *Lohengrin* with which the new era opened — for some extraordinary reason it seems to be almost obligatory to make one's début in Vienna with *Lohengrin*. Before the performance started we welcomed Weingartner with huge boards bearing the new Weingartner Fan Club's device 'Zara 63': both the club and the device were thought up on the spur of the moment. Zara in Dalmatia was Weingartner's birthplace, and 1863 was the year of his birth.

Apart from *Lohengrin* he also conducted *Die Meister-singer* and bowed 1934 out with *Die Fledermaus* on New Year's Eve. We all went out of our way to be particularly nice to him, and we standing-area habitués did our humble best to make his life in Vienna as agreeable as possible.

Weingartner lived in the Kantgasse, near the Konzert-haus and opposite the Ice Rink. I and some of my friends often used to escort him home after performances. By this time we had grown very fond of him, and he for his part was exceedingly interesting to talk to, and had given up constantly sniping at Strauss, at last realising perhaps how sensitive Vienna can be. We also took to his wife (his fifth), Carmen Studer-Weingartner. He was just over seventy, and she was barely out of her teens. She had studied conducting with him and had once conducted a concert in Vienna, wearing an outfit like a man's tail-coat tailored especially for the occasion, plus of course a white blouse. Our little fan club applauded her concert vigorously. She was an exceptionally intelligent woman, and

she produced an admirable German libretto for *Carmen* which Clemens Krauss later used in Germany.

I can also still remember an afternoon in the 'Kleiner Festsaal' of the University, where Weingartner read parts of *Faust* to a large audience, accompanied by his own incidental music to Part Two on a piano. The general impression was that it was a scholarly piece of work.

Although Weingartner's second term was so short, from the first of January 1935 to the thirty-first of August 1936, it was fraught with interest. To start with, he resumed his experiments with *Fidelio*. During his first term he had begun with the Overture 'Leonore No. 2', as at the very first performance, and then had gone straight into the A major duet with which Act One opens. Now in 1935 he started with Leonore No. 3, but in order to emphasise that the Overture 'Leonore No. 3' is not part of the final version of *Fidelio* the announcement read: 'Beethoven: Overture Leonore No. 3: followed by the opera *Fidelio*.'

Reversing the policy he adopted during his first term, Weingartner wisely embarked on his second by attending promptly to the omissions of his predecessor — invitations to prominent guest conductors. Among the array of celebrities whom he invited to Vienna were Hans Knappertsbusch, who conducted a great deal of Wagner, including a complete *Ring*, and Victor de Sabata with *Aida* and *Otello*. In *Otello* the curtain provided a good deal of entertainment by refusing to go up. Three times de Sabata started the first bars of the storm scene: the first time the curtain rose about head high, the second time about one-third of the stage was revealed, and the third time about a quarter; the fourth time at last the curtain went up the whole way and the performance could go on.

A *Tannhäuser* conducted by Furtwängler was marred by a much more serious mishap that must be almost without parallel in the history of opera. The part of Tannhäuser was being sung by the German tenor Gotthelf Pistor and, by a macabre coincidence, at the passage 'Erbarm dich mein' he suddenly lost his voice. He pulled himself together sufficiently to struggle through to the end semi-mute, but it was an eerie experience for all concerned.

Joseph Krips, who since World War II has become one of the most sought-after conductors in Europa and America, started at the Volksoper and was now conducting a lot of Mozart at the Vienna State Opera, as well as a delightful production of *The Bartered Bride* with Jarmila Novotna and Richard Tauber, and a new production of *Ariadne* with Vera Schwarz in the title-rôle: the producer was Wallerstein and the scenery was by Oskar Strnad.

But the really outstanding feature of Weingartner's second term was his invitation to Bruno Walter to come to Vienna with his version of Gluck's *Orfeo*, which had been one of the most successful attractions of the Salzburg Festival for a number of years. Walter and Margarete Wallmann were responsible for a superbly dramatic production (including a really thrilling presentation of Hades), which was particular favourite with Walter's protector Kurt Schuschnigg, the Austrian Chancellor. Later, Schuschnigg and Walter became close friends, and after the road accident in which Schuschnigg's wife Herma was killed the Chancellor attended practically every performance of *Orfeo* that Walter conducted. There was of course an obvious parallel in the tragedy of Euridice and his own bereavement. During the same period Walter also conducted an excellent production of Hugo Wolf's opera *Der Corregidor* with a cast including Novotna.

During the first year of Weingartner's second term the Vienna Opera mourned the deaths of three of its leading members who had served it faithfully for twenty years or more: Marie Gutheil-Schoder, Alfred Roller, and Richard Mayr. As a singer, Gutheil-Schoder was known to us youngsters only from what the older generation told us about her; but we had seen what she could do as a producer in *Elektra*. As for Roller, he had supplied the scenery for almost every opera we had enjoyed. But that Richard Mayr, the Vienna Opera's pride and joy as Ochs, Sarastro or Gurnemanz, should be no more was something we just couldn't believe at first. Never again to hear his 'Sölbstverständlich empfängt mich Ihre Gnod'n', or his 'Gesegnet sei, du Reiner', or in the *Musikverein* his 'O Freunde, nicht diese Töne'. Never again to see him

emerging from the stage-door wearing his squashed-in pork-pie hat, or to laugh at his brilliant extempores, as on the celebrated occasion just after notices had been put up behind the stage saying: 'No improvising'. It was a performance of *Die Walküre*, and Brünnhilde had just come leading Grane by the halter (real horses have not been used since Krauss's day) when the noble steed lifted its noble tail and relieved itself of its noble excrement, whereupon Mayr (Hunding) who had been waiting in the wings, strode up to the animal, patted it on the hindquarters, and said in his inimitable mixture of Viennese and Salzburg dialects: 'Now then old fellow, can't you read: No improvising.' Mayr was very fond of horses, and when he was not too busy often used to go for a drive in his carriage and pair or even drive some of his friends to his home at Henndorf on the Wallersee, Salzburg. Whenever he was singing at the Opera, he would turn up half an hour before the start, put on his costume and make-up, and then wait patiently until his cue came — even in *Palestrina*, in which as the Pope he didn't come on until Act Three. There was an immense crowd at his funeral, and as the cortège approached the Opera House a wind ensemble from the Vienna Philharmonic stationed in the loggia above the Ringstrasse played excerpts from the Funeral Music in *Götterdämmerung*. His coffin was then brought to his beloved Salzburg and interred in Saint Peter's cemetery.

So the Vienna Opera had to find a new Ochs, and the choice fell on Fritz Krenn, who was an admirable singer of a quite different type from Mayr. Three other first-class basses at the Opera's disposal were Herbert Alsen, who after the war organised the Mörbisch Festival in Burgenland, the German Ludwig Hofmann and the Viennese Emanuel List, who made his name in the United States and at Bayreuth. Appearances by the great Russian bass Alexander Kipnis were always festive occasions.

As regards the repertoire, all that remained for Weingartner to do was realise some of the projects planned by Krauss, who always liked to look as far ahead as possible. Whether *Orfeo* had been planned by Krauss or not is not quite clear; what is certain is that he had planned the première of Ravel's *L'heure espagnole* for February 1935.

Felix Weingartner und Clemens Krauß

— Ich beneide Sie um eines, Herr Kollega: Sie haben den besseren Vorgänger.

I envy you for one thing, you have the better predecessor.

The attractive Margit Bokor sang the part of the Spanish clockmaker's wife, Concepción, who arranges her sundry assignations in the shop during her husband's absence; when the number of her own customers accumulates alarmingly and there is a risk they will begin cannoning into each other, she hides them in the big grandfather clocks, some of which she has carted, inmates and all, into another room by the muleteer Ramiro, who happens to be paying a homely business visit to the clockmaker, and now finds himself being roped in by the attractive wife to shift surprisingly heavy furniture. But he is strong and healthy, polishes off the job without turning a hair and ends up becoming one of Concepción's customers instead of her husband's. Alfred Jerger gave a most amusing account of the part of Ramiro.

On the same bill was Mussorgsky's *Fair at Sorotchinzy*, a story about an alleged ghost that paralyses the activities of an entire fair, and a wonderful opportunity for the Vienna State Opera Ballet to bring the house down with their brilliant *Hopak*. It was a splendid evening of colourful folklore served up on the revolving stage.

Another feature of 1935 was a lovely Italian *stagione* that Krauss had prepared, just as in the old days. The cast of *The Barber of Seville* included the coloratura Toti dal Monte who as Lucia in Toscanini's visit with the Scala in 1929 had delighted even the most rabid Selma Kurz fans. Then there were *Tosca* and *Traviata* with Mercedes Capsir, as well as *André Chénier*. Yet another

world-famous Italian singer who graced Vienna with his presence in 1935 was Ezio Pinza. He was perhaps the finest Don Giovanni the world has ever known. Years later, towards the end of his days, his shapely legs and the sex-appeal of his voice still as attractive as ever, he became a leading star in musicals in the USA.

With his own premières Weingartner was less fortunate. Hubay's *Anna Karenina* was a flop, but Franz Salmhofer's first opera *Dame im Traum*, to a libretto by Ernst Descey, might well be worth a revival. The scene switches from Nice to the high mountains and back, and the story is about a woman contemplating adultery who dreams she has actually committed it, with all its tragic consequences, and as a result of the dream her marriage is saved. The actual story, a somewhat Freudian affair, is good theatre, but the lines would have to be re-written. The music is dramatically effective and contains many moments of real beauty. The work included a wonderful part for Vera Schwarz, whose voice was still as lovely as ever. Her partners were the young Czech tenor Emmerich Godin (whose part contained a lovely Serenade) and the Hungarian baritone Alexander Sved, very popular in Vienna as Rigoletto and Renato. The conductor was Joseph Krips.

With the ballet Weingartner could point to some memorable evenings. The first thing he did was to engage the outstanding dancer Margarete Wallmann as a choreographer (she had started in this capacity during Krauss's term). Franz Salmhofer had scored quite a success during Schalk's regime with his ballet *Das lachende Phantom* starring Tilly Losch, and during Krauss's regime with his ballets *Der Taugenichts von Wien* (after Eichendorff), written specially for Grete Wiesenthal, and *Weihnachtsmärchen*, in which his own music was interlarded with pieces by the Strauss dynasty. Now under Weingartner he produced a brilliant ballet entitled *Österreichische Bauernhochzeit*, which afforded Margarete Wallmann ample scope for showing what she could really do as a choreographer. It was a wonderful evening. In the same programme Karl Alwin conducted his own ballet *Symphonischer Walzer*.

It was only natural that Weingartner should conduct a

good many performances himself. In September 1934 he celebrated his fifty years as a conductor, and simultaneously his come-back at the age of seventy-one, with a performance of *Götterdämmerung*. Now in 1935 he conducted *The Merry Wives of Windsor*, *Aida*, the whole of the *Ring*, and a lot of Mozart, including *Die Entführung*, in which the Konstanze was a charming Greek soprano named Margerita Perras, who had only just been engaged. Weingartner also conducted Millöcker's operetta *Der Bettelstudent* in a full-blown operatic production with the American tenor Charles Kullman in the title-rôle. 'A lot of Wagner, a dash of Rossini, and not much Millöcker,' was one connoisseur's verdict. And Piccaver sang in *Der Zigeunerbaron*.

But Weingartner's days in office were numbered, and the end came in the person of Dr. Erwin Kerber, a member of the governing body of the Vienna Opera who had also for some years commanded an influential position in the management of the Salzburg Festival. He was a typical Salzburger, and like his fellow-countryman Richard Mayr never lost his Salzburg accent to his dying day. He had an attractive personality, was artistically-minded and an excellent administrator. *And* he wanted to be Director of the Vienna Opera, which was why Weingartner had to make way for him. Even if the old gentleman had hitherto failed to provide an overall concept, he still had plenty to offer. But after some trivial and grossly overplayed private episode Kerber managed to persuade Weingartner as kindly as possible that it was perhaps time for him to go. Weingartner complied without any fuss at all but remained at the Opera's disposal as a guest-conductor. The official announcement stated that he had resigned 'for reasons of health'. It was the first time a change of Directors had been effected without animosity. Weingartner waited patiently for a third opportunity, but in vain, and he died in Switzerland in 1942.

Kerber became Administrative Director as from the first of September 1936, and to join him as Artistic Director an invitation was sent to no less a person than Bruno Walter.

This invitation was due largely to the personal intervention of the Austrian Chancellor Kurt von Schuschnigg,

Operntheater

Sonntag den 17. November 1935

Im Abonnement — Erhöhte Preise

Neu einstudiert und inszeniert:

Orpheus

Oper in drei Akten (fünf Bildern). Musik von **Ch. W. Gluck**. Text von Calzabigi

Spielleitung: Margarete Wallmann   Dirigent: . * .

Orpheus	. . . . Kerstin Thorborg
Euridyke	. . . . * .
Eros	. . . . Margit Bokor
Ein seliger Schatten	. . . . Dora Komarek

Trauernde, Furien und Höllengeister, selige Geister, Priesterinnen und Diener des Eros

Pantomimen und Tänze ausgeführt von den Damen Pfundmayr (arme Seele in Hades), Krausenecker, Berka, Szakal, Opel; den Herren Nemeth, Binder, Raimund, den Koryphäen und dem Corps de Ballet

In Szene gesetzt von Margarete Wallmann und Bruno Walter

Entwürfe der Bühnenbilder: Robert Kautsky, der Kostüme: Ladislaus Czettel

. * . Dirigent: **Bruno Walter** a. G.

. * . „Euridyke" **Jarmila Novotna** a. G.

Nach dem dritten Bild eine größere Pause

Das offizielle Programm nur bei den Billetteuren erhältlich. Preis 50 Groschen — Garderobe frei

Kassen-Eröffnung vor 7 Uhr   Anfang 7½ Uhr   Ende 10 Uhr

Während der Vorspiele und der Akte bleiben die Saaltüren zum Parkett, Parterre und den Galerien geschlossen. Zuspätkommende können daher nur während der Pausen Einlaß finden

Der Kartenverkauf findet heute statt für obige Vorstellung und für

Montag   den 18. Rigoletto. „Rigoletto" Hr. **Mario Basiola** vom Teatre Reale in Rom als Gast. Theatergemeinde Serie A, weiße Mitgliedskarten (Anfang 7½ Uhr)

Dienstag   den 19. Tannhäuser. „Elisabeth" Frl. **Hilde Konetzni** vom Neuen Deutschen Theater in Prag a. G. Bei aufgehobenem Abonnement (Anfang 7 Uhr)

Weiterer Spielplan:

Mittwoch   den 20. Tosca. „Tosca" Fr. **Anne Roselle** a. G. Im Abonnement I. Gruppe (Anfang 7½ Uhr)

Donnerstag   den 21. Der Ring des Nibelungen. Vorabend: Das Rheingold. Theatergemeinde Serie E, gelbe Mitgliedskarten (Anfang 7¼ Uhr)

Freitag   den 22. Orpheus. Dirigent: Hr. **Bruno Walter** a. G. Im Abonnement I. Gruppe (Anfang 7½ Uhr)

Samstag   den 23. Die Zauberflöte. Bei aufgehobenem Abonnement. Beschränkter Kartenverkauf (Anfang 7 Uhr)

Kartenverkauf für alle Bundestheater (Burg-, Opern- und Akademie-Theater) an den Tageskassen: I., Bräunerstraße 14, an Werktagen von 9—18 Uhr, an Sonn- und Feiertagen von 9—17 Uhr; I., Operngasse (Operngebäude) an Werktagen von 9—14 und 15—18 Uhr und an der Abendkassa am Vorstellungstage. Telephonische Bestellungen von Sitzen (ausgenommen Säulensitze) zum Preise von S 4.— aufwärts ausschließlich unter der Telephon-Nummer R-28-3-20 von 8—18 Uhr.

Under Bruno Walter, Gluck's opera had been a permanent highlight of the Salzburg Festival since 1931. It now became the centrepiece of the second Weingartner era. Bruno Walter and Margarete Wallmann were joint producers. The notice is a curiosity. 'Eurydike' is missing, fortunately only from the title. And she is spelled wrongly in the list of the cast.

Operntheater

Im Abonnement   **Dienstag den 1. Juni 1937**   I. Gruppe

☛ **Anfang 6½ Uhr** ☚

Tristan und Isolde

von Richard Wagner
Handlung in drei Aufzügen

Spielleitung: Hans Duhan   Dirigent: • •

Tristan	Josef Kalenberg
König Marke	Alexander Kipnis
Isolde	Anny Konetzni
Kurwenal	Fred Destal
Melot	Hans Duhan
Brangäne	Enid Szantho
Ein Hirt	Hermann Gallos
Ein Steuermann	Karl Ettl
Stimme des Seemannes	Anton Dermota

Schiffsvolk, Ritter und Knappen

Schauplatz der Handlung: Erster Aufzug: Auf dem Verdeck von Tristans Schiff, während der Oberfahrt von Irland nach Kornwall — Zweiter Aufzug: In der königlichen Burg Markes in Kornwall — Dritter Aufzug: Tristans Burg in Bretagne

• • Dirigent: Generalmusikdirektor **Herbert von Karajan.** Stadttheater Aachen, a. G.

Nach jedem Aufzuge eine größere Pause

Das offizielle Programm nur bei den Billetteuren erhältlich. Preis 50 Groschen — Garderobe frei

Kassen-Eröffnung **vor 6 Uhr**   Anfang 6½ Uhr   Ende nach 11 Uhr

Während der Vorspiele und der Akte bleiben die Saaltüren zum Parkett, Parterre und den Galerien geschlossen. Zuspätkommende können daher nur während der Pausen Einlaß finden

Telephonische Bestellungen von Sitzen, R-28-320 (ausgenommen Säulensitze) zum Preise von S 4.— aufwärts werden für folgende Vorstellungen entgegengenommen.

Der Kartenverkauf findet heute statt für obige Vorstellung und für
Mittwoch den 2. Tosca. Im Abonnement I. Gruppe (Anfang 7½ Uhr)
Donnerstag den 3. Oberon. Dirigent: **Bruno Walter** a. G. (Anfang 7 Uhr)

Weiterer Spielplan:
Freitag   den 4. Der Barbier von Sevilla. Bei aufgehobenem Abonnement. Kein Kartenverkauf (Anfang 7½ Uhr)
Samstag   den 5. Der fliegende Holländer. Im Abonnement I. Gruppe (Anfang 7½ Uhr)
Sonntag   den 6. Der Schmuck der Madonna. Dirigent: Generalmusikdirektor **Hans Knappertsbusch** a. G. Im Abonnement (Anfang 7½ Uhr)
Montag   den 7. Elektra, Dirigent: Generalmusikdirektor **Hans Knappertsbusch** a. G. Theatergemeinde Serie C, rote Mitgliedskarten (Anfang ☛ 8 ☚ Uhr)

Kartenverkauf für alle Bundestheater (Burg-, Opern- und Akademie-Theater) an den Tageskassen: I. Bräunerstraße 14, an Werktagen von 9—18 Uhr, an Sonn- und Feiertagen von 9—17 Uhr und an der Abendkassa am Vorstellungstage. Telephonische Bestellungen von Sitzen (ausgenommen Säulensitze) zum Preise von S 4.— aufwärts ausschließlich unter der Telephonnummer R-28-3-20 von 8—18 Uhr.

This was Herbert von Karajan's first appearance on the conductor's rostrum of the Vienna Opera. 'Even in outward appearance his style of conducting is theatrical: as the slight figure with the narrow head and flowing mane of hair trembles with passion, draws itself up or stoops, when the conductor's baton, used to such emphasis by the right hand, releases a tornado from the orchestra, while the outspread left hand curbs the whipped up waves of sound; the style of his exposition in respect of tempo and dynamics is wholly theatrical. Crashing explosions mark the characteristics and the basic form of a performance in which the conflagration of this Wagnerian love symphony is powerfully fanned and the whole scene is suffused by the flaring lights', wrote Heinrich Kralik in the 'Neues Wiener Tagblatt'.

who was in constant touch with Franz Werfel and Werfel's wife Alma, Mahler's widow. It was over a dinner in the Grand Hotel that these three brought about the 'Direktion Bruno Walter', which sounded fine, except that the real Director was Kerber. Kerber threw himself heart and soul into his new job, and with an artistic personality of the calibre of Bruno Walter at his side, the new era might well have developed into one of the brightest chapters in the Opera's history, had not the march of political events taken such a catastrophic turn.

September 1936 was notable for the appearance of Arturo Toscanini, who conducted a marvellous *Fidelio*, with a cast including Lotte Lehmann, whom Toscanini very much admired; so much so that forswearing his usual intransigence towards singers (especially if he disliked them) he allowed her to sing the whole of the second part of Fidelio's aria 'Abscheulicher' in Act One (after the words 'der spiegelt alte Zeiten wider') transposed down a semitone. As the original also modulates a semitone down at this point, it meant that Lehmann was actually dropping a whole tone. Great was our astonishment.

One of the highlights of the Kerber-Walter era was *Oberon*, which after opening at the Salzburg Festival moved to Vienna in the autumn, with Hilde Konetzni as Rezia and Helga Roswaenge as Hüon. The Konetzni sisters were already celebrated in Vienna: Anni, a former swimming champion, had been taken on by Clemens Krauss and very soon sang her way to the fore in Wagner, while Hilde, a dramatic soprano who was the obvious successor to Lotte Lehmann, had an equally remarkable voice and an even great heart and sense of poetry. In due course she became a wonderful Marschallin in *Der Rosenkavalier*. The two sisters were generously equipped physically as well as vocally, and a duet for the two of them, as in *Walküre* or *Elektra*, was an impressive experience.

Helge Roswaenge, who had also appeared during the Schalk and Krauss regimes, was a Dane. His brilliant tenor voice, with its radiant top notes, soon made him a popular favourite. A curious feature of his technique was that between each note there was a sort of audible intake of breath, not exactly a cough and not exactly a 'bark', but an audible transition from one note to the next. Apart from his activities at the Opera he owned a small noodle factory in Austria and later took up film-producing.

A not uninteresting première was that of Jaromir Weinberger's *Wallenstein,* but it came nowhere near to repeating the success of the same composer's *Schwanda.* Max Brod translated the Czech libretto of Schiller's trilogy into German, and the three dramas were compressed into six scenes. All I can remember of the work is a military march, and Jerger as Wallenstein. A day or two later Furtwängler conducted *Die Meistersinger.*

Among other premières was Ermanno Wolf-Ferrari's sole excursion into the realms of *verismo* at its goriest, *Der Schmuck der Madonna,* conducted by Knappertsbusch, who also conducted Ottorino Respighi's opera *La fiamma.* It was a moderate success. A comic opera, *Rossini in Neapel,* put together by Bernhard Paumgartner out of bits and pieces by Rossini, did only slightly better, in spite of Tauber as Rossini and Alfred Jerger as Barbaja, the theatre manager with a taste for speculation and a good nose for money. It was the first and perhaps last time that a Vienna Opera Director (we met him in the chapter on the Kärntnertor Theatre) turned up as an operatic hero. Who will sing Karajan a hundred years from now? Equally unsuccessful was an opera by Marco Frank based on a book by Friedrich Schreyvogel entitled *Die fremde Frau,* the story of a modern woman who gradually sinks lower and lower and ends up as a murderess. *Die Sühne,* an opera by Josef Wenzel-Traunfels based on a tale by Theodor Körner, was a complete fiasco. It was about a man who returns home after the war and finds his wife with another man; the 'other man' happens to be his brother, and in attempting to kill him the returning warrior accidentally kills his own wife and is then killed by his brother ... Something for Mascagni!

During the Kerber-Walter era there were visits by Italian celebrities such as Lauri-Volpi and the world-famous Benjamino Gigli. From America came the two great Wagner singers Lauritz Melchior and Kirsten Flagstad, and from Germany Frida Leider, a notable Brünnhilde. An important new acquisition was the Yugoslav tenor Anton Dermota, who started as a lyric tenor and blossomed out during the war into a wonderful Mozart tenor. He sang the part of Florestan at the gala performance of *Fidelio* with which the Opera House re-opened in November 1955. Other acquisitions were the Greek contralto Elena Nikolaidi; Josef Witt, who, in the new production of *Palestrina* by Otto Erhart, a fugitive from Dresden, became just as much *the* Palestrina as Richard Mayr had been *the* Ochs; and Maria Reining, a Viennese, who during the Krauss regime had sung soubrette rôles and now came into her own as a lovely dramatic soprano: Elisabeth, Elsa, Sieglinde.

A landmark during 1937, the last year before Austria's independence was temporarily snuffed out, was the first appearance at the Vienna Opera of Herbert von Karajan on the first of June. He came from the Aachen Opera and conducted *Tristan.* (Between 1931 and 1937 *Tristan* was conducted by no fewer than seven top-line conductors: Strauss, Schalk, Knappertsbusch, Furtwängler, Walter, Karajan, and Böhm, whose first appearance at the Vienna Opera was in the spring of 1933.) Viennese audiences were also introduced to three singers who later became international stars: Lawrence Tibbett from the USA, a good Iago and Rigoletto; Jussi Björling, who sang in *Il Trovatore* in Swedish; and Zinka Kunz (Tosca), who later as Zinka Milanov became one of the 'Met's' very brightest stars. During his sporadic appearances at the Vienna Opera, whenever he could tear himself away from operetta or the film world, Richard Tauber explored the uttermost limits of the heroic tenor's domain (*Tiefland, Der Evangelimann, Pagliacci*).

Audiences were given a welcome Christmas present in 1937 in the form of the eagerly awaited new production of *Carmen* by Karl Ebert, who had been forced to leave the Berlin Opera and later became the founder of the Glyndebourne Festival in England. In the first and fourth acts, in each of which there were two changes of scene, he made good use of the revolving stage introduced by Clemens Krauss. Act One started in the guard-house and then moved out on to the square, and Act Four started outside the amphitheatre and ended practically in it. The conductor was Bruno Walter, and the success was prodigious. It is hard to believe that until this production this extremely popular opera was still making do with scenery dating from 1875! The Don José was the Bulgarian Todor Mazaroff, one of the most interesting discoveries of the Kerber-Walter era, who had won a prize at a Vienna Music Competition. The Carmen was the young Dane Elsa Brems. After a few performances Jan Kiepura made a guest appearance as Don José (and was the only one of the cast who sang in French). It was his last appearance at the Vienna Opera, and the Flower Song and his duet with the new Micaela (the charming Esther Réthy from Budapest) were encored. Esther Réthy developed into a very fine lyrical soprano, and after the war she was the great operetta star of the Volksoper.

Once, during Bruno Walter's term of office, some Viennese Nazis threw stink-bombs onto the stage during Act Three of *Tristan*, with such accuracy that Anni Konetzni as Isolde was unable to continue and Walter finished the 'Liebestod' with the orchestra alone. The Opera's only previous experience of stink-bombs was in 1934, when the celebrated Bayreuth baritone Friedrich Schorr, who was a Jew, was singing Wotan: Clemens Krauss interrupted the performance for an hour to clear the air and it was then resumed.

And so to 1938. In January Weingartner conducted *Der Kuhreigen* with Tauber in celebration of Kienzl's eightieth birthday, and Lehár conducted a production of *Land of Smiles* (with Vera Schwarz) transferred from the Theater an der Wien. In February Bruno Walter conducted his last première, Smetana's *Dalibor*, with lovely scenery by Kautsky showing Saint George's Church in Prague with the citadel and the old town at its foot. As the Austrian Chancellor Kurt von Schuschnigg entered his box the audience rose to its feet; he was just back from his dramatic encounter with Hitler at Berchtesgaden.

At the beginning of March despairing efforts were made to renew Bruno Walter's contract for another three years, which in view of Austria's virtually hopeless political position showed remarkable confidence in the future.

Walter's friend Ernst Lothar, who was then Director of the Theater in der Josefstadt, acted as a go-between on behalf of both the Vienna Opera and Bruno Walter, who was then conducting in Amsterdam. Telegrams were sent to Toscanini warmly inviting him to take part in the 1938 Salzburg Festival, but Toscanini declined. Perhaps he could divine the future more clearly than the rest of us.

On the ninth of March Franz Salmhofer's most successful opera, *Iwan Sergejewitsch Tarassenko* was given its first performance in a one-act version, along with Bizet's *Djamileh*. Thanks largely to Hilde Konetzni and the baritone Fred Destal, Salmhofer's work was a big success. It is the story of a heroic village blacksmith who, during the Russian peasant revolt of the 1870s, out of love for his wife hides the murderer of a Czarist sergeant, confesses to having done the murder himself, and gives his life for the other man. Unfortunately the proceedings were clouded by the ugly turn political events were taking, for it was on this very day that Schuschnigg announced a plebiscite to be held on the thirteenth of March. It never took place.

When my friend Karl Alwin raised his baton to start Tchaikovsky's *Eugene Onegin* on the evening of the eleventh of March, Schuschnigg had already broadcast news of his resignation, and the Swastika was flying over the Chancellor's office.

Next day, the twelfth, the first German troops arrived. In the evening Knappertsbusch conducted *Tristan*. Kerstin Thorborg, the statuesque Scandinavian who had been so superb in Bruno Walter's *Orfeo*, found it advisable to leave Vienna in a hurry, and in order to muster a 'glorious' cast to match this 'glorious' day the part of Brangäne had to be entrusted to Rosette Anday, which was not exactly the kind of contingency the Nuremberg Race Laws envisaged.

It was on this paradoxical note that Austrian sovereignty in the Vienna State Opera was temporarily extinguished.

Austria had ceased to exist. The main body of German troops marched in on the thirteenth of March 1938, and the State Opera was closed until the twenty-seventh of March, when Knappertsbusch conducted *Fidelio*, with Hilde Konetzni and Max Lorenz, in the presence of Field Marshal Göring. It was to be the dawn of a new era. 'Lavishly decorated with swastika flags and brilliantly lit, the Opera presents a more magnificent and festive picture than ever in its history', wrote the *Völkischer Beobachter* the following morning.

In my view, it will always be difficult to arrive at a proper assessment of the Vienna Opera's doings during World War II because, for so many people, whichever side they were on, it was a time that brings back tragic memories. Some people were living in exile, far from home, others lost their nearest and dearest on active service. There can be no one who does not look back on those years without a shudder.

Nor can the newspaper reports of those days be compared with what we had understood criticism to be up till then, because Dr. Joseph Goebbels, the Nazi Minister of Propaganda, very soon issued instructions that criticism was to make way for what he called 'reflections on art'. The Press had to toe the line, so such criticisms as have survived from those years are virtually valueless. For the singers, of course, everything in the garden was lovely; nobody got a roasting in the Press because the critics could never be quite sure that their victim was not a protégé of some party boss.

On the other hand, looking through the 1938—1945 records one cannot help being astonished by the terrific casts that the Vienna Opera managed to assemble in those days; superb singers who made international reputations after the war when they were still in their prime. The same was true of the conductors. The great names Furtwängler, Knappertsbusch, Karl Böhm — alternated with the strictest regularity. There was no particular difficulty in attracting the big names to Vienna, because most of them felt far more comfortable in Vienna than in the German part of the 'Third Reich'.

On one point everyone who lived through these years is unanimous: the Vienna Opera was an oasis of peace amid the political and military horrors of total war. As such it was screened and protected by the Nazi authorities, who were shrewd enough to realise what the Viennese felt about 'their Opera', and that in the long run only a policy of toleration would keep the house full. Accordingly the Berlin authorities issued instructions that the Vienna Opera was to be pampered and subsidised as generously as possible. Another factor that contributed to this policy was that Gauleiter Baldur von Schirach fancied himself a patron of the arts and cherished vague dreams of preserving the Austrian tradition within the framework of the 'Third Reich', a notion that cut clean across the 'assimilation' policy of Goebbels and his henchmen.

For the time being, Kerber remained in office and was an island of stability amid the hectic ebb and flow of events. But though he was a candidate for liquidation from the very first day, the authorities being well aware that he was anything but well-disposed to Nazi ideology, it was some time before he could be disposed of. He used to say that every morning when he arrived at his office he knocked on the door in case someone else was already sitting at his desk. For a time, however, he was allowed to go on occupying the Director's chair opposite a portrait of the Emperor Franz Joseph, which, if a prominent visitor was expected, could be deftly replaced by one of Adolf Hitler that was kept behind a cupboard ready for emergencies.

Like so many others, Bruno Walter was a victim of the Nazi Race Laws and had to leave the country. His office was occupied by Hans Knappertsbusch, who stayed on at the Opera and conducted some wonderful performances. Occasionally, of course (and inevitably), he sailed a bit too close to the wind, especially on one occasion when with an unprintable oath he sent an ash tray flying against a loud-speaker from which one of Hitler's speeches was being broadcast. Hitler's speeches had to be listened to by the entire staff, and for big speeches that had been announced in advance, loud-speakers were installed in the auditorium and everyone had to assemble there, though as the speech wore on the audience usually thinned out appreciably. In the case of speeches not announced in advance, rehearsals were interrupted by announcements that a speech by Hitler was about to be broadcast, and this was what had made Knappertsbusch so angry.

Hitler's first birthday in the new 'Gross-Deutschland' era was celebrated by the Vienna Opera on the twentieth of April 1938 with a performance (needless to say) of *Die Meistersinger,* conducted by Furtwängler. On a later occasion Knappertsbusch conducted *Siegfried.*

Furtwängler too had his problems. He had resigned from the post of Director of the Berlin Opera in 1934, as a protest against the ban on Hindemith. Now he was beset by acoustic difficulties, and at a rehearsal for a Philharmonic concert in the Main Hall of the Vienna *Musikverein* he glared at the swastika hangings all over the hall and said in a loud voice: 'I wonder whether it will sound all right with these decorations . . .'

The unity of the new 'Gross-Deutschland' in 1938, and even more so during the war, was to be demonstrated by comprehensive exchange schemes among various Opera Houses. The Berlin Opera brought its *Lohengrin* to Vienna with Maria Müller and Franz Völker, and in order to underline 'Gross-deutsch' unity even more heavily it also brought its own chorus which was to be amalgamated with the Vienna chorus. Later, when Böhm became Director, all Vienna's choruses became 'one big German brotherhood', and at a performance of *Die Meistersinger* the chorus was imported from the 'Opernhaus der Stadt Wien', which was the new name for the Volksoper (and a bit of a mouthful for the tram-conductors).

On the 'Grossdeutsche Reich Day', after the incorporation of Czechoslovakia in 1939, the Vienna Opera performed in Prague and Brünn, and in later years there were visits to the Netherlands, Zagreb and Bucharest after German troops had occupied these territories. The Rome Opera sent its ballet to Vienna, and the Teatro Communale of Florence gave *Falstaff* in Vienna with Mariano Stabile, who was also the producer. The whole area of Europe under Hitler's domination was criss-crossed by visiting operatic companies.

In 1939 Vienna received a visit from the Hamburg Opera, and Hans Hotter in the title-rôle of Handel's *Julius Caesar* became a popular favourite almost overnight. The producer was Karl Heinrich Strohm, the Intendant of the Hamburg Opera.

Not unnaturally, Joseph Goebbels was casting around for a new Director for the Vienna Opera, and Berlin did not take long to make up its mind that what was required was somebody amenable, not a martinet. It was realised that a rigid disciplinarian would find Viennese artists difficult to get on with.

It so happened that the above-mentioned Karl Heinrich Strohm, the Intendant of the Hamburg Opera, had been at the same school as Goebbels. Strohm was an inoffensive, quiet little man who never opened his mouth too wide and looked like a clergyman or an absent-minded professor. This was the man whom Goebbels appointed to a post once occupied by Mahler and Strauss.

The appointment must have gone to Strohm's head. At all events, the Vienna post proved too much for his sanity. In 1940, almost as soon as his appointment to Vienna was announced in Hamburg, he began to talk in a confused way, and erstwhile colleagues recall how, when bidding Hamburg farewell, he allowed himself certain observations that, as Adolf Hitler would no doubt have put it, were not quite kosher.

Accordingly, shortly after the Hamburg Opera's highly successful *Julius Caesar,* this Karl Heinrich Strohm moved into his office in the Vienna Opera House, and the inoffensive, quiet little mouse became a pompous and bombastic pocket-size dictator who lost no time in emphasising what a pig-sty Vienna was, and in outlining how he would clean the place up.

His very first action was to stir up wrath on all sides by personally ordering 'improvements' in the Opera's interior decoration. First, he had all the tapestries removed, even from the room that had been used as an office by Mahler, Strauss and Schalk. Next, he found the famous old spiral stairway from the porter's lodge to the Director's office inappropriate to his dignity, and had a new doorway opened up on the Kärntner Strasse side so that he could stalk up to his office via the Archdukes' Stairway. The door is at the Ringstrasse end of the arcade, where opera-goers collect their free seats.

Strohm made absolutely no contact with the people of Vienna. He was regarded and treated as a complete outsider, and although (or perhaps because) he always talked so big, he failed entirely to get things done, a fact that soon came to the notice of the Nazi authorities. The business of getting rid of him was made easier for them by Strohm himself, who in February 1941 disappeared into an asylum.

The unfailing test

The character tenor Peter Klein (the famous Mime) took up his appointment in Vienna during the war. At that time there was a notice in the commissionaire's office by the stage door announcing: 'Only the German Greeting is permitted here.' When the unforgettable landlord in 'La Bohème' and equally unforgettable comic Alfred Muzzarelli met his colleague in the Opera for the first time, Klein said to Muzzarelli 'Grüss Gott'. Muzzarelli looked him straight in the eye and said solemnly, 'Don't you know that we only use the German Greeting here?' Peter Klein replied in loud, stentorian tones: 'Heil Hitler!' Now Muzzarelli gazed still more solemnly into his eyes and said: 'There you are, I knew at once that you were no Nazi.'

He never completely recovered. One day, after the liberation of Vienna in 1945, he accosted three Allied officers who had not the faintest idea of conditions at the Vienna Opera, accompanied them to the stage-door of the Theater an der Wien, which was then the Vienna Opera's headquarters, led them on to the stage, and started to behave as if he were the Director: 'This is my theatre, and I need permits for all sorts of materials for my productions.' It was a grotesque scene.

The 'quiet little man' who became the big pretender and ended up as a megalomaniac was succeeded by another quiet man, who from his very first day enjoyed the confidence and goodwill of the entire staff, and long after the 'thousand-year Reich' had gone up in fire and destruction he was still in a position of authority: Ernst August Schneider, a familiar figure to all who had anything to do with the Vienna Opera during and after

World War II and one of my best friends. We call him 'Ernesto'.

Ernst August Schneider comes from Mecklenburg, was once a critic, and even lectured on the techniques of criticism. It was a certain Walter Thomas, a pupil of his in Baldur von Schirach's office, who recommended Schneider to the Gauleiter for the post of Director of the Vienna Opera.

At the time of his appointment he had already been working for some time as Chief Dramaturgist and Producer in Cologne. As Strohm's successor his terms of reference were twofold. The first thing he had to do was get rid of Kerber, who was a nuisance but in a strong position because he was so well-liked. So Schneider failed at the very first fence, because he is a man who can only make friends, not enemies. He at once realised Kerber's gifts, the two got on very well together, and they ran the Opera jointly. Secondly, the Berlin authorities had made it clear to Schneider from the very first that his appointment was only an interim one because they wanted as Director a prominent musician, and in point of fact they had been negotiating since 1941 with Karl Böhm.

After running the Opera for a time jointly with Schneider, Kerber went back to his native Salzburg in the spring of 1942 and took over the local Landestheater. During his years in Vienna Kerber had from time to time done some producing, and very well too. He had produced *Eugene Onegin* with a cast including Maria Reining and Paul Schöffler, and Louis Maillart's *Glöckchen des Eremiten*, which had not been played for years. It is a story about a bell in a lonely hermitage high up in the mountains that has the disconcerting habit of ringing whenever a wife in the neighbourhood was unfaithful to her husband. Kerber died in 1943, and the Vienna Opera honoured his memory with his production of *Turandot*.

Schneider was now in sole charge, but this experienced man of the theatre was 'too soft' for the cultural bosses in Berlin, so once again they appointed an outsider over his head, Lothar Müthel, the Director of the Burgtheater, who thereafter was to run both houses with the title of *Generalintendant*, Müthel did not go to any particular trouble over the Opera, apart from producing what from all accounts was an excellent *Fidelio*, conducted by Furt-wängler.

At last, in the spring of 1943, Karl Böhm was appointed Director of the Vienna Opera. A native of Graz, Böhm was already closely associated with the Vienna Philharmonic on the concert platform and during Clemens Krauss's term had conducted a notable *Tristan*. So once again the Vienna Opera had a professional and experienced musician at the helm. Strauss thought a lot of Böhm, and it was under Böhm that *Die schweigsame Frau* and *Daphne* had first been performed in Dresden. With Krauss in Munich and Böhm in Vienna, Strauss could be sure that his interests would be well looked after: in Kerber's day he had frequently complained about inferior casts. Böhm remained in office until the end of the war in April 1945.

Press release No. II/297/40 dated 27 April 1940 issued by the Reich Propaganda Office in Berlin.

On the occasion of the 70th birthday of Lehar on 30. 4. 1940 a particular honour will be bestowed on him. (Following information for editorial offices only, not for publication.) As the Hungarians lay claim to Lehar owing to his Hungarian nationality, but he is in fact of German extraction, he should be referred to in the Press not as the 'Hungarian' composer Lehar but as the master of German operetta. All polemics in connection with Lehar's music and person are of course undesirable.

To: *A I*	*By order*	*Stamp:*
B I	*Wittenberg*	*Reich Propaganda Office,*
D I	*Press officer*	*Berlin.*

Probably nobody will ever be able completely to disentangle all the inconsistencies of those bewildering years. Singers who came to Austria from Germany were always surprised, at any rate for a day or two, at the frequent use of the 'Heil Hitler' greeting. In German theatres the practice had been in abeyance for some time. But if they stayed at the Vienna Opera for any length of time they found that 'Heil Hitler' soon went out of fashion in Vienna too. Yet people were suspicious of each other, especially if they didn't know each other. At the same time the attraction and glamour of the Vienna Opera were more potent than ever, so that from 1938 to 1945 the artists were a much more united family than they were after the war. Politically they were for the most part left in peace, and were less badgered to join the Nazi party than people in other walks of life. The authorities, it seemed, had a soft spot for the Opera. If a performer were denounced, for instance, by a fanatically Nazi landlady for not putting out a flag during the 'Reich Theatre Festival Weeks', every effort was made to get the matter settled on the premises, so to speak. Nor was it particularly difficult for singers to be granted exemption from military service, and it was easier for singers to dodge the call-up than it was for ordinary mortals, because most of the doctors who carried out the medical examinations also had a soft spot for the Opera, and were only too willing to classify singers as being in a reserved occupation. It was desirable, of course, to be on good terms with the 'Hospitallers' in the Grosse Mohrengasse, where the medical examinations took place. Ernst August Schneider used to make a trip to Berlin every month to see that singers were not called up.

Another characteristic paradox was that although since Strohm's arrival there had been a notice at the stage-door to the effect that 'in this building the German greeting "Heil Hitler" is compulsory', the Horst Wessel song was never once played at the Vienna Opera. It is interesting to note that Horst Wessel, a member of the S.A., wrote the words (the tune is from an old ballad) at Alser Strasse 16 in Vienna, where he was lodging with a family who up to 1945 used to show visitors with pride the piano at which Horst Wessel had once pecked while writing the words. Whether or not this is an important item in the history of music is another matter.

Anecdotes and jokes against the regime went the rounds in ample numbers, both inside and outside the Opera House. Josef von Manowarda for instance, an admirable Wozzeck and Hans Sachs, but a less admirable fellow-traveller, met two other baritones, Erich Kunz and Alfred

Jerger, in a passage one day and informed them in a half-whisper out of the side of his mouth that the Führer had invented the most powerful secret weapon in history, with a range from Berlin to London. 'And back' was his colleagues' reply, in unison. Manowarda's wife, the singer Nelly Pirchhof, always wore a glass shield over the part of her hand that the Führer had once kissed.

It was only among the minor singers that informers appeared; the poorer the artist, the more rabid the Nazi. The worst of all was a certain Herr J. who always turned up at rehearsals in SS uniform and was highly dangerous. As a singer he never climbed higher than Angelotti in *Tosca*. And then all of a sudden he made a complete *volte-face* and was eventually, while still a member of the Vienna Opera, horribly beaten up at the Gestapo headquarters in the Morzinplatz.

Of the conductors, only one greeted the orchestra with 'Heil Hitler': Leopold Reichwein, who had returned to Vienna as soon as the Hitler regime took over. He committed suicide in 1945.

For the whole of the Nazi period Richard Strauss enjoyed the sort of 'poetic licence' accorded to genius. On the one hand he was definitely looked at askance by the Nazi authorities for having resigned as President of the 'Reichsmusikkammer' after getting his way about the first performance of *Die schweigsame Frau* in Dresden in 1935 with a libretto by the 'non-Aryan' Stefan Zweig. 'As far as I am concerned people only matter when they assemble as an audience. Whether they are Chinese, Bavarians, New Zealanders or Berliners is of no interest to me as long as they have paid the full price for their tickets,' Strauss wrote to Zweig, who was living in exile in Zürich. The letter was intercepted by the Gestapo and a photocopy was submitted to Hitler 'for information'. Seven years later Zweig committed suicide in South America.

The Nazis could not afford to do without the glamour of the name of Richard Strauss. At least, not for the time being; though 'one day,' promised Goebbels, 'we shall have our own music and shall no longer need this decadent old narcotic.'

Vienna's celebration of Strauss's eightieth birthday was a brilliant occasion. Strauss was sure enough of his posi-

'...in the name of the Führer'

To the head of the Press Office,   Berlin, 3. 3. 1944
Pg. Biedermann   Music Dept.
in this house.   Dr. Gk/Ga.

Dear Party Member Biedermann,

Richard Strauss will be 80 years old in July, and it is to be expected that the party newspapers will also carry long articles about him.

Reichsleiter Bormann has recently issued a confidential circular in the name of the Führer which states that all prominent party members who formally had personal contact with Richard Strauss should be broken off (sic), because Strauss has severely contravened the demands of the people's community. I recently spoke to our Reichsleiter in order to find out his opinion concerning the way in which the honour to be accorded to Richard Strauss should be handled in our newspapers and in the 'Völkischer Beobachter'. The Reichsleiter recommends that we confine ourselves to recording the fact that certain performances have taken place, and that as far as possible no long articles on Strauss should appear.

As I am only in Berlin for a short time I would request you to inform the 'VB' accordingly.

Heil Hitler!
Gk. (Dr. Gerigk).

Dr. Herbert Gerigk was the head of the music section of Dr. Rosenberg's department for 'ideological training and education throughout the NSDAP'. The offence referred to in his letter consisted in Richard Strauss's refusal to take evacuees and people who had been bombed out into his house. To the reproof that in wartime everyone must be prepared to make sacrifices, he replied that no soldier need fight on his account; all that had nothing to do with him. Whereupon Bormann commandeered the required rooms without further ado.

tion to permit himself the gesture of handing back the baton presented to him by the Gauleiter of Vienna with the remark: 'I don't like it, it's too heavy.' After the gala concert Pauline Strauss said to the Gauleiter: 'I'm giving a tea-party tomorrow but as it's only for a limited number of guests I'm afraid I can't squeeze you in.' Her relations with the Gauleiter seem to have been, to put it mildly, somewhat informal. During the ceremonies in Vienna in commemoration of the 150th anniversary of Mozart's death she went up to Schirach and said: 'My dear, I know I don't have to say "Heil Hitler" to you, help me please: I want to send our friend Ferdl in Rio a document my husband promised him, he needs it badly and he's such a nice Jew.'

In an official article put out by the Nazi Press, which was represented in force at Strauss's birthday celebrations, it was argued that Strauss was the only composer who could write a 'National-Socialist' opera, because presumably his operas would have been quite different and genuinely Teutonic if, instead of being saddled with non-Aryan librettists like Hofmannsthal and Zweig, he had managed to find 'the right man' at the outset. The real, one hundred per cent German Strauss was to be seen in the young composer of his first opera *Guntram,* a work based on a Teutonic legend in which his future wife Pauline de Ahna had sung the part of Freihild.

Interference by the Nazi authorities in the Opera's programme was on the whole relatively harmless, as for instance when it was changed in order to give Hitler, who was in Vienna, a chance of hearing his favourite opera *Tiefland.* The only irritating feature of the occasion was Hitler's insistence on having an interval after the scene in the mountains in Act One, *i. e.* before the change of scene, because he had arranged a meeting for exactly that time and refused to put it off. Another favourite of Hitler's, *The Merry Widow,* was not in the repertoire at the time, but Lehár's seventieth birthday was celebrated with *Land of Smiles,* though its librettists were just as non-Aryan as those of *The Merry Widow.* While Franz Völker was singing 'Dein ist mein ganzes Herz' the Jewish librettist Fritz Löhner-Beda had been in a concentration camp for some time, waiting for the end.

On most evenings the Vienna Opera was sold out, but the composition of the audience had changed strikingly. There were many uniforms, and the Imperial box was occupied by Nazi V.I.P.'s and (during the war years) by soldiers on sick leave. Irritation was occasionally ventilated (and tolerated by the police) in the form of heckling or audible protests. For instance during the first performance of Werner Egk's opera *Columbus* in 1942 the word 'gold' provoked a member of the audience to shout: 'We want our gold back.' Actually *Columbus* was more of a stage oratorio than an opera. The producer was Oscar Fritz Schuh, the conductor was Leopold Ludwig, and the scenery was by Reinking. One particularly fine scene was of a huge ship landing in the New World.

The simmering discontent of the upper strata of the population and of the younger generation caused modern masterpieces, which in normal times are received with interest if not applause, to be accorded a mixed reception and even booed at their first performance. It was only after several repeat performances that audiences gradually came round to them, particularly in the case of Orff's *Carmina burana,* which was given a superb performance. On the same bill was Werner Egk's ballet *Joan von Zarissa* (1942), in which Harald Kreutzberg danced the rôle of the Fool, a sort of cross between Leporello and Satan. The atmosphere of medieval France was so enchanting that it was like being transported to the world portrayed in illuminated French manuscripts. The miming of the dancers was commented on by a chorus in which some of the females wore the bonnets favoured by the French middle-classes in those days, while others wore the pointed hats, with veils, that were the prerogative of the aristocracy. They were posted in small balconies hung with coloured draperies high above the stage and held the music in their hands. It all looked rather like the stands round a tournament arena.

By all accounts, *Carmina burana* was delightful. So why the booing? Opponents of the regime said to themselves: 'Now is our chance to show you what we really think of your avant-garde pretensions, we can't be arrested, because our disapproval is directed not against Hitler but at what you usually call "degenerate art."'

The booing and shouting at the première of Rudolf Wagner-Regeny's *Johanna Balk* in 1941 were repeated at subsequent performances and were aimed at Gauleiter Schirach, and through him at the regime. As the composer was a protégé of his, Schirach attended the first performance in person. *Johanna Balk* was to be the highlight of the 1942 'Contemporary Music Week', and although it was a complete flop it was retained in the repertoire. 'Joanna doesn't go, but keeps coming back,' as one wag put it.

This was the first time the Gauleiter had deliberately sponsored a work, though admittedly a work by an able composer. The only opera the regime definitely imposed on the Vienna Opera was Rudolf Wille's *Königsballade* in 1939, just before the outbreak of the war. The young king in Wille's opera was Helge Roswaenge, but even his radiant top notes could not prevent another flop. It was a perfect illustration of Schopenhauer's dictum that 'in ethics the will is everything, but in art it is nothing'; in this case 'the will' was at all events not strong enough to rescue the work. The composer was an insignificant little man who looked like an income-tax official or a rent-collector and was a great favourite of Goebbels'.

There was a good deal of expectation before the first performance of Richard Strauss's one-act opera *Der Friedenstag* (1939) to a libretto by Hans Gregor, who later became head of the Theatrical Collection in the Austrian National Library. The production was by Rudolf Hartmann, later Director of the Munich Opera, the two leading rôles were sung by Hans Hotter and Viorica Ursuleac, and the conductor was Clemens Krauss. The setting was 1648, when the Thirty Years' War ended. The scenery was marvellous. Beneath the citadel in which the action takes place was a thirty feet high underpass through which the audience could see a grim grey tower, the pivot and symbol of the entire action. Just before the hymn to peace at the end, the tower sank into the ground to reveal the great orb of the rising sun, symbolising peace at last after thirty long years of war.

The first performance in Vienna on the tenth of June 1939, the day before Strauss's seventy-fifth birthday, was also the last (on instructions from Berlin). A man who was on the brink of starting a worldwide holocaust needed no *Friedenstag*, no dawn of peace.

A year later, in 1940, came *Daphne*, first with Maria Reining, and later with Maria Cebotari. This wonderful 'bucolic tragedy', as Gregor's libretto styles it, set at the foot of Mount Olympus, was certainly the best Vienna première in those dark years. Strauss himself had a big hand in the production, particularly in the final scene, where Daphne is turned into a laurel tree. Strauss wrote to Clemens Krauss that it must be possible for the audience to follow the transformation clearly, to see Daphne, pursued by Apollo, suddenly stand rooted to the

---

A letter from Richard Strauss dated 10 January 1940 (!)

'*As far as I can see the general opinion is that after the war Germany will be totally impoverished in any case, and even if we lose the war the question will be: whether an operatic culture and musical life will exist at all: if we should be overrun by Russia, whether any copyright will be valid, whether a Stagma* will still be in existence — in short, whether properties which are now still valued at 500,000 Marks will be worth a brass farthing in a few months' time, whether among all my works the only one to survive will perhaps be, at best, 'Rosenkavalier'.*'

* *Stagma = the German performing rights society of the time.*

---

spot as leaves and branches sprout from her hair and outstretched arms. 'Otherwise my music has no point. Daphne's transformation must be clearly visible from A to Z.'

The last time Richard Strauss conducted in the Vienna Opera was in 1942. After the performance he wrote to Clemens Krauss: 'I have just conducted dear old *Salome* here with all my old vitality and without over-exerting myself.' Once again one could see how Strauss nursed his singers and kept the orchestra down, unlike so many other conductors. Singers always had an easy passage with Strauss conducting.

The Champagne Opera

The first to conduct *Die Fledermaus* in an Opera House was Gustav Mahler in Hamburg. In Vienna Johann Strauss's work of genius was finally admitted to the precincts of the Imperial Opera in 1894 during Jahn's term. Since then it has been a fixed star in the operatic firmament all over the world, and at the Vienna Opera it is traditionally performed on New Year's Eve. Its original version was a play called *Réveillon* by Meilhac and Halévy, and the setting was neither Vienna nor New Year's Eve but Christmas Eve in Paris, as in *La Bohème*. The turbulent French feast of Christmas was incomprehensible to the Viennese public, so Strauss's librettists Haffner and Genée altered the setting to 'a resort near a big city', and converted the Paris Christmas Eve revelry into Prince Orlofsky's ball. Ever since Karajan's new production in 1960, Rosalinde and Eisenstein (shown here) have been sung by two singers who are Viennese born and bred: Hilde Güden and Eberhard Wächter. The lovely Hilde Güden started in operetta at the Volksoper and became a star of world magnitude, particularly in Mozart and Richard Strauss. In operetta she can only be heard nowadays on records — or as Rosalinde at the Vienna Opera. Eberhard Wächter, whose repertoire ranges from Amfortas to Escamillo and Posa, is so fond of operetta that he once appeared in Granichstaedten's *Orlow* at the Vienna Volksoper. He studied the part of Eisenstein with one of Vienna's most celebrated exponents of this rôle, Fred Liewehr.

The classical *Fledermaus* cast in the 1920s and 1930s was Richard Tauber as Eisenstein, Elisabeth Schumann or Adele Kern as Adele, Lotte Lehmann as Rosalinde, Alfred Jerger as Frank, and Leo Slezak as Alfred. The Frosch was sometimes Hans Moser or Ernst Tautenhayn, and once (1937) the Hungarian film comedian Szöke Szakall. Today's Frosch is usually Josef Meinrad (left), who was awarded the Iffland Ring and also excelled as Professor Higgins and The Man of La Mancha. One of the classic gags is in the scene where the drunken Governor of the prison, Frank, is found snoring with a newspaper over his face: 'The governor is groaning beneath the weight of public opinion.'

Unorthodox in all things, the Opera's head producer Otto Schenk (right) is no less so as Frosch. One of Karajan's innovations was to insist on operas being sung, wherever possible, in the original language. After his departure *The Barber of Seville* was given in German and promptly booed. In a performance of *Fledermaus* a day or two later, when Alfred, offstage, starts his aria in prison 'Ach wie so trügerisch', Schenk as Frosch burst out: 'He's got a nerve, singing in German!' (Thunderous applause). During the 1920s and 1930s the tradition of inviting someone from outside to play the part of Frosch was only observed on New Year's Eve, as the Opera had its own Frosch, the one and only Karl Norbert.

Act Two of the 1960 production of *Die Fledermaus* on New Year's Eve. Left foreground, Eberhard Wächter (Eisenstein) and Rita Streich (Adele); right Erich Kunz (Frank) and Elfriede Ott (Ida); between them Gerhard Stolze in classical operetta uniform as Orlofsky (the first time this rôle had been sung by a tenor). Producer: Leopold Lindtberg. Decor: Teo Otto. Herbert von Karajan presented brilliant Strauss, at times leaning back nonchalantly against the barrier as he listened to the dialogue. From 1963 to 1966 the New York's Eve performance was conducted with true Viennese sparkle by the veteran Robert Stolz.

The Opera Ball

To see and be seen: always an important part of the world of opera, this is nowhere more so than at the Opera Ball. The scenery is provided by the tiers of boxes, and the stage and auditorium together make an enormous dance-floor nearly 170 feet from end to end. The finishing touches are supplied by a sea of light and flowers. Tickets are booked at agencies months in advance, and the 200 pairs forming the Young Ladies' and the Young Gentlemen's Committees are drawn from Vienna's *jeunesse dorée*. At last the great evening comes, and press and TV reporters vie with each other to do the scene justice for those unable to be present: the arrival of the President and members of the Government, the entry of the Committee of Honour, the waltz dances by the Vienna State Opera Ballet, etc. It need hardly be added that the Opera Ball is the culmination of the Carnival season.

The idea of holding an Opera Ball originally came from Paris, where in the days of the can-can the proceedings sometimes became so lively that the police had to be called in to remove over-enthusiastic revellers. This sort of thing was frowned upon in Vienna, so in the 1877/78 season three 'Opera Soirées' were held at which, to discourage over-exuberance, the dancing was preceded by a concert of light symphonic music. In March 1878 the occasion was promoted to the status of an 'Opera Redoute' at which Eduard Strauss and his band provided the music. As time went on the 'Soirées' gave way to the 'Redoutes', which became a permanent feature of Carnival every year until 1899, with the exception of 1889, the year of Crown Prince Rudolf's death at Mayerling. The old tradition was revived briefly in 1924, but the first real *Opera Ball* was in 1935. Up to then it only existed in Heuberger's operetta.

The first Opera Ball after the reconstruction of the Opera House was in 1956. Since then it has become more and more brilliant every year. For the magnificent banks of flowers along the balustrades of the boxes 14,000 carnations are flown in from the Riviera two days before. The crowns worn by the Young Ladies' Committee are slightly different each year. The 6,000 revellers have seven bands to dance to, and the Lucullan delicacies are provided by five different restaurateurs; all together 1,000 persons are employed on the night of the ball.

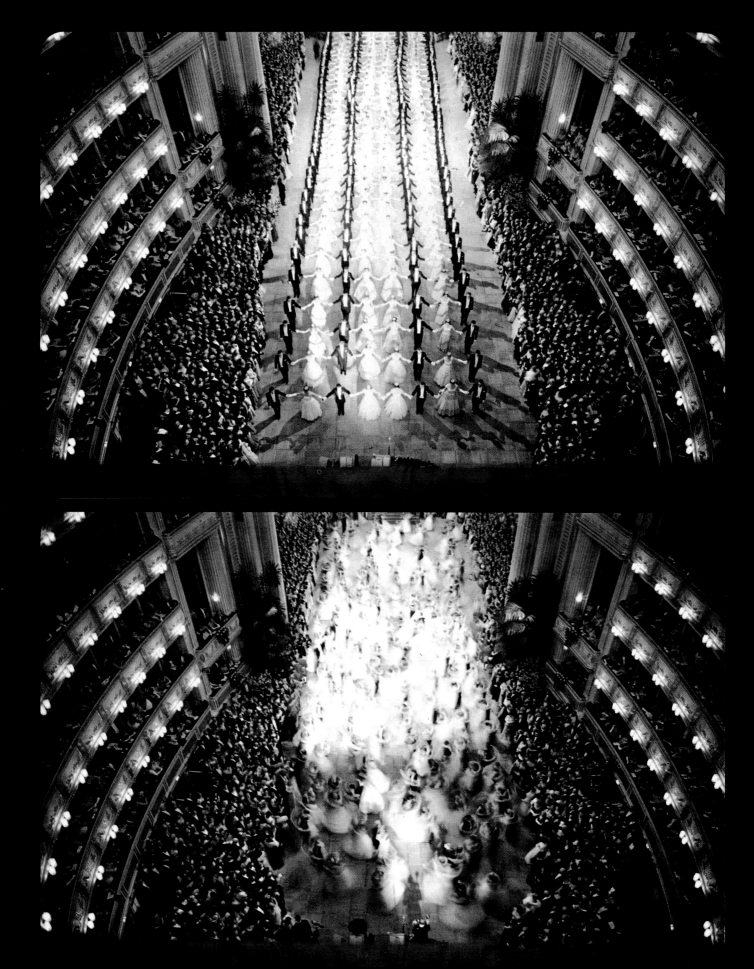

In celebration of Strauss's eightieth birthday in 1944, there was a series of performances of his operas, but by this time he himself was conducting only in the concert hall. The culmination was an *Ariadne* that can scarcely have been excelled for sheer brilliance. Maria Reining was Ariadne, Alda Noni was Zerbinetta, the 'young God' Max Lorenz was Bacchus, and the conductor was Karl Böhm. It was of this performance that the well-known live recording was made.

The same year saw the production of *Capriccio*, with a highly original libretto by Clemens Krauss. The setting is a country-house near Paris, and the work consists of a discussion between music-lovers and professional musicians on which is more important in an opera, the words or the music. The result is an opera full of poetry and intellect. As the theatrical manager La Roche, with his elaborate theories on how to run a theatre, Paul Schöffler scored a great triumph, and it has been one of his finest rôles ever since. The conductor was Karl Böhm, the scenery was by Hartmann, and the Countess was Maria Cebotari.

In commemoration of the 150th anniversary of Mozart's death Vienna was treated to a 'Mozart Week of the German Reich' (what a title!). The Munich Opera brought *Così fan tutte* with Krauss conducting and Hilde Güden (surprisingly enough) as Despina, and Richard Strauss conducted his own version of *Idomeneo*. He was visiting Vienna fairly frequently about this time and was always ready to give advice to anyone conducting one of his operas. Once during a rehearsal of *Salome* he sat just behind Knappertsbusch, who at the end of Salome's dance made a broad ritardando in 3/4, whereupon there was a gruff voice at his ear, '*Richard* Strauss, not Johann.'

An outstanding feature of this 'Mozart Week' was Gustaf Gründgens's production of *Die Zauberflöte*, which had already been given in Berlin. 150 years after the first production in the Freihaus Theater on the thirtieth of September 1791, with Schikaneder himself as the first Papageno, the work was staged as a fairy-tale. The presentation was partly realistic and partly symbolic. On the one hand the 'enormous snake' wriggled and reared most realistically, on the other hand Tamino, instead of actually playing his flute, brandished it above his head as if it were the conductor's baton, and instead of coming out of the instrument the notes seemed to float out of the air from somewhere far away. The three boys were suspended in a sort of basket covered with flowers.

The original dialogue was restored almost *in toto*, but Papageno's traditional punch lines were dispensed with. Many producers have started out to 'purge' *Die Zauberflöte,* but the result never lasts longer than the first night. By the second all the good old gags are back, such as Papageno's celebrated warning when the Priests take Papagena away from him in Act Two: 'Sir, I beg you not to interfere in my family affairs.' Against gags like this no producer can prevail. Helge Roswaenge was Tamino, Maria Reining was Pamina, Erna Berger was the Queen of the Night, and Knappertsbusch conducted.

For audiences in general the most successful novelty during the war was *Der schwarze Peter* (1939) by Norbert Schultze, the composer of 'Lili Marleen'. The Vienna Opera was the eighty-first theatre to stage it. It is a fairy-tale opera for children in which there is a rich kingdom and a poor kingdom, with a Prince in one and a beautiful Princess in the other. They get married and live happily ever after. Anton Paulik, who had conducted the first performance of *Gräfin Mariza* at the Theater an der Wien in 1924 and was now at the State Opera, warmed the hearts of thousands of children with his conducting of this delightful little piece.

Looking through the programmes of those days one can only be amazed at the array of first-class artists on the Vienna Opera's staff. To start with there was Furtwängler, who on one occasion acted as a producer (of *Tristan*), and right in the middle of the war requested the same authentic stage-designs that Roller and Mahler had created in 1903.

Hans Knappertsbusch conducted mostly Wagner, and in those days Wagner was the backbone of the repertoire of every Opera House in Germany. He conducted a lot of Strauss too, as well as Humperdinck's *Königskinder*. Böhm also conducted Wagner, and in 1943 embarked on his term as Director with *Die Meistersinger*. Occasionally he also conducted Mozart and Verdi. The 130th anniversary of Verdi's birth was celebrated in 1943 with a 'Verdi Week' of which the most interesting feature was probably *Macbeth* with Elisabeth Höngen as Lady Macbeth (Böhm calls her in his diary 'the greatest tragedian in the world') and Schöffler and Hotter alternating as Macbeth. There were also new productions of *Un Ballo in Maschera* and *Otello*, both conducted by Böhm and produced by Oscar Fritz Schuh with scenery by Caspar Neher. Maria Reining was Desdemona and Max Lorenz was a brilliant Otello (he was helped with his make-up by none other than Willi Forst!).

Oscar Fritz Schuh was appointed Head Producer; he first came to Vienna with Strohm from Hamburg. Two prominent stage-designers were Caspar Neher and Wilhelm Reinking, who is now Chief Stage-Designer at the Berlin Opera. Schuh and Neher produced *Figaro* and *Così fan tutte* in the Redoutensaal of the Hofburg, so making the first contribution to the Vienna Mozart style which came to its full flowering in the immediate post-war years at the Theater an der Wien.

Among other interesting new productions were *Falstaff* conducted by Clemens Krauss on a visit from Munich, and Franz Schmidt's *Notre Dame* produced by Koloman von Nádasdy, later Director of the Budapest Opera. The part of Quasimodo was sung by Herbert Alsen in a positively horrifying mask.

There was also a new production of *Bohème* that made good use of the revolving stage, and a brilliant *Aida* conducted by Vittorio Gui, with Set Svanholm (a wonderful Siegfried) as Radames and Daniza Ilitsch as Aida. The latter got into serious trouble when it came out that she had been hiding a British parachutist in her apartment.

Paul Schöffler was splendid in a long overdue first Vienna performance of Borodin's *Prince Igor*. Schöffler also appeared in Handel's *Rodelinde*, partnered by Esther Réthy. The performance took place in the Redoutensaal, which was put to full use during the war. It was part of an attempt at a Handel renaissance in Vienna, following the visit of the Hamburg Opera with *Julius Caesar*; but apart from brilliant performances by Schöffler and Réthy it never really caught on.

Programme planning was very much affected by the many anniversaries that came round during the war. Apart from the Richard Strauss celebrations already referred to there were a number of other illustrious names on the list. 1938, for instance, was the fiftieth anniversary of the first performance of Josef Bayer's ballet *Die Puppenfee*, and the commemorative performance conducted by Anton Paulik was its 675th. In 1939 and 1944 there were gala performances of *Palestrina* in celebration of Hans Pfitzner's seventieth and seventy-fifth birthdays. Josef Witt sang the part of Palestrina, and it was a moving scene when the frail old man, trembling with emotion, came on to the stage at the end to take his bow and hold out his hands to Witt in gratitude. Witt was also a brilliant Eisenstein and later became a favourite producer and teacher.

In 1940 there were three anniversaries: the seventieth anniversary of the first Vienna performance of *Die Meistersinger;* the centenary of the birth of Tchaikovsky, which was commemorated with *Eugene Onegin;* and the eightieth birthday of Emil Nikolaus von Reznicek, which was celebrated by taking into the repertoire a new version of his *Donna Diana*. The Donna Diana was Else Schulz, an uncommonly attractive singer from Vienna, athletic yet ethereal; the way she moved was a joy to watch. She was a good Salome and an enchanting Rosalinde.

Another eightieth birthday, four years later, was that of Eugen d'Albert, so Hitler's favourite opera *Tiefland* was trotted out again with Maria Nemeth as Marta.

To commemorate the centenary of Otto Nicolai's forming of 'the entire orchestral personnel of the Imperial Theatre by the Kärntner Thor' into the world's most celebrated orchestra, the one and only Vienna Philharmonic, the Opera gave a gala performance of *The Flying Dutchman;* and on the seventy-fifth anniversary of the opening of the Opera House, on the twenty-fifth of May 1944, Böhm conducted the Furtwängler and Lothar Müthel production of *Fidelio* with Anni Konetzni and Paul Schöffler. Before the performance the Burgtheater actor Raoul Aslan recited a prologue by the then Poet laureate Josef Weinheber.

But over all these occasions there hung the lowering

clouds of total war. As early as 1942 the Opera had to be closed from time to time for lack of coal, and after the Stalingrad 'disaster' of 1943 it was shut for three whole days. The programmes contained instructions to the audience on what to do in the event of an air-raid. It was the gnawing anxiety about the way the war was going that led the Berlin authorities to put on as comprehensive a show of gaiety as possible all over the 'Reich',

---

Genius, Know Thyself

While Richard Strauss was composing 'Capriccio' he had innumerable conferences with his librettist Clemens Krauss. One day during such a meeting there was a ring at the door. It was the postman with a payment on royalties. Proudly, the composer showed his friend the very large sum of money: 'I've earned that on the one song 'Heimliche Aufforderung'.' Clemens Krauss: 'And Schubert died a pauper.' Strauss: 'But he will live the longer.'

---

which was one reason why operetta featured so prominently in the Volksoper's programmes during the war. Vienna was also lucky in having Anton Paulik at hand, for he was probably the best operetta conductor there was. He conducted *Eine Nacht in Venedig, Die Fledermaus* and *Land of Smiles*, while Böhm conducted *Der Zigeunerbaron*. In the Redoutensaal Oscar Fritz Schuh and Paulik put on *Wiener Blut*, and Alexander Steinbrecher made an arrangement of Suppé's *Boccaccio*.

Operas and operettas were no more immune to 'Aryanisation' than shops and villas were. The *Orpheus* ballet by the 'banned' Margarete Wallmann was replaced by a new one by Rosalia Chladek in which Julia Drapal, who was one day to be Prima Ballerina, scored her first real success as one of the lost souls in Hades. And Korngold's version of *Eine Nacht in Venedig* had to give way to one by Anton Paulik and Rudolf Kattnigg. Where once Jeritza had sung a 'laughing song' from *Ritter Pasman*, Maria Reining now sang an arrangement of Johann Strauss' 'Wo die Zitronen blühn' to comply with the Nuremberg racial laws; being only one eighth Jewish, Johann Strauss just got by.

During the war many of Vienna's most popular favourites were at their zenith. Maria Reining, originally a soubrette, was at her very best in youthful dramatic rôles such as the Marschallin, Elsa, Elisabeth and Daphne; Maria Cebotari, who died such a tragically premature death after the war, was also a wonderful Daphne as well as an unforgettable Violetta; Peter Klein, a character tenor who arrived with Strohm from Hamburg and was still a star in the Karajan-Hilbert era, was perhaps the best Mime in the business, and is now an excellent teacher at the Conservatorium der Stadt Wien; Erich Kunz, Viennese born and bred, came to Vienna from Breslau, made his début as Beckmesser, and immediately won all hearts with his humour and wonderful powers of characterisation, which also make him an incomparable Papageno and Dr. Bartolo; and the radiantly lovely Esther Réthy, who was engaged by Bruno Walter and excelled as Eva, as Sophie, and in all kinds of operettas. Richard Strauss was a great admirer of hers, and she was his first suggestion for Daphne. Hilde Konetzni's voice was at its brilliant best; and Max Lorenz, the great Wagner tenor, also sang in Italian operas for a while, his Otello being one of the finest since Slezak's day. Wenko Wenkoff, a Bulgarian tenor, was very successful for a time, and Elisabeth Höngen, engaged by Böhm, scored a triumph as Carmen. Irmgard Seefried made her first public appearance as a ten-year-old prodigy in her native Bavarian town of Bad Wörishofen by singing Schubert's 'Allmacht' solo with a massive mixed choir! She started in Vienna as Eva but soon blossomed out into Vienna's foremost Mozart singer (Susanna, Pamina, Zerlina). She is the wife of the violinist Wolfgang Schneiderhan. Elisabeth Schwarzkopf started as a coloratura soprano, as Rosina in *The Barber of Seville* (Böhm 1944) and soon rose to international fame as a lyric soprano. Emmy Loose soon became a very good Mozart soubrette (Blondchen, Despina, etc.), and Christl Goltz, who was later to achieve fame as Salome and Elektra, also made her début during the war in *Die Frau ohne Schatten*.

Other prominent sopranos and contraltos were the mezzo-soprano Piroska Tutsek, the Greek mezzo-soprano Elena Nicolaidi, Gertrude Rünger (she had sung Klytaemnestra under Clemens Krauss and returned to Vienna as Elektra), and Marta Rohs, whose charming Cherubino, Octavian and Silla (in *Palestrina*) are still remembered with pleasure. The tenor Karl Friedrich was on the threshold of his career, and the basses Adolf Vogel and Fritz Krenn were at their peak. Vogel was particularly good in comic opera, and Krenn was Vienna's best Ochs since Richard Mayr.

Erika Hanka was engaged by Director Schneider as ballet-mistress and dancer, and after the war she was very successful as a choreographer and built up the new State Opera Ballet almost single-handed. Erich von Wymetal, son of Wilhelm von Wymetal, followed in his father's footsteps and became a producer. Ulrich Roller, Alfred Roller's son, proved himself a talented stage-designer but was killed on the Russian front early on. Leopold Ludwig and Wilhelm Loibner developed into efficient conductors, the latter also being an excellent pianist. He started as a répétiteur, and, ever since his *Falstaff* with Jerger, he has been a pillar of the Vienna Opera as a *Kapellmeister*. Rudolf Moralt, a nephew of Richard Strauss, embarked on an all too brief career as a conductor. Before the première of *Daphne*, which Moralt was to conduct, Clemens Krauss asked Knappertsbusch if he had ever seen Moralt at work. Knowing how conceited Krauss was, Knappertsbusch replied without batting an eyelid: 'Oh yes, he's very good — much better than I am, and almost as good as you.'

Vienna was 'honoured' by being selected as the venue of the 'Reich Theatre Festival Weeks' every June. The choice may have been dictated by politics; or was it intended as a compliment?

Some idea of the wealth of talent at the Opera's disposal can be gleaned from the fact that there were two first-class Brünnhildes permanently available (Anni Konetzni and Helena Braun); four Hans Sachses (Hans Hotter, Paul Schöffler, Josef Herrmann and Karl Kamann); and four Siegfrieds (Max Lorenz, Set Svanholm, Joachim Sattler, and Dr. Julius Pölzer, who sang in the *Götterdämmerung* that Knappertsbusch conducted on the thirtieth of June 1944, when Valhalla in flames was a foretaste of what was in store for the Opera House).

STAATSOPER WIEN

Freitag, den 30. Juni 1944

Preise II

DER RING DES NIBELUNGEN

Ein Bühnenfestspiel für drei Tage und einen Vorabend von Richard Wagner

Dritter Tag:

Götterdämmerung

In drei Aufzügen und einem Vorspiel

Musikalische Leitung: Hans Knappertsbusch

Spielleitung: Erich v. Wymetal

Personen der Handlung.

Siegfried	Dr. Julius Pölzer *Staatsoper München*
Brünnhilde	Helena Braun *Staatsoper München*
Gutrune	Daga Söderqvist
Hagen	Herbert Alsen
Gunther	Carl Kronenberg *Staatsoper München*
Alberich	Adolf Vogel
Waltraute	Elisabeth Höngen
Die drei Nornen	Else Schürhoff / Elena Nikolaidi / Daniza Jlitsch
Die drei Rheintöchter	Esther Réthy / Aenne Michalsky / Elena Nikolaidi
Die drei Mannen	Egyd Toriff / Karl Ettl / Roland Neumann

Bühnenbilder und Kostüme nach Entwürfen von Alfred Roller

Nach jedem Aufzug eine größere Pause

Anfang 16 Uhr   Ende 21 Uhr

Das Publikum wird gebeten, sich vor Beginn der Vorstellung beim Erscheinen unserer verwundeten Frontsoldaten in der Mittelloge von den Plätzen zu erheben.

Bei Fliegeralarm Ruhe bewahren! Es ist Vorsorge getroffen, daß alle Besucher Platz in den Luftschutzräumen finden. Richtungspfeile beachten! Die Sitzplätze ohne Hast verlassen und allen Anordnungen der Luftschutzorgane Folge leisten!

In the summer of 1944 came the 'twentieth of July' attempt to assassinate Hitler. Following the declaration of 'total war' the Opera remained closed, but there were concert performances for soldiers on leave, and Böhm made some recordings in the *Musikverein* with what was left of the ensemble. It was during one of these recording sessions on the twelfth of March 1945, just after 11 a. m., that the air-raid sirens started wailing, and in accordance with official instructions everyone 'proceeded' to the air-raid shelters in the Opera House. These were fortunately under the Ringstrasse side of the building, which was the only part to escape destruction after a series of direct hits. The stage, the auditorium and all the rehearsal rooms were completely burnt out.

As soon as he heard the news that the Opera House was on fire, Ernst August Schneider, who was still playing a lively part in the running of the Opera while on active service (in the ranks) at Mödling, hurried to Vienna to see what could be done. And it was a good thing he did, because most of the firefighters were Ukrainian auxiliaries who had no idea that what was going up in flames was not just another building, and consequently were not exactly over-exerting themselves. But as soon as there appeared on the scene a figure in German uniform who seemed to know what was to be done and issued common-sense instructions, they worked heroically.

Two minutes before the bombs fell a small group in the air-raid shelter were whiling away the time by discussing with a blend of piety and humour what the staff of the Vienna Opera, from the Wagner tenors to the humblest stage-hand and the most junior typist, could arm themselves with if ever they were called upon to defend their beloved Opera House.

The weapons at the Opera's disposal were listed one by one. 'There's everything we could possibly want,' claimed one optimist, 'fifty muzzle-loaded rifles left over from the war against Prussia in 1866, complete with bayonets; a thousand swords; and infantry, cavalry and students' sabres, some of them from Maria Theresia's day, not to mention the stock of fourteenth- and fifteenth-century troopers' cuirasses.' Someone else remembered the gilt-trimmed aluminium helmets, inset with precious

---

---

stones, which had been handed down from Winkelmann to Aagard-Oestvig and Schmedes. Only Slezak and Franz Völker always wore their own (outsize) helmets. 'And all absolutely bullet-proof,' put in a third optimist, 'especially Siegfried's helmets with the genuine goose-feathers, and the Valkyrie helmets of best-quality straw.'

'Apart from all these, we've got the oldest armour in the whole of Vienna, all the paraphernalia worn by the knight in *Puppenfee*, complete with anti-rust devices so that the knight can move his arms and legs at the witching hour of midnight.' 'None of it is any good,' sighed a less optimistic member of the chorus. 'Surely there must be something we could use?' 'Of course there is — the Mexican saddle that Jeritza used to gallop in on in *La fanciulla del West*.'

The next minute the whole stock was in ashes. But the Vienna Opera survived. From the very first it had always risen above its Directors. Now it was to rise even above politics.

Franz Salmhofer Heads the Vienna Opera in the Theater an der Wien 1945—1955, Hermann Juch in the Volksoper 1946—1955

In Search of My World

During World War II I was far from my native land. My very first evening as a refugee in the United States I spent in the standing-area at the 'Met'. I returned to Vienna in 1946, failed to find either my friends or my family, and gazed upon the ruins of the Opera House I had virtually grown up in.

Moments of the deepest revulsion are very often followed by a reaction in the direction of self-delusion, a temptation to behave as if everything were just as it always had been. So I went to the opera. The Vienna Opera was now provisionally accommodated at the Theater an der Wien and the Volksoper. I dropped in at the Volksoper to see *Tosca* with a cast including Maria Nemeth, Alfred Jerger and (if I remember rightly) Josef Kalenberg, who all seemed to be in good voice. Just like the 1930s... And then I realised it was no use trying to delude myself: the world I had known was no more. I recalled a young American soldier next to me in the standing-room at the 'Met', who at the point where old Giovanni Martinelli erupted with his great outbursts of despair towards the end of Act Three of *Otello*, leaned across and asked: 'What the hell's he so excited about?' At the time I regarded him as an uncouth lout; now I reproached myself for my attitude. We had more important matters to bother our heads about than Scarpia's attitude as the knife strikes home, or the volley that finishes off Cavaradossi. *Verismo* opera can only flourish in times of lasting peace; in times when the *verismo* of everyday life is only too immediate, it makes no impact.

And Wagner? Until then I had always been an ardent Wagnerite, and I am again now. But just at that time words like 'Heil, König Heinrich' were positively nauseating because of the involuntary association of the word 'Heil' with someone else. Pathos is only tolerable in unemotional times. In the immediate post-war years the stage was ripe for simple humanity and the cultivation of style. Recent history had set the scene for a great artistic revolution, which had inevitably to originate in post-war Vienna, the great Mozart renaissance.

I had not been back in Vienna long before it was borne home to me that I had a lot to catch up with. I was like a student who has missed a couple of terms. Not that I had lost contact with Vienna during those seven ghastly years. There had been letters, and sometimes even newspapers. But for a dedicated opera fan there are other more informative sources of information. I once had an opportunity of talking to some German prisoners who were full of the latest gossip of how the Konetzni sisters were singing better than ever but were not getting noticeably slimmer despite wartime rationing; of a wonderful new Hans Sachs named Paul Schöffler and a charming new Eva from Bavaria called Irmgard See-fried; of Strauss's latest work, a sort of course in musical aesthetics and literary history in operatic form; of Maria Reining's going over to young dramatic rôles. And if only you could hear Hans Hotter! No wonder, when I arrived back in Vienna, that I was a bundle of inferiority complexes, because I couldn't even recognise the new stars on the street!

But not for long. I enjoy recalling an intimate restaurant near the Hotel Bristol that euphemistically called itself the 'Künstlerklub', the Artists' Club, and now and again even managed to produce an 'under-the-counter' steak. It was here that I got my first close-up of many of the new deities. In one corner downstairs there would be the film director Ernst Marischka with a new and altogether phenomenal conductor named Herbert von Karajan, with whom he was planning a film of the *Saint Matthew Passion*. One of the regular customers upstairs, being fed by bevies of adoring females, was Hans Hotter.

For the first time in 150 years the Vienna Opera was playing in two separate theatres every evening. The idea had been toyed with for some time, and in the 'artistic testament' that he bequeathed to his friend Karl Böhm in April 1945, Richard Strauss put forward concrete proposals for sharing the repertoire between the Opera House and the Theater an der Wien.

By 1946 the whole vast complex of State Theatres (the Burgtheater, the Akademietheater, and the two separate theatres housing the State Opera) was under a central 'State Theatres Administrative Office' run by Egon Hilbert, a former police official who regarded the theatre world, and especially the Opera, as his private and per-

166

Opening night in the Theater an der Wien on 6 October 1945. Max Lorenz, who should have sung Florestan, was in the west of Austria and could not cross the bridge over the Enns river, the notorious frontier between the American and Russian zones of occupation.

sonal domain. His love for the Opera was all-consuming, even if it was lavished more on its running than on its standards. He had suffered all the privations of Dachau concentration camp during the war, but there were stories of how he used to contrive to make his way to Munich on transport duty and sneak into the Opera.

Among his comrades in the camp were Leopold Figl, who was to become Chancellor of the Second Austrian Republic; Felix Hurdes, who was to be appointed Minister of Education; and town councillor Matejka. Amid the misery of the concentration camp these four passed the time in a spirit of desperate optimism, by planning how the post-war world was to be shared out amongst them, and Hilbert was allotted the State Theatres. Hilbert set to work 'con fuoco e con brio', working an average of twenty-five hours a day (or so it was alleged). In these early post-war years this remarkable man who, as Director of the State Opera, was to come to an end that would not be out of place in a Shakespearean tragedy, certainly got things done. He had to work with two Directors (one at each of the theatres the Vienna Opera was playing at) whom he would have preferred to see reduced to the stature of puppets with no wills of their own. Many months before Hilbert's arrival Franz Salmhofer had somehow managed at the Theater an der Wien to conjure up a repertoire out of nothing; and Hermann Juch was appointed Director of the Volksoper by Hilbert himself.

Hilbert's original plan, which was never realised, was based on a clear distinction between the fare provided at the two theatres: opera at the Theater an der Wien, operetta at the Volksoper. Under Hilbert the two theatres were completely independent of one another. Each had its own singers under contract, albeit with a proviso that they had to sing at the other theatre if required. The Vienna Philharmonic Orchestra was assigned to the Theater an der Wien and the Volksoper formed an orchestra of its own. The only artists the two theatres shared were the ballet under Erika Hanka, which had to perform in both theatres as required.

The Volksoper was the first of the two theatres to get going again. By the fourteenth of April 1945 hostilities in Vienna were at an end and the period of Russian occupation began. On the twenty-seventh of April Dr. Karl Renner proclaimed the restoration of the Austrian Republic and Alfred Jerger was designated commissary head of the Vienna Opera. The commander of the Russian garrison issued characteristically crisp instructions: 'Give us opera.' Which Jerger did. The Volksoper, which during the war had been called the 'Opernhaus der Stadt Wien', had emerged unscathed, props and all, whereas the State Opera had lost practically all its scenery and costumes. On the first of May there was a performance of *Figaro* at the Volksoper conducted by Joseph Krips, in which Sena Jurinac made her début as Cherubino. But *Figaro* was not really a good choice for this particular time. The occupation forces had an eye for gold, and after each interval the scene opened on a few less gilt chairs or golden curtains. What was required was an opera featuring less elegant social circles. So two weeks later Jerger pushed his 'Austrian miracle' a stage further by putting on *Bohème* with Anton Dermota as Rodolfo, Sena Jurinac as Mimi, and Irmgard Seefried as Musette. Somehow or other, by June there were performances every evening. There were no trams, so information about rehearsals had to be delivered on foot. There was no electric current, but the show went on. People kept going out of pure enthusiasm. The stage-hands were paid nothing, but every one of them was imbued with a dynamic sense of mission to rebuild the Vienna Opera from scratch. There was little or nothing to eat, yet not a single première was affected by illness.

Franz Salmhofer was appointed Director of the Vienna State Opera in June 1945. He had been *Kapellmeister* at the Burgtheater for many years and had spent the previous month at Ybbs on the Danube. Now he returned to Vienna without a piece of luggage and in Austrian-style leather shorts, in which attire he was officially confirmed in office by the State Secretary for Education. The mantle of Mahler and Strauss descended upon the shoulders of a musician of striking personality who was Viennese born and bred, an erstwhile member of the Vienna Boys Choir, and a pupil of Franz Schrenker.

As a composer he had already had a few ballets and two operas performed at the Vienna Opera with considerable success. His first action was to summon all the available singers and orchestral players to a meeting by the main stairway in the Opera House, which was the only part of the house that had survived the fire. After a short speech in which he instilled into all and sundry a feeling

Gottfried von Einem's Opera 'Danton's Tod' was produced at the Theater an der Wien in 1947. (Caricature by Winnie Jakob.)

of pride at having a country to belong to once again, he set about assuring himself at first hand that to give any sort of performance in the ruins of the Opera House was quite out of the question. It was not until after this memorable little ceremony that he resolved to see about staging operas at the Theater an der Wien; because he was well aware that the Volksoper alone provided a far from adequate remedy. The Theater an der Wien belonged to the Vienna Municipality, so Salmhofer secured permission to use it from Burgomaster Körner, who later became President of Austria.

It was here, in the Theater an der Wien, that *Fidelio* and *Der Waffenschmied* were first performed, that Meyerbeer conducted, that Vienna heard *Bohème*, for the first time as well as *Fledermaus* and *The Merry Widow* conducted by Johann Strauss and Lehár respectively.

One day Salmhofer and his technical staff presented themselves at the stage-door of the Theater an der Wien in the Lehárgasse and introduced themselves to the old woman caretaker, who was doing well by growing mushrooms on the stage: 'Good morning, ducks; we're the new landlords!' And she was the first person he took on — as a lavatory attendant.

The theatre was in an advanced state of dilapidation and had not housed a performance since 1939. It was still completely empty, except for the rats. Salmhofer's talent for improvisation in getting the theatre into shape was ingenious, to say the least. First, he put the State

Opera Chorus to work as carpenters, decorators and tailors.

Fortunately the indispensable Vienna Philharmonic Orchestra, whose dissolution during the war had been averted only by the intervention of Furtwängler, had survived intact. So had their music. As for the rest, the resourceful Salmhofer had to use his wits. If he was short of money, he hired out the chairs in the Redoutensaal at exorbitant

---

Director to the Rescue

During the first months after the end of the war Director Franz Salmhofer hit on some highly unconventional schemes when it came to helping his beloved artists to acquire the bare necessities of life. 'Something's got to be done!' he stormed. 'I need bacon for Welitsch, coal for Lorenz, petrol for Schöffler!' Next door to the Theater an der Wien stood a house of dubious reputation which used to be frequented by occupation troops. One day, loaded with the desirable goodies, an allied van once again drove up to the door and the chauffeur and his companion disappeared into the house, whereupon Franz Salmhofer, disguised as a workman, clambered on to the vehicle with a number of stage-hands and began to unload bacon for Welitsch, coal for Lorenz and petrol for Schöffler. When one of his helpers was bold enough to ask his boss whether they were not committing a theft, Director Salmhofer raised the bent index finger of his right hand (his most frequently imitated gesture) and announced in tones full of righteous indignation: 'Please take note of this fact — the Vienna Opera does not steal!'

---

fees to certain Allied officers who liked the feeling of sitting on gilt chairs. And when the electric current failed for the umpteenth time he went to the Electricity Works in person and had the Theater an der Wien linked to the special cable that served the Russian Kommandatura.

On the sixth of October 1945 he opened with *Fidelio*. The walls of the dungeon were the walls of the theatre itself and some of the scenery was from the Volksoper's *Aida*. The Director's office was on the fifth floor, and neither the Vienna Municipality, which owned the building, nor the State, which was responsible for running the State Opera, was prepared to have the lift repaired. The great 'Theater an der Wien era' had dawned.

There was no love lost between Hilbert and Salmhofer. Both were fanatical enthusiasts, but whereas the latter was a fanatical professional, the former was a fanatical amateur. Each talked loud and long (and in a shrill voice) without listening to what the other was saying. It may even have been the constant bickering between these two explosive personalities that was the reason everything went so well at the Theater an der Wien.

The singers much preferred Vienna to devastated Germany, and many of them were falling over each other to acquire Austrian citizenship. And at the time travel permits were very hard to get.

The Theater an der Wien soon proved to have several sterling qualities. It was small and intimate, and for the first time the audience was able to appreciate the singers' acting powers. At first it was feared that the acoustics would restrict the repertoire to smaller-scale operas, but these misgivings were soon set at rest. Salmhofer had the orchestra pit temporarily enlarged by removing two rows of stalls, and although for instance it was never big enough for more than five desks of first violins, both *Die Meistersinger* and *Elektra* sounded fine.

The conductor of the opening *Fidelio* was Joseph Krips. As the third member of the Salmhofer-Hilbert-Krips trio of enthusiasts he was from the very first (*de facto* though not *de jure*) the Opera's Chief Conductor.

During the war Krips had been banned from conducting in Vienna on racial grounds and had taken a job in a champagne factory, but many artists used to pay him furtive visits and handsome rewards for his practical help and advice.

During the 'Theater an der Wien era' it was Krips who was most instrumental in promoting Mozart for the first time from a stop-gap to number one box-office attraction. There was such a rush to get seats for a performance of *Don Giovanni* with Ljuba Welitsch, Hilde Konetzni, Irmgard Seefried, Paul Schöffler and Anton Dermota that the police and riot squads were kept busy for hours. Krips also conducted a wonderful *Così fan tutte* and (in January 1948) the long-awaited production of *Die Zauberflöte* in which Wilma Lipp made her sensational début as the Queen of the Night.

Krips also conducted some Verdi (*Aida* in Italian with Welitsch in 1946) and *Prince Igor* with Paul Schöffler in 1947, as well as some Strauss, notably *Ariadne* in 1947 with Maria Cebotari and Sena Jurinac. *Aida* was produced by Lothar Wallerstein, who had been abroad during the war, and *Die Zauberflöte* and *Così fan tutte* by Oscar Fritz Schuh.

An invaluable support for Krips was the always reliable Rudolf Moralt, who in 1946 conducted a performance of *Die Entführung* in celebration of the 950th year of Austria's existence, the cast including Elisabeth Schwarzkopf (Konstanze), Anton Dermota (Belmonte), Ludwig Weber (Osmin), Emmy Loose (Blondchen), and Peter Klein (Pedrillo). The part of Selim Bassa was played by an actor who was later to become a star of world magnitude: Curd Jürgens.

The problem of where to find conductors in the immediate post-war years was particularly acute because for one reason or another many of the great names were banned by the Allied authorities — Böhm, Krauss and Karajan; and Furtwängler and Knappertsbusch because they were Germans and therefore not allowed to enter Austria. Böhm was cleared fairly soon, and one of my most pleasant memories is of him conducting a new *Turandot* at the Theater an der Wien in 1948 with Maria Cebotari, Irmgard Seefried (Liu) and Helge Roswaenge. The producer was Wallerstein, who had also been responsible for the first Vienna production in 1926, and he had the 'Son of Heaven' serenely enthroned high above his subjects in a splendidly colourful spectacle like an old fairy-tale.

In connection with the Allied ban there were often the most absurd discrepancies and inconsistencies. I remember how Elisabeth Schwarzkopf, then a wonderful coloratura singer, was once banned by the British but cleared by the French, and later banned by the Russians and cleared by the Americans. On one occasion one of the occupying powers made representation to Salmhofer that it would be advisable for a worthy, plump little diva from Poland who was not exactly in the first flush of youth to sing the part of Gilda in *Rigoletto*. Before she had sung more than a few notes Salmhofer managed to get hold of

Emmy Loose to take over the part, because 'when the plump little Pole comes on in her nightdress everyone will roar with laughter'. The Allied officers duly protested and Salmhofer blandly informed them that it was an act of mercy: 'What would have happened if she had had a stroke?'

On most, but not all, of the Vienna Opera's tours abroad the conductors were Krips and Böhm. By a curious paradox, it was the four-power occupation of Austria that was largely instrumental in re-introducing Austrian art and culture to the world at large. In 1946 the French occupation authorities negotiated a visit by the Paris Grande Opéra with Debussy's *Pelléas et Mélisande* at the Theater an der Wien. Irene Joachim, a grand-daughter of the famous violinist, scored a great success as Mélisande. The conductor Roger Désormière was so taken by Vienna's Mozart productions that he arranged the Vienna Opera's first invitation in 1947 — to Nice and Paris in a French military train.

Later the same year came a visit to Covent Garden with Krips and Clemens Krauss as conductors. During the visit there was a reunion with Richard Tauber, then living in London, who sang a glorious Don Ottavio. Though he was mortally ill and had only one lung, Salmhofer invited him to take part in the new Vienna production of *Die Zauberflöte* in the spring of 1948, but he never appeared on the stage again and died four months after his swan-song in *Don Giovanni*.

In the following years the Vienna Opera paid regular visits to Brussels, to the May Festival at Wiesbaden, to Paris, and to Italy, usually with Mozart, but also with *Wozzek*, *Elektra*, and *Der Rosenkavalier*.

It was the Golden Age of Mozart. During the 1947-48 season Mozart accounted for one-sixth of the repertoire of the two houses, one hundred performances in all. After him came Johann Strauss, Puccini, Offenbach, Richard Wagner, and then Richard Strauss, with only twenty-five performances. The new 1948 *Zauberflöte* alone was given thirty-three times during the season.

As the Vienna Opera had started from scratch in 1945, each new opera taken into the repertoire meant a completely new production, so the repertoire was as yet

1. Dermota. 2. Taddei. 3. Salmhofer. 4. Oeggl. 5. Kunz.

In June 1948 there was a strange football match on the Wacker-Platz in Meidling, a suburb of Vienna: Vienna Philharmonic v. State Opera singers. Result: the orchestra won by 7 to 3. The singers' eleven was captained by Erich Majkut as goalkeeper (in years gone by Alfred Piccaver and Franz Völker used to play goal). His team-mates were Anton Dermota, Karl Friedrich, Giuseppe Taddei, Peter Klein, Erich Kunz, Ljubomir Pantscheff, Hans Braun, Georg Oeggl, Erik Kaufmann ... Director Franz Salmhofer was goalkeeper for the Philharmonic. And how often does this happen: the losers were carried from the field on the shoulders of the victors and spent the rest of the evening signing autographs.

by no means comprehensive. The singers certainly had to work hard: in the course of the 1947-48 season Peter Klein made 146 appearances, Jerger 124, Emmy Loose 88, Sena Jurinac 83, Hilde Konetzni 68, Wilma Lipp 58, Ljuba Welitsch 53, and Irmgard Seefried 47.

One by one the old favourites were finding their way back. Knappertsbusch arrived in April 1947 to conduct *Salome* with Cebotari and Paul Schöffler and was accorded an ovation that went on for minutes on end. Shortly afterwards he conducted *Der fliegende Holländer* with Hans Hotter and Anni Konetzni. There had been general astonishment at the ban on such a 'notorious' anti-Nazi as Knappertsbusch. One evening immediately after the war there was a performance of *Die Meistersinger* in Munich with Knappertsbusch conducting. The proceedings started with an American officer coming on the stage and making an interminable speech. What followed is best described in Knappertsbusch's own words: 'I was just standing there, and I suppose my right hand must have twitched — anyway, there was a sudden terrific C major chord from the whole orchestra.' Next day he was banned.

In December 1949 Clemens Krauss conducted a new *Meistersinger* with Schöffler a superb Sachs, Erich Kunz an incomparable Beckmesser, and Dermota a most lyrical David. Krauss also conducted works I never knew him to conduct when he was Director, notably *Boris Godunov*, and in 1953, to commemorate the 140th anniversary of Wagner's birth, *Tristan* with Anni Konetzni and Set Svanholm. Clemens Krauss died towards the end of the Theater an der Wien era while on tour in Mexico. Karl Böhm's appointment as Director of the Vienna State Opera in the reconstructed Opera House had just been announced, although Clemens Krauss had been expressly designated for the post by Dr. Kolb, the Minister of Education. Some people still maintain that Krauss's bitter disappointment was the cause of his fatal heart attack far from home.

In the same year, 1954, I made my first TV appearance in Germany and was therefore able to pay my last respects to Wilhelm Furtwängler at his funeral in Heidelberg. The year 1954 was like 1949 in that we said farewell to many great artists. My beloved Richard Strauss was cremated at Garmisch in September to the accompaniment of the Waltz from *Rosenkavalier*. The previous May Hans Pfitzner died in Salzburg after the Vienna Philharmonic Orchestra had generously come to his assistance by having the ailing old man brought from Ger-

---

If possible, with ceiling

When Erich W. Korngold came to Vienna in 1950 to help prepare the première of his last opera 'Die Kathrin' in the Volksoper, he absolutely couldn't get used to the new trend of 'implied' scenery. The stage designer Walter von Hoesslin had designed a room for Kathrin, naturally without a ceiling. 'Where's the ceiling?' asked E. W. K. Hoesslin explained that a modern, intellectual visitor to the theatre who saw this room would imagine the ceiling for himself. Korngold couldn't get the thing out of his mind, and a few weeks later he wrote to Hoesslin (who had a property at Waidring in the Tyrol): 'I am coming to spend the day with you to have another talk about the scenery. Please book me a hotel room. If possible, with ceiling.'

---

many to Austria to spend the evening of his life near Salzburg. He lived to hear a gala performance of *Palestrina* in celebration of his eightieth birthday, with Krips conducting and a cast including Hotter as Borromeo, and that wonderfully intelligent tenor Julius Patzak (another one-time habitué of the standing-area in the gallery) as Palestrina. In 1949 Lothar Wallerstein died in New Orleans, and in June of the same year we assembled by the main staircase in the Opera House for the funeral of Maria Cebotari, a lovely and accomplished singer (and successful film star) from Rumania who had excelled as Turandot and Salome at the Theater an der Wien. Only a few weeks before she succumbed to a malignant disease she had appeared as Laura in *Der Bettelstudent* at the Volksoper.

Two careers of world renown — all too brief, alas — began at the Theater an der Wien. I have never forgotten the tremendous impression the Bulgarian singer Ljuba Welitsch made on me when I first heard her as Giulietta in *Tales of Hoffmann*. In those days she had the most sensually exhilarating voice since Jeritza, and a superb stage-presence. Her *Salome* became the talk of New York as well as Vienna, and she was also a magnificent Tosca, Aida, Donna Anna, Tatiana, Manon and Musetta. Comparisons between her and Jeritza were suggested particularly by *Jenufa* which she sang with a Czech company conducted by Jaroslav Krombholc. Where Jeritza surpassed Welitsch was in the variety of her tone-colour. But it should be borne in mind that Welitsch did not come to the fore, as Jeritza did, in an age when there were Strauss, Puccini or Korngold to write operas specially for her particular personality. Ljuba Welitsch is a delightful person to know, and even in less happy days later on, when she lost her voice (far too early), retired from the operatic stage and married a Vienna policeman, she never quite lost her sense of humour, and it was not long before she was making a new career in TV and on the films.

In September 1949 there was a performance of *Aida* with Set Svanholm as Radames in which a new and very young Amonasro made his début and took Vienna by storm: George London. This exceptionally good-looking, slim and elegant American had in his early days sung 'extracts' at concerts with Mario Lanza. Actually the Vienna Opera can claim to have discovered him, following an audition he gave during one of the Opera's visits to Brussels. Almost overnight he became the new heart-throb of every girl in the audience, particularly in *Don Giovanni*, where his wonderful vibrato and handsome figure showed up to particular advantage. From Vienna he went to the 'Met' and Bayreuth. He was perhaps at his best as Escamillo, Dr. Miracle, and Boris (which he sang in Moscow in Russian). His was another career that was all too brief; in 1968 this highly intelligent, well-read and cultured singer became Director of Programmes at the newly-established Kennedy Center for the Performing Arts in Washington.

During the Theater an der Wien era Vienna enjoyed visits from many of the world's leading conductors. In 1947 Otto Klemperer conducted *Don Giovanni*, and Sir John Barbirolli *Aida*; in 1949 Georg Solti conducted

Tristan (as did Eugen Jochum a year later); and in 1950 Fritz Busch conducted *Otello*. Krips had just departed, and Salmhofer wanted Busch as his successor, but unfortunately Busch died shortly afterwards. In 1951 Erich Kleiber conducted *Der Rosenkavalier*, with Fritz Krenn as an excellent Ochs, and in 1953 John Pritchard conducted *La Forza del Destino*. Wilhelm Furtwängler conducted *Die Walküre* and *Tristan* in 1952, and in 1953 a concert of excerpts from *Götterdämmerung* in commemoration of the seventieth anniversary of Wagner's death, was well as a new *Fidelio* with scenery by his old collaborator Herbert Graf, who later became Director of the Zurich and Geneva Opera Houses.

At that time the critics still concentrated their attentions mainly on the singers, although the Age of the Producer, with its alternations of glamour and ineptitude, was only just round the corner. In 1952 Gustaf Gründgens was to produce Stravinsky's new opera *The Rake's Progress,* but just as rehearsals were due to start he asked to be released from his contract, because 'nowadays I can earn five times as much in Italy.' So Günther Rennert took over and made a successful début with this extremely interesting work, based on Hogarth's etchings, in which the composer blends traditional forms with the successive stages of his own development. Rudolf Schock (long before he went over to films) was Tom, Erna Berger was Anne, Jerger was Nick Shadow and Elisabeth Höngen was Baba the Turk, beard and all. Stefan Hlawa contributed some highly original sets. On the other hand, Stefan Beinl's production of *Lohengrin* in 1948 was the first of a long series of atrocities committed on this unfortunate opera. In Act Three Lohengrin came into a stage in almost total darkness ('Am Mittag hoch steht die Sonne!') against a backcloth of a Byzantine Gralsburg, though the audience is not to know of Lohengrin's being a knight of the Holy Grail until after he has declared his identity in his 'narration'. Even a superlative cast including Julius Patzak, Maria Reining, Karl Kamann (Telramund) and Herbert Alsen (King Henry) could do little to save the show. But on the first night there was a real sensation: Krips was taken ill and Knappertsbusch deputised at short notice.

In 1949 Adolf Rott perpetrated assaults on two of opera's most tempestuous heroines. In *Elektra* Roller's magnificent castle at Mycenae was supplanted by Kautsky's cold and colourless setting, and Aegisthus was vulgarly tossed through an open trap-door; while as for *Tosca*, in Act Two Scarpia's room was right next to Cavaradossi's cell, and in Act One there was an enormous and quite pointless picture of the Marchesa Attavanti. (When Jeritza returned to Vienna to sing *Tosca* she refused to put up with it and insisted on having most of the scenery altered.)

But in 1951 Adolf Rott, who always seems to be storming the heights in one production and plumbing the depths in the next, was responsible for an admirable production of Menotti's *The Consul.* Though it had not quite the warmth of the American production I saw, Rott's adroit use of the revolving stage conjured up some effective impressions in this tragedy of a refugee, with its distant views of the horrors of the concentration camp, scenes of people being hunted by the secret police, and a vision of hundreds of mass-graves. The conductor was Meinhard von Zallinger, and Hilde Zadek scored one of the triumphs of her life as Magda Sorel, along with Laszlo von Szemere as a conjuror who actually did tricks on the stage. Hilde Zadek, an outstandingly intelligent person, was also very good in Italian opera. Perhaps her greatest success of all was in 1954 as the good-natured but occasionally bloody-minded Pauline/Christine in *Intermezzo*, with Alfred Poell, who really did look exactly like Richard Strauss.

Of the contemporary operas performed during the Theater an der Wien era, *The Consul* was the greatest success, along with the new version of Salmhofer's *Ivan Tarassenko* with Welitsch, Schöffler and Roswaenge. This is not to say that there were no other interesting first performances of contemporary works. In 1950, for instance, Josef Gielen produced Honegger's dramatic oratorio *Jeanne d'Arc au bûcher* with a libretto by Claudel. It was an evening of modern theatre at its best — a miscellany of mime, singing, dancing, the spoken word, choruses, jazz and folk-song. In the middle of the stage was Jeanne (Alma Seidler) chained to the stake, and all around were fantastic figures of nightmare visions and childhood memories, culminating in Jeanne's death and apotheosis in the form of a church service with real incense. The choir was posted on platforms on either side of the stage. Clemens Krauss conducted, and the Burgtheater actor Raoul Aslan was particularly impressive as Frère Dominique.

During these years there was close co-operation between the Vienna Opera and the Salzburg Festival, and many Festival productions moved to Vienna in the autumn, notably Gottfried von Einem's first two operas, produced at Salzburg by Oscar Fritz Schuh. The first, in 1947, was *Dantons Tod* conducted by Ferenc Fricsay, with Paul Schöffler as Danton and Maria Cebotari as Lucille. Although this work was one of the most pronounced successes in the post-war German-speaking operatic world, several critics lambasted its 'merciless dissonances' and referred to it as 'musical Desperanto'. The second was *Der Prozess* (1953), based on Kafka's novel, conducted by Heinrich Hollreiser with a cast including Max Lorenz and Lisa della Casa.

The most agreeable part of my process of 'catching up with the times' was making the acquaintance of Richard Strauss's last operas, though I had managed to get hold of piano scores in America. In 1950 Rudolf Moralt conducted a production of *Daphne* in which the world of the sun-god and the laurel-tree was pitch-dark! Anneliese Kupper was too heavily built, not an inch a nymph, and it was not until I saw Hilde Güden's wonderful performance as Daphne a good many years later that I was able to come to terms with this particular opera. A year later Rudolf Hartmann's Salzburg production of *Capriccio* came to Vienna, conducted by Karl Böhm, and it was my first opportunity of enjoying Schöffler's superb performance as La Roche. The Countess was Christl Goltz, at that time Vienna's most fascinating exponent of 'intellectual' parts.

The following year (1952) Clemens Krauss conducted another of Rudolf Hartmann's Salzburg productions, *Die Liebe der Danae*. This opera was to have had its first performance at the 1944 Salzburg Festival, but owing to 'total war' it never got beyond a dress rehearsal with

Viorica Ursuleac, Horst Taubmann, and Hans Hotter. The 'satirical mythological' libretto about the miracle of the golden rain was concocted by Joseph Gregor from an old draft of Hofmannsthal's. Although *Danae* and *Der Friedenstag* are demonstrably the poorest operas Strauss ever wrote, for some strange reason *Danae* made a great impression on me, and even now, almost twenty years later, the big G flat duet for female voices 'Wie himmlischer Regen' still sticks in my mind.

Maria Jeritza came back to Vienna. In 1948 she had got married in Saint Patrick's Cathedral in New York, her husband (the third) being Irving P. Seery. I liked him very much and was very upset to hear of his death a year or two ago. It was his fondest wish to see his beloved Maria on the stage again — ever since her years at the 'Met' he had been one of her most ardent admirers. Between 1950 and 1953 she sang Tosca and Salome several times at the Theater an der Wien, and at the Volksoper, where she started on her illustrious career, she sang in *Cavalleria Rusticana* and *La Fanciulla del West*. She donated all her fees to the fund for the reconstruction of the Opera House.

At her first appearance in *Tosca* at the Theater an der Wien I was in a box with Korngold, and we both felt as if we were being transported back thirty years. Jeritza was still a fascinating singer and gave the younger generation another glimpse of the vanished world of *verismo* opera. Again there was the same storm of applause after her performance of Tosca's prayer while lying on the ground. In *Cavalleria* she had the eight steps up to the church increased to twelve so that, as in the good old days, at the words 'a te la mala Pasqua' she could contrive a more spectacular fall. In *La Fanciulla* she insisted on being mounted on a horse, so for rehearsals three trusty steeds were borrowed from the police. Jeritza rode round the stage on the first two, but the third was absolutely against the whole thing and reared, and Jeritza had such a bad fall that on the first night she was unable to sit on a horse. There were six or seven horses in all in this production, and their frequent whinnying put the singers off, so much so that Hilbert once rang the stage-manager Hoesslin: 'I hold you personally responsible for

Burgtheater actor Fred Liewehr be-came a star in operetta at the Volks-oper. (Caricature by Winnie Jakob.)

seeing that there's none of this infernal neighing at this evening's performance!'

It seemed as if all Vienna was demonstrating its undy-ing affection for Jeritza. There were crowds round her hotel all day long, and sometimes she would come out on to her balcony and throw her fans — umbrellas! Mr. Seery, as it happened, owned an umbrella factory in the United States.

As of 1946 the second Opera Director alongside Salm-hofer, and of equal status, was Dr. Hermann Juch at the Volksoper. He comes from Tyrol, and his father was a former Minister of Finance. Juch had been employed by the State Theatres ever since the 1930s. In 1941 Strohm appointed him to succeed Kerber as head of the artistic side of the State Opera.

In 1945 the Volksoper became State property, thus embarking on another chapter in its unusual history. It was opened as a 'legitimate' theatre in 1898 in com-memoration of the fiftieth anniversary of Franz Joseph's accession. From 1904 to 1916 it enjoyed a period of great prosperity as a purveyor of light opera under the shrewd management of Rainer Simons from Mainz. He was the first to perform *Tosca* (which Mahler detested) in Vienna, and also ventured to put on *Salome* after it had been banned by the censor from the Opera House. He also launched such celebrated singers as Jeritza, Emil Schipper and Josef von Manowarda. There ensued a further brief period of prosperity (1919—1924) under Felix von Weingartner and his deputy, Karl Lustig-Prean, which included a lot of Wagner. From then on it was one crisis after another until World War II, when the Volks-oper operated as the 'Opernhaus der Stadt Wien'. It was here that Ljuba Welitsch made her début as Salome.

After the war, the question arose as to what the Volks-oper was to be used for. Juch was against Hilbert's plan of State-subsidised operetta and was in favour of grand opera. Nevertheless, the highlights of Juch's term of office were light opera, and under pressure from Hilbert he had to acquiesce in grand opera's being the preserve of the Theater an der Wien. His next idea was to make the Volksoper Vienna's 'Opéra Comique', and he worked out a comprehensive and exceedingly interesting plan that resulted in a complete and triumphant renaissance of clas-sical operetta, performed by leading opera-singers and actors with the best producers of the day. Oscar Fritz Schuh, for instance, produced *Die Fledermaus* and *Der Opernball*, Hubert Marischka *Der Zigeunerbaron*, Hans Jaray *Wiener Blut*, Theo Lingen Offenbach's *Die Bandi-ten*, and Axel von Ambesser *La belle Héléne*.

Juch's outstanding discovery as an operetta producer

was Adolf Rott, whose 1949 production of *Der Bettel-student* on a 'rotating' stage ushered in a new era of producing operetta as a spectacular 'show'.

The celebrated opening is a sort of merry-go-round: the singers stand on pedestals like statues in a baroque garden and sing the opening bars of their main songs while the stage revolves, an idea Hoesslin derived from the captivating open-air theatre (1737) in the Schönborn garden. In this epoch-making production Maria Cebotari was Laura and the Burgtheater actor Fred Liewehr become an operetta star overnight in the title-rôle; nowadays his Eisenstein in *Die Fledermaus* is as much of a classic as Girardi's Verschwender was in Raimund's play of that name. In the same production Kurt Preger as Ollendorf established himself as the comedian with the most robust voice that Vienna operetta has ever known, and the lovely Esther Réthy became Vienna's leading operetta diva.

The Volksoper during Juch's administration has often been called the Bayreuth of operetta. In *Fledermaus* alone Hilde Güden, Sena Jurinac und Gerda Scheyrer all sang the part of Rosalinde, Rita Streich and Wilma Lipp were alternatives as Adele (the regular star in the part was Elfie Mayerhofer) and there was Anton Dermota as Alfred. In Willy Forst's production of *Orpheus in the Underworld* Max Lorenz was Orpheus and Hans Moser was Jupiter. In *Der Zigeunerbaron* Hilde Konetzni was Saffi and Laszlo von Szemere was Barinkay. In *Eine Nacht in Venedig* Helge Roswaenge was the Duke. Among the cast of *Gasparone* were Hermann Uhde and Willy Domgraf-Fassbaender; Hilde Zadek and Wilma Lipp appeared in *Der Vogelhändler*, and Ljuba Welitsch in *Giuditta*.

Musically, the moving spirit behind this renaissance was Anton Paulik, now an Old Master of Vienna Operetta. After moving from the Opera House to the Volksoper he had the great good fortune to inherit the services of that great artist Walter von Hoesslin, who had been Technical Director in charge of scenery at the 'Opernhaus der Stadt Wien' and had studied with Max Reinhardt and Oskar Strnad. It is very rare for such an outstanding stage-designer as Hoesslin to be Technical Director as well.

Wilhelm Loibner began in 1934 as an accompanist, and as repertoire conductor he became a pillar of the house. He is married to the soprano Ruthilde Boesch. (Caricature by Winnie Jakob.)

Hoesslin is entirely devoid of jealousy and has been glad to set many other stage-designers on the road to success.

Actually it was Paulik, Esther Réthy and Hoesslin who first led Juch's thoughts in the direction of operetta, often during 'gastronomic conferences' at the 'Linde' restaurant. But Juch could also point to some interesting performances in the domain of opera: *Schwanda the Bagpiper* in a revolving-stage production by Lothar Wallerstein (now back in Austria) conducted by Erich Leinsdorf, a pupil of Toscanini, with Walter Höfermayer as the Bohemian bagpiper; *Tannhäuser* and *Der Freischütz* conducted by Knappertsbusch; *Don Carlos* conducted by Böhm; and *Faust* conducted by Otto Ackermann (the cast was later joined by George London). Herbert Waniek's production of *The Merry Wives of Windsor* on a Shakespearean stage, and Benjamin Britten's realisation of *The Beggar's Opera*, conducted by Meinhard von Zallinger, were both full of originality, as were Kienzl's *Der Kuhreigen*, conducted by Felix Prohaska in which two 'discoveries' were made — Theresa Stich-Randall and Waldemar Kmentt; and *Fra Diavolo* with the operetta star Per Grundén.

Among the more unusual evenings were Adolf Rott's epoch-making production of Orff's *Die Bernauerin* with Käthe Gold and Fred Liewehr from the Burgtheater, and Gershwin's *Porgy and Bess* by an all-American company

The final scene of *The Magic Flute* with (from left to right) Gottlob Frick, one of the greatest Wagner basses, as Sarastro; Hilde Güden, the charming Mozart and R. Strauss singer, as Pamina; and Anton Dermota, a worthy upholder of the Vienna Mozart tradition, as Tamino. The conductor is Wilhelm Loib- ner. The production opened in 1962 at the Theater an der Wien under Karajan. The producer was Rudolf Hartmann, then the Director of the Munich Opera, and the scenery was by Günther Schneider-Siemssen. The temple of Sarastro is a solution along abstract lines.

Above: from Act One of *Le Nozze di Figaro* with (from left to right) Eberhard Wächter as the Count, Wladimiro Ganzarolli as Figaro, Gertrude Jahn as Cherubino, Olivjera Miljakovic as Susanna, and Murray Dickie as Basilio. The producer was Leopold Lindtberg, and the scenery was by Teo Otto. The conductor in this photograph is Joseph Krips, though on the first night in 1967 it was Karl Böhm. The giddy height the chorus was asked to sing from caused a good deal of discussion at the time.

Above right: *Falstaff,* Act Two, a room in the Fords' house, with Wladimiro Ganzarolli as Falstaff and Wilma Lipp, formerly a dazzling Queen of the Night and now a star in lyrical parts, as Mistress Ford. The conductor is Argeo Quadri. The first night in 1966 was Leonard Bernstein's debut in Vienna as a conductor. The production, scenery and costumes were all by Lucchino Visconti, who brought all his experience as a film-director into play when devising the transition in Act Three from outside the Garter Inn to Windsor Park.

Below right: *Don Giovanni* with (from left to right) Eberhard Wächter, whose repertoire ranges from Amfortas to Eisenstein, as Don Giovanni; Herbert Lackner, a product of the Conservatorium, as Masetto; and Wladimiro Ganzarolli as Leporello. This production was in 1967 and the conductor was Joseph Krips. Luciano Damiani's scenery illustrates some of his favourite motifs, such as a large expanse of sky and in the background the small one-story houses seen from above.

Tristan und Isolde. The very effective scenery for August Everding's production in 1967 was by Günther Schneider-Siemssen, a master of abstract scenery (*Pelléas et Mélisande* and the *Ring* at the Salzburg Festival) as well as of realism (*Jenufa*). This is a scene from Act Three with Otto Wiener as Kurwenal. One can perhaps afford to dispense with the 'beetling castle' stipulated by Wagner, and with my favourite 'spreading lime tree'; but I sorely miss the 'vast sea horizon' that Wagner wanted. In *Tristan* as in the *Flying Dutchman*, if an almost limitless expanse of sea is not among the protagonists the 'melancholy strain' loses its point.

(1952), in which William Warfield scored a great success as Porgy and Leontyne Price, now a star of the first magnitude, made her Vienna début as Bess. Audiences raved, all except Clemens Krauss, who ostentatiously walked out of his box — a protest that Gershwin's music has managed to survive.

One sad disappointment was the fiasco of Korngold's latest opera, *Die Kathrin*. It was to have been put on in 1938 with Jarmila Novotna and Jan Kiepura, but it was a victim of Hitler's 'Anschluss'. It also was handicapped by a terribly commonplace libretto and belonged to an age that is beyond recall, but there is some agreeable music in it. Korngold was very downhearted at the way his native Vienna seemed to have forgotten him. At each of *Kathrin*'s seven performances he hoped against hope for applause after Kathrin's (Maria Reining) Letter Song, and when it was not forthcoming he murmured to himself: 'They're all Nazis.' To cheer him up, I got myself a gallery ticket at each of the last three performances and saw to it that applause was forthcoming.

So many outstanding performances during the Theater an der Wien era keep coming to mind: the Desdemona of Carla Martinis, for instance (another brilliant but tragically short career), or Rudolf Christ as the foppish Baron Lummer in *Intermezzo* and as Wenzel in *The Bartered Bride*, both of them masterpieces of subtle humour. Then there were Ludwig Weber's tremendous Boris, Karl Kamann as the Sheriff in *La Fanciulla del West*, Elisabeth Höngen as Pique Dame, the delightful Elfie Mayerhofer as Adele — and the stage-hands' strike that kept all the State Theatres closed for a month early in 1950.

Two international careers were launched in those days and have gone full steam ahead ever since. We watched Lisa della Casa grow from Zdenka to a resplendent Arabella, and our glorious Sena Jurinac from Octavian to the Marschallin.

People forget so quickly nowadays. How many remember the early appearances of stars who later became world-famous in other rôles; of Windgassen for instance as Pinkerton (1954), or the beardless and much too youthful-looking King Henry of Theo Adam (1954), both of them at the very beginning of their careers? I well remember Walter Berry as Silvano in *Un Ballo in Maschera*, Eberhard Wächter as the English Lord in *Fra Diavolo*, Otto Edelmann as Pali the gipsy in *Der Zigeunerbaron*, and Karl Dönch as the lawyer Dr. Blind in *Die Fledermaus*. I recall Dagmar Hermann (Octavian), Hans Braun (Posa), Adolf Vogel, Georgine von Milinkovic (Fricka), Günther Treptow (Tristan), and Josef Gostic in *Die Liebe der Danae*.

'Wozzeck' — 1930 and 1952

After the first performance of 'Wozzeck' at the Vienna Opera after the war (1952) Friedrich Torberg, writing in the 'Wiener Kurier', compared the audience with the one at the Vienna première in 1930:
'*Those who clap now, would have remained silent 20 years ago, those who are silent now would still have hissed 20 years ago, and 20 years ago those who hissed now would not have gone in at all. A few left during the intervals. In 20 years' time they will presumably come back to hiss. But of course it is quite possible that, on the contrary, they might have clapped 20 years ago and that in the meantime the whole thing has become too old-fashioned for them.*'

During all this time Egon Hilbert, in his capacity as head of the Administration of the State Theatres, maintained his autocratic regime. Some admired him, others detested him; some found him ridiculous, others oppressive; people imitated his soprano voice — yet despite all the friction and bickering the Hilbert-Salmhofer-Juch trio imprinted its stamp on a great epoch in the history of the Vienna Opera. Gradually, Hilbert was drifting more and more inevitably towards a head-on collision with the Minister of Education, Dr. Kolb; and eventually in October 1953 the Minister had to suspend the super-dynamo Hilbert for deliberately overstepping the bounds of his authority, and he was moved to Rome as head of the Austrian Cultural Institute. But he could not live without 'his' Opera; after a few years he was back in Vienna as Intendant of the Vienna Festival. He soon scored two sensational successes with Otto Schenk's productions of *Lulu* and *Dantons Tod* at the Theater an der Wien.

Hilbert's successor as head of the Administration of

the State Theatres in 1953 was Ernst Marboe, who was then head of the Federal Press Service. I had the utmost admiration for this highly cultured and gifted personality (who was also an excellent writer). Marboe was toying with the most revolutionary plans for the Vienna Opera but died prematurely before he could realise more than their early stages. Personally I had every reason to be extremely grateful to him, because it was he who in 1955 appointed me to the post of dramaturgist in charge of production under Salmhofer at the Volksoper. In 1955, the year the Opera House re-opened, the Volksoper became a State theatre independent of the State Opera. Marboe had wanted to use it for musicals, operetta, and light opera, but by the time he took over the Administration of the State Theatres in 1953 his terms of reference were concentrated on the re-opening of the Opera House. In February 1954, it was officially announced that Karl Böhm was to be the new Director of the Vienna Opera with a five-year contract as from the first of September 1954, stipulating that he was to spend seven months a year in Vienna. The future of the Vienna Opera seemed rosy and assured, and in celebration of Böhm's appointment the younger generation organised a torch-light procession that stretched from the Theater an der Wien to the Schwarzenbergplatz. How differently it all turned out . . .

In some ways the Theater an der Wien era was prophetic. The Mozart trend was consolidated, and the supremacy of the producer, who during the following ten years was to be inflated to the stature of a dictator, was already casting its first shadows. But in most respects it was an era of farewell. It represented the last sunset glory of ensemble, soon to be undermined by jet aircraft and LP records, both of which meant that the same singers were in constant demand all over the world. It was also the end of Italian opera sung in German — from now on 'Wie eiskalt ist dies Händchen' had to give way to 'che gelida manina'. Tempi passati.

Heute nacht zogen sie aus . . .

Heute nacht wurde es in der Linken Wienzeile und in der Dreihufeisengasse lebendig. Die Tore des Theaters an der Wien öffneten sich und heraus schritten in wallenden Gewändern und unter Waffengeklirr all die Opernfiguren, die hier seit zehn Jahren Unterschlupf gefunden hatten. Sie zogen, nachdem sich der Vorhang über die „Zauberflöte" gesenkt hatte, ringwärts, um sich noch vor der „Coronation" in ihrem neuen feudalen Quartier heimisch niederzulassen

Tonight they moved house . . .
On the Linke Wienzeile and the Dreihufeisengasse tonight all was life and colour. The doors of the Theater an der Wien opened and a procession emerged. In flowing garments and to the rattle of arms out came all the characters in opera that had found a roof over their heads during the past ten years. Hardly had the curtain fallen on the 'Zauberflöte' than they moved off towards the Ring to take up their new feudal quarters, secretly, in time for the 'Coronation'.

The long-awaited fifth of November 1955 dawned at last. I had paid the prescribed 5,000 Schillings and was in my seat for the opening performance in Vienna's rebuilt Opera House: *Fidelio*. All round the House the streets were thronged by thousands of people listening to the relay on the radio, many of them following in miniature or piano scores. It had already been a year of great celebrations: there had been the signing of the State Treaty on the fifteenth of May, and in October the last of the occupation troops had departed. So one had the feeling that the 5,000 Schillings were a patriotic investment. And that very morning there had been an official ceremony at which all the members of the Vienna State Opera assembled on the stage and Ernst Marboe made a moving speech to the guests of honour (including van der Nüll's grand-daughter), who had come to Vienna from the four corners of the earth. The Minister of Education presented Karl Böhm with the key to the Opera House, and Karl Böhm conducted the *Meistersinger* Overture and 'The Blue Danube'. The Vienna Philharmonic Orchestra was in brilliant form.

For the House itself it was a very successful début. The original plan had been to rebuild the Opera House exactly as it was before its destruction, including all its elaborate ornamentation. But no sketches were available, and on aesthetic grounds, too, the two architects, Erich Boltenstern and Otto Prossinger, decided to restore as much as possible of the original structure, but to modify the interior decoration and fittings in accordance with the taste and standards of the 1950s. The four tiers and the boxes were retained, though the third tier boxes were done away with, as were the notorious pre-war balcony seats directly behind a pillar, from which very little could be seen of the stage. The basic colour-scheme was the old red, gold and ivory.

New police regulations in case of fire meant that the capacity had to be reduced from 3,100 to 2,211. The interior decoration was much less opulent than it had been during the Makart era; and whereas before 1945 the workshops, stores and heating-plant had all been accommodated in the House itself, nowadays they are dispersed, and the heating and hot water are piped from a plant in the Hofburg. The new House has an up-to-date hydraulically operated sliding stage and elevators as well as a revolving stage, so that changes of scene can be effected vertically as well as horizontally; yet only very occasionally has a producer seen fit to avail himself of all the new facilities.

The intervals in *Fidelio* at once gave us an opportunity to appreciate the splendid new foyers, laid out in the shape of a large U, 394 ft. long and almost 30 ft. wide. At the centre is the old foyer (with the Moritz Schwind paintings) that survived the fire. On the Kärntner Strasse side, where the Director's office used to be, is the large Tapestry Hall, and on the Operngasse side, in place of the old staff quarters, is the Marble Hall and Buffet. The work of reconstruction cost 260 million Schillings, most of which was raised from taxes, the remainder being provided by contributions from all parts of the world.

Scanning the boxes through opera glasses, we sought out the honorary members of the Vienna Opera: Bruno Walter, Lotte Lehmann, Helene Wildbrunn, Anni and Hilde Konetzni, Emil Schipper, Maria Nemeth, Hans Duhan, Gusti Pichler. Alfred Piccaver had aged almost beyond recognition, and he must have known it, because he kept well in the back-ground in his box. He had returned from London to die in Vienna, and not long afterwards we were walking in his funeral cortège. Maria Jeritza was a conspicuous absentee: she had just married and was piqued because the official invitation did not include her husband.

5,000 Schillings have the physical effekt of sharpening the critical faculties of eyes and ears. Karl Böhm conducted superbly, and of the cast at the historic opening performance at the Theater an der Wien in 1945 there remained Irmgard Seefried as Marzelline and Paul Schöffler as Pizarro. Anton Dermota, then Jacquino, was now Florestan, and the new Leonore was Martha Mödl, a great artist whose performance fell short of the best of which she has been capable before and since. The cast was illustrious enough in all conscience, but the production! Even at that early date I had a premonition that the age of the producer, with its innumerable horrors and its all too infrequent delights, had already dawned. At the

second scene's opening for instance, Pizarro appeared wearing a fiery red wig à la Franz Moor. But for no apparent reason the order of the scenes was changed and Pizarro came on alone, *before* his soldiers, who came sloping in casually in groups at intervals later on. Poor Schöffler had to sing his 'Ha, welch ein Augenblick!' *before* receiving the letter that prompts it! Who and what we owed it to that Tietjen, the former *Generalintendant* of the Berlin Opera, a conducter as well as a producer, had to be invited to produce this gala *Fidelio,* is something we may never know.

The 'Opera Festival' was on a tremendous scale and included eight premières in three weeks. The second première, on the sixth of November, was *Don Giovanni,* and again the conductor was Böhm. The producer was Oscar Fritz Schuh and the scenery was by Caspar Neher. George London sang the 'champagne' aria in front of a very pretty curtain; apart from that it was something of an abstract production in which the audience was asked to imagine that three chandeliers hanging from the rigging-loft could convert a square in a Spanish town into a splendid banqueting hall. Lisa della Casa sang Donna Anna, Sena Jurinac Donna Elvira, Irmgard Seefried Zerlina, Dermota Don Ottavio, Walter Berry Masetto and Ludwig Weber the Commendatore.

Next came *Die Frau ohne Schatten,* again superbly conducted by Böhm. This was the first performance at which there were quite a number of empty seats, a sign that the inflated prices had overshot the mark. The standing-area was practically deserted. The producer was Hartmann and the scenery was by Emil Preetorius, whom even this fantastic fairy-tale could not inspire to avail himself of all the ultra-modern stage devices the new Opera House had to offer. He simply repeated the extremely primitive scenery he had already used in Berlin and Munich. This was the beginning of the highly lucrative practice of getting the maximum 'wear' out of scenery by using it in as many different theatres as possible. The cast included Rysanek as the Empress, Höngen as the Nurse, Goltz as the Dyer's Wife, Weber as Barak, and Hopf as the Emperor.

This was followed by Adolf Rott's production of *Aida,*

which was as dark as one of the seven plagues of Egypt and included stage action during the overture (it lasted very few performances). Radames was presented as a ghost. For the scene that is supposed to be played in Amneris's room the scenery of the following triumphal feast scene was used. The conductor was Rafael Kubelik, who is a wonderful conductor in the concert-hall, but this was his first *Aida.* Rysanek was Aida, Madeira was Amneris, Hopf was Radames, Gottlob Frick was Ramphis, and Czerwenka was the King.

Then came *Die Meistersinger,* produced by Herbert Graf and conducted by Fritz Reiner, the celebrated conductor from Hungary. He did not go down at all well with the audience, mainly because he kept his eyes glued to the score all the time. As he was Chief Conductor of the Chicago Symphony, and Karl Böhm conducted in Chicago in February, there was not unnaturally a good deal of gossip about an 'exchange arrangement', though surely there was no need for either Böhm or Reiner to stoop to such a practice in this context. (The cast: Schöffler as Sachs, Seefried as Eva, Kunz as Beckmesser, Murray Dickie as David, Frick as Pogner, Braun as Kothner, and Anday as Magdalena.)

The greatest successes were the last three premières.

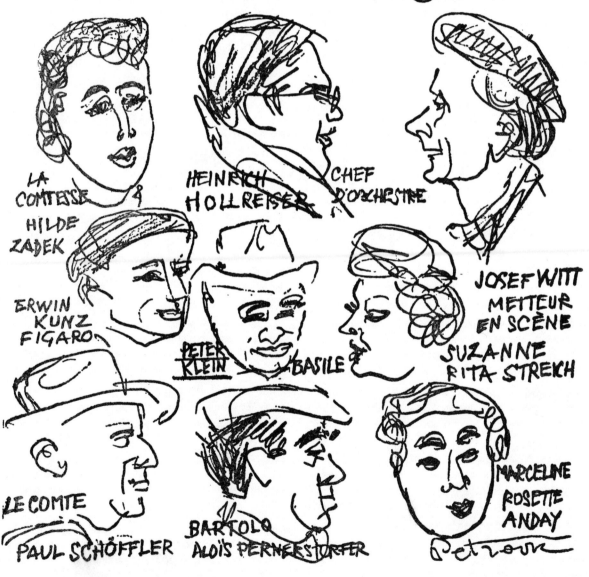

Hans Knappertsbusch conducted a wonderfully Viennese *Rosenkavalier*, produced by Josef Gielen with Roller's traditional scenery. Maria Reining was the Marschallin, Jurinac was Octavian, Güden was Sophie, Böhme was Ochs, Poell was Faninal, and Terkal was the Italian singer. Next came a superb *Wozzeck*, conducted by Böhm and produced by Schuh with scenery by Caspar Neher, with Berry as Wozzek, Goltz as Marie, and Lorenz as the Drum Major. This was followed by an evening of ballet with *Giselle*, and the world première of Boris Blacher's *Der Mohr von Venedig*, with choreography by Erika Hanka. Dirtl was Othello, Zimmerl was Desdemona, Adama was Iago, and the conductor was Heinrich Hollreiser.

There were also two glorious concerts: on Sunday the thirteenth of November Bruckner's *Te Deum* and Beethoven's Ninth (with the chorus of the Opera) conducted by the veteran Bruno Walter. On the following Sunday Böhm conducted Mozart's *Requiem* in a special performance given by the State Opera Choir 'in memory of our dead'. Raoul Aslan opened the performance with a recitation of the ode 'An die Menschheit' by Friedrich Hölderlin.

The heady delights of an 'Opera Festival without parallel', of 'our Opera House as the world's stage', of 'the Opera Festival as the insignia of our freedom', and of the 'musical coronation', were followed by a blinding hangover. There had been performances that, musically at any rate, were of a very high standard. But neither Knappertsbusch nor Reiner nor Kubelik belonged to the Vienna Opera, and for a house-warming party it is unusual, to say the least, to have to borrow the furniture.

The weeks after the gala was over were, therefore, a distinctly lean period. The gala performances had been planned well in advance, but now the Vienna Opera's 'own' admirable producer Josef Witt was saddled with the thankless task of transferring the repertoire productions from the Theater an der Wien. Most of them did not travel well. Furthermore, many of the stars decamped after the gala performances, and at the repertoire performances some of the casts were distressingly poor. Some of these performances were advertised as 'new produc-

tions', which was an exaggeration, to say the least. Others were billed as 'special productions at increased prices of admission'. Two of the very few interesting performances during this period were the *Tristan* of February 1956 conducted by André Cluytens and a really excellent *Manon Lescaut* (Puccini) in which Günther Rennert's impressionist production, Stefan Hlawa's pastel-coloured scenery, and Erni Kniepert's lovely costumes all contributed to a wonderful evening, with Martinis as Manon and Schock as Des Grieux.

Nevertheless, the criticism levelled at the Director mounted day by day. Böhm duly conducted the Chicago Symphony concerts, and people agreed that the one really perfect piece in the Vienna Opera's repertoire was 'Böhm in America'. On the twenty-eighth of February 1956 Böhm landed back at Vienna Airport, and in an interview there with the music-critic Karl Löbl uttered the notorious words: 'I've no intention of sacrificing my career to the Vienna Opera.' Local patriots of course took this very much amiss; on the other hand, Böhm was at least being perfectly honest. After all, what conductor ever *has* sacrificed an international career to the Vienna Opera? I mean in actual fact, not in sentimental interviews. Mahler never aspired to an international career as a conductor, Schalk was a purely local celebrity, Clemens Krauss (partly for political reasons) never really attained international stature, and Furtwängler always wriggled out of being tied to Vienna. Anyway, — Karl Böhm was greeted with a storm of booing when he came on to conduct *Fidelio* on the first of March 1956, was deservedly applauded for his performance of the 'Leonore No. 3' Overture, and resigned as Director the following day. A day or two later there were more catcalls before *Elektra*, because Böhm had said that the demonstration on the first of March had been organised by 'hooligans'. Böhm was still available as a conductor, and in the following years his work at the New York 'Met' earned his recognition as a conductor of international stature. In Vienna too he was never more popular as a conductor than in the years following his dramatic resignation.

Within six months of its spectacular re-opening the Vienna Opera found itself once again without a Director.

I can recall many enjoyable conversations with Ernst Marboe, head of the State Theatres Administration, during the 1955-56 season. Many of them took place on the way out to Hinterbrühl, where Marboe used to enjoy kicking a football about with his children and his friend, the bass singer Ljubomir Pantscheff. The name Herbert von Karajan kept cropping up over and over again.

Karajan had never conducted at the Theater an der Wien (according to a rumour, Hilbert had sworn that only over his dead body should Karajan be admitted to the Vienna Opera), but his series of concert performances of opera with the Vienna Symphony Orchestra in the *Musikverein* had caused a furore.

In spring 1956 I had been responsible, at the Volksoper, for the production of the first 'musical' in Austria: *Kiss me, Kate!* I followed it up with another proposal: for many years now there had been no full-scale Italian *stagione* as in the old days, so why not put one on at the Volksoper under Salmhofer? I put the idea up to Marboe at Hinterbrühl. He looked me straight in the eye and said: 'All right. But the *stagione* must finish by the eleventh of June at the latest.' I asked why, and was told to mind my own business. I duly saw the Volksoper *stagione* through in the early part of June. It included the Vienna débuts of the world-famous tenor Mario del Monaco and of the excellent conductor Argeo Quadri, who later took over all the Italian repertoire at the State Opera as well as at the Volksoper. On the twelfth of June the superb Milan Scala ensemble started a season at the State Opera with *Lucia di Lammermoor* produced and conducted by Herbert von Karajan. It was Vienna's first *Lucia* since Toscanini's visit with the Scala ensemble in 1929, and people started queuing up the evening before, armed with camp-stools and rugs. Callas sang the part of Lucia and when Karajan came on at the end to take his bow, she dropped him a deep curtsey and kissed his hand. Giuseppe di Stefano was a wonderful Edgardo, and the Sextet was encored. The next evening the ensemble performed Giorgio Strehler's production of Cimarosa's *Il matrimonio segreto* at the Akademie Theater, with a wonderful cast including Graziella Sciutti as Carolina and the lovely contralto Giulietta Simionato as Fidalma. The

same day Marboe announced that Karajan was to be the Vienna Opera's 'artistic manager' (he preferred to do without the title of 'Director'). Egon Seefehlner, who had done so much for Vienna's musical life during his many years as manager of the Konzerthaus and had then moved to the Opera to be Deputy Director under Karl Böhm, was now given the title of 'Secretary General'. Now I knew why Marboe had told me to mind my own business at Hinterbrühl. Böhm maintains that Marboe had already decided on Karajan before the campaign against Böhm really got going.

For Karajan, the appointment was the culmination of his career as the world's *Generalmusikdirektor*. Since 1950 he had held a prominent position at the Scala both as a producer and as a conductor; in 1955 he succeeded Furt-wängler as chief conductor of the Berlin Philharmonic Orchestra, with which he scored a triumphant success in America as well as in Europe; since 1956 he had been 'artistic head' of the Salzburg Festival; he was also permanent 'Concert Director' of the Vienna 'Gesellschaft der Musikfreunde' and had for many years put in a lot of hard work with the Vienna Symphony Orchestra. On top of all this he was also the permanent conductor of the Philharmonia Orchestra of London.

It was common knowledge that nobody had devoted more thought to the problems of opera in the twentieth century than Herbert von Karajan. His ideas were centred on problems peculiar to the present day, and, by Viennese standards at any rate, they were revolutionary. By and large they were sometimes more a matter of brilliant intuition than of concepts thought out on logical lines, with all their practical implications. Yet there is no denying that many of the principal items in the 'Karajan programme' — performing operas in their original language, for instance, and diluting the ensemble principle by a constant infusion of guest artists — have outlasted his actual term of office.

Karajan's theory and policy were roughly as follows. What with LP records, radio and TV, the leading stars are in constant demand all over the world, and, thanks to present-day airline schedules, can be on tap at a moment's notice. The ensemble opera of the old days, in which artists were available for long periods on end and could play, or rather sing, their parts in a standing repertoire consisting of many different works, would have to make way for a succession of ensembles engaged for short periods. In other words, a team of star artists would have to be assembled for a limited period and for a limited number of individual productions. This would assure that each production was of an exceedingly high standard. After the last performance the members of the ensemble would disperse and go their several ways. Karajan's plan entails close co-operation between the world's leading Opera Houses as regards dates and fees. It is also — both practically and artistically — a cogent argument in favour of operas sung in the original language, because obviously the singers at every theatre must sing in the same language.

In Vienna Karajan's ideas gave rise to a good deal of criticism because ensemble has always been an important feature of the Viennese tradition. Nevertheless, they might have found more ready acceptance if they had not been propagated as entailing a sort of 'Opera Trust', instead of merely a more co-ordinated degree of joint planning. The former concentration on ensemble meant that the repertoire could always be counted upon to include most of the accepted masterpieces, even if it was not always possible to assemble the ideal cast for any given performance. What Karajan's ideas amounted to was that an opera should be put on only when the world's finest cast was available.

Karajan's first step towards realising this somewhat revolutionary plan was to conclude an agreement with the Milan Scala for three years from 1956; in fact it was not until Karajan's resignation in 1964 that the Scala regarded the arrangement as terminated. This much-discussed agreement came about as follows. In the course of various talks before his appointment Karajan said to Kamitz, the Austrian Minister of Finance: 'I warn you, I'm going to cost you an awful lot of money!' Kamitz arranged a special grant for Karajan to cover disbursements to conductors, producers and singers not on the rolls of the Vienna Opera. As the fees stipulated by the 'Scala Agreement' were very high by Viennese stand-ards, singers under contract to the Scala were either called upon to sing in Vienna too if required, or they were given a contract by the Scala for performances in Vienna (as happened, for instance, in the cases of Birgit Nilsson, Elisabeth Schwarzkopf and Leontyne Price). At regular intervals the Vienna Opera paid the Scala lump sums in settlement of disbursements by the Scala on Vienna's behalf, plus a small percentage to cover their expenses and services. Another clause in the agreement was that each House was to make scenery available to the other at preferential rates. In practice, however, there were one or two snags. In Vienna, many operas still had not been prepared in their original language, so that Vienna also had to draw on the Scala for singers for minor rôles, and the Scala very often sent second-rate singers for leading rôles when better singers were available in Vienna. In those days the programme leaflets were apt to look like a membership list of the Sicilian Mafia or the population register of a village in Calabria.

The notion of close co-operation between Vienna and Milan is not the 'totally un-Austrian monstrosity typical of modern business methods' that many people declared it to be. On the contrary, it is the logical development of an old Austrian tradition. Before 1848, for example, there was even a time when the Vienna Opera and the Scala were under joint management (see the chapter on the Kärntnertor Theatre). During the last years of the Monarchy there were plans for extending this co-operation to several other opera houses, and Karajan also called on the opera houses of the world to collaborate. Moreover, the Vienna Opera has always derived a great deal of its glamour from artists under long-term contracts — Piccaver, Lehmann, Jerger, etc., whereas in the old days the highest-paid international stars such as Caruso, Gigli, or Chaliapin only paid fleeting visits to Vienna. By means of his 'Scala Agreement' Karajan succeeded in inducing such top stars as Franco Corelli, Giuseppe di Stefano, Ettore Bastianini, Giulietta Simionato and Antonietta Stella, to name only a few, to spend much longer continuous periods in Vienna than had previously been the case.

The top Italian singers were paid at Italian rates for

Obviously, as soon as these highly paid stars impinged on the Vienna Opera, with its lower fees but far more frequent appearances, there was bound to be friction. In Vienna, 10,000 Schillings (with pension rights) was the absolute top fee for artists of the highest calibre, whereas it was not unusual for an Italian artist to be paid one million Lire (about 40,000 Schillings). Many fees adjusted to equal those of the Italians. (Today, 40,000 Schillings in no longer the top fee even in Vienna.) A lot of ill-feeling was also caused by the fact that the Italians' fees were paid in Italy and therefore evaded the Austrian tax.

As regards the scenery supplied by Milan, it did not exactly set the Danube on fire; in fact some of it, for *Traviata* for instance, was on hire in Vienna for so long that it would have been cheaper to build it in Vienna in the first place. There were one or two bizarre episodes: in 1958 the scenery for Hindemith's *Mathis der Maler* was built in Italy at the Vienna Opera's expense and then hired out by Vienna to the Scala, where the première was held *before* the first Vienna performance.

The objection may of course be raised that all these details are of no interest to the general public, that all that matters is what one sees and hears 'on the night'. There were some indescribably lovely performances of Italian opera under Karajan. His second new production (April 1957) was *Otello,* Karajan himself producing and conducting. The scenery was by Wilhelm Reinking, and the costumes by Georges Wakhevitch. Mario del Monaco was a superb Otello, but it was Leonie Rysanek who stole the show. Anselmo Colzani as Iago attracted some booing, and at the repeat performance Paul Schöffler was much better. Karajan conducted marvellously, but in the Storm Music the orchestra was drowned by the thunder, which was over-amplified. Karajan also conducted a new *Tosca,* produced by Margarete Wallmann, with Renata Tebaldi (and later Leontyne Price), Tito Gobbi as Scarpia, and a new Italian tenor on the Vienna Opera's books, Giuseppe Zampieri, as Cavaradossi (1958). Among repertoire performances Karajan conducted were *Madame Butterfly* (1958) with Sena Jurinac, and *Aida* (1959) with Tebaldi, Simionato, Gobbi and the new tenor Eugenio Fernandi. The Chief Conductor of the New York Philharmonic,

singing in Vienna. Not being an ensemble theatre, the Scala engages its singers from one production to the next, and pays them relatively high fees as compensation for the limited number of appearances they are guaranteed.

185

Tanz auf vielen Hochzeiten: Karajan ‚BZ' (Berlin)

How happy could he be with either: Karajan

Dimitri Mitropoulos, was perhaps the only really great conductor Karajan was anxious to secure for the Vienna Opera; Mitropoulus conducted *Manon Lescaut*, a new *Madame Butterfly* (1957) with Jurinac, produced by Josef Gielen, and a new *La Forza del Destino* (1960) produced by Margarete Wallmann, with Antonietta Stella, Giuseppe di Stefano, Giulietta Simionato and Ettore Bastianini. Francesco Molinari-Pradelli conducted a new *Turandot* (1961) with a wonderful cast including Birgit Nilsson, Leontyne Price (Liu) and Giuseppe di Stefano. In 1960 Lovro von Matačić conducted a new production of *André Chénier* with Renata Tebaldi, Franco Corelli and Ettore Bastianini; a new *Cavalleria* with Christl Goltz as Santuzza; and a new *Pagliacci* produced by Paul Hager with scenery by Jean-Pierre Ponelle, and with Jon Vickers as Canio, Aldo Protti as Tonio, Eberhard Wächter as Silvio, and Wilma Lipp as Nedda (for the first time). There were some splendid feasts of *bel canto* and some distinctly mediocre evenings too, but one soon got used to judging the Vienna Opera by its 'finest hours' rather than by the standards of its everyday performances. Before the war there had been 'little seasons' before and after the 'high season'. Under Karajan it was the 'little seasons', September, May and June, that produced

the most brilliant occasions, because in those months both the 'Met' and the Scala were closed.

Looking back, one tends to identify Karajan's term as the 'Italian era', but there were some highly interesting evenings of German opera too. Karajan produced and conducted seven different Wagner operas; the whole of the *Ring, Tristan, Tannhäuser* and *Parsifal*. From the very first there was some totally unjustifiable opposition to Karajan as a producer — on principle. 'What right has a *Kapellmeister* to dabble in producing? People should stick to their own jobs!' This bigoted attitude betrays a total ignorance of theatrical history. In the old days, nearly all great conductors of opera acted as their own producers: Toscanini at the Scala, Jahn and Mahler at the Vienna Opera. Karajan has a perfect right to be judged solely by results. Although he had often produced at the Scala before trying his hand at it in Vienna, it was during his time at the Vienna Opera that he really matured as a producer. Unfortunately the principles on which he went to work were totally unfamiliar to his colleagues at the Vienna Opera, and caused a good deal of difficulty in its day-to-day running. To Karajan, production means interpreting the music by technical media. He orders a seemingly endless sequence of rehearsals so as to work out a detailed lighting pattern for the entire work. Bar by bar, infinitely subtle nuances of lighting are devised, and to co-ordinate them with the music at rehearsals Karajan usually has recourse to tape-recordings of the work in question, conducted by himself of course, with extras acting as stand-ins. The singers are drilled at piano rehearsals and on the rehearsal stage; only relatively late do they attend rehearsals on the main stage, where the first thing they do is learn to co-ordinate their movements to 'their' light. Ever since the days of Mahler people have been complaining that the stage is too dark, and Karajan's lighting is frequently criticised as providing more darkness than light. There was also some surprise that Karajan should need (allegedly) up to seventy-five lighting rehearsals for a performance in pitch darkness. (Birgit Nilsson says that in Karajan's productions one could easily slip away for a cup of coffee and no one in the audience would notice.)

The picture of the year with no problems

Karajan did not like to be photographed. After his resignation the photographers had an easier time. (Caricature by Rudolf Angerer.)

Das Bild des Jahres ohne Schwierigkeiten

Be that as it may, there can be no doubt whatever that Karajan is an outstandingly gifted producer. That he has a highly personal style of his own has been amply demonstrated at the annual Salzburg Easter Festival, which he organised after turning his back on Vienna.

His first Vienna première was *Die Walküre* in April 1957, with which he embarked on his new production of the *Ring*. On this occasion he is said to have been satisfied with 'only' twenty-five lighting rehearsals. This production of the *Ring* was handicapped from the very first by Emil Preetorius's stage-designs, which vacillated between classical and neo-Bayreuth without any individuality of their own (for his Salzburg Easter Festivals Karajan works with the extremely talented designer Günther Schneider-Siemssen). In Act One, instead of just the door of Hunding's house, the whole back wall flew open to

reveal the kind of sky one finds in travel brochures. But the fight between Hunding and Siegfried was marvellous, and so was Wotan's farewell to Brünnhilde. Musically, the performance already presaged the unemotional, almost chamber-music quality of Karajan's later performances of Wagner that has aroused so much controversy. Hans Hotter was Wotan, Jean Madeira (later Ira Malaniuk) was Fricka, Leonie Rysanek was Sieglinde, Ludwig Suthaus was Siegmund, and Gottlob Frick was Hunding. Among the Valkyries were Christa Ludwig and Ljuba Welitsch! Of Birgit Nilsson as Brünnhilde one critic could only say 'Helmets off, gentlemen!' Later, the part was taken over by Martha Mödl. In *Siegfried*, which followed at Christmas 1957, the forest had shrunk to a single bough, the dragon was something between a shadow and a phantom, and Birgit Nilsson awoke from her long sleep in a modish gown with tight sleeves and a zip-fastener. A touch of realism was given to Wolfgang Windgassen's 'Forging Song' by a gigantic bellows in the background. Hans Hotter sang the Wanderer, Gustav Neidlinger sang Alberich, Peter Klein was his usual incomparable Mime, Hilde Rössel-Majdan was Erda, and this *de luxe* cast even included Wilma Lipp as the Forest-Bird. But the Wanderer was not one-eyed, and the passage of dialogue with Siegfried in Act Three referring to his having only one eye was cut, which caused a storm of criticism. Vienna's Christmas present in 1958 was *Rheingold*, in which the singing Rhine Maidens were supplemented by dancers (or rather swimmers) from the Ballet in a very impressive projection of the depths of the Rhine; yet for all the tips from the conjuror Kalanag, Alberich was no more invisible when wearing the Tarnhelm than he had been in previous productions. Ten genuine anvils from a trade school lent realism to Nibelheim, and the lighting was Karajan's best yet. Hans Hotter was Wotan, Alois Pernerstorfer was a brilliant Alberich, Eberhard Wächter was Donner and was later promoted to Wotan, and Wolfgang Windgassen was Loge. To complete the *Ring*, *Götterdämmerung* arrived in June 1960, with Birgit Nilsson and Wolfgang Windgassen.

Musically, the Wagner performances were perhaps Karajan's finest in Vienna. Once he even deputised for Keilberth and conducted *Die Meistersinger*. In June 1959 he produced and conducted *Tristan* with Birgit Nilsson and Wolfgang Windgassen, and this was followed by *Parsifal* in April 1961. Heinrich Wendel's scenery included a marvellous transformation by which the trees of the first scene became the pillars of the Gralsburg, but in the semi-darkness all the Flower Maidens' efforts to seduce Parsifal, to Erich Walter's choreography, were doomed to founder. This was the celebrated performance with two Kundrys, Elisabeth Höngen in Acts One and Three and Christa Ludwig in Act Two: effective maybe, but very much open to criticism, as Wagner definitely had in mind the transformation of a *single* character, and if a theatre lacks the resources to portray this, then it has no right to be in business.

Karajan's last Wagner production was *Tannhäuser* in January 1963 with the same team: Hans Beirer as Tannhäuser, Eberhard Wächter as Wolfram, Gre Brouwenstijn as Elisabeth, Christa Ludwig as Venus, and Gottlob Frick as the Landgrave. The production included many good touches, though in the Venusberg scene the ballet overdid the gymnastics, and at the end of Act One the real hounds that Wagner insisted on were rather too much of a contrast to the oratorio-like attitudes taken up by the chorus, whose costumes looked like uniforms. But the real live falcons borne on bound wrists by real falconers from the Falconers' Club were most impressive.

From the very first day he took office until long after his resignation, Karajan was Vienna's number one topic of conversation. The Russians no longer mattered, nor did China, compared with the news that Karajan had bought his third racing-car. A calm and objective discussion of Karajan was an impossibility, feelings ran too high. People were either fanatical admirers or fanatical opponents. It was either love or hate, there was nothing in between, though his most ardent admirers sometimes found their enthusiasm waning in face of the fanatical intolerance of his devotees. Conversely, the equally fanatical intolerance of his detractors converted potential critics into uncritical supporters. In short, the entire population was divided into two camps. People who in normal times could not have been induced by wild horses to set foot in the Opera, travelled miles to attend a Karajan performance ('Of course I don't know anything about music, but obviously the man's a magician'). Then there was the celebrated 'Karajan trance' of his early years: before starting a concert he would stand stock still in front of the orchestra, bent slightly forwards, eyes closed, arms across his chest, his head sunk in meditation; either one was fascinated or one just smiled. Yet later, when he abandoned this pose, people missed it.

Although Karajan frequently deserved the criticism he got, a great deal of it was due to pure jealousy: 'Just look what he earns!' Mingled with relatively good-humoured banter like 'world-champion in conducting', 'the Greta Garbo of the rostrum', or 'the twenty-second century conductor' were genuine anger at *Carmen* sung in French and sarcasm about his villa at Saint-Tropez. There was no

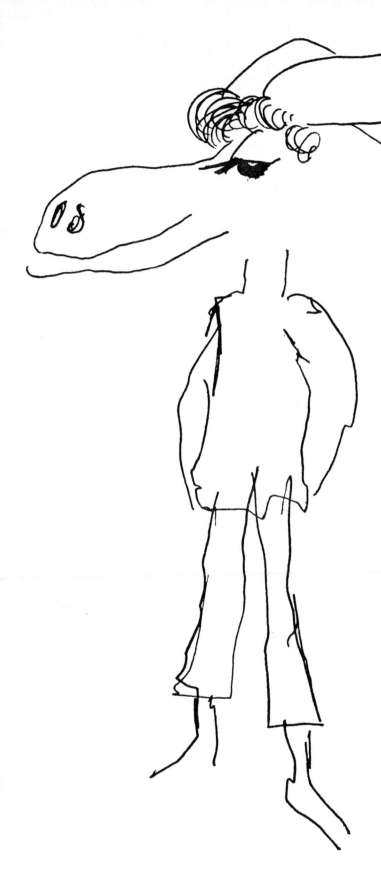

Erich Kunz als Bottom in Benjamin Britten's 'Midsummer Night's Dream', 1962. (Caricature by Winnie Jakob.)

harm, of course, in his skiing in the Engadine if he wanted to, but why on earth must he choose to fly to the skiing grounds in a helicopter? ('Franz Schalk would never have done a thing like that!'). People who regulary let their own villas for exorbitant rents boiled with moral indignation if Karajan leased somebody his private aeroplane. 'Did Gustav Mahler need Yoga for concentration and relaxation?' And when Karajan was voted Vienna's best-dressed man, it was just 'cheap publicity'. And worst of all 'he squanders our precious Schillings' abroad by having his Salzburg costume made by a Milan tailor!

Even his tax problems were all at once the concern of every good Austrian music-lover. Karajan was careful never to spend more than 180 days a year in Austria, otherwise he would have been deemed to be domiciled in Austria and would have had to pay Austrian tax on all his earnings from whatever source. A lot of people would have been only too glad if the tax authorities had made things difficult for him over his 'Buchenhof' property at Mauerbach near Vienna. The most die-hard reactionaries became convinced Republicans overnight and indulged in caustic comments on Karajan's aristocratic 'von'. People with none too edifying records themselves started delving back into his activities during the 'Third Reich' (like Furtwängler, Krauss, Böhm and Knappertsbuch he had been banned by the Allies for quite a time after the war). Yet the very same people still harped on the superiority of the Germanic race: Karajan's father was a doctor in Salzburg, his grandfather was called Karajanis or Karajanopoulos, a Macedonian or Armenian or something. The ignorant professed to be experts. Remarks like 'Karajan's extravagance is ruining Austria', or 'It's thanks to Karajan that the Vienna Opera enjoys a worldwide reputation', were volunteered by people who wouldn't have been able to tell the difference between the *Meistersinger* Overture and the 'Blue Danube Waltz' even if you played them both right through.

Under Karajan the running of the Vienna Opera was more expensive than it had ever been before, and cheaper than it has ever been since. But Karajan never re-engaged Callas, because she wanted a fee of 2,500 dollars. His own salary was 6,000 Schillings a month as 'artistic

Otto Wiener in the title rôle of Hindemith's opera 'Cardillac'. (Caricature by Winnie Jakob.)

manager' and 18,000 Schillings every time he conducted. After his departure costs were doubled, and by 1969 the State Opera (including pensions) was costing the Austrian tax-payer about half a million Schillings a day.

Karajan's most beautiful production was without question Debussy's *Pelléas et Mélisande* (1962) with Hilde Güden, largely because the scenery was by a kindred spirit of his, Günther Schneider-Siemssen. In the same year he replaced Tietjen's controversial *Fidelio* with a new production of his own, also in collaboration with Schneider-Siemssen. Christa Ludwig's Leonore was her début in a soprano part. There were some interesting productions of contemporary opera: in 1958 Stravinsky conducted one performance of *Oedipus Rex* in person, and at another performance the narrator was Jean Cocteau (with his sleeves rolled up). This was followed in 1961 by Orff's *Oedipus der Tyrann* produced by Günther Rennert with Gerhard Stolze as Oedipus. Previously there had been Hindemith's *Mathis der Maler* (1958) produced by Adolf Rott, with Paul Schöffler as Mathis and the composer himself conducting one performance. Poulenc's *Die Gespräche der Karmeliterinnen* in 1959 (it was per-

formed in German), based on Bernanos' *Die begnadete Angst*, was notable for Margarete Wallmann's production; usually more of a 'shop-window display' artist, she here produced a most moving scene of the nuns' execution. Also in 1959 came Pizzetti's *Murder in the Cathedral* (also performed in German) with Hans Hotter as Becket, Karajan conducting, and the composer making a personal appearance; and Benjamin Britten's *Midsummer Night's Dream* conducted by Hollreiser and produced by Werner Düggelin. In 1960 the Städtische Oper Berlin treated Vienna to Schoenberg's *Moses und Aaron* conducted by Hermann Scherchen and produced by the Berlin Opera's General Intendant, Gustav Rudolf Sellner.

The most interesting revival of a half-forgotten work was Monteverdi's *L'Incoronazione di Poppea* (1963) in a 'modern' realisation by Kraack with Sena Jurinac as Poppea, her first appearance as a 'femme fatale'. The work was admirably produced by Günther Rennert, who had also produced Rossini's *Cenerentola* in 1959 with Christa Ludwig, Alberto Erede conducting, as well as a delightful *Bartered Bride*, conducted by Jaroslav Krombholc with a cast including Irmgard Seefried and Waldemar Kmentt, and with Oskar Czerwenka in great form as Kezal. On New Year's Eve 1960 Karajan conducted a new *Fledermaus* with Hilde Güden and Eberhard Wächter, the producer being Leopold Lindtberg. Act Two was enlivened by Erich Kunz as Governor of the prison interpolating some Viennese songs, and Giuseppe di Stefano giving a rendering of 'Dein ist mein ganzes Herz' in impeccable German (for a fee of 1,000 dollars). Josef Meinrad was delightful as Frosch, and Rita Streich as Adele.

Rudolf Moralt, the Vienna Opera's most loyal and reliable staff conductor, died in 1958, shortly after conducting a performance of the ballet *Josephslegende*, which was Prima Ballerina Julia Drapal's farewell performance after twenty-five years with the Vienna State Opera Ballet. Karajan induced Krips to return after five years' absence, and other conductors who appeared during this period were George Szell, Antonio Votto, Lovro von Matačić, Oliviero de Fabritiis, Georges Prêtre, Janos Ferencsik, Tullio Serafin, Heinz Wallberg, Hans

Swarowsky, Berislav Klobucar, Heinrich Hollreiser and Wilhelm Loibner.

Few people ever got to know the real Karajan behind the publicity 'image'. He has always been an individualist, and hated press and radio interviews, though in recent years he has become more amenable and less intolerant. The circles he preferred to move in were neither musical nor Viennese gossip-mongering society, but the international *haute-volée* of the Engadine, where he established a permanent domicile at St. Moritz.

During his term of office there was a great deal of glamour, one or two real crises, and a lot of storms in tea-cups. People got excited about the most trivial matters so long as Karajan was involved in them. Not so trivial was his refusal to allow the Austrian television service to relay *Der Rosenkavalier* live from the New Festival Theatre at Salzburg on the grounds that live relays distort the performance. This refusal was due to a previous relay of *Cenerentola* which he bitterly regretted ever having sanctioned.

Karajan signed an exclusive contract with Deutsche Grammophon, for whom 'his' Berlin Philharmonic recorded. The Vienna Philharmonic is under contract to a British firm, and when Karajan urged them to ease out of this commitment so that they could record with him, a Viennese journalist termed it 'Balkan behaviour'. Karajan sued him and won.

Karajan abhors unauthorised photographs, either of his productions or of himself. In America it is the normal practice for photographs of a 'musical' to be taken by a photographer who has the sole rights and is just as much under contract as the stars. In Austria, however, this is not the practice, and on one occasion in Salzburg Karajan is said to have personally assaulted a photographer who was taking photographs without his permission. For days afterward people talked about 'Propellor Herb, the shutterbug smacker'.

The first crisis during Karajan's term blew up early in 1962. The technical staff demanded a new collective agreement including higher pay and a revision of the overtime schedule. The negotiations were conducted by the State Theatres Administration, now no longer

'*Ohne meinesgleichen — wo wäre das Theater?*' Paul Schöffler as Director La Roche in '*Capriccio*'. (*Caricature by Winnie Jakob.*)

run by Karajan's friend Ernst Marboe, who had died suddenly and prematurely of a heart-attack in 1957. For some time there was no progress; the stage-hands refused to work more overtime than they were obliged to (too little for the production schedule) and rehearsals became increasingly precarious. At this juncture Karajan brought off a brilliant coup: in January 1962, when a solution seemed as far off as ever, he showed that he, too, could 'do it on the cheap' by staging his finest production, *Pelléas et Mélisande*, with comparatively few rehearsals. As the negotiations dragged on with no sign of a settlement the Minister of Education, Heinrich Drimmel, asked Karajan to preside over them himself. The next thing that happened was that an agreement was suddenly reached while Karajan was away from Vienna for a couple of days. Karajan felt that he had been by-passed and claimed that the terms of the agreement were impracticable because the stage-hands, instead of accepting a fixed and specified amount of overtime, merely bound themselves 'to volunteer to work unlimited overtime as occasion demanded', a formula that became known as the 'on request' clause. The real reason why an agreement was reached so suddenly was to save the Opera Ball, which, for all State functionaries, is a social occasion of the first magnitude but for Karajan was a matter of no importance.

Early in February Karajan resigned in protest, and public opinion was almost entirely behind him. There was even a sympathetic strike of the entire artistic and technical personnel, and during a performance of *Un Ballo in Maschera* the unfortunate Tullio Serafin was the innocent victim of noisy demonstrations in favour of Karajan.

Karajan was prepared to withdraw his resignation on two conditions: first, the immediate appointment of a co-Director who enjoyed his complete confidence, and second, that the State Opera should be divorced from the State Theatres Administration's budget should, until Jauner had made in 1875). The Minister of Education, Dr. Drimmel, who was by no means whole-heartedly pro-Karajan but was well aware how much Karajan meant to the State Opera ('the greatest freedom for the loftiest art') took steps to ensure that both conditions were met. Karajan's co-Director was Walter Erich Schäfer, General Intendant of the Stuttgart Opera, a distinguished, erudite and most cultivated man of whom Karajan had a high opinion (as well as laughing at his racy Swabian jokes). But to be on the safe side, Schäfer had his Stuttgart contract extended to 1967 before proceeding to take a furnished flat in Vienna and to run the two Operas simultaneously.

The Opera's separation from the State Theatres Administration was propounded in a statement issued by the Ministry of Education, in the form of an 'addendum'. It stipulated that sums allocated for certain items in the State Theatres Administration's budget should, until further notice, be credited to the State Opera to cover the latter's immediate requirements. Or in common parlance, so long as it kept within its budget, the State Opera did not have to secure the State Theatres Administration's approval for every Schilling it spent. The new regulations applied to all artistic personnel on contract (with the exception of the 'permanent bodies', the chorus, the orchestra, and the ballet), to all visiting artists, to scenery, and to all overtime, ect., by the artistic and technical personnel.

So Karajan came back. Besides Schäfer he had Albert Moser as Secretary-General to assist him. Moser had been running the Styrian Music Society very successfully for a number of years before Marboe appointed him to a post in the State Theatres Administration, and at the State Opera he succeeded Egon Seefehlner, who moved to Berlin as Deputy Director. When Karajan mounted the rostrum to conduct *Aida* in March 1962, he found a sheaf of red roses waiting for him. There was enormous enthusiasm, and after Act Two the entire stalls accorded him a standing ovation. Previously Karajan had assembled 600 members of the staff in the auditorium and thanked them for their loyalty. The storm was over — but it was not long before more thunderclouds appeared on the horizon.

During the weeks that followed there were visits of the Marquis de Cuevas Ballet Company and the London Festival Ballet, and two interesting performances by the Württemberg State Opera of Stuttgart under Ferdinand Leiter: Rennert's production of Rossini's *Il Turco in Italia*, with the late Fritz Wunderlich, who met such a tragically premature end, and Wolfgang Fortner's *Bluthochzeit* based on a play by Garcia Lorca, with a brilliant performance by Martha Mödl. Then came Karajan's new *Fidelio,* and a *Figaro* with Lisa della Casa as the Countess and Geraint Evans as Figaro. In the summer Karajan conducted the gala performance of *Die Zauberflöte* with which the renovated Theater an der Wien re-opened. Another lovely evening at the Theater an der Wien was Strauss's *Intermezzo* with a superb performance by Hanny Steffek as Christine and with Hermann Prey, who has since become a TV star, in good voice as *Kapellmeister* Storch.

The autumn of 1962 was graced by some lovely Italian singing from Corelli and Price, Simionato and Stella, and di Stefano and Bastianini. Within the space of a few months there was a choice of Boris Christoff, Nicolai Ghiaurov, and Cesare Siepi as King Philip in *Don Carlos*!

In 1963 came Karajan's new *Tannhäuser* and *L'Incoronazione di Poppea;* in May the première of Tchaikovsky's ballet *The Sleeping Beauty,* with choreography by Vaslav Orlikovsky; and later a minor sensa-

From Adolphe Adam to Igor Stravinsky

The Ballet
of the Vienna State Opera

Susanne Kirnbauer
as Princess Aurora
in Tchaikovsky's
Sleeping Beauty (1966).

Adolphe Adam's *Giselle*, in Coralli's original choreography, has been in the standard repertoires of ballet companies the world over ever since 1841.

Top: Erika Zlocha as Giselle in the scene with Prince Albrecht (Richard Adama) and Hilarion (Erwin Pokorny). — Below: in the celebrated ensuing variations in Act One. — Right page: Fanny Elssler as Florinde in Casimir Gide's Ballet *Le diable boiteux* (engraving by Andreas Geiger, 1836).

And. Geiger sc.

Fanny Elßler in der Cachucha.

Left: Else von Strohlendorf, the first prima ballerina (1920 to 1924) of the Vienna State Opera who was a product of the Opera's own ballet school and corps de ballet. Hitherto only foreigners, mainly Italians, had been engaged as prima ballerina, but the tradition came to an end with the appointment of Strohlendorf.

Right: Gusti Pichler, prima ballerina from 1924 to 1935, in Schubert's *Deutsche Tänze*. She was Strohlendorf's successor, and for over ten years between the two world wars her fragile beauty won her as many admirers among ballet fans as her technical proficiency. In 1938 she was made an honorary member of the Vienna State Opera, an honour that until then had only been conferred upon singers. She is now living in London, but after the re-opening of the Vienna Opera in 1955 she was often in Vienna and was able to assure herself at first hand that she was by no means forgotten.

Top: Edeltraud Brexner as Juliet in Prokofiev's *Romeo and Juliet.* She joined the Vienna Ballet in 1957. In 1960 she was presented with the Fanny Elssler Ring, an award endowed by the former solo ballerina Riki Raab. She was also appointed to the Vienna Opera Ballet's teaching staff. — Left: Julia Drapal, prima ballerina 1949—1958, as Potiphar's Wife in Richard Strauss's *Josephslegende,* with Olga Fiedler as the favourite slavegirl. Julia Drapal was also an enchanting performer in the State Opera's productions of operetta in the Volksoper between 1945 and 1955.

Above: *Symphonischer Walzer* by Karl Alwin (1935): Poldy Pokorny (left), Willy Fränzl, and Julia Drapal. — Below left: Gusti Pichler and Willy Fränzl in the first performance of Richard Strauss's *Schlagobers* (1924). — Below right: *Don Juan* by Gluck with Erwin Pokorny as Don Juan and Lucia Bräuer as Zerline.

Top: *Der Moor von Venedig* by Boris Blacher (1955). From left to right: Edeltraud Brexner (Bianca), Richard Adama (Iago), Christl Zimmerl (Desdemona), Willy Dirtl (Othello), Lucia Bräuer (Emilia). — Left: Edeltraud Brexner and Karl Musil during a rehearsal. — Below: From Gottfried von Einem's *Medusa:* Karl Musil (Perseus) and Christl Zimmerl (Medusa).

Next page: A scene from Stravinsky's *Le sacre du printemps* with Christl Zimmerl and the corps de ballet.

The crisis. The psychiatrist said: 'Tell me the whole story from the beginning.' And Herbert von Karajan began... (see below). (Caricature by Erich Sokol in the 'Arbeiter-Zeitung' of 14 June 1964.)

„Wissen Sie, am Anfang erschuf ich Himmel und Erde..."
'Well: In the beginning I created Heaven and Earth...'

tion that was the talk of the town for days. A performance of *Die Meistersinger* had to be cancelled when the audience were already in their seats because the tenor Wolfgang Windgassen had not been informed of the change of programme and there was nobody to replace him (according to the original programme it was to have been *The Flying Dutchman* that evening).

In June Karajan conducted a new *Don Giovanni*. Teo Otto's bronze-coloured sets conjured up a dark romantic atmosphere and the producer was Oscar Fritz Schuh. The Commendatore never appeared but was represented by a voice and a projection! Two excellent Don Giovannis alternated, Eberhard Wächter and Cesare Siepi; Leontyne Price (the Volksoper's Bess at one time) was a superb Donna Anna, and Donna Elvira was a new part for Hilde Güden. So within the short space of seven years there had been two new productions of *Don Giovanni*, two of *Fidelio* and two of *Tannhäuser*. In the old days productions used to last 30 years and more. The number of works performed grew smaller and smaller, (forty-two in the 1961-62 season as against eighty-four in Schalk's 1926-27 season) and the same old repertoire works were refurbished over and over again, with yet a third *Don Giovanni* making its appearance in 1967.

In June 1963 came the event that almost everyone had been expecting for some time: Schäfer, who never really felt at home in Vienna, was forced to realise that there was no future for him at the Vienna Opera and returned to Stuttgart for good, ostensibly for reasons of health.

Almost at the same time Franz Salmhofer resigned as Director of the Volksoper, also for reasons of health. He was succeeded by Albert Moser, who is now my boss. At the State Opera, Karajan suggested Egon Hilbert as co-Director.

The news broke like a bombshell, and it hardly needed second sight to venture the opinion that 'it can't possibly last'. In point of fact the suggestion, put forward on the advice of the producer Paul Hager, was a quite unaccountable sign of weakness on Karajan's part. Hilbert was a great favourite with the Press, especially the anti-Karajan Press, and as Intendant of the Vienna Festival, and earlier still in the Theater an der Wien era, he had certainly achieved superlative results. But how could two such strikingly incompatible personalities possibly work together? Hilbert talked a lot, wrote a lot, was given to interminable memoranda and a great deal of fuss; without an atmosphere of excitement he could not exist. Karajan on the other hand disliked putting things in writing and was a man of few, but crisp, words. If people started to shout, he would leave the room. He is one of the quietest men imaginable: even at rehearsals he keeps his voice almost down to a whisper, which is why everyone is so attentive. What Karajan wanted at this juncture was someone to take the administrative chores off his hands; whereas what Hilbert wanted was to be a full-blown Director of the Vienna Opera with full authority in artistic matters. What Karajan wanted was an *ad hoc* assembly of stars for limited periods; what

Hilbert wanted was the ensemble of the good old days. The result — during the one and only year of this strangely assorted couple — was a mixture of classical tragedy and the broadest farce, though admittedly there were one or two wonderful evenings.

In October 1963 preparations for a new production of *Bohème* were going ahead. Karajan had already scored a resounding success with Zeffirelli's production of *Bohème* at the Scala, with Mirella Freni as Mimi and Gianni Raimondi as Rodolfo. So he proposed to put on the same production in Vienna; transfers of this kind are in Karajan's view an essential feature of the opera world of to-day. And this same production of *Bohème* was given in Munich and Moscow as well as on television.

It is customary in Italy for full-fledged *Kapellmeister* to act as prompters. As well as singing the actual notes they also mime the singers' gestures, so that the less the singers know about their parts, the more indispensable is an alert 'maestro suggeritore', and under the terms of the agreement with the Scala Karajan engaged a certain Armando Romano for a not inconsiderable fee. The Austrian Trade Unions protested and had the labour permit withheld. At the première early in November 1963, Director Hilbert himself gallantly led the 'maestro suggeritore' through the enemy's lines to his post. The Trade Unions countered by calling an immediate strike. The two Directors appeared in front of the curtain, Karajan in tails and Hilbert in a dinner jacket. Hilbert read out a résumé of the facts of the case, stressed his loyalty to Karajan, and sealed it with a kiss (no one who saw the episode will ever forget Karajan's face). The audience, asked to go home, protested vigorously. There was some disorder and a first-class sensation all over Europe.

The episode split little Austria into two irreconcilably hostile factions. My grocer, who had never been to the Opera in her life, regarded it as uncivilised to deny Karajan his 'mastro zutscherritohre'. My bootmaker on the other hand, who had also never been to the Opera in his life, regarded it as an impertinence that this Karajan should squander the taxpayers' money on a 'mestro dschuzerridoore'. A number of illustrious stars, including Franco Corelli, Leontyne Price, Ettore Bastianini, Anto-

nietta Stella, Giulietta Simionato, Mirella Freni and Gianni Raimondi signed a declaration that they could not sing without a 'maestro suggeritore'. A day or two later Karajan decided to go ahead without the aforesaid 'maestro suggeritore' and the première of *Bohème* with Freni and Raimondi was one of the greatest triumphs of his career at the Vienna Opera. For Karajan it had been a trial of strength. And when Karajan's lovely Salzburg production of *Il Trovatore* was transferred to Vienna, complete to Teo Otto's scenery with its air of mystery, and the brilliant bit of stage-business when the huge flag slowly unfurled over the camp, neither Franco Corelli nor Eberhard Wächter, who was a splendid Luna, had the

slightest difficulty in managing without a 'maestro suggeritore'.

It is interesting to note that in their findings of the second of June 1964 (Zl. 408/64) the Administrative Courts came down unequivocally on Karajan's side. They held that performances of Italian operas in the Vienna Opera with leading Italian singers conducted by a world-famous conductor were important occasions for music-lovers not only in Austria but all over the world. This was indisputable. But the Courts also found that there was not the slightest threat of Vienna's regular prompter losing his job or even that his services might be curtailed. There could therefore be no objection to the issue of a labour permit for a 'maestro suggeritore', whose presence undoubtedly contributed to raising the standard of the performance as a whole.

For the last phases of this extraordinary dual Director-ship somebody invented the brilliant title of 'Die unheim-liche Ehe' (*Die heimliche Ehe* is the German title of Cima-rosa's opera *Il matrimonio segreto*, but *unheimlich* is not the opposite of *heimlich*; it means 'eerie' or 'sinister'). Hilbert's opening salvos were directed at Karajan's pri-vate secretary André von Mattoni, whom Karajan had made a member of the management of the Opera and who is without question the most loyal and self-effacing person imaginable. Then there were meetings (documented by the minutes) at which Karajan claimed that Hilbert was not entitled to call himself 'Staatsoperndirektor': his proper title was 'Direktor der Staatsoper'! Two grown men actually committed themselves to paper on such footling trivialities! The last straw was when Hilbert slammed down the receiver during a telephone conversa-tion with Karajan. From then on the two corresponded only in writing. The climax came at a performance of *Tannhäuser* on the seventeenth of May 1964. It was a repeat performance of Karajan's own production, and Hilbert put it down for that day knowing perfectly well that Karajan had a concert with the Berlin Philharmonic in the *Musikverein* that evening. Karajan requested Hil-bert to put *Tannhäuser* off. Hilbert refused, and on the seventh of May arranged for the head of the Belgrade Opera, Oskar Danon, to conduct it, which he did to a chorus of 'Hilbert must go' from the audience. On the eighth of May Karajan resigned as from the end of the season 'for reasons of health', stating that whether he could remain at the Vienna Opera's disposal as a conductor and producer would depend on what artistic assurances 'the new Director or Directors' would guarantee. On the twenty-first of May Karajan conducted a performance of *Fidelio* at which Florestan's question 'Who is the Governor of this prison?' was answered from the gallery with a shout of 'Hilbert'.

Karajan's phrase 'the new Director or Directors' was a reference to the legal tangle that in the last instance precipitated Karajan's departure. There was a clause in Hilbert's contract to the effect that he 'could' resign in the event of Karajan's doing so. Karajan on the other hand was of the view that the administration was essentially a joint or dual one and that if one Director resigned the other one was automatically out of office; and the former Minister of Education, Drimmel, later stated that this was what had in fact been agreed — orally. But Drimmel was no longer in office, and his successor, Theodor Piffl-Perčević, was unable to find any written document stipulating that Karajan's resignation would automatically include Hilbert's.

In June 1964 came Karajan's new production, conducted by himself, of *Die Frau ohne Schatten*, with scenery by Schneider-Siemssen and costumes by Ronny Reiter. It was an interesting production with some effective use of the traps for vertical changes of scene. Leonie Rysanek was the Empress, Christa Luwig was the Dyer's Wife, Grace Hoffmann the Nurse, Walter Berry Barak, and Jess Thomas the Emperor. It was a *deluxe* cast from top to bottom, with stars such as Fritz Wunderlich and Lucia Popp in very minor rôles. Karajan was in superb form and there was much enthusiasm and chanting of 'We want Karajan'. The only blemishes were some misguided cuts and transpositions in the second act. The repeat performance with Gundula Janowitz as the Empress and Otto Wiener as Barak was Karajan's farewell appearance at the Vienna Opera.

During this last month of the 1963-64 season there were some wonderful performances. In June Karl Böhm reap-

peared after a long absence to conduct *Tristan*, there was a lovely *Turandot* with Birgit Nilsson and Mirella Freni, and Lisa della Casa gave a delightful performance in a new production of *Arabella*, with Mimi Coertse as Fiakermilli, conducted by Joseph Keilberth.

So Karajan departed, and Hilbert stayed on. Once again Vienna let a genius go. The Karajan years may have been turbulent and storm-tossed, but at least they included moments of genuine greatness. For people who since his departure have had 'other things to worry about' Karajan made the Opera something to look forward to and to look up to. True, the applause was sometimes elicited by little tricks of stage-management. In *Götterdämmerung*, for example, the curtain came down before Siegfried's journey to the Rhine, a long time before Wagner intended, immediately after Siegfried's and Brünnhilde's final 'Heil'; there was no chance for Brünnhilde to listen to Siegfried's horn-call and wave him farewell, but there was more time for the orchestral interlude ('I never noticed it before', was a frequent comment). A trifle perhaps, but still... Then people sometimes wondered why, if Karajan was prepared to engage the most expensive artists from all over the world, he never engaged a Wagner producer but adopted a 'do-it-yourself' policy. Now, a good deal later, we can see that as a result of neo-Bayreuth hardly any of the leading producers will touch Wagner with a barge-pole, and if they do, the result is seldom a success. Again, people tend to say nowadays that as a conductor Karajan was marvellous but as a Director — well, they are not so sure. But it's not quite as simple as that. Maybe Karajan lacked an overall intellectual concept and a systematic programme (so for that matter did all the other Directors except Mahler and Clemens Krauss), but he was a marvellous 'producer' in the present-day sense. He knew how to put the show over. He also brought to the Vienna Opera many international stars who have since made Vienna their home.

After Karajan's departure there was no reversion to the pre-Karajan practice of singing Italian operas in German (except for Hilbert's unpopular attempt, mentioned in the next chapter), and no dilution of the Opera's hard-won independence from the State Theatres Administration.

Heinrich von Kralik after Karajan's resignation. 'Die Presse', 13 May 1964 (extract). (Translation on page 215.)

Umschau nach dem Richtigen

Einem neuen Staatsoperndirektor müßte die Wiedergewinnung Karajans gelingen

Was der Wiener Oper ihre Eigenart und wohl auch ihre Überlegenheit verleiht, liegt in der Tatsache, daß sie keine Manager-, sondern eine Künstler- und Dirigentenoper ist. Seit rund hundert Jahren sind es mit wenigen peinlichen Ausnahmen große Künstler gewesen, die in der Direktionskanzlei das Schicksal der Oper lenkten. Die Tradition der Wiener Oper ist eine Künstlertradition, die ihre Kraft und Bedeutung nicht aus dem Moment ängstlichen Beharrens schöpft, sondern aus der Fähigkeit, sich in ständigem Wechsel zu erneuern. Daß etwa der Blütezeit unter Jahn und Richter das gänzlich anders geartete, geradezu entgegengesetzte Opernerlebnis der Mahler-Zeit folgen konnte, ist für die sozusagen biologische Beschaffenheit des Institutes sehr bezeichnend.

In ähnlicher Weise trug Karajan neue Ideen, neue Gedanken, neue Pläne ins Haus, die zeigen, daß sein Künstlertum ein vielschichtiges und weitschauendes ist, und daß seine Dirigentenkapazität nur eine Teilfunktion bildet. Seiner Idee von einer international gelenkten Interessengemeinschaft der großen Opernhäuser gehört die Zukunft. Wie schön wäre es gewesen, wenn die Zukunft von Wien aus ihren Ausgang genommen hätte, und wenn nicht den ersten schüchternen Versuchen, wie sie der Vertrag mit der Scala vorsieht, nach kleinlicher Buchhalterart eine scheinbare Passivbilanz im Saldokonto vorgerechnet worden wäre.

Neu und ungewöhnlich war es auch, daß Karajan, nach allen Regeln der Kunst, gelernter Musiker, die Aufgaben von Regie und Inszenierung, in die er sich erst einzufühlen und einzuarbeiten hatte, selbst in die Hand nahm. Er brachte damit auch in der szenischen Realisierung des Opernspiels wieder das Musikerrecht zur Geltung, das in bedenklichem Ausmaß von einer weniger musikalischen Theater- und Schauspielregie usurpiert worden war. Nach etlichem Tasten und gewiß nicht immer geglückten Versuchen hat er in den letzten Jahren auch als Inszenator seinen persönlichen Stil, seine klare und sichere Form gefunden. Die von ihm musikalisch und szenisch geleiteten Aufführungen von „Pelléas und Melisande", „Troubadour" oder „Tannhäuser" geben davon das rühmlichste Zeugnis und zeigen die glückhafte Erprobung seiner Methode in drei sehr verschiedenen Stilbereichen. Sie führen aus dem Chaos, in welchem sich die Operninszenierung derzeit allenthalben befindet, zu künstlerisch gesicherter Ordnung. Sie werden vielleicht in ähnlicher Weise Geschichte machen wie die Mahler-Roller-Aufführungen zu Beginn unseres Jahrhunderts.

Heinrich K r a l i k

Whether one likes Karajan or not, he has a very important place in the history of the Vienna Opera as a Director. After his resignation in the summer of 1964 he said in an interview: 'It is my duty to apply the highest possible standards to my performances and to the artistic potentialities available. I enjoy showing just what the mobilisation of all the forces at my disposal can bring about. People must be given a goal. Racehorses enjoy racing, but it has to be given an incentive. This is something I shall never go back on. If I felt that the horse was no longer responding to the challenge I should give up.'

Interviewer: 'But in Vienna you did give up.'

Karajan: 'Yes, because there's no race-horse there, only an old cart horse.'

This was where Karajan was wrong. He had every reason to be proud of what he had achieved in Vienna, but no first-class Director has ever raised the Vienna Opera from mediocrity to world class single-handed, and no third-class Director has ever reversed the process. It is the resilience of the Opera itself that matters; the Directors merely act according to their lights. It was only after Jahn's brilliant 'gastronomic' years that Mahler imposed his concept of 'intellectual' theatre, and Karajan, it must not be forgotten, had the marvellous Theater an der Wien era to build on.

And after Karajan's departure Leonard Bernstein showed with his brilliant *Falstaff* and *Rosenkavalier* that the 'old cart horse' could still raise a fair turn of speed.

So Karajan departed and Hilbert stayed on. As co-Director with Karajan his contract would have expired in 1968, but it was later extended to 1970. But before then Hilbert was to be the first Director of the Vienna Opera to die in office.

Personally I do not think that Hilbert intended from the very first to ease Karajan out. By inviting him to be Director of the Vienna Opera Karajan had offered him the fulfilment of his life's ambition. Hilbert's whoop of delight was perfectly genuine, and so perhaps was the famous embrace in front of the curtain after the announcement of the cancellation of *Bohème*. At the start he was almost obsequious to Karajan but soon changed his tune when he saw that Karajan couldn't stand the sight of him and was tired of his long-winded tirades and interminable memoranda. So, like Elektra, Hilbert decided to go it alone ('Nun denn, allein') and may well have echoed Angelotti's 'Finalmente' in *Tosca*.

Hilbert's first season opened on the first of September 1964 with stentorian shouts of 'we want Karajan' from the standing-area, followed by *Figaro*. Never before have there been so many disturbances and demonstrations in the Vienna Opera.

Previously, Hilbert had been crusading for a return to German-language ensemble theatre and the Mozart cult of the Theater an der Wien era. But as sole Director his first move was to get the Italian singers back. And most of them obliged. But they were a much more expensive luxury now than they had been before the agreement with the Milan Scala was abrogated. Now that they were engaged directly by Vienna they demanded higher fees to counterbalance the disadvantage of not being taxed at the lower Italian rates. So Hilbert embarked on a super-Karajan policy, but without Karajan.

One trump-card with which Hilbert hoped to get his own back on Karajan was the re-engagement of Giuseppe di Stefano, whom Karajan had turned down for *Bohème* in Milan in 1963, because he could no longer sing his aria 'in tono', complete with top C. There was a time when di Stefano was one of the greatest tenors of the century. So Hilbert offered di Stefano a contract for a considerable number of appearances at 2,000 dollars a time, without deductions. Di Stefano duly arrived in Vienna in September and gave one or two really good performances before the effect on his voice of wine, women and song — not to mention the Casino in the Favoritenstrasse — became embarrassingly apparent. On the morning of the dress rehearsal of *Carmen* di Stefano backed out, though his exact words are still in dispute. James King deputised. The Vienna Opera took di Stefano's defection as applying to his contract as a whole; but six months later di Stefano suddenly turned up in Vienna (he was singing in *Land of Smiles* in Berlin at the time) and put in a claim for the performances he was still due to give under his contract. The Ministry of Finance refused to sanction a proposed settlement for 800,000 Schillings, and at the time of this writing the matter still rests there. This time, Hilbert had made no memorandum.

There was a real sensation in October 1964 when Aurel von Milloss, who was in charge of the State Opera Ballet, secured Rudolf Nureyev to dance in *Swan Lake* and to be responsible for the choreography as well, with Margot Fonteyn as Odette. When Milloss returned to Rome and Vaslav Orlikovsky took over the ballet in 1966, the two stars danced together again in *Marguerite*

et Armand, a ballet based on *La dame aux Camélias* to music by Liszt, with choreography by Frederick Ashton.

Unfortunately Hilbert was not an artist. He was a fanatically keen manager, but not a professional; his knowledge of the international singers' market was superficial. He was a super-dynamic bundle of energy, and the Opera was his whole life (the running of it, not the artistic side). He took a special delight in achieving the impossible. With his falsetto and fortissimo marathon monologues he invariably got what he wanted: dates from the singers, money from the Government, concessions from the Trade Unions. 'The Opera is more important than we are' was his favourite motto. He was firmly convinced he had a hot-line to God Almighty, whom he was always invoking in his harangues. If you had an appointment with him to discuss rehearsal dates, you would as likely as not be regaled with an ardent religious discourse. On his desk were two telephones. If the right-hand one rang, he would pick up the left-hand one and say: 'Just a moment, the other telephone's ringing,' then pick up the right-hand one, still holding the left-hand one to his ear, and say 'Hang on for a moment, I've got someone on the other line'; then he would return to the left-hand one and say 'All right, the caller on the other line's not there', and slam the right-hand receiver down.

Hilbert wanted to renovate the entire Mozart repertoire, but things went against him. *Die Zauberflöte,* of which Karajan had given a break-neck performance at the re-opening of the Theater an der Wien, was a particularly pathetic victim of the transfer to the Opera House in September 1965. The new *Entführung* in October 1965 was interrupted by shouts of 'poor Mozart', and even the incomparable Fritz Wunderlich was unable to save it. Günther Rennert's charming production of *Così fan tutte* in the Landestheater at the 1960 Salzburg Festival was a complete flop when it was transferred to Vienna and sung in German, despite the efforts of Karl Böhm and a brilliant cast (Güden, Ludwig, Sciutti, Kmentt, Berry, Dönch). *Figaro* in 1967 was one of Leopold Lindtberg's more controversial productions, and *Don Giovanni* in 1967, in an equally controversial production by Otto Schenk, was greeted with booing. Hilbert's idea of singing

Karl Dönch is the most famous Beckmesser today both at the Vienna Opera and at the Metropolitan. The Doctor in 'Wozzeck' which he has been singing in Vienna since 1952, is also one of his brilliant parts in both houses. (Caricature by Winnie Jakob.)

Italian operas in German started off with *The Barber of Seville* in 1966, and the very first words were drowned in a chorus of protest: 'Rossini in German? A disgrace.'

Hilbert engaged the producer Wieland Wagner, whose ideas had stirred up a great deal of controversy among audiences and critics alike. In principle there is no objection to vagaries of fashion — mini-skirts one year, maxi-skirts the next. Unfortunately, theatrical productions last somewhat longer. Was it really necessary for Wieland Wagner to murder four masterpieces so diabolically that anyone in the audience using ear-plugs would have been unable to identify them? In May 1965 there was actually applause for his *Lohengrin*, that in Act One without a spark of animation plodded on like an oratorio to its leaden-footed ending before a kind of blue-stained

Leonard Bernstein (above) made his début with 'Falstaff' in 1966 in the production by Luchino Visconti. Maestro Argeo Quadri is in charge of the Italian repertoire both at the Vienna Opera and at the Volksoper. (Caricatures: Winnie Jakob.)

Heinz Wallberg, General Director of Music in Wiesbaden and repertoire conductor in Vienna. (Caricature by Winnie Jakob.)

Robert Stolz at 83 years of age took over 'Fledermaus' after Herbert von Karajan. (Caricature by Winnie Jakob.)

glass window scenery. In Act Two the audience is supposed to see 'the door of the Minster' on the right. In Wieland Wagner's production the audience looked in vain: he had had the quaint idea of imagining the Minster to be the auditorium, so that the wedding-procession moves towards the front of the stage until the curtain (the threshold of the Minster) falls just before the procession reaches the footlights! One of the climaxes of this Act is Ortrud's invocation of heathen gods. Richard Wagner directs that it must be sung on the steps of the Minster (the last throes of paganism's resistance to Christianity). The older generation are used to comparing what they see on the stage with what they know is authentic; the younger generation are unable to defend themselves against such desecrations of what Richard Wagner in-

tended. 'Schreckliches wird geschehen' ('Something terrible is going to happen') warns the Page in *Salome*, and even this is a euphemism for Wieland Wagner's November 1965 production. To start with there was no moon, and the action seemed to be taking place in some huge sewer littered with slabs of rock and rubbish-bins, and the audience had to sit the whole unsavoury business out until Anja Silja as Salome, in blue jeans and a bikini, put an end to it with a blood-curdling shriek as she was being impaled by the executioner. In *Elektra* in December 1965 Karl Böhm's wonderful conducting and the superb performances of Regine Resnik (Klytaemnestra), Birgit Nilsson (Elektra) and Leonie Rysanek (Chrysothemis) managed to save something from the wreck of a production that might well have been ultra-modern two generations ago. Toward the end, for instance, Chrysothemis bawled her cry of 'Orestes' straight into her brother's face long after he should have taken to his heels to escape the Furies.

After Wieland Wagner's tragic death his widow, Gertrude, made her first and last attempt to follow in her late husband's footsteps in Vienna in 1967 with an unintentionally hilarious copy of the Bayreuth production of *Der Fliegende Holländer*. The audience responded with booing, catcalls and laughter, in accordance with the old Teutonic practice of visiting one person's sins (Gertrude's) upon the whole family, Richard and all.

Hilbert was a daemonic military commander who unfortunately knew little about strategy. His one obsession was that the position must be held to the last man (the words sound familiar!). So he held it, and the last man was himself. He was indeed a 'remarkable case'. He was quite incapable of listening to what the other person was saying, yet suggestions one had put to him often cropped up later as his own. He hardly ever attended auditions or listened to a new work being played over; but when he did, he often hit the nail on the head in a matter of seconds. His reactions were instantaneous. If he wanted to speak to someone he would manage to get hold of him by hook or by crook even if the victim was on a sleigh-tour in the Arctic.

Hilbert was the first legal official to be Director of the Vienna Opera, yet he was the most anti-juridical Director in the Opera's history. He was a past-master in the art of not honouring contracts if it was in the Opera's interest (as he conceived it) to break them.

He positively adored his singers, even to the extent of congratulating Elisabeth on a superb performance in *Tannhäuser* in the interval after the first act. If he needed a certain artist, the singer in question would (much to his own surprise) be paid a fee far in excess of what he had asked. Another of Hilbert's eccentric methods of raising a singer's fee without being asked to was to guarantee him or her a relatively large number of appearances at an agreed fee, then inform him orally that

'Ich bin nicht müde, Tetrarch.'
Anja Silja as Salome. (Caricature by Winnie Jakob.)

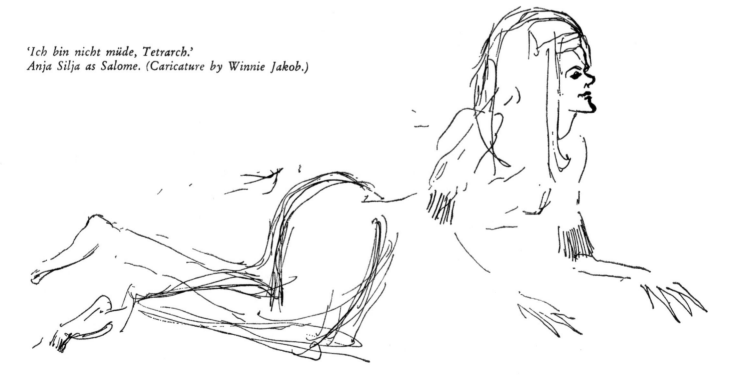

Christa Ludwig (above in a caricature as Dorabella) began as Cherubino in Vienna in 1955 and went on to Carmen, but also to Fidelio, Ariadne and to Marie in 'Wozzeck'. In 1968 she was the Marschallin in 'Rosenkavalier' under Leonard Bernstein, who accompanied Christa and her husband Walter Berry (who sang Ochs) at a memorable concert of Mahler songs in the Konzerthaus. (Caricature by Winnie Jakob.)

there was no need for him to appear so often, and eventually pay him the difference.

By 1967 Press attacks were almost continuous. At the same time Hilbert's health was deteriorating dramatically from one day to the next. Complete chaos seemed inevitable. To the new head of the State Theatres Administration, Erwin Thalhammer, fell the thankless task of trying to impress upon Hilbert the advisability of resigning of his own accord. Seemingly at death's door, Hilbert accompanied his beloved State Opera on its tour to the World Exhibition in Montreal in the summer of 1967. In his macabre race against death Hilbert had one last hurdle to negotiate, to make sure that his third wife Gretl, to whom he was devoted, was properly provided for. The grotesque tangle of his matrimonial affairs was paraded for all to enjoy. He married his first wife in church, then married his second in a registry office, and not in church, before the Vatican had annulled his first marriage. Finally, he married Frau Gretl in church, but not at a registry office, before he was divorced from his second. A lovely case for budding lawyers to get their teeth into! Not until Hilbert had secured the payment of his Director's salary to Frau Gretl up to the date his contract expired in 1970 did he sign a form of resignation in January 1968 with effect from the first of February. Having done so, he got into his Government chauffeur-driven car outside his house in Penzing, and fell back dead.

One particularly tragic element in the Hilbert story is that most people refused to give him the personal credit for the many brilliant successes he could point to. They just refused to believe he had it in him. For example: Hilbert appointed as head producer a Viennese of genius from the younger generation, Otto Schenk. I am very proud of the fact that it was on my suggestion that my good friend Otto put on his first production at the Volksoper during Salmhofer's term. Hilbert was Intendant of the Vienna Festival at the time, and shortly afterwards Schenk brought him two sensational successes with his productions of *Lulu* and *Dantons Tod* at the Theater an der Wien.

Schenk's productions at the Vienna Opera were of

world stature: *Jenufa* with Sena Jurinac (1964); *The Rake's Progress* with Anneliese Rothenberger, Eberhard Wächter and Waldemar Kmentt (1965); *Carmen* with Christa Ludwig (1966, and how marvellously she put over the Habañera as a chanson); *Tales of Hoffmann* (1966) with Anja Silja in all four female leads (and particularly effective as the 'dead-pan' doll with a huge blue bow), Waldemar Kmentt, and Otto Wiener with a wonderfully realistic limp.

Schenk's secret is something that cannot be imitated: he strikes up a close friendship with the singers he is working with, studies their behaviour in private life, and lets them act on the stage as they would in real life.

Hilbert was also responsible for one of the greatest sensations in the Vienna Opera's history, the visit of Leonard Bernstein in 1966. True, the idea was first mooted by the Vienna Philharmonic, and the negotiations were conducted by the orchestra's manager Helmut Wobisch. With his phenomenal *Falstaff* Bernstein became the idol of the Viennese public in record time. And Hilbert, who was always preaching the virtues of ensemble, had to admit that Luchino Visconti's lavish production with predominantly Italian singers was the greatest single event during his term in office. The following year Bernstein returned to the Vienna Opera to give a memorable performance of Mahler's Second Symphony with the Vienna Philharmonic Orchestra.

Hilbert also took two contemporary works into the repertoire: *Katerina Ismailova* (1965) in the presence of Schostakovitch himself, and Gottfried von Einem's *Dantons Tod* (1967) produced by Harry Buckwitz and with a brilliant performance by Eberhard Wächter. In 1967 August Everding made his bow as a Wagner producer with a *Tristan* in which Tristan was sung by Jess Thomas, and in 1964 *Palestrina* was Hans Hotter's first production in Vienna, and the late Fritz Wunderlich's last brilliant rôle.

During Karajan's time there had been many brilliant premières and many mediocre repertoire performances; under Hilbert many of the premières misfired, but some of the repertoire performances were marvellous. It is also to Hilbert's credit that he introduced to Vienna Nicolai

Senior producer at the Vienna Opera, sub-tenant on television, producer at the 'Met', ten times sold out 'Humorist on the Naschmarkt' in the Konzerthaus, Salzburg Festival's Thisbe and partner in night-long arguments on the sense and non-sense of opera — mio Otto! (Caricature by Winnie Jakob.)

Ghiaurov, perhaps the greatest living bass, and discovered Jeanette Pilou at a casual audition.

But all to no avail. Whenever anything went wrong it was laid at Hilbert's door, and whenever things went right it was a proof that the Vienna Opera could rise above anything.

Perhaps one day it will be possible to write the history of the Vienna Opera in *Fledermaus* gags. At all events Erich Kunz hit the nail on the head when he said: 'Not every Director is a Karajan — and not every Karajan is a Director.'

Our Wishes: For Him and For Ourselves

Dr. Heinrich Reif-Gintl
Director of the State Opera
Since 1968

28 March 1969, midnight

I can still hear the hissing and booing with which a large part of the audience received the producer Luchino Visconti when he appeared before the curtain tonight after the première of Verdi's 'Simone Boccanegra'. Bare, cold walls with no Old Genoa, no fight between the patricians and plebeians, masks reminding one of astronauts. A heated discussion broke out during the interval because some people thought it very modern. An American producer declared: 'I like it, because it doesn't look like an opera.' Why, may I ask, should an opera not look like an opera?

The new Director of the Vienna Opera is Heinrich Reif-Gintl, and we, the older generation of opera-goers, give him a large starting capital of trust and confidence. Apart from Schalk, he is the only other Director to have worked his way up in the House. In 1923 he began working in the Intendant's department, in 1927 Schalk arranged a transfer from what he called the 'General-Dillettanz' to Administrative Secretary in the Opera. 'Can you tell the difference between a major key and a door key?' asked Schalk by way of an entry examination, which Reif-Gintl passed without difficulty; he is not only a lawyer but also plays the violin, viola and horn. He served under eight Directors, became Hilbert's Vice-Director, in 1968 acting Director, and in 1969 his appointment was confirmed.

Reif-Gintl knows and loves the Opera and understands his métier. His first appointment was generally welcomed: he gave Horst Stein, Director-General of Music in Mannheim, who made a name in Vienna as a conductor of Wagner, the title of 'First Conductor' — an innovation at the Vienna Opera — with a contract that calls for his presence in the house for seven months of the year.

During 1968, Reif-Gintl's year as acting Director, the budget allowed for very few premières: apart from the evening of ballet with *Daphnis and Chloe* and *Sacre du Printemps* (choreography: Vaslav Orlikovsky) there were three operas already programmed by Hilbert. In March, to begin with, there was the long-delayed Viennese première of *Die schweigsame Frau* by Richard Strauss, in the production by Hans Hotter with Mimi Coertse, Renate Holm und Oskar Czerwenka, and with Silvio Varviso as conductor. The new *Rosenkavalier* was put on in April under the unorthodox and imaginative direction of Leonard Bernstein.

At that time the maestro from Boston was commuting between his *Rosenkavalier*, the 'Atrium' discotheque, his concert with the Philharmonic Orchestra and my production of *West Side Story* in the Volksoper. He told us how much he would have liked to conduct *The Queen of Sheba* in Vienna. What a pity that this opportunity — it would have been a historic occasion — was missed: it is the most modern artists who will bring about a revival of the one-time popular repertoire operas, not the older die-hards who feel so up-to-date when (usually without knowing them) they despise Goldmark, Meyerbeer and Bellini as old-fashioned. Moreover, of late we can once again boast of genuine grand opera voices in our own ensemble and among the regular guest artists.

Rosenkavalier under 'Lennie' re-created a thoroughly international Baroque Vienna: Christa Ludwig from Berlin, Gwyneth Jones from Wales, the coloured singer Reri Grist. The Viennese were Walter Berry, Erich Kunz, Waldemar Kmentt and, as producer, Otto Schenk. Finally, in December, there followed the tremendous Schenk production of *Lulu* by Alban Berg under Böhm, with Anja Silja in the greatest rôle of her life.

We expect a great deal from Heinrich Reif-Gintl. I give him my most heartfelt good wishes.

And herewith I take my leave. I came to love my work on the Vienna Opera, because in the course of it I was able to live my whole life over again.

'Everybody has something of the dancer in him', says Rudolf von Laban, but whether every opera connoisseur has something of the ballet connoisseur in him is quite another matter. At ballet performances I have always been an 'interested' spectator, and I can remember some wonderful evenings of ballet. I have also enjoyed reading articles on ballet (provided they were not too technical) and talking to enthusiasts to whom ballet means as much as opera does to me.

Ballet came to Austria from northern Italy towards the end of the sixteenth century and was taken up by the Imperial Court because it symbolised power and glory. The Emperor Leopold I, himself an amateur composer and conductor, was the real founder of what is now the Vienna State Opera Ballet. In order to be one of the Court dancers it was necessary to have been trained at the Paris Académie de Danse, which was the Mecca of the classical ballet, to come from a good family, and to be well-connected. Here as elsewhere the supremacy of the male sex was absolute. Women had to wait until the late seventeenth century before being admitted as dancers, but once they were admitted they soon caught up with their male rivals, and by the nineteenth century it was the female dancers whose supremacy was absolute. It was only very recently that male dancers regained parity with their female colleagues.

In Baroque Vienna the professional dancer was given plenty to do. A good part of the programme at both the Imperial Theatres, the 'Ballhaus by the Burg' and the Kärntnertor Theatre, was devoted to ballet, and the company was directed by three of the most celebrated choreographers of their time, Franz Hilverding (who created the *ballet d'action*), Gasparo Angiolini and Jean Georges Noverre. In next to no time Vienna was eighteenth century Europe's second centre of ballet after Paris. A Viennese *corps de ballet* was trained, but the choreographers and solo dancers were invariably foreigners.

The culmination of Viennese Baroque ballet was the *Schau- und Maschinenballett*, an elaborate form of entertainment in which the dancers were subordinated to lavish spectacle and the exploitation of ingenious stage devices. It was Angiolini who discovered the potentiality of the dance as an expression of individuality, and the human being as a portrayer of feelings, and it was in collaboration with this great reformer of ballet that Gluck, the great reformer of opera, created the first tragic ballet, *Don Juan*.

Jean Georges Noverre was summoned to Vienna by the Empress Maria Theresia and at once asked for permission 'to destroy all the masks, burn all the wigs, and tear up all the crinolines'. What he aspired to was an expression of human thoughts and emotions through the medium of the dance. In 1767 he founded a 'school of stage-dancing' for the training of his dancers. The school still exists, only in a somewhat different form: it is now directly associated with the Opera, and only dancers who have attended it are accepted by the State Opera Ballet.

In the nineteenth century the Opera Ballet had a home of its own at the Kärntnertor Theatre, where around the turn of the century the ballet-master was the celebrated Salvatore Vigano of Naples. His wife, a Viennese, was the first to dance in flesh-coloured tights without a voluminous costume and crinoline. It was for Vigano and his wife that Beethoven wrote his *Geschöpfe des Prometheus* (1801). It was not long before the ballet too felt the impact of romanticism. The stage positively teemed with water-sprites, spirits of the air, forest-elves, and the like all circling round the ballerinas, sylphs of gossamer delicacy in transparent tulle skirts and the very latest flat satin shoes with padded toes, gliding ethereally through the moonlight. Everything was subordinated to the glorification of the ballerina. Even her male partner was little more than just an extra leg.

The epitome of this romantic style was the young Italian dancer Maria Taglioni. She was born in Stockholm, started her career at the Kärntnertor Theatre, and was at the top of the tree until she was challenged by a Viennese dancer named Fanny Elssler.

Fanny Elssler was a typical suburban Viennese girl, from Gumpendorf to be precise. Her father was Haydn's valet and copyist and her mother used to carry Fanny to the ballet school in a basket on her back, so that she should not hurt her precious feet on the rough cobbles. The lovely little blue-eyed girl became the incarnation of unbounded sensuality, and her dancing and her private life made her one of the most talked-of women in Europe. At the age of sixteen she had presented an Italian duke with a child, and two years later she became the mistress of old Friedrich von Gentz. She revolutionised the art of dancing, was the first to imbue it with a dramatic element, and was the pioneer of modern mime.

In every way she had her feet more firmly on the ground than Maria Taglioni, which was why she was able to make certain folk-dances 'respectable'. Her Cachucha (a wild dance from Spanish harbour taverns) in Gide's ballet *Der hinkende Teufel* took audiences by storm all over Europe, and later in America too. After seeing her dance, the German writer Friedrich Rückert wrote: 'What are we going to do when we are angels in heaven if there is such dancing here on earth?' And she was actually awarded the honorary degree of 'Doctor of Dancing' by Oxford University.

In 1851 she retired from the stage, and once again it was a question of having recourse to foreigners for the leading positions in the Opera Ballet. The last Prima Ballerina at the Kärntnertor Theatre was Claudine Couqui of Milan; Richard Wagner once interrupted a rehearsal of *Tristan* to pay her a compliment.

The revolution of 1848 entailed drastic economies, but it's an ill wind that blows no good, and one of its effects was a revolution against the star cult, followed by the cultivation of an ensemble spirit, its chief apostle being the brother of one of the stars, Paul Taglioni.

For the time being the move into the new Opera House in 1869 put paid to efforts to build up a distinctive Viennese ballet style. The first ballet programme in the new house on the sixteenth of June 1869 was a creation by the outstandingly successful two-man team of Paul Taglioni (libretto) and Paul Ludwig Hertel (music) about the last King of the Assyrians, *Sardanapalus*.

The Taglioni-Hertel partnership turned out ballets that went back to the days of the old elaborate *Maschinenballets*. Heaven, Earth and Hell; the world of spirits and demons and the world we live in were presented with a fantastic wealth of scenery and costumes. Never for an instant was the eye left unfeasted.

During the first two years in the new house the partnership produced three such spectacles: *Flick und Flock, Satanella* and a full-scale ballet named *Fantasca* about the abduction and rescue of a Spanish grandee's daughter.

All these ballets were immensely popular, and commanded a place in the repertoire right up till 1900, by which time *Sardanapalus* had enjoyed one hundred, *Satanella* seventy-eight, and *Fantasca* no fewer than 154 performances.

Another particular favourite was *Excelsior,* with music by Romualdo Marenco and a libretto by the well-known dancer and choreographer Luigi Manzotti. It presented portrayals of some of mankind's most important discoveries, with 'Englightenment' competing with 'Ignorance' for the souls of the human race. This was the sort of ballet that thrilled two whole generations of ballet fans, and it ran for no fewer than 329 performances.

Ballets destined for entertainment pure and simple had completely ousted the more refined romantic ballets, and there was no demand for elves and nymphs in plain white tulle. No wonder that between 1869 and 1945 Adolphe Adam's *Giselle,* for instance, one of the most exacting romantic ballets with a title-rôle that is one of the most dreaded tests of a ballerina's quality, was staged only fourteen times.

The man who gave the Vienna Opera Ballet a new lease on life was the Viennese Josef Hassreiter. As balletmaster he succeeded in founding a sort of 'Viennese style', with the help of the composer Josef Bayer and the stage-designer Franz Gaul. One of their dancers was Berta Linda, who later became the wife of the painter Hans Makart. This trio produced a great number of highly successful ballets, all of which were overshadowed by a work which can still be seen today (and not only in Austria): Bayer's and Hassreiter's *Die Puppenfee*. No ballet has ever caused such a run on box-offices all over the world. And the underlying idea is so simple, just a toyshop in which the dolls and toys suddenly come to life and introduce themselves to the audience with a series of dances. Between its first performance in 1888 and the end of World War II in 1945, it was presented at the Vienna Opera alone no fewer than 700 times; and in

1958, only three years after the re-opening of the Opera House, it was revived in a new production. Again and again there would be the familiar poster outside the Opera:'... followed by *Die Puppenfee*.' Even Giuseppe Verdi had to put up with the first performance of *Falstaff* at the Milan Scala in 1893 being followed by *La fata delle bambole*.

Gustav Mahler was not particularly interested in ballet, but he did discover the Wiesenthal sisters, who are sure of their place in the history of the ballet for their interpretations of Viennese waltzes.

Hassreiter was the first ballet-master to fill all the leading positions in the *corps de ballet* with products of the Opera's own ballet-school. Until his time the Prima Ballerina had always been a foreigner, usually an Italian; but this tradition was finally broken by the appointment of Else von Strohlendorf, the first genuine Viennese product of the Opera's ballet-school to be awarded the title of Prima Ballerina. Since then this coveted distinction has been accorded only to Gusti Pichler, Julia Drapal, and Edeltraud Brexner.

Other successful and very popular ballets by Josef Bayer were *Sonne und Erde* and *Rouge et Noir*, the latter illustrating the experiences of a young man of good family who becomes a compulsive gambler. *Sonne und Erde*, a lavish spectacle, ran until 1927 (363 performances in nearly forty years).

Another elaborately staged ballet was *Die goldene Märchenwelt*, 'a fantastic ballet-mime in ten scenes and an introduction', introducing Little Red Riding-hood, Snow-White, the Sleeping Beauty and a number of other well-known figures from Grimm's fairy-tales. It certainly gave the whole *corps de ballet* plenty of scope to show what they could do and included some agreeable music by Heinrich Berté, who for his part in composing *Das Dreimäderlhaus* (the Viennese original of *Lilac Time*) was later nicknamed 'Schu-berté'.

The end of World War I and the general dislocation of values that followed led to a temporary decline in the State Opera Ballet's standing. It may well be that the dance needs a stable social background more than any other form of art. In Vienna, the renaissance of classical ballet brought about by Diaghilev and his 'Ballets Russes' made little impact. And this in spite of visits during the Weingartner and Gregor eras, before the end of the Monarchy, of some of the legendary stars of the equally legendary Marinsky Theatre of St. Petersburg — Anna Pavlova, Mathilde Kchesinska, Tamara Karsavina, Vaclav Nijinsky. The last time Diaghilev and his 'Ballets Russes' came to Vienna was in 1927, during Schalk's term.

The first sign of a wind of change to infuse some life into the Vienna Opera's ailing ballet was when, during the second half of his period as Director, Richard Strauss summoned from Berlin the very versatile dancer and choreographer Heinrich Kröller, who had done a lot for classical ballet in Germany. But his efforts to inject new life into the Vienna Ballet were short-lived: lack of funds completely ruled out any large-scale project. Still, Kröller was able to make his contribution to the annals of Viennese ballet with the Vienna première of Strauss's ballet *Josephslegende*, and with the world première of *Schlagobers* (both these ballets have been discussed in the chapter on the Strauss-Schalk era). As Joseph, Willy Fränzl fully lived up to his reputation, and Gutheil-Schoder mimed the part of Potiphar's wife. In *Schlagobers* the stars were Fränzl, Gusti Pichler and Tilly Losch.

The period between the two World Wars was notable more for the quality of the star performers than for the standard of the works they danced in, none of which enjoyed more than a modest success except three lovely ballets with music by Franz Salmhofer: *Das lockende Phantom* starring Tilly Losch, who after leaving Vienna made a name for herself in Hollywood; *Der Taugenichts in Wien* (1930) after Eichendorff, with Grete Wiesenthal; and *Österreichische Bauernhochzeit* (1934) with choreography by Margarete Wallmann. Other prominent dancers at this time were Hedy Pfundmayr, who succeeded Gutheil-Schoder as Potiphar's wife; Riki Raab; and Adele Krausenecker. The solo dancers were Willy Fränzl and Tony Birkmeyer, both of whom were descended from dancers who had been associated with the Opera for many years.

I have a very large family. The reason I have never got married is that no woman could bear having to live with all my favourite Lohengrins and Mimis, Papagenos and Klytemnaestras. They are all my cousins, brothers, aunts and nephews — my family in fact.

In my childhood, operatic stars were remote and unapproachable beings, but this changed abruptly in 1925 as a distant (but genuine) aunt invited Lotte Lehmann to my distant uncle's birthday party, whereupon the uncle promptly got a divorce and married Lotte Lehmann. My relatives were all against her, but I flouted their opposition and took her side, and from then on my family has dominated my existence.

In 1936 Jan Kiepura asked me to go on a world tour with him as his private secretary. During his triumphs at the New York 'Met' and in Paris I was waiting in the wings, and he would dictate letters on the beach at Nice or in a sugar plantation in the middle of Cuba. I was very fond of him and am very proud of the photograph with the dedication: 'Whenever you mention the word *family*, think of us.' In Hollywood I visited Maria Jeritza and later spent a month or two at her villa in New Jersey. At the open-air opera in the Zoological Gardens in Cincinnati I stood behind Jarmila Novotna: the music was sometimes drowned by the roaring of the lions. Although I am a teetotaller I sacrificed my principles and went to a Heuriger with Ernst Marboe and Maria Callas after a Vienna performance of *Lucia di Lammermoor*. In Beirut I acted as compère to a recital by Gerda Scheyrer, and when Ruthilde Boesch was appearing in my show in Texas I was able to introduce her to her future husband Wilhelm Loibner, who was on the temporary staff of Austin University at the time. I have done a TV show with Regina Resnik and arranged recording sessions with Paul Schöffler. With Richard Tauber I shared a nostalgic exile in London during the last year of the war, and I had the privilege of introducing Anneliese Rothenberger to the Shah of Persia during an interval at a performance of *Fledermaus* in which she was a brilliant Adele. Emmy Loose's husband was my throat-doctor (in my profession I have to do a lot of talking) and was absolutely invaluable. I am not a gambler, but at the Trieste races Anna Moffo said why didn't I put something on her horse; without batting an eyelid I put a hundred thousand lire or so on the wretched animal and lost the lot.

I wonder how many times the family has foregathered at Otto Schenk's place: Eberhard Wächter, Evelyn Lear, Thomas Stewart, Gundula Janowitz, Lucia Popp, Heinz Holecek; or have been guests of Rita Streich, Mimi Coertse, or Renate Holm? Then there was the marvellous party after the first night of Otto Schenk's *Tosca* at the New York 'Met' in 1968 with Birgit Nilsson and Franco Corelli; and an unforgettable evening with Leonard Bernstein at Christa Ludwig's and Walter Berry's villa at Klosterneuburg after Bernstein had conducted *Der Rosenkavalier*.

I was recently engaged on a long and fruitless search for somewhere to live. One day I came upon a villa in which for some strange reason I immediately felt at home. Was it the view, the position, or the air? Anyway, I moved in, and it was only later that I found out that my immediate neighbours include Hilde Zadek, Eberhard Wächter, Gwyneth Jones and Lotte Rysanek!

I have so many cherished memories of my family, memories that I can revive merely by glancing through the many family albums I have accumulated. This is one of them.

Franz von Dingelstedt
(1867—1870)

Johann Herbeck
(1870—1875)

Franz Jauner
(1875—1880)

Wilhelm Jahn
(1881—1897)

Gustav Mahler
(1897—1907)

Felix von Weingartner
(1908—1911/1934—1936)

Hans Gregor
(1911—1918)

Richard Strauss
(1919—1924)

Franz Schalk
(1918—1929)

Clemens Krauss
(1929—1934)

Erwin Kerber
(1936—1940)

Heinrich Strohm
(1940—1941)

Ernst August Schneider
(1942—1943)

Karl Böhm
(1943—1945/1954—1956)

Franz Salmhofer
(Vienna Opera in the Theater
an der Wien 1945—1955)

Hermann Juch
(Vienna Opera in the Volksoper
1946—1955)

Herbert von Karajan
(1956—1964)

Egon Hilbert
(1964—1968)

Heinrich Reif-Gintl
(1968—   )

Theodor Reichmann (Wotan)   Amalie Materna (Brünnhilde)   Hermann Winkelmann (Dalibor)   Emil Scaria (Wotan)

Ernest van Dyck (Des Grieux)   Marie Renard (Carmen)   Gustav Walter (as Romeo in *Roméo et Juliette* by Gounod)   Bertha Ehnn (Margarethe)

Antonie Schläger (as Valentine in Meyerbeer's *Les Huguénots*)   Paula Mark (Nedda)   Marie Wilt (in the title rôle of Donizetti's *Lucrezia Borgia*)   Wilhelm Hesch (Falstaff)

Leo Slezak (Tannhäuser)

Erik Schmedes (Evangelimann)

Adelina Patti (private photograph)

Selma Kurz (Mignon)

Lucille Marcel (Elektra)

Anna Mildenburg (Klytemnaestra)

Marie Gutheil-Schoder (as Esmeralda in *Notre Dame* by Franz Schmidt)

Lucie Weidt (as Elisabeth in *Tannhäuser*)

Leopold Demuth (Don Juan)

Pauline Lucca (private photograph)

Rosa Papier (Sieglinde)

Friedrich Weidemann (Wotan)

Alfred Piccaver
(André Chénier)

Lotte Lehmann
(in *Manon* by Massenet)

Richard Tauber (Don José)

Jarmila Novotna (as Marie in
The Bartered Bride)

Emil Schipper (Gunther)

Maria Olczewska
(private photograph)

Alfred Jerger (Jonny)

Rosette Anday (Carmen)

Richard Mayr (Ochs)

Viorica Ursuleac (Marschallin)

Josef von Manowarda (Philipp)

Gertrude Rünger (as the Nurse
in *Die Frau ohne Schatten*)

Koloman von Pataky
(private photograph)

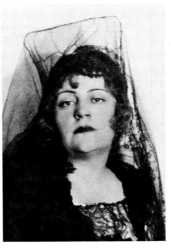

Maria Nemeth (Donna Anna)

Karl Hammes (as Charles
Gérard in *André Chénier*)

Margit Schenker-Angerer
(Octavian)

Elisabeth Schumann
(private photograph)

Lotte Schöne (Sophie)

Marie Gerhart
(private photograph)

Adele Kern
(private photograph)

Alexander Sved (as Wilhelm
Tell in the Volksoper)

Vera Schwarz (as Renate in
Dame in Traum
by Franz Salmhofer)

Fritz Krenn (Kaspar)

Elena Nicolaidi (Azucena)

Richard Schubert (Loge)

Laurenz Hofer
(private photograph)

Josef Kalenberg (as Siegfried
in *Götterdämmerung*)

Ella Flesch
(private photograph

Max Lorenz (Aegisthus)

Erich Zimmermann (David)

Franz Völker (as Sou-Chong
in *The Land of Smiles*)

Gunnar Graarud (as Menelas
in *Die ägyptische Helena*)

Set Svanholm (as Siegfried in
Götterdämmerung)

Todor Mazaroff (as Alfredo in
Traviata)

Helge Roswaenge (Don José)

Trajan Grosavescu (Don José)

Helene Wildbrunn (Fricka)

Rose Pauly (Marie in *Wozzeck*)

Wilhelm Rode (Doktor Mirakel)

Hermine Kittel (Brangäne)

Kerstin Thorborg (private photograph)

Margit Bokor (Alice Ford)

Georg Maikl (Don Ottavio)

Wanda Achsel-Clemens (Alice Ford)

Bella Paalen (private photograph)

Hermann Wiedemann (Beckmesser)

Hermann Gallos (as Andres in *Wozzeck*)

Hans Duhan (private photograph)

Enrico Caruso
(as the Duke in *Rigoletto*)

Titta Ruffo (private
photograph)

Mattia Battistini
(private photograph)

Feodor Chaliapin
(Boris Godunov)

Beniamino Gigli (Radames)

Aureliano Pertile
(private photograph)

Maria Callas
(private photograph)

Ezio Pinza (Figaro)

Kirsten Flagstad
(private photograph)

Lauritz Melchior (Tannhäuser)

Toti dal Monte
(private photograph)

Jussi Björling (private
photograph)

Julius Patzak (Palestrina)

Herbert Alsen (Commendatore)

Maria Cebotari (Frau Fluth)

Elisabeth Höngen (Azucena)

Rudolf Schock (as Bacchus in *Ariadne*)

Christl Goltz (Dyer's Wife)

George London (Eugene Onegin)

William Wernigk (as Missaïl in *Boris Godunov*)

Carla Martinis (as Amelia in *Un ballo in maschera*)

Hilde Rössel-Majdan (as Meg Page in *Falstaff*)

Hans Braun (as John Sorel in Gian-Carlo Menotti's *The Consul*)

Peter Klein (Mime)

Sena Jurinac (Octavian)

Irmgard Seefried (as the
Composer in *Ariadne*)

Wilma Lipp (Zerbinetta)

Hilde Güden (Zerbinetta)

Hilde Zadek (as Magda in
The Consul
by Gian-Carlo Menotti)

Esther Réthy (as Lisa in
The Land of Smiles)

Walter Berry (Papageno)

Christa Ludwig (Dorabella)

Hanni Steffek (as Christine in
Intermezzo)

Dagmar Hermann
(as Nancy in *Martha*)

Renate Holm (Papagena)

Gerda Scheyrer (as Gabriele
in *Wiener Blut*
in the Volksoper)

James King (Erik)

Astrid Varnay (Herodias)

Karl Kamann (as Jack Rance
in *Fanciulla del West*)

Emmy Loose (Blondchen)

Anton Dermota (Des Grieux)

Ljuba Welitsch
(in Massenet's *Manon*)

Ludwig Weber (as Timur in
Turandot)

Martha Mödl (Eboli)

Jeannette Pilou (Micaela)

Maria Reining (as Lisa in
The Land of Smiles)

Anni Konetzni (Marschallin)

Hilde Konetzni (Marschallin)

Erich Kunz (Papageno)

Lisa della Casa (Donna Anna)

Paul Schöffler (Don Pizarro)

Hans Hotter
(as Borromeo in *Palestrina*)

Gerhard Stolze (as Nero in
Monteverdi's
L'incoronazione di Poppea)

Eberhard Wächter (Count Luna)

Gottlob Frick (King Mark)

Otto Wiener
(as La Roche in *Capriccio*)

Biserka Cvejic (as Olga in
Eugene Onegin)

Walter Kreppel (Rocco)

Otto Edelmann (Holländer)

Murray Dickie (as Valzacchi
in *Rosenkavalier*)

Giuseppe di Stefano (as Alvaro in *La forza del destino*)

Franco Corelli (André Chénier)

Giulietta Simionato (as Ulrica in *Un ballo in maschera*)

Nikolai Ghiaurov (Mephisto)

Cesare Siepi (Philipp)

Renata Tebaldi (Aida)

Antonietta Stella (Tosca)

Tito Gobbi (Scarpia)

James MacCracken (Otello)

Birgit Nilsson (Elektra)

Anja Silja (Salome)

Wolfgang Windgassen (Tristan)

Oskar Czerwenka (Kezal)

Regina Resnik (as Mrs. Quickly in *Falstaff*)

Rita Streich (Susanna)

Karl Dönch (as Fra Melitone in *La forza del destino*)

Mimi Coertse (as Aminta in *Die schweigsame Frau*)

Gundula Janowitz (Fiordiligi)

Lotte Rysanek (as Hanna Glawari in the *Merry Widow* in the Volksoper)

Leonie Rysanek (as the Empress in *Die Frau ohne Schatten*)

Anneliese Rothenberger (Mimi)

Fritz Wunderlich (Palestrina)

Lucia Popp (Queen of the Night)

Waldemar Kmentt (Erik)

Willy Fränzl, now dignified with the title of Professor, still makes a contribution to the State Opera Ballet by training the dancers in the opening Polonaise and by supplying the choreography for the Ballet's waltz at the annual Opera Ball. For a time Fränzl and Birkmeyer were in charge of the company, and so for an even shorter time was Margarete Wallmann, who quickly became popular as an excellent dancer and later devised the admirable choreography for Bruno Walter's performance of Gluck's *Orfeo* in 1935. At performances in Germany Wallmann's choreography was superseded by Rosalia Chladek's, in which Julia Drapal made her début as one of the 'lost souls in Hades'.

The most important ballet première during the war was Werner Egk's *Joan von Zarissa*, starring Harald Kreutzberg. After the brief intermezzo of the well-known dancer and choreographer Helga Svedlund, Director Ernst August Schneider made the important acquisition of Erika Hanka as head of the Vienna State Opera Ballet.

Erika Hanka, an officer's daughter, was born in Croatia and trained in Vienna and in Germany, where she was a member of the celebrated Ballets Jooss. Next she moved to Düsseldorf, where her talent for choreography was discovered. By the time she arrived at Hamburg she was a ballet-mistress, and in 1941 she moved to Vienna.

What she found there was not particularly encouraging, owing to the decimation of the male dancers, many of whom were prisoners-of-war or wounded or on active service. Four years later the destruction of the Opera House robbed the Ballet of all its essential training and rehearsal rooms. By the time the war at last came to an end, training could only be resumed under the most austere conditions imaginable — unheated premises and wildly unreliable electricity supply, to name only two — in the cellars under the Theater an der Wien.

It is impossible to praise too highly Erika Hanka's achievement in fitting her company to tackle the modern repertoire in such a short space of time. In the immediate post-war years she staged ballets of the calibre of Stravinsky's *Petrouchka*, Mussorgsky-Ravel's *Pictures at an Exhibition*, Hindemith's *Nobilissima visione*, de Falla's *Three-cornered Hat*, and Rimsky-Korsakov's *Capriccio Espagnol*, ballets that had seldom or never been performed in Vienna before.

One of her really great achievements was a double-bill consisting of Gluck's *Don Juan* and Strauss's *Josephslegende*, the former danced by Lucia Bräuer, Arnold Jandosch and Erwin and Poldi Pokorny, and the latter by Carl Raimund as Joseph, Willy Fränzl as Potiphar and Julia Drapal as Potiphar's wife. Both ballets were superbly performed.

The first step towards a revival of the classical ballet was Delibes's *Coppélia* with Julia Drapal as Swanilda.

Looking back, one can only be amazed at Erika Hanka's almost incredible resolution and the amount of sheer hard work she got through. As well as supplying the interludes ballet in the operas at the Theater an der Wien and in the operas and operettas at the Volksoper, the *corps de ballet* had to present programmes of their own at the Theater an der Wien, and occasionally at the Volksoper too, for ten long years before the Opera House reopened. In every post-war season Erika Hanka had to provide choreography for one complete programme of ballet and for an average of five or six operas or operettas in two different theatres, not to mention her responsibility for the repertoire, for the daily training and rehearsal schedules, and especially for bringing on young talent. From 1946 on there was also the Ballet's commitment at the Bregenz Festival to be coped with. It was Erika Hanka who really brought the Vienna Opera Ballet back to life after World War II, and her lamentably premature death was an almost irreparable loss.

After Gusti Pichler's retirement in 1935 the title of Prima Ballerina was not filled until 1949, when it was awarded to Julia Drapal, an artist with a wonderful temperament, a great stage personality, intuitive acting ability and a gamut ranging from dramatic passion to Viennese humour (the latter as the shoemaker's apprentice in the ballet in *Der Zigeunerbaron* at the Volksoper, for instance, one of Erika Hanka's most fascinating choreographies; or as the little imp in *Höllische G'schichte* for

209

which Hanka also supplied the libretto to music by Johann Strauss). Its first performance at the Volksoper on the fourteenth of June 1949, the fiftieth anniversary of Johann Strauss's death, meant that the link with the 'Viennese style' of the Hassreiter-Bayer ballets had now been reforged.

There could be no better proof of Erika Hanka's vitality and versatility than her programme in the last five years before the Opera House re-opened. In December 1950 she offered a new production of Stravinsky's *Fire Bird* at the Theater an der Wien, together with the first performance of Theodor Berger's *Homerische Symphonie*. The production of the former was both subtle and exotic, with the costumes and Stefan Hlawa's scenery flaunting every possible fiery nuance. In *Homerische Symphonie*, Hlawa's prehistoric scenery was exciting and at the same time menacing, especially in the underworld scenes, with crowds of people dancing on a surface above which a huge extinct planet was suspended. The craters of its extinct volcanoes poised directly above the heads and uplifted arms of the dancers seemed to promise instant catastrophe, and the segment of the globe suspended amid grey hangings conveyed an impression of the vast invisible expanse of a celestial body long dead.

In *Fire Bird* the stars were Julia Drapal as the Firebird and Carl Raimund as Kashchei. With them was a young dancer making his début as the Prince, Willy Dirtl, of whom great things were expected. These expectations were amply fulfilled eighteen months later in Gottfried von Einem's *Rondo vom Goldenen Kalb,* with choreography by Erika Hanka, first at the Volksoper, then at the Theater an der Wien, and eventually at the 'new' Opera House. The cast also included Lucia Bräuer and Carl Raimund, and with Lisl Temple, Dirtl danced a marvellous *pas de deux*. In Rimsky-Korsakov's *Scheherezade* he was every bit a match for his illustrious partner, Julia Drapal, and the audience were in raptures over the almost incredible lightness, elegance and agility of his leaps.

Werner Egk followed up his wartime *Joan von Zarissa* with a ballet based on *Faust*, and entitled *Abraxas,* that Vienna saw on the twentieth of June 1953. This was perhaps the first postwar ballet of real significance, and at its first performance in Munich some of the love scenes caused such a scandal that the work had to be taken off after only five performances. In Vienna the performance passed off without incident. With Erwin Pokorny as Faust, Lucia Bräuer as Archisposa, Lisl Temple as Margarethe, Willy Dirtl as a tiger and Lucia Schwab as a snake, the performance was a great triumph for the State Opera Ballet, and from then on Edeltraud Brexner, who made her début as the female Mephistopheles 'Bellastriga', was obviously an aspirant to all the leading rôles.

The programme of the last ballet première (10 May 1954) before the re-opening of the Opera was Prokofiev's *Classical Symphony* with Margaret Bauer, Edeltraud Brexner and Willy Dirtl; Stravinsky's *Orpheus* with Erwin Pokorny, Margaret Bauer and Julia Drapal; Rossini's *La boutique fantasque* with Julia Drapal and Carl Raimund as can-can dancers; and Borodin's *Polovtsian Dances* with Julia Drapal, Lucia Bräuer and Willy Dirtl.

A year later the State Opera Ballet at long last was granted a privilege that in Baroque times was its bread and butter, so to speak; that of contributing to a festive occasion, in this case the ceremonies attending the signing of the Austrian State Treaty on the fifteenth of May 1955. Edeltraud Brexner and Willy Dirtl were to dance the 'black swan' *pas de deux* from Tchaikovsky's *Swan Lake* on an open-air stage outside Schönbrunn Palace in the presence of representatives of the four Allied Powers and the Austrian Government. The dress-rehearsal went splendidly but the actual performance never took place as the stage was under water following a torrential rain.

Three weeks later, on the sixth of June, Brexner and Dirtl received ample compensation for this disappointment: they danced the same *pas de deux*, only in Petipa's original choreography, in the Theater an der Wien. The applause rose to a crescendo as, in the Coda, Brexner executed the prescribed thirty-two *fouettés* at a breathtaking speed within the circumference of a man's hand (or so it seemed), and Willy Dirtl went through his leaps with a virtuosity that seemed to defy the laws of gravity.

The performance proved that now at last there was a real audience for ballet in Vienna, thanks to all the constructive pioneer work done by Erika Hanka. It also proved that after a lapse of twenty or thirty years Vienna could once again succumb to the fascination of classical ballet. Until now, the only opportunities of seeing good classical ballet in Vienna had been the occasional visits of the Marinsky Theatre Company.

It was with a view to including more classical ballet in the repertoire and to giving the ensemble a more thorough training in classical technique that in the previous year Erika Hanka had engaged the dancer and choreographer Gordon Hamilton, a native of Sydney, who had been a solo dancer with leading companies in London and Paris.

On the sixteenth of September 1955 the Ballet gave its last programme in the Vienna Opera's provisional headquarters at the Theater an der Wien. The programme consisted of the Divertissement from Delibes' *Sylvia*, Tchaikovsky's *Black Swan* and Rossini's *La boutique fantasque*. By the time the State Opera Ballet moved into the reconstructed Opera House it was well trained in all branches of the ballet repertoire, and the solo dancers had been reinforced by some highly promising new talent including (for a year or two) the American Richard Adama.

On the twenty-ninth of November 1955 it was the turn of the Ballet to make its contribution to the re-opening ceremonies. Adolphe Adam's romantic classical ballet *Giselle* with the original choreography by Jean Coralli, enchanted all who saw it. In the world première of Boris Blacher's *Der Mohr von Venedig*, a version of *Othello* with a libretto and choreography by Erika Hanka, the company showed that it was now sufficiently up-to-date to tackle contemporary ballets, and in the rôle of Othello, Willy Dirtl scored a triumphant success as an actor, quite apart from his dancing. The up-and-coming Christl Zimmerl made her début as Desdemona, and it was at once clear that here was a great ballerina in the making. Lucia Bräuer was Emilia, Richard Adama was Iago, and Edeltraud Brexner was Bianca.

At the première of *Giselle* the part of Giselle was danced by Margaret Bauer. At a repeat performance on the fourth of December this exacting part was danced with complete technical and natural assurance by a completely unknown and very young dancer named Erika Zlocha. Another new discovery.

Gordon Hamilton discharged his duties with characteristic Anglo-Saxon thoroughness, and the classical repertoire that had been neglected for so long was being continually expanded. 'Divertissements' were concocted out of the original choreographies of Tchaikovsky's *The Sleeping Beauty* and *Casse-Noisette*, containing *pas de deux* for Brexner and Adama and ample opportunities for talented rising stars such as Erika Zlocha, Dietlinde Klemisch, Karl Musil and Paul Vondrak to distinguish themselves. Other extracts included the *pas de trois* from Act One and the whole of Act Two of *Swan Lake*, the *pas de deux* from the last act of Minkus's ballet *Don Quixote* and a *pas de trois* from *Pasquita*, the latter in Balanchine's choreography. Other ballets taken into the repertoire for the first time were *Les Sylphides* to music by Chopin, and *Spectre de la rose* to Berlioz's orchestration of Weber's *Invitation to the Dance*. In addition, all the best programmes from the Theater an der Wien period were retained for presentation in the Opera House.

The year 1957 opened with some highly promising co-operation between Erika Hanka and the producer Günther Rennert, who on the tenth of March offered a fascinating production of Carl Orff's triptych *Carmina burana*, *Catulli carmina* and *Trionfo di Afrodite*. In the first of these, Brexner, Bräuer, Zlocha, Adama, Vondrak and the *corps de ballet* scored such a success that the work was retained in the repertoire for many years in its own right, without the other two.

In May the State Opera Ballet produced another programme consisting of *Joan von Zarissa*, with Willy Dirtl as Joan and Edeltraud Brexner as Isabeau, and the world première of Erika Hanka's *Hotel Sacher* to music by Hellmesberger arranged by Max Schönherr. Here at long last was a new ballet in the traditional 'Viennese' style. As an affected and wrought-up operatic diva Brexner had the audience roaring with laughter; Erika Zlocha was a sweet and charming Viennese flower girl; the uncommonly versatile Lucia Bräuer was the operatic diva's highly temperamental sister; while Willy Dirtl and Richard Adama vied with each other as a waiter and a smart young officer, respectively. Despite one or two changes in the cast, *Hotel Sacher* can still be relied upon to be a draw whenever it is put on.

From 1956 on there were annual 'Ballet Weeks', an institution that was particularly close to Erika Hanka's heart because they gave her company a chance to measure themselves against other international companies. In September 1956 the visitors were Georges Balanchine's New York City Ballet. Six years later this famous company paid Vienna a second visit, again in the autumn, but this time at the Theater an der Wien, though at the invitation of the Vienna State Opera. In November 1957 Vienna welcomed the 'Grand Ballet du Marquis de Cuevas' and Antonio with his Spanish Ballet. In 1958 it was the turn of the Georgian Ballet from the Soviet Union, and in November 1959 and March 1962 the Cuevas Ballet paid Vienna two further visits with programmes including the Helpman-Larrain full-length production of Tchaikovsky's *The Sleeping Beauty*. In 1960 the visitors were Maurice Béjart's 'Ballet du XXième Siècle' from the Brussels Théâtre Royal de la Monnaie, in 1962 the London Festival Ballet, and at the end of May 1965 the world-renowned Bolshoi Ballet from Moscow.

On the sixteenth of November 1957 Erika Hanka demonstrated once again, and for the last time, all her great qualities as a creator of modern ballet. During the 'Ballet Weeks' she staged an extremely individual production of Béla Bartók's *The Miraculous Mandarin*, with Willy Dirtl and Dietlinde Klemisch in the leading parts, and also created choreography for the world première of Gottfried von Einem's *Medusa*, which was a triumph for Christl Zimmerl. Between these two contemporary works Gordon Hamilton presented as his last important contribution to the Vienna State Opera Ballet Act Two of *Swan Lake* in Lev Ivanov's choreography, with Brexner as Odette. Towards the end of the Hanka era, in 1957, Brexner was awarded the title of 'Prima Ballerina' in succession to Julia Drapal, and in 1960 she was the first to be awarded the 'Fanny Elssler Ring' endowed by the former solo dancer Riki Raab for the outstanding Austrian ballerina of the day. Never before in the Ballet's history had two successive dancers been awarded the title of Prima Ballerina in the course of the same balletmaster's term of office.

Just as Vienna was congratulating itself on possessing a ballet fully up to international standards, came the news of Erika Hanka's sudden death on the fifteenth of May 1958, followed shortly afterwards by that of Gordon Hamilton. In commemoration of all that Erika Hanka had done for the State Opera Ballet for so many years there was a memorial performance of some of her best choreographies — *Der Mohr von Venedig*, *Medusa* and *The Miraculous Mandarin* — on the thirteenth of June 1958.

The show must go on. In November 1958 Dmitrije Parlić, ballet-master and one-time first solo dancer at the Belgrade Opera, commanded attention with his very first choreography in Vienna, Bizet's *Symphony in C*, a ballet in the classical style without a story. He did his best to follow in his predecessor's brilliantly successful footsteps, but his time with the Vienna Opera Ballet was too short for him to be able to influence its fortunes to any appreciable extent. His principal gift to Vienna, and his greatest personal success, was his production of Prokofiev's *Romeo and Juliet* on the twenty-sixth of March 1960, which was one of the events of the season and the first full-length ballet Vienna had been given for many years. Edeltraud Brexner and Richard Adama were Juliet and Romeo respectively, Willy Dirtl was Tybalt, and Lucia Bräuer was the Nurse.

The year before, Vienna had offered Raffaello de Banfield's one-act ballet *Le Combat*. In its brief thirty minutes it illustrates the tragic love of Tancred and Clorinda and was a great success for both Brexner and Parlić. On 30 April, barely a month after the première, Erika Zlocha and Karl Musil took over the name-parts in *Romeo and Juliet*. The latter was already giving promise of the international stature he was later to attain. The love scenes between him and Zlocha were particularly moving. The scenery was by Georges Wakhevitch, who had already designed the scenery and costumes for *Giselle*, the Othello ballet, *Le Combat*, etc. He always preferred rich colours, especially a russet brown, which was as appropriate to the atmosphere of Verona and the tragedy enacted there as it was to the equally tragic atmosphere of *Der Mohr von Venedig*.

One interesting choreographer invited to Vienna from Hanover was Yvonne Georgi, who in 1959 staged *Evolutionen*, Vienna's first ballet with electronic music. Three years later, in celebration of Stravinsky's eightieth birthday, she produced his *Agon* and *Apollon musagète*. In 1961 the Vienna Opera's Artistic Director, Herbert von Karajan, himself conducted the first Vienna performance of a ballet to the music of Gustav Holst's *The Planets*, with choreography by the Wuppertal ballet-master Erich Walter.

But the occasional guest choreographer was no replacement for Erika Hanka.

Karajan was looking for a new permanent ballet-master as successor to Dmitrije Parlić. He now engaged Aurel von Milloss, a Hungarian by birth, who as a dancer and choreographer had spent most of his time in Italy where he was instrumental in forming an up-to-date national ballet. Milloss had already visited Vienna in October 1941 with his Ballet of the Royal Opera of Rome, and although Italy was at war with Russia he had, with Mussolini's backing, danced the name-part in *Petrouchka* by Stravinsky, whose works were banned. Milloss was more interested in modern than in classical ballet, and his outstanding attribute was his intellect, which is perhaps why he found it difficult to make much headway in Vienna. Nevertheless, Vienna had reason to be grateful to him for his very interesting choreographies to music by Stravinsky, Bartók, Prokofiev and Ravel *(Estro arguto, Estro barbarico, Salade, Les noces, Bolero)* as well as for introducing a number of celebrated choreographers and dancers. Vienna's Balanchine repertoire — *Serenade, Vier Temperamente*, and *Apollo*, is also largely due to Milloss.

In May 1964 Ninette de Valois showed Vienna her ballet *Checkmate* to music by Sir Arthur Bliss, Georges Balanchine introduced his choreography of Hindemith's *Vier Temperamente*, and Leonide Massine, who in 1958 had polished up Fokine's production of *Petrouchka* for the Vienna Opera, put on a new production of de Falla's *Three-cornered Hat*.

In October 1964 came the first appearance in Vienna of Rudolf Nureyev, a great star whose frequent appearances with the State Opera Ballet are still as much of an attraction as ever. It was through him that Viennese audiences came to appreciate the rare delights of classic ballet with his full-length productions of Tchaikovsky's *Swan Lake* and Ludwig Minkus's *Don Quixote*, and with a revival of *Giselle*. In all three ballets he danced the principal rôle himself. Among great ballerinas who paid visits to Vienna at this time were Margot Fonteyn, Svetlana Beriosova and Yvette Chauviré.

The present head of the Vienna State Opera Ballet, Vaslav Orlikovsky, is a Russian with a striking personality who was previously in charge of the Basle Ballet. He has given Vienna excellent productions of Britten's *Prince of the Pagodas*, Tchaikovsky's *Sleeping Beauty*, Stravinsky's *Sacre du Printemps*, and Ravel's *Daphnis et Chloe*. Karl Musil has made an international name for himself as a classical and lyrical ballerino whose world-wide engagements are a reminder that Vienna has now a ballet of its own to be reckoned with. Susanne Kirnbauer has followed his example: during a visit by the Vienna State Opera Ballet to the 1968 Ballet Festival in Paris, she was awarded the prize sponsored by the association of literary and ballet critics for the best performance, in the face of redoubtable competition from all parts of the world. Successes like these also do honour to the entire company and to the school that trained its members in the first place.

Today, the Vienna State Opera Ballet has a reputation to live up to. Vaslav Orlikovsky is conducting a resolute campaign against the tendency to regard the ballet as the 'younger sister', as nearly always happens to any company, however brilliant, that has to supply the ballet interludes in performances of opera. Now that old-style ensemble theatre is finding it more and more difficult to adapt itself to contemporary conditions, the Vienna State Opera Ballet is one of the last oases of genuine ensemble in the operatic world of today.

Translations

From page 66:

RULES FOR VISITORS TO THE COURT OPERA
(Regulations pursuant to the law forbidding late arrival.)

§ 1. A cannon will be fired in the Imperial & Royal Arsenal at 5 p.m. daily as a signal to visitors to the Court Opera, that they should begin their preparations at home. On days when performances commence at 6:30 p.m. the signal will be given at 4:30.

§ 2 At 6 p.m. or 5:30 respectively, a second shot will give warning to ticket-holders who are resident in the outer suburbs that their journey to the Court Opera should now start. It has been arranged with Viennese householders that the *concièrges* shall inform such tenants as intend to visit the Opera on that day as soon as the 6 p.m. or 5:30 p.m. shot has been fired, and shall urge the said tenants to leave the house immediately.

§ 3. As the tramway and omnibus system, particularly during the current pipe-laying operations, is exceptionally prone to involvement in traffic blocks and thus may cause ticket-holders in vast numbers to arrive late, all owners of season-tickets and ticket-holders are obliged *on their word of honour* never to board one of the said vehicles to travel to the Opera once the above mentioned signal has sounded.

§ 4. Standing about and chatting in the cloakrooms before the commencement of each performance are forbidden in the interests of accelerated movement of persons through the cloakrooms. Critics who have attended the dress rehearsal are most specifically forbidden to detain the audience of first nights by indulging in prophecy in the cloakrooms.

§ 6. At 7 p.m. precisely, or at 6:30 as the case may be, a steam whistle within the Opera House will announce the commencement of the performance. Whoever has not reached his seat by that time will have to bear the consequences as threatened in the Director's Rules dated 2 November.

§ 7. After the curtain has risen, members of the public are strictly enjoined to preserve their sense of illusion. To that end, namely the retention of illusions in the auditorium, the following measures will be followed:

a) Engaged couples, who are commonly prone to disturb their neighbours and distract attention from the stage by indulging in lively discussion, will be denied entry, and the doorkeepers will be instructed accordingly. Persons of both sexes entering in couples are required to give evidence of their marital status by showing their marriage certificate.

b) Strikingly beautiful ladies who might tend to attract the glances of gentlemen, may be refused entry to the auditorium.

e) Opera glasses may only be trained on the stage. Any person who turns his glass upon the auditorium during a performance and thereby relinquishes his sense of illusion, will be required to pay a fine of fifty Kreuzer each time for the benefit of the pension fund.

f) Hard sweets may only be enjoyed during a performance in such a way that the confect be laid between the tongue and the gums without the assistance of the teeth, there pressed soundlessly in the 'i'-position of the tongue against the roof of the mouth and maintained in this position until such time as the sweetness has flowed past the base of the tongue and landed soundlessly in the throat.

g) Coughing, clearing of the throat and sneezing can only be permitted during a fortissimo. Immediately before the commencement of a crescendo the leader of the orchestra will indicate by a sign with his bow that members of the audience may bring out their handkerchiefs in anticipation of a cough or clearing of the throat.

h) Critics who are fond of bringing their scores to the Opera are strictly forbidden to turn the pages in view of the resulting noise. On no account is it permitted to follow the score of an opera other than the one which is being performed; in such a case the hurried leafing over pages would be even more disturbing.

i) During the intervals lady attendants in the buffets are to ensure that no customer is permitted to consume more than *one* caviare roll or the like; over-rich nourishment during the intervals leads all too easily to indigestion which may dispel the illusion in the following act.

§ 9. Smoking outside the Opera House before the start and after the end of the performance is permitted.

§ 11. Those critics who customarily provide two newspapers with a review on the same evening are kindly permitted, where an unabbreviated Wagner performance is concerned, to facilitate the carrying out of their duties by writing one review *before* the performance.

§ 12. The attention of visitors to the Opera is expressly drawn to the prohibition whereby that section of the audience which owing to late arrival must await the conclusion not only of the Overture but the entire first act outside the entrances, will on no account be accorded a separate performance of any sort or kind.

Vienna, 8 November 1897.

L. A. Terne

From page 74:

Apart from the mania for newspaper notices and the craze for publicity of some singers and their lawyers (who always have to represent someone in order to have their names mentioned in the Press), Mahler's relationship to these artists could also be explained by some other mistake which is common to all absolute governments. There is no reason why Gustav Mahler should be the only autocrat who remains exempt from it. The more he wanted to stand on his own the more he had to rely in some respect on others and therefore it could have happened that influences became active in him and through him which he himself was not aware of. And moreover — a man of such authoritarian character as Mahler fortunately is — should be nobody's friend. At any given moment, when one party was for him there was bound to be one against him. If everyone and everything would have opposed him he would not have given up the fight so soon. And, as with every autocrat, Mahler was surrounded by too many lesser intellects not to sometimes have ignored an honest judgement. But an artist needs nothing more than the honesty of the opinions offered to him. Although the French minister Guizot once said: If I am right I need no friends', the same does not apply to an artist. When he resigned all the superfluous people who crowded around him fell back; who knows how many who signed this ridiculous proclamation against him would not be willing at the same moment to sign one against his successor? Now Mahler goes away to regain all the artistic freedom his ecstatic nature needs. He deserved and found both praise and criticism, but taken as a whole he has the right to claim fame and, what is more, love. He should not part from us without being assured that the great many Viennese who were able to enjoy and appreciate his achievements will preserve this feeling of honesty and gratitude.

Dr. D. J. Bach

214

From page 75:

To the worthy members of the Imperial Opera House

The time has come to put an end to our cooperation. I have to part from the workshop I have come to love and say herewith farewell to you.

Instead of achieving something whole and complete as I had dreamed of, all that I leave behind me is unfinished and imperfect: this is the fate of mankind.

It is not up to me to judge those people who have come to appreciate my work and to whom it was dedicated. Nevertheless I may assure them at this moment that I meant well and aimed high. Success was not always granted to my endeavours. Nobody is so much liable to become a victim of the 'resistance of the matter' — 'the malice of the object' than the practising artist. But I always dedicated my entire strength to subordinating my person to the subject, my inclinations to the duty. I did not spare myself and therefore had the justification to demand the utmost from others. In the turmoil of the struggle, in the heat of the moment, you and I could not avoid injuries and errors. But when finally we achieved a task and solved a problem we forgot all the difficulties and misery and felt richly rewarded, even without obvious signs of success. We all advanced a step forward and with us this institution on which we have concentrated all our efforts.

My heartfelt thanks to all those who my supported efforts in this difficult and often thankless task, who assisted me and struggled with me. Please accept my sincere wishes for your future and for the prosperity of the Imperial Opera House, whose fate will never cease to be the object of my lively interest and sympathy.

Vienna, December 7, 1907.

Gustav Mahler

From page 197:

THE SEARCH FOR THE RIGHT MAN

The next Director of the Vienna Opera will have to succeed in bringing Karajan back.

The Vienna Opera owes its individuality and indeed its superior rank to the fact that it is not a manager's opera house but is dominated by its artists and conductors. During the last hundred years or so the men who guided the destinies of the Opera from the Director's office were, with a few awkward exceptions, great artistic personalities. The tradition of the Vienna Opera is an artistic tradition, which draws its strength and importance not from cautious conservatism but from a capacity for perpetual renewal through change. It is highly characteristic of the — as it were — biological composition of the institution that the blossom-time under Jahn and Richter should have been followed by a totally different, positively antithetical experience of opera during the Mahler epoch.

In rather the same way Karajan brought to the Vienna Opera new ideas, new plans, a new way of thinking, showing that within his artistic personality, which is both complex and farsighted, conducting represents only a part of the whole. The future lies in his conception of an internationally controlled community of interests linking all the great opera houses. How splendid it would have been if the first hesitant steps in the shape of a contract with the Scala in Milan had not been checked by small-minded book-keeping showing an apparent debit balance in the profit and loss account.

An equally unusual innovation was the way in which Karajan, a trained musician according to every rule in the book, personally took over the functions of stage management and production, into which he had first to feel his way, studying as he went along. This had the result, even on the scenic side of operatic production, of bringing to the forefront the prerogatives of the music which had been usurped to an unwarrantable extent by a less musically-orientated school of dramaturgical and histrionic production. During recent years, learning by trial and error and after a few not always very fortunate experiments, he has found his own personal style as a producer and his own sure form of expression. The productions of *Pelléas et Mélisande*, *Il Trovatore*, or *Tannhäuser*, in which both the musical and scenic spheres were under his control, are most praiseworthy examples of this, and show him testing out his methods in three very different departments of style. They lead the way out of the chaotic conditions which prevail in operatic production everywhere at the present time, and on to firm artistic ground. They may make history just as the Mahler-Roller productions did at the beginning of our century.

Heinrich Kralik

Index of Names

Numbers in brackets mean that the name in question is to be found on that page in the text of a caption to an illustration. Roman numbers relate to the picture section.

List of Pictures